LEARNING, MARGINALIZATION, AND IMPROVING THE QUALITY OF EDUCATION IN LOW-INCOME COUNTRIES

Learning, Marginalization, and Improving the Quality of Education in Low-Income Countries

Edited by Daniel A. Wagner, Nathan M. Castillo, and Suzanne Grant Lewis

OpenBook Publishers

https://www.openbookpublishers.com

© 2022 Daniel A. Wagner, Nathan M. Castillo and Suzanne Grant Lewis. Copyright of individual chapters is maintained by the chapter's author.

This work is licensed under an Attribution-NonCommercial 4.0 International (CC BY-NC 4.0). This license allows you to share, copy, distribute and transmit the text; to adapt the text for non-commercial purposes providing attribution is made to the authors (but not in any way that suggests that they endorse you or your use of the work). Attribution should include the following information:

Daniel A. Wagner, Nathan M. Castillo and Suzanne Grant Lewis, *Learning, Marginalization, and Improving the Quality of Education in Low-income Countries*. Cambridge, UK: Open Book Publishers, 2022. https://doi.org/10.11647/OBP.0256

Copyright and permissions for the reuse of many of the images included in this publication differ from the above. This information is provided in the captions and in the list of illustrations.

In order to access detailed and updated information on the license, please visit https://doi.org/10.11647/OBP.0256#copyright

Further details about Creative Commons licenses are available at http://creativecommons.org/licenses/by-nc/4.0/

All external links were active at the time of publication unless otherwise stated and have been archived via the Internet Archive Wayback Machine at https://archive.org/web

Digital material and resources associated with this volume are available at https://doi.org/10.11647/OBP.0256#copyright

Every effort has been made to identify and contact copyright holders and any omission or error will be corrected if notification is made to the publisher.

ISBN Paperback: 9781800642003
ISBN Hardback: 9781800642010
ISBN Digital (PDF): 9781800642027
ISBN Digital ebook (epub): 9781800642034
ISBN Digital ebook (mobi): 9781800642041
ISBN Digital ebook (XML): 9781800642058
DOI: 10.11647/OBP.0256

Cover design by Anna Gatti.

Preface

The education goal—Goal 4—of the 2030 UN Sustainable Development Goals places a strong emphasis on "ensuring inclusive and equitable quality education and promoting life-long learning opportunities for all." This goal recognizes that though great gains have been made in improving access to education in the two decades since the first set of UN goals in the year 2000—a major accomplishment—such success is not enough. Schooling must be of good quality and effective learning for all children, and in all locales. The achievement of quality education has been especially difficult for those who are poor and marginalized in low-income countries—those at the bottom of the pyramid.

This volume—*Learning, Marginalization, and Improving the Quality of Education in Low-income Countries*—is based on papers presented at an international virtual conference, Learning at the Bottom of the Pyramid 2 (LBOP2), held online in November/December 2020, and co-hosted by the University of Pennsylvania and IIEP-UNESCO. About 150 experts and observers—including researchers, policymakers and practitioners—participated in the conference. Topics included both thematic issues (e.g., metrics and financing) and national case examples (India, Ivory Coast, Kenya and Mexico), which broadly focused on better understanding children's learning in low-resourced settings worldwide, along with ways that new policy approaches can improve learning.

This volume is the second in a series on "learning at the bottom of the pyramid." The first conference, LBOP1, was held at the University of Pennsylvania in Philadelphia on March 2–3, 2017, and resulted in the 2018 book *Learning at the bottom of the pyramid: Science, measurement and policy in low-income countries*, published by IIEP-UNESCO.

The LBOP initiative continues to raise substantial issues of concern to international agencies, foundations, policymakers, education specialists, and the public at large. It is clear that in order to achieve quality education for all, a better understanding of learning in low-income societies will remain a high priority.

Dan Wagner
UNESCO Chair and Professor of Education
University of Pennsylvania

Karen Mundy
Director, IIEP-UNESCO

Contents

Preface		v
Contributor Biographies		xi
Acknowledgements		xxi
Introduction *Daniel A. Wagner*		1
1.	Diversity and Equity in Education: Policy, Practice, and Options for Reaching Children at the Bottom of the Pyramid *Lauren Pisani and Amy Jo Dowd*	13
2.	Education on the Move: How Migration Affects Learning Outcomes *Jo Kelcey, Ozen Guven, and Dana Burde*	45
3.	Teaching at the Bottom of the Pyramid: Teacher Education in Poor and Marginalized Communities *Kwame Akyeampong*	77
4.	Improving the Impact of Educational Technologies on Learning Within Low-Income Contexts *Nathan M. Castillo, Taskeen Adam, and Björn Haßler*	113
5.	Reducing Inequality in Education Using "Smaller, Quicker, Cheaper" Assessments *Luis Crouch and Timothy S. Slade*	149
6.	Not All Pyramids Are the Same: Relative Learning Exclusion and Its Evolution Over Time *Dirk Van Damme, Tijana Prokic-Breuer, and Stan Vermeulen*	181
7.	Financing Education at the Bottom of the Pyramid *Samer Al-Samarrai and Luis Benveniste*	193

8. Mexico: Education and Learning at the Bottom of the Pyramid — 223
   Sylvia Schmelkes del Valle, Héctor Robles Vásquez, and Annette Santos del Real

9. India: Learning in the Margin: Reflections on Indian Policies and Programs for Education of the Disadvantaged — 277
   Rangachar Govinda

10. India: Learning Challenges for the Marginalized — 293
    Udaya Narayana Singh, Rajarshi Singh, and Padmakali Banerjee

11. India: The Role of Civil Society Organizations and Scalable Technology Solutions for Marginalized Communities — 309
    Rajarshi Singh, Annapoorni Chandrashekar, and Nishant Baghel

12. Ivory Coast: Children at the Bottom of the Pyramid and Government Policies — 323
    François Joseph Azoh and Zamblé Théodore Goin Bi

13. Ivory Coast: Promoting Learning Outcomes at the Bottom of the Pyramid — 343
    Kaja Jasińska and Sosthène Guei

14. Kenya: Education, Learning, and Policy-Framing for Children at the Bottom of the Pyramid — 361
    Sara Ruto, Ann Gachoya, and Virginia Ngindiru

15. Kenya: Free Primary and Day Secondary Education Policies and Their Contributions to Learning at the Bottom of the Pyramid — 381
    Emmanuel Manyasa and Mercy G. Karogo

16. Kenya: Disability and Learning at the Bottom of the Pyramid — 397
    John K. Mugo, Diana Makau, and David K. Njengere

17. Kenya: Education in Marginalized Communities — 417
    Joyce Kinyanjui

Afterword: The Challenge Ahead for Learning at the Bottom of   439
the Pyramid
Rachel Hinton and Asyia Kazmi

List of Illustrations   443
List of Tables   449
Index   453

Contributor Biographies

Taskeen Adam is a Senior Research Lead at EdTech Hub and Associate Manager at Open Development and Education. She has a wealth of experience from South Africa, Rwanda, India, Niger and the UK. Her research focuses on justice-oriented design frameworks for inclusive and equitable EdTech interventions, with a specialization in online learning and technology-supported teacher professional development. Her doctoral research highlights that historical injustices, cultural imposition, and economic dependence continue to play a significant role in education. Taskeen is committed to bridging the digital divide, decolonizing education and countering digital neo-colonialism.

Kwame Akyeampong is Professor of International Education at the Open University, UK. Kwame began his academic career in Ghana at the University of Cape Coast. Until his appointment at the University of Sussex in 2004, he served as the Director of the Institute of Education at the University of Cape Coast, and later as Professor at the University of Sussex. He has published widely in international journals on education and development. From 2011 to 2013, Kwame served as senior policy analyst with the Education for All Global Monitoring Report team in UNESCO, Paris.

Samer Al-Samarrai is a senior economist working in the World Bank's Global Education Practice. Prior to joining the World Bank in 2011, Samer worked at UNESCO and as a Research Fellow at the Institute of Development Studies in the UK. He has published widely and was a co-author of the World Development Report 2018: Learning to Realize Education's Promise and several of UNESCO's annual Global Education Monitoring Reports.

François Joseph Azoh has a Doctorate in psycho-sociology of education. He is a teacher researcher at the l'École Normale Supérieure in Abidjan. He is also working as a psychotherapist and trainer, affiliated with various research and education organizations at the regional and national levels in Ivory Coast.

Nishant Baghel is Director, Technology Innovations at Pratham Education Foundation. He leads digital initiatives that typically connect the disconnected across rural parts of India. He specializes in leveraging advanced technologies for rural EdTech and creating learning opportunities for all. He oversees programs that reach more than 500,000 children and have been recognized by the World Economic Forum as the only 'School of Future' from India.

Padmakali Banerjee, a Ph.D. in Psychology, was a Fellow, Somatic Inkblot Series (FSIS–US). She is the Pro-Vice-Chancellor, Amity University Haryana, and a recipient of the 2018-Greenbuild Leadership Award from USGBCI. She developed an 'Optimism index' to measure optimism quotient. Her book "The Power of Positivity—Optimism and the 7th Sense" (SAGE) is a popular choice globally. Her research model PEROMA is used for counseling, educating, and training amongst the organization and general public.

Luis Benveniste is the Human Development Regional Director for Latin America and the Caribbean at the World Bank. He was a co-author of the World Development Report 2012: Gender Equality and Development. Luis´s research interests focus on teacher policies and student assessment practices. Luis has worked on a wide variety of education projects in Latin America and the Caribbean, Africa and East Asia and Pacific. He holds a Ph.D. in International Comparative Education from Stanford University.

Dana Burde is Associate Professor and Director of International Education at NYU Steinhardt; Affiliated Faculty with NYU Politics, NYU Abu Dhabi, Columbia University's Saltzman Institute of War and Peace Studies; Center for Economic Research in Pakistan; and founding Editor-in-Chief of the INEE-NYU *Journal on Education in Emergencies*. Burde's research on how to increase access to quality education for underserved populations, including girls, and how governments educate their citizens. Her book, *Schools for Conflict or for Peace in Afghanistan* (Columbia University Press) won the 2017 *Grawemeyer Award for Ideas Improving World Order*.

Nathan M. Castillo is an Assistant Professor of Global Studies in Education at the University of Illinois at Urbana-Champaign. Dr. Castillo is an international education development scholar whose research interrogates learning equity in the Global South and how appropriate uses of technology can improve learning, instruction, and assessment in low-income contexts. Nathan has served as an advisor to UNICEF, UNESCO, USAID, the Inter-American Development Bank, and several international, non-government organizations. After completing service in Guatemala with the United States Peace Corps, Dr. Castillo received a Master's from Harvard University, and a Ph.D. from the University of Pennsylvania.

Annapoorni Chandrashekar is a Senior Manager, Digital Innovation at Pratham Education Foundation, where she is responsible for program management and communications of PraDigi. An engineer by education, an entrepreneur, and filmmaker, she believes that learning to learn is a critical 21st-century skill. Her experience of bootstrapping and working for Ed-tech ventures drives her urgency and enthusiasm to take open learning initiatives to all communities and diverse learners.

Luis Crouch is a Senior Economist at RTI's International Development Group. He is on the board of directors of various NGOs and public bodies. He specializes in education policy, decentralized finance and education statistics and planning. Recently he has become interested in early grade reading and targeted Early Childhood Development, as key entry-points in education systems' quality response. He has authored many reports, technical and journal, and contributed to various technical books.

Amy Jo Dowd has led research teams at Save the Children and the LEGO Foundation. A graduate of Stanford (MA) and Harvard's (MEd, EdD) Graduate Schools of Education, she is passionate about using rigorous research to improve practice in international education and development.

Anne Gachoya is the Deputy Director Education at the Directorate of Policy, Partnerships & EACA, Ministry of Education in charge of coordinating education reforms in the Ministry and the National Educational Sector Support Program (NESSP) development. Ann sits in the Technical Committee of the National Curriculum Reform Policy Framework. She is a professional educational planner experienced in quality assurance and standards, education management, policy design, formulation and implementation of policies and programs.

Zamblé Théodore Goin Bi is a professor – researcher in the Department of Sociology at the Peleforo Gon Coulibaly University in Korhogo, Côte d'Ivoire. He teaches the sociology of education. He is also the President of the Scientific Council of the Association Ivoirienne de Recherche en Éducation (AIRE).

Rangachar Govinda is a Distinguished Professor at the Council for Social Development. He was Vice Chancellor, National University of Educational Planning, New Delhi and has taught at the University of London (as Visiting Professor), M.S University Baroda and IIEP, UNESCO, Paris. He has published extensively, including the India Education Report and Who Goes to School: Study of Exclusion in Education. His research interests include primary education, decentralized management, policy analysis, human rights, and democracy.

Suzanne Grant Lewis is Chair of Education Sciences and Policy at Education.org, a foundation building an independent, global resource for evidence-informed decision-making and implementation in education. Her work with LBOP began as Director of the UNESCO International Institute for Educational Planning (IIEP) overseeing the offices in Paris, Buenos Aires, and Dakar (2014-2021). Prior to this she worked in philanthropy and academia. She is passionate about bridging the worlds of research, policy, and practice through more inclusive, relevant evidence.

Sosthène Guei works as ECD Research Associate for the Jacobs Foundation on the TRECC (Transforming Education in Cocoa Communities) Program in Côte d'Ivoire. In this framework, he supports and informs TRECC mandated research projects and interventions with the overall objective of improving outcomes for children and youth in

Côte d'Ivoire. Sosthène has a keen interest in sustainable development issues, specifically in child and youth development through quality education. He is also the local coordinator for the International Society for the Study of Behavioral Development (ISSBD) and supports in the implementation of a 3-year research capacity building program with Ph.D. students in Côte d'Ivoire.

Ozen Guven, Ph.D., is an applied social science researcher working on teacher effectiveness, child protection, migration and forced displacement, emergencies, equity and inclusion in education. Dr. Guven conducts research and evaluation in the United States and in low- and middle-income countries. She worked as a consultant for USAID, DFID, Save the Children, American Institutes for Research, and others. She is currently an advisor with Education Northwest.

Björn Haßler is the director of Open Development & Education, and Technical Director at EdTechHub. He is an advocate for international cooperation and development, Global Public Goods, open development practices, Open Access and Open Education and their role in global equity. He specializes in sustainable and scalable approaches for program implementation to improve educational outcomes — across primary, secondary, and higher education.

Rachel Hinton is a social anthropologist with expertise in refugees and equity in education. She leads the strategy and design of education research at the UK FCDO—including the RISE and EdTech Hub programs. Her research spans Nepal, India, and Ghana and she has taught courses on refugees and migration, South Asia, and childhood studies. Rachel is co-author of the book *Inclusive Aid*. Rachel is a Visiting Fellow of Practice at BSG, University of Oxford.

Kaja Jasińska is the Director of the Brain Organization for Language and Literacy Development (BOLD) Laboratory at the University of Toronto (Applied Psychology and Human Development). Dr. Jasińska studies the neural mechanisms that support language, cognitive, and reading development across the lifespan using a combination of behavioral, genetic, and neuroimaging methods. Her research aims to understand how early-life experiences change the brain's capacity for learning, focusing on environments with poverty-related risk (e.g., rural communities; LMICs).

Mercy G. Karogo is the former Acting Chief Executive Officer of the Kenya National Examinations Council. She has extensive experience in the education sector where she started as a secondary school teacher before becoming a Lecturer at the Kenya Polytechnic, now known as the Technical University of Kenya. She has held a number of other senior management positions in a career spanning approximately 30 years.

Asyia Kazmi is the Global Education Policy Lead at the Bill and Melinda Gates Foundation. Asyia's 25-year career in education began as a mathematics teacher in the UK. Before joining the Gates Foundation, Asyia was in PwC leading the Girls' Education Challenge, a £800m fund set up by the UK's Department for International Development to support the education of 1.5 million girls in 17 countries. Her areas of expertise include teaching, learning, and assessment; school improvement; and large-scale program management. Asyia has a Masters in Applied Mathematics from Imperial College London and a Doctorate in Education on teaching and learning mathematics from Institute of Education, University College London.

Jo Kelcey (Ph.D.) is a post-doctoral researcher at the Lebanese American University in Beirut, Lebanon. She has extensive experience working on humanitarian and development education programs across several continents for multilateral agencies, non-government organizations, and donor organizations. Her research includes humanitarianism and education, migration and education, and knowledge production in crisis affected contexts.

Joyce Kinyanjui (Ph.D.) is the Managing Director of ziziAfrique, an organization that carries out educational research to contribute to the body of knowledge and to inform policy and practice. Her research and professional interests lie in inclusive education, girls' education, assessments for teaching and learning and accelerated learning. She has over 30 years of experience working in the education sector.

Diana Makau is a Principal Research Officer in the Kenya National Examinations Council (KNEC). She coordinates quality assurance of assessments undertaken by KNEC at Basic Education level. This involves analyzing and reporting on an all-inclusive range of big data at primary and secondary education levels. She has also been involved in various engagements in assessment both locally and internationally. Her area of specialization is educational measurement and evaluation.

Emmanuel Manyasa is the Executive Director of Usawa Agenda, a not-for-profit organization engaged in research and advocacy in education, with special focus on equity, and a Global Education Monitoring Report (GEMR) 2021 Fellow. He holds a Ph.D. in development economics. He has over 18 years of experience in teaching, research, consultancy and training across Africa spanning several sectors including: education and training; economic development; strategic planning and management; program evaluation; and feasibility analysis. His core research interests are in equity in education, policy analysis, economic development and development planning.

John Mugo is the Executive Director of Zizi Afrique Foundation. He works on the holistic development of children and youth, to equip them with competences for learning, working and living. Based in Nairobi, John works on generating large-scale evidence on values and life skills, and linking evidence to wider system change. Formerly, John headed the Uwezo learning assessments in East Africa, and chaired the Department of Special Needs Education at Kenyatta University.

Karen Mundy is Director of UNESCO's International Institute of Education Planning. She is on leave as Professor of International and Comparative Education at the University of Toronto, and is an expert on education in the developing world. She previously served as Chief Technical Officer at the Global Partnership for Education. At the University of Toronto, Dr. Mundy has been a Canada Research Chair and the Associate Dean of Research and Innovation. She has published six books and numerous articles and book chapters.

Virginia Ngindiru is a senior manager at Zizi Afrique Foundation, coordinating the Foundational Literacy and Numeracy as well as the Youth portfolios in the organization. Previously, Virginia was a manager in the same institution, overseeing implementation, monitoring and advocacy of the Accelerated Learning Program. The program seeks to hasten acquisition of foundational literacy and numeracy competencies for children furthest behind, through innovative, child-centered pedagogies. Previously, Virginia served similar initiatives at the Women Educational Researchers of Kenya and Voluntary Services Oversees (VSO) Kenya.

David K. Njengere is the CEO, Kenya National Examinations Council (KNEC). He is an education researcher with a Ph.D. in Education, well grounded in Curriculum Design and Development; and large scale assessments. He has been instrumental in conceptualization, design and implementation of Competency Based Curriculum and Competency Based Assessment in Kenya. Dr. Njeng'ere also works in other education reforms at national, regional and global level.

Lauren Pisani, Ph.D., has over 10 years of experience in international education and child development. In her role at Save the Children, Lauren led research and evaluation of early learning and development programs around the world. In addition, Lauren was instrumental in creating the International Development and Early Learning Assessment (IDELA), and she managed resources and research related to the tool.

Tijana Prokic-Breue, Ph.D., is Director and co-founder of Education Lab Netherlands, a project of Research Centre for Education and the Labour Market at Maastricht University and Free University of Amsterdam. She is an adviser on comparative quantitative research with focus on educational quality and equity.

Héctor Robles Vásquez has a Ph.D. in Agricultural Economics and Demography from Pennsylvania State University. He is a specialist at the Mexican Educational System. From 2005 to 2019, at the National Institute for the Evaluation of Education (INEE-Mexico), he led the design and construction of the national system of indicators for compulsory education.

Sara Ruto is the Chief Administrative Secretary at the Ministry of Education in Kenya. Previously, Sara was the Chief Executive Officer of the People's Action for Learning (PAL) network. This network comprises civil society organizations that conduct citizen led assessments and actions to improve learning outcomes in Africa, Asia, and the Americas. As PAL CEO, Sara led the accelerated learning program that sought to provide improved learning outcomes for children left behind. Sara was Chair of the Kenya Institute of Curriculum Development.

Annette Santos del Real has a Ph.D. in Education, and is an executive director with experience coordinating educational research and evaluations on a state and federal level within Mexico to create a culture of evaluation to better inform policymakers how to implement effective educational programs and policies.

Sylvia Schmelkes del Valle is a Mexican Sociologist with an MA in Educational Research and Development at the Universidad Iberoamericana in Mexico City. She was Academic Director of the Centro de Estudios Educativos for 10 years. She has also been a professor and researcher in the Departamento de Estudios Educativos of the Centro de Investigación y Estudios Avanzados, Instituto Politécnico Nacional, and in the Instituto de Investigación y Desarrollo de la Educación of the Universidad Iberoamericana Mexico City, which she headed (2007–2013). She has written on the right to education, educational quality, values education, intercultural education, and adult education. At present she is Academic Provost of Universidad Iberoamericana in Mexico City.

Rajarshi Singh is the Director of Programs at People's Action for Learning (PAL) Network, a south-to-south partnership of 15 member organizations working towards supporting children's foundational learning across 14 countries in Africa, Asia, and the Americas. He focuses on program management and monitoring, evaluation, and research. He managed projects across Africa (Kenya and Sierra Leone) and Asia (India and Nepal) for multiple clients like the World Bank, UN Women, international NGOs, USAID, and governments. He holds a Ph.D. in Computational Mechanics from Carnegie Mellon University.

Udaya Narayana Singh is a poet-linguist-educationist, and translation theoretician, Udaya Narayana Singh is currently Dean, Faculty of Arts, Amity University Haryana at Gurgaon. He served as a Professor and Pro-Vice-Chancellor of Visva-Bharati, Santiniketan. Earlier, he was the Director of India's Central Institute of Indian Languages, Mysore (2000–09), where he had set up the National Translation Mission. He was awarded the Sahitya Akademi Award for Poetry in 2017, and has published over 180 research papers and 58 books.

Timothy Slade currently serves as a Senior Research Education Analyst with the International Education team at RTI International. In past lives he has served as an expatriated project director in Kenya and Malawi, a headquarters project manager for various education interventions and research programs, and as an adult educator and classroom teacher. His formal academic training is in data science, early grade reading, international studies, French language, and human physiology.

Dirk Van Damme (Ph.D., Ghent University) served as Senior Counsellor in the Directorate for Education and Skills at the OECD in Paris, and Head of the Centre for Educational Research and Innovation. Before joining the OECD in 2008, he was professor of educational research (Ghent University, Belgium) and comparative education (Free University Brussels, Belgium, visiting professor at Seton Hall University, NJ, USA). His current interests are the science of learning, comparative analyses of educational systems, lifelong learning, and higher education policy and evaluation. He currently is Senior Research Fellow of the Center for Curriculum Redesign in Boston, MA (USA).

Stan Vermeulen, Ph.D., is a postdoctoral researcher at the Research Centre for Education and the Labour Market (ROA) at Maastricht University. He works on the "Education Lab Netherlands" project, in collaboration with the Dutch Inspectorate of Education and the Free University of Amsterdam (VU). His research mostly concerns teacher labor market outcomes, teacher quality, and the intergenerational transmission of skills.

Daniel A. Wagner is the UNESCO Chair in Learning and Literacy, and Professor of Education at the University of Pennsylvania. He is Founding Director of the International Literacy Institute, co-established by UNESCO and the University of Pennsylvania, Founding Director of the federally-funded National Center on Adult Literacy, and Founding Director of Penn's International Educational Development Program. Dr. Wagner has extensive experience in national and international educational issues, and has served as an advisor to UNESCO, UNICEF, World Bank, USAID, DFID/FCDO, and others on international development issues.

Acknowledgements

We would like to acknowledge the significant support of the co-organizers of the LBOP2 International Conference and co-hosts of the virtual event: University of Pennsylvania Graduate School of Education/International Educational Development Program and IIEP-UNESCO. We would also like to thank the following organizations for their kind and generous support: the UK Foreign, Commonwealth & Development Office (FCDO); the Bill & Melinda Gates Foundation; the EdTechHub; the Jacobs Foundation; the University of Pennsylvania; Penn's International Literacy Institute; Penn's UNESCO Chair in Learning and Literacy; and Penn's Perry World House. Thanks also to conference co-coordinators Sydney Dinenberg and Camilla Petrakis. We would also like to express our appreciation to the staffs of IIEP (Amelie Gagnon, Aurélia Courtot, Claire Kaplun, and Alexandra Waldorn) and PennGSE/IEDP (Kim Eke, Lauren Scicluna, and Charles Washington), as well as GSE IEDP students (Anahita Kumar, team leader, with Aanchal Gidra, Walid Hedidar, Tessa Kilcourse, Noora Noushad, and Yang Tingting Rui). Very special thanks to Elizabeth Baird for her outstanding editing of the chapters of this volume. Further, we would like to thank Alessandra Tosi and her staff at Open Book Publishers for their support and special attention in the production of this volume; and, it was through Lionel Gossman's wisdom and encouragement that we embraced OBP's free and open access publishing approach. Finally, we would like to acknowledge the time and energy of the many speakers, writers, and panelists who helped to enrich the conversations and debates during and after the LBOP2 conference.

Introduction

Daniel A. Wagner

The fourth United Nations Sustainable Development Goal (SDG4) calls for *inclusive, equitable,* and *quality* education. While certainly a noble endeavor on the surface, it is important to ask how these three characteristics can actually be measured and achieved. To help answer such an essential question, this volume brings together the research of experts from universities, non-governmental organizations, and national government think tanks and agencies who are pioneering new approaches to reach vulnerable children and youth—those who are "learning at bottom of the pyramid" (LBOP).

The chapters herein are based on papers presented at the second international conference on this topic, co-hosted (virtually) in December 2020 by the University of Pennsylvania and IIEP-UNESCO entitled "Learning at the Bottom of the Pyramid", or LBOP2. This event built on a framework from an earlier conference and book (Wagner, Wolf, & Boruch, 2018). Contributors prepared seven thematic papers on key sub-topics of LBOP, which lay out strategies to improve learning outcomes in low-income countries. Country-specific professionals prepared four national case studies, each utilizing this framework, which are based on research undertaken in India, Ivory Coast, Kenya, and Mexico.

Let us begin with a description of two learning contexts that help delineate the meaning of learning at the bottom of the pyramid.

South African classrooms: Two contexts of learning[1]

Shayandime Primary School is located in a small rural village in the northern province of Limpopo, South Africa. Just a few dozen miles

---

1 This section draws from Wagner & Castillo (2014). Author's note: the school names have been changed, and these profiles combine details from several schools.

from the border of Zimbabwe, the area is dotted with traditional houses called *rondavels*, an adapted version of the southern African-style hut. In spite of the occasional broken window, the school is not without resources. It is one of many establishments in the region that received a donation of desktop computers, and upper-primary learners spend time working on basic typing activities. However, disadvantaged learners with weak English proficiency have limited access to the computers, since no programs have been written in their local language, Venda. In the classroom, learners spend most of their time copying sentences from the chalkboard, and rarely participate in activities that support child-centered creativity and critical thinking skills.

By contrast, four hours away in the provincial capital of Polokwane sits Central Elementary School. It has brick paths around the perimeter and a state-of-the-art computer lab, with flat-screen monitors and a smart board with projector. The computer lab, which rivals that of the local university, was acquired in part through revenue earned by renting out the school's event hall to the community. There are no broken windows, the teachers present structured lesson plans, and the parents are an integral part of the school culture. Given its appealing learning environment, the provincial officials proudly exhibit this urban school to visiting national and international education planners. Many students have mobile phones, and give the appearance of being motivated to learn and to be connected to South Africa's future.

Comparisons of rural and urban contexts in low- and middle-income countries (LMICs) often consist of these types of observations of infrastructural and social differences. The South Africa Annual National Assessment (ANA), administered at the end of each school year, measures progress in learner achievement in Grades 1–6 and 9 (e.g., DBE 2013). The ANA inevitably confirms the type of subjective vignette described above. South African schools are categorized according to a poverty index based on the relative wealth or poverty of the community and are grouped into quintiles. Rural Shayandime Primary belongs to the lowest quintile. When the ANA was conducted there, only five learners in Grade 3 scored above the national norm, while the large majority scored in the bottom 10 percent, creating a skewed distribution. By contrast, Central Elementary ranks in the middle (third) quintile with normally distributed scores; these are somewhat below the national urban norms for the mathematics and home language reading competencies for Grade 3.

These contrasts of LBOP2 are typical in many LMICs, almost creating two worlds of education: one for the relatively well-off, and one for those without. Over the past two or three decades, an avalanche of new research has confirmed this relative bifurcation of learning worlds (Wagner, 2018; Wagner et al., 2018).

The search for inclusion and equity

The two schools above raise a fundamental question: how can countries promote greater inclusion and improve learning equity, as called for in SDG4? Two actionable perspectives seem increasingly evident: first, countries must *raise the floor* of learning outcomes of the poor and marginalized, rather than primarily focusing on average national scores; and second, countries must *close the gap* in learning disparities between those at the bottom and those at the top of the scale. Both are needed to support the achievement of all learners, and both are broadly addressed in the thematic papers contained in this volume. Indeed, it was this framework that fueled discussions at the LBOP2 conference and led to each of the papers in this volume.

Thematic papers: Towards raising the floor

In many countries today, the strong focus of public policy is on the "middle" or norm—whether referring to income, years of schooling, or learning outcomes. This is understandable since the majority population in most countries (and its largest voting bloc, one might add) is comprised of "average" people who are, politically and statistically, in the middle group of any population. However, such a focus on the middle comes with educational, social, and economic costs.

A Minister of Education might rightly ask the following question: can the needs of the poor be better addressed by raising outcomes for the middle of the population—thereby "lifting all boats", as the saying goes. Or, by contrast, should the focus be on addressing the needs of the very poor directly, the approach we term *raising the floor*?[2] With the advent of

---

2 First described in Wagner and Kaur (2006).

SDG4, and the current COVID-19 pandemic, greater attention is being paid to learning levels, and especially to those learners with the lowest outcomes (UNESCO, 2021; Wagner et al., 2018; World Bank, 2021).

In the three subsections below, we lay out several broad issues that are highly pertinent to how to raise the floor: (1) who are the children left behind; (2) learning in the classroom; and (3) improving metrics on learning.

Who are the children left behind?

In this volume, we have tried to identify which children are most at risk, and for what reasons. Across the globe, and especially in LICs, there is little question that human diversity drives major differences in learning. In *Chapter 1*, Pisani and Dowd lay out a broad definition of diversity at the BOP, highlighting three major dimensions of diversity: (1) gender disparities—with a case study in Afghanistan; (2) disability—with a case study in Tamil Nadu (India); and (3) language of instruction—with a case study in Kenya. Overall, the authors show that policy and investment need to progress beyond a "one size fits all" approach to disadvantage, and recognize that producing equitable learning outcomes for all children requires different levels and types of inputs for different groups.

Another key population of children at risk is those displaced due to internal or external migration. As Kelcey, Guven, and Burde point out in *Chapter 2*, access to quality education can help migrants navigate the uncertainties of geographical displacement and contribute to the social and economic development of their host states. Yet data on migrants' learning outcomes remain inadequate and collected in inconsistent ways. Employing two case examples (in Lebanon and Ecuador), the authors show that official policies for migrant children differ, or are interpreted differently, at the school level, and that students' wellbeing and sense of belonging are also connected to learning achievement.

Learning in the classroom

Improving the quality of children's learning necessitates a close look at teachers' roles and responsibilities. But, as with their learners, teachers are quite diverse, as are the contexts within which they work. Many of these contexts, especially in LMICs, are rife with challenges.

In *Chapter 3*, Akyeampong focuses on some new and unprecedented obstacles that teachers face. Even as "teacher quality" has improved by increasing teacher training in some better-off communities, student populations have grown dramatically. As a result, class size and the overall diversity of students has led to less time learning, and a drop in learning achievement, especially at the BOP. In addition, during the global pandemic, we have seen huge impacts on children's access to good-quality education, especially with the push towards remote (virtual) learning.

Information and communication technologies (ICTs) can transform how we can support learning through real-time data collection and analytics. In *Chapter 4*, Castillo, Adam, and Haßler point out that ICTs are becoming cheaper and more powerful each year, with access expanding to nearly every part of the education sector. Particularly, mobile phones are outpacing other types of technology—even in low-income contexts—opening up opportunities to move away from "traditional" teaching materials (such as textbooks, chalkboards, and notebooks), while improving teacher training and data collection for real-time assessments. The authors suggest that emerging technologies should employ a reciprocal model whereby student input helps optimize the model and the model, in turn, helps optimize user skills through continuous, formative analysis.

Improving metrics on learning

Measurement (or metrics) has been central to conversations about learning at the BOP. As noted in the first LBOP volume (Wagner et al., 2018), such an analysis requires an understanding of the demographics of the sample, as well as a reliable way to measure learning. In this volume, three chapters explore what kinds of metrics are required in order to create reliable, valid, and comparable tools. Crouch and Slade, in *Chapter 5*, propose using a variety of "smaller, quicker, cheaper" (SQC; after Wagner, 2011) assessments, particularly since their use has grown in recent years. They point out that in one of the latest signs of that interest, the World Bank (2019) is seeking to cut the proportion of 10-year-old non-readers in lower-middle-income countries by half, from around 50 percent to around 25 percent, by 2030. But how to ascertain whether such a goal is feasible—what types of metrics will be required?

By using a large EGRA (early grade reading assessment, oral reading fluency) dataset from Kenya, the authors show that a Gini coefficient (and other measures of inequality for learning) can reliably measure the gap between readers and non-readers. In sum, Crouch and Slade found that when one correlates improvements in the average levels of reading fluency with changes in inequality, these improvements are highly related to reductions in inequality.

In *Chapter 6*, Van Damme, Prokic-Breue, and Vermeulen propose an innovative measure of learning at the BOP, called "learning exclusion"— which they define as the relative distance in learning outcomes between the lowest 10 percent of performers and the median in a country's population. A larger gap would indicate that learners at the bottom are relatively more excluded from what a nation's population considers to be the norm. A smaller gap would suggest that learners at the bottom are more integrated into the skill profile of a nation's population. The authors used outcomes from six rounds of PISA scores between 2000 and 2018 to measure learning exclusion, and found that some countries that scored poorly in terms of learning exclusion in 2012 showed remarkable progress over time, while others remained stagnant. The exclusion of a learner is not, they found, primarily defined by his or her absolute performance in global terms, or by his or her distance from the top performers—but rather by the deviation from what a society considers to be the norm.

For each goal of the SDGs, there is a clamor for more resources, and SDG4 is no exception. But what about the equity concerns of spending? Should financial resources be spent "across the board" on all goals, or should some areas receive extra attention—and more funding? In *Chapter 7*, Al-Samarrai and Benveniste consider a framework for what they term "spending equity". They find that total public education spending tends to be unequally distributed, particularly in low-income countries. Further, they note that it is common for the poorest and wealthiest quintiles to have similar enrollment rates in public *primary* schooling, but a far greater proportion of children in the wealthiest quintile are enrolled in public *tertiary* institutions. Thus, since per-student expenditure is much higher in tertiary institutions, this tends to skew the distribution of public education funding in favor of wealthier quintiles, particularly in low-income countries. Improving metrics for determining where spending should be targeted will improve support for those at the bottom of the pyramid.

National case studies: Towards closing the gap

The global benchmarks set by the UN Sustainable Development Goals are expected to be carried out at the national level, typically through government agencies. However, it is important to recognize that there are multiple stakeholders that implement education in every country, and adaptation of strategies and policies to local contexts, languages, and other factors is essential for success. Teachers, families, and non-governmental agencies offer critical insights into how learning can be supported effectively. Promoting local, scalable, and collaborative policies and approaches is a cornerstone of improved learning, and necessary to help close the learning gap in low-income countries. This volume's second section provides case studies, distributed over four countries, that dive deeper into issues of localizing the LBOP approach within national educational systems.

Mexico (*Chapter 8*), is the first of these national case studies. Schmelkes, Robles, and Santos provide an overview of the demographics of social vulnerability, and how these data map on to low learning levels. The authors demonstrate that Mexico has not managed to guarantee: (a) universal access to school; (b) universal completion of compulsory education; or, (c) basic levels of learning to progress in school. This implies what they term a "social debt", especially to children in conditions of social vulnerability. They point out that the heritage and diversity of Mexico comes in part from its native indigenous populations, whose languages can be organized into 68 linguistic groups. Indigenous children who attend school almost always receive instruction in Spanish, and in these circumstances, children take much longer to learn to read and write, and their mastery of the content included in the curriculum is consequently much lower. The authors conclude that some Mexican government policies and programs have been put into place to mitigate the effect of poverty on education, but most continue to privilege access and permanence in education, rather than learning.

In India, three case studies provide varying perspectives on key aspects of education at the BOP. In *Chapter 9*, Govinda provides a set of reflections on policies and programs for education of the disadvantaged in India. He begins by asking a fundamental question: what if all children gain access to school (India's overarching goal), but the majority fail to acquire even the basic skills of literacy and numeracy after several years of schooling? Indeed, he notes that Indian policy has always embedded concern for quality within a framework of equity and social justice, but translation of that intent into reality has proved elusive, particularly for disadvantaged children. In *Chapter 10*, Singh, Singh, and Banerjee examine disadvantage through the lens of language diversity in India. Nearly 96 percent of India's mother-tongues are spoken by only four percent of the population, but early grade education, textbook production, and teacher training programs rarely take into account these linguistic minorities, despite constitutional provisions that require schools to impart education in every child's mother-tongue. They conclude by noting that academic, socioeconomic, and psychological support systems that take into account India's heterogenous populace are required to achieve resilience and lifelong learning of children. Finally, in *Chapter 11*, Singh, Chandrashekar, and Baghel consider the role of civil society organizations (CSOs) in promoting innovations in marginalized communities, particularly using ICTs. They note that CSOs often act as subject matter experts, support capacity building, and often represent marginalized communities by serving as advocates while promoting fundamental rights and values. As one example, they describe Pratham's PraDigi Open Learning program that has reached hundreds of thousands of Indian children across multiple states. They conclude that such ICT platforms blend technology, children's curiosity, and traditional social structures to engage communities in children's learning.

In the Ivory Coast, there are two case studies concerning LBOP. In *Chapter 12*, Azoh and Goin Bi provide a review of government policies, with a focus on how to identify the vulnerable populations that face the most barriers to education and learning. The authors describe the demographics by poverty, gender, disability, and national citizenship—and how each dimension challenges children's learning at the BOP. National educational policies in the Ivory Coast have responded to such problems of disadvantage by integrating local schools (Islamic, community, handicapped) into policy frameworks that are helping to reduce gaps over time. Complementing the above approach, Jasińska and Guei (in *Chapter 13*) find that impoverished rural communities are often denied access to quality education, where only 14 percent of sixth-grade students attain sufficient competency in both math and language. The authors review several research-based programs that incorporate three broad strategies: (1) changing classroom structures to better meet children's learning needs; (2) leveraging educational technologies to provide access to quality education; and (3) systematically addressing poverty. In one example of the latter, the authors detail a cash transfer program that offers families small amounts of financial support to ease economic hardship, thereby promoting school attendance rather than work on plantations. Integrated interventions that include poverty reduction transfers and innovative pedagogical approaches offer new ways to address the causes of inadequate learning outcomes among Ivory Coast's most vulnerable children.

In Kenya, four case studies are included. In *Chapter 14*, Ruto, Gachoya, and Ngindiru write about the policy framing of education and learning equity among school children. They note that the inequitable distribution of learning opportunities has historical, sociocultural, and economic underpinnings, particularly in Kenya's arid north. While the positive ingredients needed for a functional education system are available in terms of textbooks and teachers, the most important issue is one of inequitable opportunity for building a resilient system that works for all children—where policies should move from being input-driven to becoming outcome-based. In *Chapter 15*, Manyasa and Karogo focus on recent trends in free primary and secondary education, and whether this is effective for quality learning. Based on multiyear data collection, the authors found that children at the bottom of the pyramid constitute a significant percentage of all children, and yet despite being in school, their learning levels remain low. Indeed, while Kenyan government policies have facilitated children's access to school, their study shows that little learning happens in the early years of schooling, leading to disadvantages along children's entire school journey. Mugo, Makau, and Njengere, in *Chapter 16*, consider ways of improving learning among those with disabilities in Kenya, showing also that there is an over-representation of over-age children in schools. Further, despite the accommodations for disabilities already in place, end-of-cycle examinations continue to marginalize learners with disabilities, and hold them back. Finally, Kinyanjui (in *Chapter 17*) provides a comparative analysis of children's marginalization across multiple counties in rural Kenya as related to school enrollment rates, with particular attention paid to poverty, language barriers, gender, and more. Recently, the pandemic has also impacted learning, as only about 20 percent of Kenyan students have regular access to digital learning. Kinyanjui, as with others in the Kenyan case, find that there are many interconnected and continuing causes of marginalization that remain obstacles for learning at the bottom of the pyramid.

Conclusions

Collectively, the papers of this volume try to clarify how we can improve learning in low-income countries and in poor and marginalized communities, among populations at the bottom of the pyramid. They also demonstrate multiple approaches to both raising the floor and narrowing learning gaps. Even so, much needs to be done to achieve improved learning equity.

Better situated *diagnostics* are clearly important. As the saying goes: "If you cannot measure it, you cannot manage it."[3] This principle is widely cited in many fields, and it is becoming increasingly central to how educational policymakers, researchers, and practitioners think about their work. Measurement is crucial, even if not everyone agrees on what and how to measure. As this volume shows, credible research evidence depends on measurement, and should be an essential component for all substantive development efforts. Yet experts frequently do not have enough valid, reliable, and disaggregated data to evaluate how their initiatives will work over time, across contexts, and specifically for populations at the bottom of the pyramid.

Field-based partners and other local stakeholders, as well as national ministries of education, will be central to the next phase of work on LBOP issues. As noted earlier, this type of involvement in LBOP efforts cannot be taken for granted. BOP learners have remained disadvantaged for decades and even centuries, often for the kinds of reasons that are

---

3 Attributed to Peter Drucker, a major figure in corporate management. No citation is available. See also Wagner (2018, p. 240).

explored in multiple chapters of this volume. While researchers may understand, at a distance, the challenges of overcoming marginalization, at the local level such problems are endemic and difficult to change. Thus, an activist LBOP approach would need to include at least the following components: local and culturally adapted instruments and interventions; a focus on valid measurement tools that emphasize disaggregation at their core; ICT tools that promote personalized and adaptive learning content informed by real-time data capture; and longitudinal designs that will enable the study of change over time. Finally, and necessarily, cross-disciplinary and cross-sector collaborations will be required to scale up future visions of improving learning for those at the bottom of the pyramid.

As we move forward into the remaining years of the 2030 UN SDG targets, it is clear that social and economic inequalities will persist, and even increase, unless we maintain a serious focus on learning among the poor. Only by transforming the way learning is understood in contexts at the bottom of the pyramid can we begin to understand how to better promote learning equity for those hardest to reach. One thing is clear: progress on issues of learning equity will take considerable effort, persistence, understanding, and collaboration.

References

Department of Basic Education (DBE), South Africa. (2013). *Report on the annual national assessment of 2013: Grades 1 to 6 & 9*. Pretoria: DBE. http://www.education.gov.za/LinkClick.aspx?fileticket= Aiw7HW8ccic%3D&tabid=36

Prahalad, C. K. (2006). *The fortune at the bottom of the pyramid: Eradicating poverty through profits*. Upper Saddle River, NJ: Wharton School Publishing.

UNESCO. (2021) *Reimagining our futures together: A new social contract for education*. Paris: UNESCO.

Wagner, D. A. (2011). *Smaller, quicker, cheaper: Improving learning assessments in developing countries*. Paris/Washington: UNESCO-IIEP/FTI-Global Partnership for Education. http://unesdoc.unesco.org/images/0021/002136/213663e.pdf

Wagner, D. A. (2018). *Learning as development: Rethinking international education in a changing world*. New York/London: Routledge.

Wagner, D. A., & Castillo, N. M. (2014). Learning at the bottom of the pyramid: Constraints, comparability and policy in developing countries. *Prospects: Quarterly Review of Comparative Education*, 44(4), 627–638.

Wagner, D., & Kaur, I. (2006). *Out-of-school children and youth in the MENA region*. Background paper for the Middle East and North Africa (MENA) Regional Report. Washington, DC: World Bank.

Wagner, D. A., Wolf, S., & Boruch, R. F. (Eds.) (2018). *Learning at the bottom of the pyramid: Science, measurement, and policy in low-income countries*. Paris: UNESCO-IIEP. http://unesdoc.unesco.org/images/0026/002655/265581E.pdf

World Bank. (2019). *Ending learning poverty: What will it take?* Washington, DC: World Bank. https://openknowledge.worldbank.org/bitstream/handle/10986/32553/142659.pdf?sequence=6&isAllowed=y

World Bank. (2021). *Realizing the future of learning: From learning poverty to learning for everyone everywhere*. Washington, DC: World Bank.

1. Diversity and Equity in Education

Policy, Practice, and Options for Reaching Children at the Bottom of the Pyramid

Lauren Pisani and Amy Jo Dowd

Introduction

Despite calls for "Education for All", there is a global learning crisis at every level of education, and the COVID-19 pandemic has only exacerbated the challenge of realizing Sustainable Development Goal 4 (SDG4)—that all children complete free, equitable, and quality primary and secondary education leading to relevant and effective learning outcomes. Prior to the pandemic, there were 250 million children at the pre-primary level in low- and lower-middle-income countries (LMICs) at risk of not realizing their developmental potential (Black et al., 2016), and at the primary and secondary levels, more than 617 million children and adolescents were not achieving minimum proficiency in reading and mathematics (UNESCO Institute for Statistics, 2018). In addition, 200 million adolescents were not enrolled in secondary education, and out-of-school rates had been essentially stagnant since 2012 (UNESCO Institute for Statistics, 2018). These challenges were disproportionately affecting disadvantaged children—those living in poverty, those with disabilities, girls, and those learning in a second (or even third!) language (Rose et al., 2017; World Bank, 2018).

In the fall of 2020, 1.7 billion children faced closed, interrupted, or uncertain access to schooling, and emerging data suggest that 40 percent of low- and middle-income countries (LMICs) have not taken steps to support learners at risk of exclusion during the COVID-19 pandemic (UNESCO, 2020) (see Figure 1). The short- and long-term effects of COVID-19 on learning are unknown, but experts warn that they will likely exacerbate the divide between advantaged and vulnerable children that existed prior to 2020. In the short-term, differences in learning levels prior to school closures, access to remote learning opportunities and materials (e.g., access to the internet), and responsibilities at home such as chores and childcare could lead to learning loss (Carvalho & Hares, 2020). In the long-term, economic shocks to individual families and national education systems threaten both the access and quality of school post-pandemic (Save the Children, 2020; UNESCO, 2020). For example, prior to COVID-19, education spending inequities showed an average of 10 percent of public education budgets in LMICs spent on the poorest 20 percent of learners (UNICEF, 2020). Now, the estimates predict an education financing gap of $77 billion in LMICs (Save the Children, 2020).

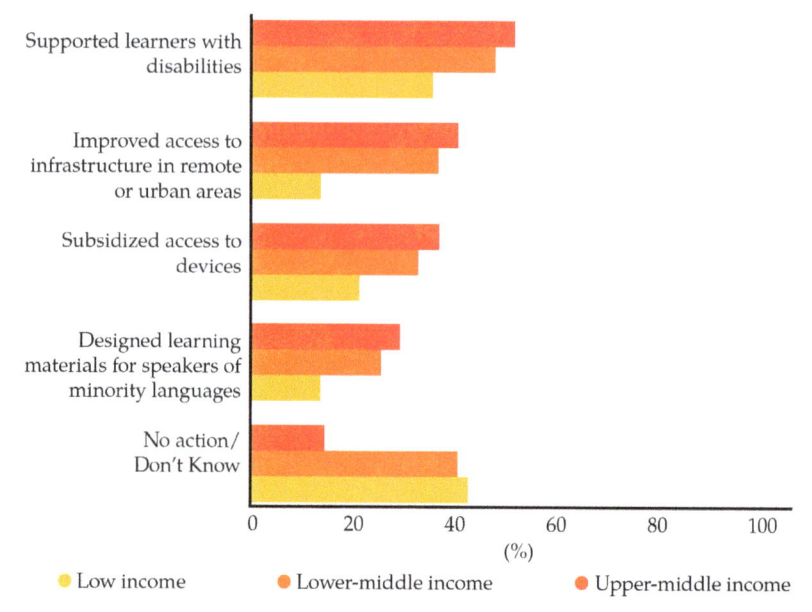

Fig. 1. Proportion of LMICs taking measures to include disadvantaged populations in distance learning during the COVID-19 pandemic in 2020. Source: UNESCO (2020).

Wealth-driven gaps in learning grow with each level of education (Rose & Alcott, 2015), and these shortfalls have led to calls for progressive universalism (Education Commission, 2016), or attention to quality education expansion, with priority given to the lowest levels of schooling (including pre-primary education) and to those at the bottom of the pyramid (Wagner et al., 2018). In this way, as access to quality preschool and schooling expands and learners thrive, level by level, all children are supported to achieve their potential. Such policies would pave the way for more equitable education systems, but we must also support the millions of children who are out of school in our current systems. This number will only grow due to COVID-19, and a substantial proportion of children around the world will require additional support in order to master the foundational literacy, numeracy, and social emotional skills that will allow them to effectively enter the workforce.

Disparities will persist until education systems strengthen the connections between equity-focused policy and practice. Countries across the globe strive to provide access to quality instruction, but many struggle to implement those policies effectively and universally. For example, basic education expansion in Tanzania intentionally focused on improving access for girls, and while this effort was successful it also deepened educational inequality for the rural poor, as well as disabled children (Baum et al., 2019). This case shows that equity-focused policy implementation is feasible, but a focus on one dimension may not be holistic enough to raise enough children from the bottom of the pyramid (Wagner, 2018). On the other hand, where rich young Bangladeshi men are 10 times more likely to attend higher education than poor young Bangladeshi women, there is a disconnect between equity goals and education budget allocations (Ilie & Rose, 2016).

Systems need to develop differentiated strategies that take the diversity of their student body into account. They must recognize that some children face additional challenges during their educational journeys. If we fail to consider and act on the factors that affect whether or not children attend school and are engaged while there, we risk the gaps between vulnerable and advantaged children growing larger and larger. Importantly, these issues intersect and some factors, like poverty and location, can multiply or reduce the impact of other factors on children's learning outcomes. Contextualized targeting of policy is challenged by a relative lack of data—especially for disability and language differences—but makes iterative testing of policy and implementation no less important.

Potential solutions relate not only to policy (e.g., girls have the right to education in all areas of the country), but also to school systems themselves (e.g., access to appropriate latrines for girls), as well as culturally held norms existing in children's communities (e.g., value of education for girls vs. boys). Prioritizing how to move towards progressive universalism requires not only data, but concentrated effort to use it and leverage political will to implement pro-equity policy, and monitor its impact on for learning and equality of outcomes over time. This data-based approach will vary by context, requiring local solutions and an iterative approach to evidence, practice, and policy.

In this paper, we explore examples of such efforts along four different equity dimensions—poverty, gender, disability, and language—using global data and particular country case studies. We know that these issues intersect for many children at the bottom of the pyramid, and present available data showing this reality. We discuss how each dimension affects children's learning experiences in pre-primary, primary, and secondary schooling and how challenges can grow as students at the bottom of the pyramid progress through education systems. This approach allows us to explore how disadvantage accumulates over time, discuss the interplay between issues of access and quality, and elucidate examples of efforts to improve quality, expand outreach, and innovate to include more children and support their learning.

Poverty at the bottom of the pyramid

Poverty and its relationship to learning outcomes for children at the bottom of the pyramid requires special attention. Poverty is the leading factor that drives educational disadvantage, and it has the power to exacerbate or alleviate the relationship between other types of disadvantage and learning outcomes. On its own, wealth has a strong relationship to school enrollment both between and within countries. Low-income countries have out-of-school rates that are consistently higher than lower-middle, upper-middle, and high-income countries (UNICEF, 2019; Wagner et al., 2018; World Bank, 2018). Within countries, poor children are significantly more likely to be out of school than wealthy children, and poor girls in low-income countries are the least likely in the world be accessing education (UNICEF, 2019; World Bank, 2018). The COVID-19 crisis has exacerbated these challenges as many systems moved to distance learning, but in LMICs only 20 percent of households have access to the internet and around half have access to radio or television (Carvalho & Hares, 2020). The related economic crisis is estimated to mean that an additional 90 to 117 million children will be living in poverty, and between 7 and 9.7 million will drop out of school (Save the Children, 2020).

Poverty also has a clear link with learning outcomes from the earliest ages. Multi-country studies identify poverty as a key driver of low cognitive development in 3–4 year old children living in low- and middle-income countries (LMICs) (Black et al., 2016; McCoy et al., 2016). Similarly, meta-analyses using data from the International Development and Early Learning Assessment (IDELA) find a significant positive relationship between family wealth and learning and development for children aged 3–6, with an effect size ranging from one to three months of development per additional household asset (Save the Children, 2018). Assessments of children's performance in primary school across various LMICs have also highlighted the strong link between children's socioeconomic status and their learning outcomes (Rose & Alcott, 2015; Wagner et al., 2018). Thus, whether among young children or those in primary school, poverty fundamentally challenges the equality of learning outcomes.

There are exceptions where students in poor countries have strong learning outcomes and poor children in other countries are closer to performing on par with their wealthier peers. In order to promote best practices in this area, it's important to understand how governments and policymakers are driving better educational equity for the children they serve, and whether and how corresponding progress is made at the bottom of the pyramid as well. Recent PISA results demonstrated that children's learning outcomes are resilient to poverty in many high-income countries, but this generally occurs in countries with stronger education systems overall (OECD, 2019). Lessons learned from countries with weaker systems and fewer resources who have taken on poverty in their education systems can inform many others who are still working toward this goal.

Case study: Ethiopia

Ethiopia has invested substantially in improving conditions for children in recent years, especially in the domains of health and education. Public services and policies supporting children, including health and nutrition services, child protection, and access to education have increased. The country's first National Children's Policy was approved in 2017 and provides a framework for implementing the Conventions on the Rights of the Child. Additional pro-poor policies and initiatives within the Ministry of Education's Sector Development Programs have targeted improving quality and equity of educational services for all children (Pankhurst et al., 2018; UNICEF, 2017).

Access to both pre-primary and primary enrollment in Ethiopia has been growing faster than many other African nations. However, the gaps in access and learning outcomes for the richest and poorest remain large. For example, the proportion of children out of school was cut by approximately half in a decade, but in 2016, 39 percent of the poorest had never been to school, compared to 7 percent of the richest (see Figure 2). Similarly, the proportion of children completing primary school in Ethiopia has grown substantially over a short period, but still only 25 percent of the poorest complete this level of education compared to 76 percent of the richest children.

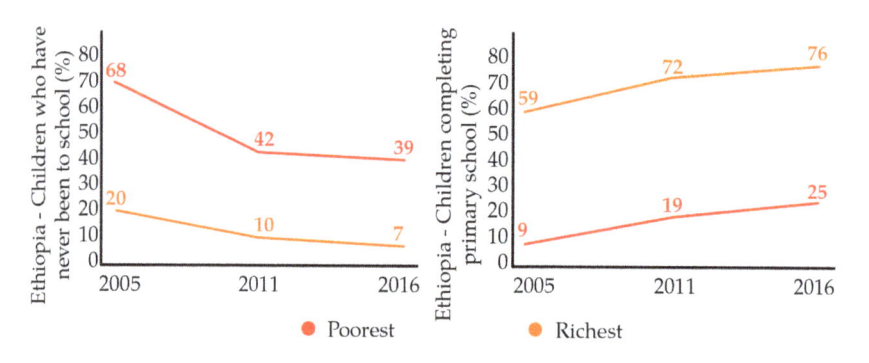

Fig. 2. Access and learning by wealth over time in Ethiopia. Source: Created by authors with data from the World Inequality Database on Education.

Multiple studies of early childhood education in Ethiopia have found that poorer children have weaker learning and development outcomes than their wealthier peers (Dowd, Borisova, Amente, & Yenew, 2016; Save the Children, 2017). Further, longitudinal research from the Young Lives study demonstrates that learning gaps between wealthy and poor children that emerged during early childhood persisted over time and were associated with grade progression, primary school completion, and learning outcomes at the end of primary school. By the end of primary school, the Young Lives study found that most children were performing at two or three grade levels below curricular expectations. The widest gaps were observed between children in urban and rural communities in mathematics, and between poor and wealthy children in English (Pankhurst et al., 2018).

Multiple initiatives are underway in Ethiopia to improve children's learning from the early childhood period onward. Many of these initiatives involve leveraging families and communities to supplement school-based programs, or extend reach where schools are not effectively operating. One such program trained parents to deliver early literacy and mathematics content to preschool-aged children who did not have access to pre-primary classes (locally called O-Classes), and found that children whose parents participated in this home-based ECE program displayed learning gains comparable to those of children enrolled in government O-Classes (Borisova et al., 2017). Further, a study of the same program found that children who attended government O-Classes and whose parents attended the home-based training learned more over the course of a school year than children who attended O-Classes only, with those from the poorest families gaining more than their wealthier peers (Dowd et al., 2016).

The benefits of engaging parents and communities has been tested and found to be effective at the primary level as well. A study of literacy programs from multiple countries, including Ethiopia, found that children who participated in community reading activities (e.g., book borrowing, reading clubs, etc.) displayed stronger gains in reading comprehension than their classmates who did not participate in these activities (Dowd et al., 2017a). Additional research on this topic has demonstrated that programs which include community reading activities have larger impacts on children's higher-order literacy skill development (i.e., fluency and comprehension) than teacher training alone (Friedlander et al., 2019).

At least one-third of the youth in Ethiopia are out of school at the upper-primary and lower-secondary level, overwhelmingly those from poor families. Approximately 10 percent of these children dropped out of school, but an additional 25 percent never attended at all (Bashir et al., 2018). Effective coordination and appropriate funding for alternative education programs at scale is severely lacking. However, there is promising evidence from a number of small-scale programs which mix educational inputs with life-skill training and mentoring (Inoue et al., 2015). For example, the Youth-in-Action program implemented in Ethiopia and four other African countries found that youths could develop critical work readiness skills in a relatively short period of time, and that more active family involvement and support magnified the benefits of the program (D'Sa, 2018).

Ethiopia has been progressive in its social policies and has prioritized improving educational outcomes for children, but realizing education progress for all 58 million children, including those at the bottom of the pyramid, will continue to be a challenge. This is especially true given the humanitarian crises that have affected Ethiopia in recent years and will likely continue to impact schooling and learning for millions of children. Unfortunately, this reality is common in LMICs, and substantial progress for the poorest will require additional pro-poor targeting and innovation.

One innovation that is cost-effective and has proven to be impactful in East and Southern Africa, as well as other regions of the world, is to more strategically leverage children's time outside of school for learning (Dowd et al., 2017b). Globally we see that improvements in access to education tend to take the path of least resistance; they begin with the easiest to reach—wealthier, more urban communities—and progress to harder-to-reach communities (Wagner, 2018). If we sit back and wait for schooling to come to everyone, we will waste decades of learning for children at the bottom of the pyramid. Indeed, if school disruptions due to the pandemic endure, more and more children will be without access than there were even just a decade ago. Families and communities can be mobilized now to improve learning outcomes for children at all levels of education. COVID-19 has left families hungry for resources to enable their participation in ensuring learning continuity. Greater involvement of parents and communities can also help to improve demand and accountability from policymakers for poor quality education (Rose & Alcott, 2015).

In addition, we know that time spent while children are in school is not optimal and there is much work to be done to improve the quality of education everywhere, but especially for the poorest. Ministries of Education must become more innovative in their pro-poor targeting of quality improvement initiatives (Wagner et al., 2018). A recent study from Malawi showed that supplementing administrative records on teacher placement with geo-spatial data created a more objective database of school remoteness on which to build policies for more equitable deployment of teachers and incentives (Asim et al., 2019). Having objective data driving policy improves enforcement and accountability, and preliminary results from Malawi demonstrate promising improvements in regulation of teacher placement and class size in poor communities. While there are many challenges, new ideas and creative innovations to test abound.

Gender disparities at the bottom of the pyramid

Gender parity in educational outcomes has been a top global policy priority for decades, but disadvantages for girls persist. The Millennium Development Goals set the target that: "By 2015, children everywhere, boys and girls alike, will be able to complete a full course of primary schooling". Progress toward gender parity was made and the most recent global statistics suggest that today there is relative gender parity in enrollment from pre-primary through secondary education (UNESCO, 2015b; UNICEF, 2019; World Bank, 2018). However, gender disparities in completion and learning still exist, especially for the poorest, and gains in equity are stalling or even regressing in some places (Psaki et al., 2018; World Bank, 2018).

Gender disparities in enrollment and learning outcomes worsen as girls progress through education systems. Few gender differences in these categories have been identified at the pre-primary level, and it's more common for learning outcomes to favor girls where there are differences (Save the Children, 2018; UNICEF, 2019). Results from large-scale learning assessments at the primary and secondary level display some trends of girls outperforming boys in reading and boys outperforming girls in mathematics, but overall do not display a consistent advantage for girls or boys. However, data from household surveys find that 15–19 year old girls who have completed primary education are more likely to lack basic literacy skills than boys with the same level of education (Psaki et al., 2018). One reason that girls at older ages experience lower learning outcomes is their absence from school due to menstruation and gender-based violence. Girls in LMICs often face a lack of appropriate sanitation resources to effectively manage menstruation while at school, and this can lead to increased absenteeism and disengagement (Mason et al., 2013; Miiro et al., 2018; Sommer et al., 2016). In addition, as girls age, instances of gender-based violence, early marriage, and pregnancy increase and negatively affect enrollment, attendance, and learning (Ellsberg et al., 2014; Erulkar & Muthengi, 2009; Nanda et al., 2014).

In locations where societal norms perpetuate large gender disparities in enrollment and learning, disadvantages for girls are persisting or even widening (Psaki et al., 2018). Estimates of the impact of the COVID-19 pandemic for girls include an increase in early marriage for around four million girls (World Economic Forum, 2020) and secondary school dropout for 20 million young women (MalalaFund, 2020). One example of a country that has made strides, but also continues to struggle with gender equality in education is Afghanistan.

Case study: Afghanistan

In 1999, Afghanistan was the lowest-ranking country in terms of gross enrollment rates for girls, with less than four percent of girls enrolled in school (UNESCO, 2015a). After the fall of the Taliban in 2001, reconstruction of the education system became a priority for the country as well as international donors, and Afghanistan ratified policies that support universal enrollment for boys and girls through Grade 9 (Human Rights Watch, 2017; Jones, 2008). Large investments were made in improving access and quality of education programs for all children, especially girls. Statistics about the gains in primary school enrollment and completion for girls are disputed, but UNESCO reported that the country succeeded in enrolling 72 girls for every 100 boys by 2015 (UNESCO, 2015b). However, as in other contexts, large disparities exist within the country, and poor girls living in rural areas are the least likely to access education.

Educational inequality in Afghanistan is driven by issues at the policy, school, and community levels. At the policy level, the Ministry of Education has endorsed plans supporting girls' education, but lacks the authority and resources to enforce these policies. At the school and community levels, school locations and a lack of female teachers prevent families from sending their girls to school. Most of Afghanistan is rural farmland, and children tend to live long distances from the nearest school. Families typically feel less comfortable allowing their girls to travel long distances to attend school compared to their boys. In addition, there are substantially fewer female teachers than male teachers, and families often feel uncomfortable having their daughters in close contact with unfamiliar men. At the community level, deeply held cultural beliefs and traditions that place little value on education for girls prevent families from demanding better educational conditions for their daughters.

One of the main strategies adopted by the government for improving the enrollment for all children, but especially girls, has been to build more schools. Administrative data from the Ministry of Education showed that many children lived five kilometers or further from the nearest primary school and that these schools typically did not have appropriate facilities for girls or female teachers. As a result, substantial efforts were made to improve infrastructure (i.e., build more schools in rural areas and improve facilities for women and girls) (Human Rights Watch, 2017; Jones, 2008). A randomized trial that studied the effectiveness of this strategy found that building a school in a rural village did significantly improve enrollment and learning outcomes for all children, and that the effects were even larger for girls (Burde & Linden, 2013).

Another strategy leveraged by non-governmental organizations and endorsed by the government has been to increase provision of home- or community-based education. A study of the perception of these programs by local stakeholders found that they are culturally acceptable and valued alternatives to government-based schools (Kirk & Winthrop, 2008). Community-based schools represent the only possibility for education for many girls in Afghanistan, and also provide additional opportunities for adult women to hold respected roles as teachers in their communities. However, without integration and oversight by the Afghan Ministry of Education, these programs lack alignment with government curricula, key resources, and quality oversight.

The condition of girls' education in Afghanistan is one of the most extreme in the world, and the recent change in government as of August 2021 may well make matters significantly worse. However, aspects of the dynamics found here are present in many other contexts. Globally, we find that persistent gender discrimination in education is not driven by national policies, but rather by school resource limitations and strongly held cultural beliefs. There are countries within which boys are now at an educational disadvantage, but research finds that this tends to occur in higher-functioning systems (i.e., higher income), whereas girls tend to be at a disadvantage in lower-functioning systems (lower income) (Psaki et al., 2017). Therefore, when considering how to progress toward improving education for those at the bottom of the pyramid, improving the quality of education systems in LMICs and effectively engaging communities are the most relevant ways forward for improving education for the most disadvantaged girls.

Similar to the results of the Burde and Linden (2013) study in Afghanistan, recent global research also finds that the most effective programs for improving girls' access to education focus on providing schools that are closer to girls' homes and decreasing the cost of schooling (Evans et al., 2019). Families place a lower value on education for girls, especially in patriarchal societies (Kaul, 2018), even though the private and social returns of education for girls are actually higher than for boys (Psacharopoulos & Patrinos, 2018). These types of interventions may be effective in areas where girls are struggling the most because they help to reduce the social and financial risks of sending girls to school.

In addition, alternative approaches—like community-based schools that employ local women as teachers—could help provide educational services in communities where weak government systems are not functioning. Solutions that work outside government systems are not ideal, but in the short- to medium-term they may represent the only realistic option for some children at the bottom of the pyramid. Finding effective alternative approaches will be especially critical in contexts of conflict and instability, where it is often unknown when state-supported services will resume. Studying the effectiveness of alternative educational approaches, as well as designing processes for aligning them as much as possible with government standards, is important for maximizing the potential benefits of these initiatives (Meyers & Pinnock, 2017).

In terms of improving learning outcomes once girls are enrolled in school, different types of initiatives have been shown to be promising for different age groups. A recent meta-analysis of 177 studies of both general education interventions and targeted gender-based interventions found that general interventions which raise the quality of schooling for all children tended to have the largest impact on girls' learning outcomes in early primary grades (Evans et al., 2019). As girls progress through their schooling, improving infrastructure and sanitation has been found to improve engagement in learning (Mason et al., 2013; Miiro et al., 2018; Sommer et al., 2016). Finally, meaningful engagement with community members around the value of educating girls could help to improve families' willingness to invest in education for their girls, and to increase demand for these services.

Disability at the bottom of the pyramid

Children with disabilities—who have "long-term physical, mental, intellectual or sensory impairments which in interaction with various barriers may hinder their full and effective participation in society on an equal basis with others"—represent another group of learners at the bottom of the pyramid (UNCRPD, 2007). In the education sphere, they can face challenges both in accessing education and in being well-supported once they arrive. Very few children with disabilities across the globe access pre-primary education, and among primary- and lower-secondary-school-aged children, those with disabilities are estimated to be out of school at rates that are much higher than children without disabilities (Education Commission, 2016). Access gaps widen from Grade 1 onwards, and are often about twice as large as the gap associated with rural residence or high poverty (Filmer, 2008). Kuper et al. (2014) also show disabled children's lower probability of schooling among more than 900,000 children across 30 countries, and find them more likely to pursue pre-primary and primary than secondary education. Further, those with learning and communication impairments were least likely to attend school compared to children with other types of disabilities (e.g., physical, vision, hearing); see also Mugo et al. (this volume) on education and disabilities in Kenya.

Once in school, children with disabilities may face apathy, uncertainty, and exclusion, leading to lower rates of completion and gaps in learning outcomes that widen over time (World Bank, 2019). As a result of the COVID-19 crisis, they are now even less likely to be in school or to gain foundational skills, and their parents may have heightened concerns about their return to school (World Bank, 2020). As discussed in the section above, (where raising overall educational quality is found to be key to raising girls' learning outcomes), it is important to consider the overall quality of the education systems that children with disabilities have access to (Singal, 2019a). Overcrowded classrooms, insufficient materials and teacher support, limited parental support, and no or low levels of local evidence are global challenges that affect all students' learning, and need to be considered systemically alongside more disability-specific issues like assistive technologies and teacher attitudes. On this last point, a review of studies from a variety of countries on primary school teachers' attitudes towards the inclusion of children with disabilities in regular classroom settings shows teachers are primarily neutral or negative, depending on their training and experience with such students (De Boer, Pijl, & Minnaert, 2011). Thus, improving educational quality for all children and engaging with attitudes—whether of parents, teachers, or both—can help address the challenges of disabled learners at the bottom of the pyramid.

Case study: India

In India, a supportive, inclusive policy environment places the education of children with disabilities as a central concern of its *Sarva Shiksha Abhiyan* (SSA) program, ensuring educational access and quality for children aged 6–14 years old. The program, however, faces challenges with both implementation and enforcement, resulting in children with disabilities being out of school at a rate five and a half times the general rate. When children do enroll, they are more often boys who rarely progress beyond primary schooling (Singal, 2009; UNESCO, 2019). These challenges have resulted in the pursuit of inclusive education via both mainstream schooling (overseen by the Ministry of Human Resource Development) as well as special schools (overseen by the Ministry of Social Justice and Empowerment, often implemented by NGOs). These two ministries and many additional partners have overlapping goals and age groups for which each state determines how to invest (UNESCO, 2019), which leads to implementation challenges. For example, a 2007 World Bank report noted that, while the policy provides support for aids and appliances, in practice people with disabilities rarely knew about it, or else paid to get it—transferring a right into a privilege. Though more recent evidence shows low-income parents accessing these resources and improved attendance, it remains difficult to meet basic needs and ensure that teachers have the capacity to support all children's learning (Singal, 2016).

Teacher training under SSA is primarily in-service and focused on identification of children with disabilities and management (as opposed to pedagogy); support for adapting teaching and learning materials is scarce (Singal, 2009). There are also gaps in teacher attitudes, as well as curriculum and pedagogy to support their learning effectively. For example, a positive attitude towards inclusion has been documented to have the strongest links to prior acquaintance with a person with a disability (Parasuram, 2006). Thus, the system has supportive policies, but personal relationships seem to frame acceptance in the classroom.

India's public early childhood system, the Integrated Child Development Services (ICDS), and privately managed preschools alike have very limited numbers of children with disabilities (Kaul et al., 2017). This has been longstanding: only 10 percent of people with disabilities between the ages of 3 and 35 have attended a preschool program (Government of India Ministry of Statistics and Programme Implementation, 2019) and 75 percent of five-year-olds with disabilities do not attend any educational institution (UNESCO, 2019). The presence of children with disabilities in preschool is more common in urban than rural areas, highlighting the intersectional nature of this access. In addition, ICDS teachers are not trained in how to work with children with disabilities (Alur, 2002).

Early detection of delays is important to enable timely intervention, but these practices are limited by infrastructure as well as capacity in the ICDS centers (UNESCO, 2019). Tackling this challenge head on is the Samarpan Early Intervention Center model of Madhya Pradesh, established in 2010, that aims to identify, screen, treat, and rehabilitate children with developmental delays or physical disabilities (National Institute for Transforming India Aayog & UNDP, 2015). Focused on early identification and action, it addresses social, visual, speech, hearing, mental, and physical development under one roof, aiming to remove or reduce detected delays. This program became a model for national roll-out in 2013. Since then, it has evolved to have district coordinators, distribute teaching and learning kits, experiment with mini-centers to expand access, and build hostels to facilitate short-term residential family training. It also addresses attitudinal barriers by using street theater, wall paintings, pamphlets, and advertisements to raise awareness about disability, remove feelings of embarrassment, and build sensitivity and acceptance in hopes that people will shed their inhibitions and seek support for their children (National Institute for Transforming India Aayog & UNDP, 2015). Thus, even responses built upon the developmental priorities of identification and intervention should integrate actions aimed at changing attitudes towards children with disabilities.

In the schooling system, even though the first years of the century saw an increase in the enrollment of children with disabilities (Singal, Jeffery, Jain, & Sood, 2011), one-fourth of Indian children with disabilities aged 5 to 19 do not attend any educational institution (UNESCO, 2019), with barriers including accessibility, curriculum, and pedagogy, as well as parent and teacher attitudes. The challenges of teacher attitudes range from lack of training, confidence, resources, and administrative support, to fears about whole-class impact, as well as limited prior contact with children with disabilities. Importantly, research in diverse country contexts has shown that such attitudes and fears can be shifted via week-long pre-service training, especially for those who do not have the advantage of knowing a person with a disability (see, for example, Sharma & Nuttal, 2016). Further, parents of children with disabilities from all socioeconomic strata are increasingly supportive—in attitude and action—of their children's education, but their engagement is not particularly well-organized (Singal, 2016; Singal & Jain, 2012). Thus, models and actors exist for concretely moving forward and implementing the supportive policy that exists in India, but thus far success has varied state-by-state alongside variation in investment (see Figure 3).

Bihar
- 2014-15 (A): 27
- 2015-16 (A): 28
- 2016-17 (BE): 36
- 2016-17 (RE): 36
- 2017-18 (BE): 42

Chhattisgarh
- 2014-15 (A): 104
- 2015-16 (A): 122
- 2016-17 (BE): 176
- 2016-17 (RE): 151
- 2017-18 (BE): 211

Maharashtra
- 2014-15 (A): 35
- 2015-16 (A): 44
- 2016-17 (BE): 48
- 2016-17 (RE): 41
- 2017-18 (BE): 49

Tamil Nadu
- 2014-15 (A): 589
- 2015-16 (A): 530
- 2016-17 (BE): 682
- 2016-17 (RE): 686
- 2017-18 (BE): 663

Uttar Pradesh
- 2014-15 (A): 306
- 2015-16 (A): 243
- 2016-17 (BE): 325
- 2016-17 (RE): 302
- 2017-18 (BE): 295

West Bengal
- 2014-15 (A): 42
- 2015-16 (A): 53
- 2016-17 (BE): 36
- 2016-17 (RE): 36
- 2017-18 (BE): 73

Millions of Rupees

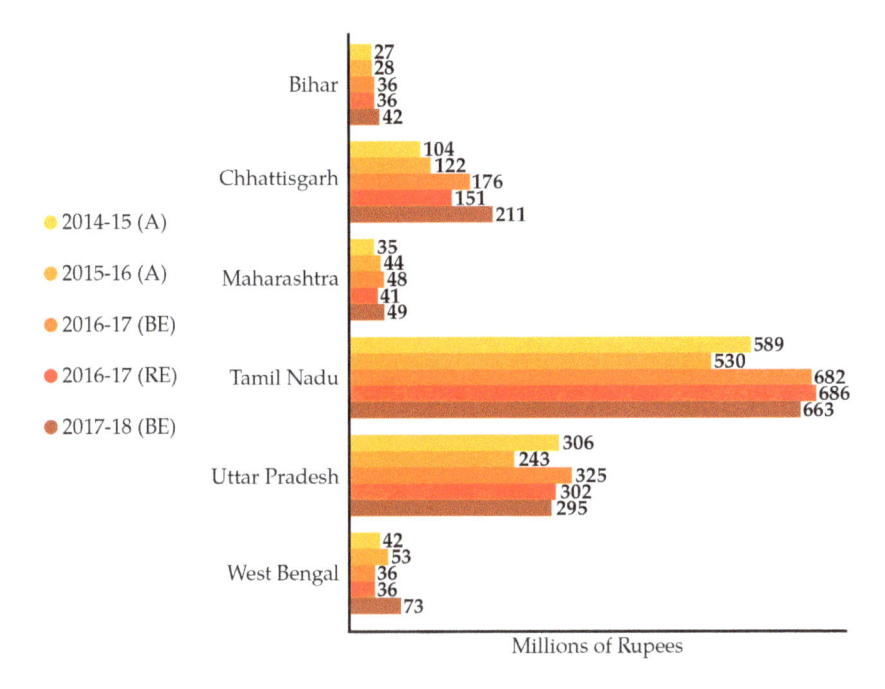

Fig. 3. Budgetary interventions for primary and secondary school education for children with disabilities—selected states (millions of Rupees).

Figure 3 suggests that a disabled child among Tamil Nadu's 68 million residents is likely to enjoy greater investment than one among Uttar Pradesh's 204 million, where investment in children with disabilities was less than one percent of the SSA budget (UNESCO, 2019). Investment in professional and attitudinal development has not yet occurred, leaving many teachers feeling unable to respond to the needs of children with disabilities. This deficit leads to low classroom engagement, low levels of learning, and dismal transition rates into upper primary and beyond (Singal, 2019b). Indeed, only one in five Indians with a disability aged 15 or older has attended secondary school or higher education; only one in four is in the labor force (Government of India Ministry of Statistics and Programme Implementation, 2019). Research carried out in Madhya Pradesh contrasts such frustrating employment outcomes with disabled young people's own sense of the value of schooling. The youth see their education as having enhanced their social skills and networks, especially in terms of confronting stigmatization, while their parents were more likely to label schooling a failure because it did not lead to a job (Singal et al., 2011). Either way, the main challenge of *how* to deliver on India's long-standing vision of inclusive education remains.

Whether in the ICDS or in the classrooms of primary or secondary schools, children with disabilities in India are increasingly included, but often still marginalized (Singal, 2019a). SSA supports their presence but lacks pervasive early intervention options, clear teacher training and support mechanisms, and consistent and adequate budgetary allocations to make the vision a reality. Still, children with disabilities gain skills and networks—the more education they have, the greater these are—especially boys; however, these investments inconsistently lead to employment or independence, leaving the children, families, and teachers alike frustrated. The policy-practice connection for disabled children at the bottom of the pyramid is under-funded and under-implemented to date, but possibilities for leveraging greater learning exist to be tested.

Language of instruction at the bottom of the pyramid

Many nations' education policy statements uphold a child's right to learn in the language that they speak at home. In classrooms across the globe, however, the reality is that the language of instruction is very often determined by the priorities of head teachers, teachers, and parents. These local decision-makers determine whether the classrooms in their communities feature a foreign language or local language(s) (Trudell, 2007). In many settings, local attitudes and priorities tend to favor international languages, given their believed economic value and prestige. Whether it's French in Mali or English in Vietnam, education occurs in international languages officially as early as the first few grades of primary school, and in practice often from the start, leaving children who do not speak them at the bottom of the pyramid.

The languages that children hear in the classroom often change across pre-primary, primary, and upper-primary/secondary schooling, such that children experience instruction in two, sometimes three, languages in different dosages and to different purposes across their school careers. Even in pre-primary education where local languages are more commonly used, it is not an absolute (Bronteng, Berson, & Berson, 2019). These shifts and changes in focus and exposure make it unsurprising that overall learning is poor. The challenges of languages at the bottom of the pyramid are so long-standing that they affect both the teachers who learned the foreign language incompletely as they went through the system as well as their current students. Indeed, a recent survey across seven countries in Africa showed that only 11 percent of fourth-graders were able to read a paragraph in their national (international) language, and only one in 10 of their teachers had mastered their own students' language curriculum (Bold et al., 2017).

Case study: Kenya

Kenyan language policy states that the medium of instruction in pre-primary education is the language of the catchment area. It also states that literacy is taught in the lower primary grades in the first language of the learner, with English and Kiswahili (where it is not the language of the catchment area) taught as subjects, and English is the medium of instruction beginning in Grade 4 (Kenya Institute of Curriculum Development, 2019). However, implementation can be quite different from policy. The majority of 72 pre-primary and primary teachers from across the Kisii, Kericho, and Bondo counties interviewed by Begi (2014) report leading their classes in English, a situation that Begi links to key inputs like training (one-quarter of teachers are trained in how to use their mother-tongue in the classroom), materials (one-third have culturally relevant materials), and official support (only 55 percent of pre-primary teachers, and less than 40 percent of primary teachers, feel supported in using their mother-tongue). This situation is made worse by the fact that only 34 percent of Grade 4 language teachers have the minimum subject knowledge (Bold et al., 2017). Thus, without optimal support in local or national languages, only 26 percent of Kenyan fourth-graders can read a paragraph, and their average reading comprehension score is 40 percent correct (Bold et al., 2017). While students and teachers alike struggle, norms like the informal use of students' language to convey meaning being considered a sign of poor teaching (Trudell, 2004) can only make things worse.

Kenyan parents value education, but not all have the reading skills or the awareness of the importance of oral language for literacy development to contribute to foundational reading skills from a child's first years. For example, a study from Uwezo (2015) estimates that, on average, 45 percent of mothers of school-aged children cannot read English at a second-grade level, and that this proportion could be as high as 90 percent in the highly impoverished Northern Eastern Province. This leads to a situation in which young Kenyan children have little support from their closest caregivers in navigating shifts between languages in their early years of schooling.

Recent research findings present a viable option for addressing this challenge with young children. A cluster-randomized control trial demonstrated that a program that provided training and dialogic reading materials, with books featuring colorful pictures and familiar content related to children's daily lives (that had been adapted for a low-literacy population), boosted children's book-related vocabulary significantly, especially among children with illiterate caregivers (Knauer, Jakiela, Ozier, Aboud, & Fernald, 2019). Interestingly, additional input (i.e., refresher training or a home visit) did not further enhance these outcomes, suggesting that this could be a low-cost and scalable model to replicate in other contexts. While this intervention measures only one developmental aspect of being school-ready, reading and discussing books with parents or other caregivers has myriad benefits that contribute to holistic development (Mendelsohn et al., 2018).

At the primary level, Free Primary Education in Kenya still excludes the poorest families (Oketch & Ngware, 2010), and Kenyan policy delineates the use of mother-tongues for instruction in Grades 1–3, with both Kiswahili and English as subjects. In reality, however, English dominates instruction in these grades, leading to low levels of English-reading mechanics and little comprehension, and even in the face of more limited instruction, better comprehension in Kiswahili and mother-tongues (Trudell & Piper, 2014). At home, most parents do not have the skills to interpret their students' learning data (Lieberman, Posner, & Tsai, 2014)—lessening the level of home support for the transition to the next level of schooling. The result is a system in which young children are taught intensively in a language that the vast majority of them do not speak, so it is not that surprising that only three in 10 Grade

3 students can do Grade 2 schoolwork (Uwezo, 2016). These results are worse for poor children and children living in rural areas, many of whom use neither English nor Kiswahili in their daily lives outside of the classroom, as those in urban areas do (Piper & Miksic, 2011).

Even if teachers believe that students should be taught in their mother-tongues, they themselves may not speak the language of the area, which makes acting on that notion challenging, if not impossible. Further, a multilingual classroom negates the ability to choose one mother-tongue to speak, leading to a reliance on Kiswahili or English instead of local languages (Muthwii, 2004). Responses to these issues that test language policy options, like the two versions of the Primary Math and Reading Initiative (PRIMR) (one of which tested use of English and Kiswahili, and another the use of those languages as well as mother-tongues) show that mother-tongue instruction leads to the acquisition of higher-order reading skills like fluency and comprehension (Piper, Zuilkowski, & Ong'ele, 2016). Scaling this solution would require the political will and resourcing to tackle the challenges of teacher-student language matches and multilingualism, noted above. Teacher training and allocation based on language ability along with shifts in political will and resourcing would help ensure that the four proven PRIMR intervention components (teacher training and guides, student books, and instructional coaching) deliver on high-quality language policy implementation.

From Grade 4 onwards, when the medium of instruction in Kenya officially shifts to English, the nature of the language challenge becomes intergenerational—not only within families but also across generations of teachers and learners in the schools. The access issue has mostly resolved itself via the attrition of students who cannot speak enough English to continue. Challenges are heightened because "the language teacher is a non-native speaker who has been taught and trained by non-native users of English mak[ing] the task of teaching ... a very difficult one; indeed a nightmare" (Kioko & Muthwii, 2001, p. 206). Kembo-Sure and Ogechi (2016) document the difficulties that teachers of science and mathematics have when they themselves face challenges in both English proficiency and in the mastery of the math and science concepts that they are teaching. The resulting classroom interactions do not effectively facilitate learning. Thus, solutions must combine elements of student and teacher support in order to result in better instruction and outcomes. One such opportunity consists of using an assessment of Mathematical Knowledge for Teaching (Miheso-O'Connor Khakasa & Berger, 2016) to discover teachers' strengths and weaknesses in teaching the Kenyan secondary math curriculum, and using this proactively to overcome identified challenges. Curiously, the framework does not consider English language proficiency but could be strengthened—and provide more holistic solutions for teachers and their students—by doing so.

Where a mismatch between language policy and language use in schools in Kenya exists, children, especially those at the bottom of the pyramid, struggle to learn. Parents are unable to support their children's learning and teachers may not have mastered the content when learning in a second or third language themselves. Further, due to limitations in access to English speakers as well as practice opportunities, many teachers may not have mastered enough English to effectively support learning. These challenges multiply across generations of teachers and students, and across levels of education.

Unfortunately, as evidenced by the cross-country studies noted above, this situation is not unique to Kenya. Any solution must address all parties. The solutions reviewed above—from dialogic reading between parents and children at the pre-primary level, to well-supported mother-tongue implementation in Primary Grades 1–3 and the possibility of targeted professional development in upper-primary and secondary schooling—offer several promising options for addressing these challenges (Knauer et al., 2019; Miheso-O'Connor Khakasa & Berger, 2016; Piper, Zuilkowski, & Ong'ele, 2016). If such efforts at all levels of education target those struggling most, they could progressively contribute to improving learning for those at the bottom of the pyramid.

Conclusion

Children at the bottom of the pyramid are often dealing with more than one dimension of disadvantage. With global GDP expected to contract by 4.9 percent as a result of COVID-19, international, national, and household spending on education will likely decline as well—disproportionately affecting the most marginalized learners (IMF, 2020). In order to make meaningful progress toward the UN goals set for 2030, we must take larger, more innovative steps forward. Education systems need to recognize the diversity in their student populations, prioritize early investment and enrollment for the most marginalized, and take more meaningful steps toward implementing proven policies that can improve access and learning for all. Strategies that show promise include more fully leveraging the resources that currently exist in disadvantaged communities, investing in teachers, using administrative data more strategically, and developing more targeted policies for children at the bottom of the pyramid.

Stronger engagement of parents and communities can ease some of the disconnections between policy and practice, and improve educational outcomes for the most disadvantaged children. Empowering families around their children's education will help increase demand for higher quality services and hold policymakers accountable for these disconnections (Rose & Alcott, 2015). Strengthening the connection between schools and families can also help school administrators and teachers better understand the needs and demands of the communities they serve, and can help parents better understand educators' practices to promote learning. Conversely, failing to meaningfully engage families in their children's education can inhibit the results of effective classroom reforms. For example, a randomized control trial of a new teacher-training program for pre-primary students in Ghana with three study arms (control, teacher training only, and teacher training with parental awareness) found that adding parental awareness meetings counteracted the positive effects of the program that were found in the study arm that involved teacher training only. That is, study results showed significant positive effects on learning in the teacher-training study arm, and no effects in the study arm with teacher training and parental awareness sessions. Interviews with parents revealed that many parents disagreed with the emphasis the program had placed on child-centered, play-based pedagogy and felt strongly that pre-primary classes should focus on academics and discipline (Wolf et al., 2019).

Research from all levels of education finds that effective engagement of parents and communities can substantially enhance the learning that takes place in classrooms (Friedlander et al., 2019; D'Sa, 2018; Dowd, Borisova, Amente, & Yenew, 2016; Dowd et al., 2017b; Özler et al., 2016). In addition, in situations where children are out of school, especially in the early childhood period, parents and communities can fill an important gap in early learning support for the most disadvantaged children (Borisova, Pisani, Dowd, & Lin, 2017). This reality has been heightened by COVID-19 as children of all ages were learning from home. Many interventions and systems across the globe made a shift to some form of distance learning, placing parents in an even more central role in their children's education. Emerging evidence collected during COVID-19 lockdowns also suggests that supporting parents' mental health and wellbeing is critical for supporting children's wellbeing and learning during times when they have less access to the supports typically provided by schools and other institutions (Center for Translational Neuroscience, 2020; Yoshikawa et al., 2020). Building stronger synergies with families leverages a critical cadre of resources that already exist in communities around the world.

Children at the bottom of the pyramid are often those who enter classrooms with different or additional needs, and teachers must be better equipped to reach the wide range of children they serve. For example, any child is likely to struggle with mastering the language of instruction if their teacher does not fully grasp that curriculum, but those who do not speak this language outside of school or those with learning delays or disabilities are differentially affected. At a minimum, these children need teachers who have mastered the curriculum, and ideally their teachers should be equipped with additional strategies and resources to support their unique learning needs. Systematically improving pre-service and in-service support for teachers is critical for improving learning outcomes for all children, but especially the most disadvantaged.

A promising technique for driving large-scale improvement for children at the bottom of the pyramid is better use of administrative data. Each year, more and more data are generated about children's access and learning outcomes, but little of it is transformed into useful information for governments. For example, the approach of using existing administrative records and geo-spatial data to inform allocation of teachers in poor communities in Malawi is a helpful example of how data can be leveraged to hold policymakers accountable and improve learning conditions for children at the bottom of the pyramid (Asim, Chimombo, Chugunov, & Gera, 2019). Data must also be leveraged to understand which solutions work, for whom, and under which conditions. The profile of the most disadvantaged children differs depending on the context, as do the primary drivers of their educational outcomes. In order to accelerate and improve efficiency in investments for children at the bottom of the pyramid, we must be continuously testing and learning about not only whether new solutions work, but also how and why.

Policies that target the most disadvantaged children in their particular contexts, and recognize that these children require more than the status quo, will be critical for improving learning outcomes for all. Policy and investment need to progress beyond a "one size fits all" approach, and recognize that producing equitable learning outcomes for all children requires different levels of inputs for different groups. This is essential, as forecasts suggest that a reduction in national education budgets of $22 billion in 2020 could grow to $55 billion in 2021 (Save the Children, 2020). Humanitarian contexts are especially challenging and ongoing investment is needed to reach the estimated 104 million out-of-school children living in areas affected by violent conflicts and political instability pre-COVID, as well as those who have joined their ranks in 2020 (UNICEF, 2018).

Children who are typically marginalized—girls, the poorest, those with disabilities, and those from different language or ethnic groups—and fare even worse in these contexts. To date, governments in LMICs, as well as international donors, have been prioritizing the "reach" of an investment over the depth or the profile of the children being served. This has driven the large improvements in coverage that have been achieved since the 2015 UN Millennium Development Goals, but now we need to shift the conversation from quantity to quality.

References

Alur, M. (2002). "They did not figure": Policy exclusion of disabled people in India. *International Journal of Inclusive Education*, 6(2), 101–112. https://doi.org/10.1080/13603110110091625

Asim, S., Chimombo, J., Chugunov, D., & Gera, R. (2019). Moving teachers to Malawi's remote communities: A data-driven approach to teacher deployment. *International Journal of Educational Development*, 65, 26–43. https://doi.org/10.1016/j.ijedudev.2018.12.002

Bashir, S., Lockheed, M., Ninan, E., & Tan, J.-P. (2018). *Facing forward: School for learning in Africa*. Washington, DC: World Bank.

Baum, D. R., Hernandez, J. E., & Orchard, A. (2019). Early childhood education for all: A mixed-methods study of the global policy agenda in Tanzania. *Early Years, 39*(3), 260–275. https://doi.org/10.1080/09575146.2019.1572075

Begi, N. (2014). Use of mother tongue as a language of instruction in early years of school to preserve the Kenyan culture. *Journal of Education and Practice, 4*(3), 37–49.

Black, M. M., Walker, S. P., Fernald, L. C. H., Andersen, C., DiGirolamo, A., Lu, C., ... & Grantham-McGregor, S. M. (2016). Early childhood development coming of age: Science through the life course. *The Lancet, 6736*(16), 1–14. https://doi.org/10.1016/S0140-6736(16)31389-7

Bold, T., Filmer, D., Martin, G. H., Molina, E., Stacy, B., Rockmore, C., ... & Wane, W. (2017). *What do teachers know and do? Does it matter? Evidence from primary schools in Africa* (World Bank Policy Research Working Paper No. 7965). https://doi.org/10.13140/RG.2.2.22383.23201

Borisova, I., Pisani, L., Dowd, A. J., & Lin, H.-C. (2017). Effective interventions to strengthen early language and literacy skills in low-income countries: Comparison of a family-focused approach and a pre-primary programme in Ethiopia. *Early Child Development and Care, 187*(3–4), 1–17. https://doi.org/10.1080/03004430.2016.1255607

Bronteng, J. E., Berson, I. R., & Berson, M. J. (2019). Public perception of early childhood language policy in Ghana: An exploratory study. *Early Years, 39*(3), 310–325. https://doi.org/10.1080/09575146.2019.1631759

Burde, D., & Linden, L. L. (2013). Bringing education to Afghan girls: A randomized controlled trial of village-based schools. *American Economic Journal, 5*(3), 27–40. https://doi.org/10.1257/app.5.3.27

Carvalho, S., & Hares, S. (2020). *Six ways COVID-19 will shape the future of education*. Center for Global Development. https://www.cgdev.org/blog/six-ways-covid-19-will-shape-future-education

Center for Translational Neuroscience. (2020). How long can the levee hold? *Medium*. https://medium.com/rapid-ec-project/how-long-can-the-levee-hold-2a2cd0779914

D'Sa, N. (2018). *Supporting rural youth to leverage decent work: Evidence from the cross-sectoral Youth in Action program*. https://resourcecentre.savethechildren.net/node/14228/pdf/sc_pathways_to_opportunity_oct_2018_web_0.pdf

De Boer, A., Pijl, S. J., & Minnaert, A. (2011). Regular primary schoolteachers' attitudes towards inclusive education: A review of the literature. *International Journal of Inclusive Education, 15*(3), 331–353. https://doi.org/10.1080/13603110903030089

Dowd, A. J., Borisova, I., Amente, A., & Yenew, A. (2016). Realizing capabilities in Ethiopia: Maximizing early childhood investment for impact and equity. *Journal of Human Development and Capabilities, 17*(4), 477–493. https://doi.org/10.1080/19452829.2016.1225702

Dowd, A. J., Friedlander, E., Jonason, C., Leer, J., Sorensen, L., Guajardo, J., ... & Pisani, L. (2017a). Lifewide learning for early reading development. *New Directions for Child and Adolescent Development,* (115), 31–49. https://doi.org/10.1002/cad

Dowd, A., Pisani, L., Dusabe, C., & Howell, H. (2017b). *Leveraging the enthusiasm of parents and caregivers for lifewide learning.* https://www.unicef.org/esa/sites/unicef.org.esa/files/2018-09/EducationThinkPieces_3_Parents-and-caregivers.pdf

Education Commission. (2016). *The Learning Generation: Investing in education for a changing world.* Global Campaign for Education. https://report.educationcommission.org/wp-content/uploads/2016/09/Learning_Generation_Full_Report.pdf

Ellsberg, M., Arango, D. J., Morton, M., Gennari, F., Kiplesund, S., Contreras, M., & Watts, C. (2014). Prevention of violence against women and girls: What does the evidence say? *Lancet, 385*(9977), 1555–1566. https://doi.org/10.1016/S0140-6736(14)61703-7

Erulkar, A., & Muthengi, E. (2009). *Evaluation of Berhane Hewan: A program to delay child marriage in rural Ethiopia.* Guttmacher Institute. https://www.guttmacher.org/journals/ipsrh/2009/03/evaluation-berhane-hewan-program-delay-child-marriage-rural-ethiopia

Evans, D. K., Yuan, F., Filmer, D., Ganju, E., Goldstein, M., Jakiela, P., ... & Yorke, L. (2019). *What we learn about girls' education from interventions that do not focus on girls* (Working Paper No. 513). Center for Global Development. www.cgdev.orgwww.cgdev.org

Filmer, D. (2008). Disability, poverty, and schooling in developing countries: Results from 14 household surveys. *World Bank Economic Review, 22*(1), 141–163. https://doi.org/10.1093/wber/lhm021

Friedlander, E. W., Arshan, N., Zhou, S., & Goldenberg, C. (2019). Lifewide or school-only learning: Approaches to addressing the developing world's learning crisis. *American Educational Research Journal, 56*(2), 333–367. https://doi.org/10.3102/0002831218792841

Government of India Ministry of Statistics and Programme Implementation. (2019). *Persons with disabilities in India.* New Delhi.

Human Rights Watch. (2017). *"I won't be a doctor, and one day you'll be sick": Girls' access to education in Afghanistan.*

Ilie, S., & Rose, P. (2016). Is equal access to higher education in South Asia and sub-Saharan Africa achievable by 2030? *Higher Education, 72*(4), 435–455. https://doi.org/10.1007/s10734-016-0039-3

IMF. (2020). World economic outlook update June 2020. *World Economic Outlook, 2*(6). https://www.imf.org/en/Publications/WEO/Issues/2020/06/24/WEOUpdateJune2020

Inoue, K., Di Gropello, E., Taylor, Y. S., & Gresham, J. (2015). *Out-of-school youth in sub-Saharan Africa: A policy perspective* (Directions in Development: Human Development). Washington, DC: World Bank.

Jones, A. M. E. (2008). Afghanistan on the educational road to access and equity. *Asia Pacific Journal of Education, 28*(3), 277–290. https://doi.org/10.1080/02188790802267423

Kaul, V., Bhattacharjea, S., Chaudhary, A. B., Ramanujan, P., Banerji, M., & Nanda, M. (2017). The India early childhood education impact study. New Delhi: UNICEF.

Kembo-Sure, E., & Ogechi, N. O. (2016). Literacy through a foreign language and children's rights to education: An examination of Kenya's medium of instruction policy. *Nordic Journal of African Studies, 25*(1), 92–106.

Kenya Institute of Curriculum Development. (2019). *Basic education curriculum framework*. Nairobi.

Kioko, A. N., & Muthwii, M. J. (2001). The demands of a changing society: English in education in Kenya today. *Language, Culture and Curriculum, 14*, 201–213. https://doi.org/10.1080/07908310108666622

Kirk, J., & Winthrop, R. (2008). Home-based school teachers in Afghanistan: Teaching for tarbia and student well-being. *Teaching and Teacher Education, 24*(4), 876–88. https://doi.org/10.1016/j.tate.2007.11.014

Knauer, H. A., Jakiela, P., Ozier, O., Aboud, F., & Fernald, L. C. H. (2019). Enhancing young children's language acquisition through parent–child book-sharing: A randomized trial in rural Kenya. *Early Childhood Research Quarterly*, 1–12. https://doi.org/10.1016/j.ecresq.2019.01.002

Kuper, H., Dok, A. M. Van, Wing, K., Danquah, L., Evans, J., Zuurmond, M., & Gallinetti, J. (2014). The impact of disability on the lives of children: Cross-sectional data including 8,900 children with disabilities and 898,834 children without disabilities across 30 countries. *PLoS ONE, 9*(9). https://doi.org/10.1371/journal.pone.0107300

Lieberman, E. S., Posner, D. N., & Tsai, L. L. (2014). Does information lead to more active citizenship? Evidence from an education intervention in rural Kenya. *World Development, 60*, 69–83. https://doi.org/10.1016/j.worlddev.2014.03.014

Malala Fund. (2020). *Girls' education and COVID-19*. https://malala.org/newsroom/archive/malala-fund-releases-report-girls-education-covid-19

Mason, L., Nyothach, E., Alexander, K., Odhiambo, F. O., Eleveld, A., Vulule, J., ... & Phillips-Howard, P. A. (2013). 'We keep it secret so no one should know': A qualitative study to explore young schoolgirls attitudes and experiences with menstruation in rural Western Kenya. *PLoS ONE, 8*(11), e79132. https://doi.org/10.1371/journal.pone.0079132

McCoy, D. C., Peet, E. D., Ezzati, M., Danaei, G., Black, M. M., Sudfeld, C. R., & Fink, G. (2016). Early childhood developmental status in low- and middle-income countries: National, regional, and global prevalence estimates using predictive modeling. *PLOS Medicine, 13*(6), e1002034. https://doi.org/10.1371/journal.pmed.1002034

Mendelsohn, A. L., Cates, C. B., Weisleder, A., Johnson, S. B., Seery, A. M., Canfield, C. F., ... & Dreyer, B. P. (2018). Reading aloud, play, and social-emotional development. *Pediatrics, 141*(5), e20173393. https://doi.org/10.1542/peds.2017-3393

Meyers, J., & Pinnock, H. (2017). *Guide to the accelerated education principles*. UNHCR. https://www.unhcr.org/59ce4fc77

Miheso-O'Connor Khakasa, M., & Berger, M. (2016). Status of teachers' proficiency in mathematical knowledge for teaching at secondary school level in Kenya. *International Journal of Science and Mathematics Education, 14*, 419–435. https://doi.org/10.1007/s10763-015-9630-9

Miiro, G., Rutakumwa, R., Nakiyingi-Miiro, J., Nakuya, K., Musoke, S., Namakula, J., ... & Weiss, H. A. (2018). Menstrual health and school absenteeism among adolescent girls in Uganda (MENISCUS): A feasibility study. *BMC Women's Health, 18*(1). https://doi.org/10.1186/s12905-017-0502-z

Muthwii, M. J. (2004). Language of instruction: A qualitative analysis of the perceptions of parents, pupils and teachers among the kalenjin in Kenya. *Language, Culture and Curriculum, 17*(1), 15–32. https://doi.org/10.1080/07908310408666679

Nanda, P., Datta, N., & Das, P. (2014). *Impact of conditional cash transfers on girls' education*. IMPACCT.

National Institute for Transforming India Aayog & UNDP. (2015). *Good practices resource book*. New Delhi: OneWorld Foundation.

OECD. (2019). *PISA 2018 results (Volume I): What students know and can do*. https://doi.org/10.1787/5f07c754-en

Oketch, M., & Ngware, M. (2010). Free primary education still excludes the poorest of the poor in urban Kenya. *Development in Practice, 20*(4), 603–610. https://doi.org/10.1080/09614521003763095

Özler, B., Fernald, L. C. H., Kariger, P., Mcconnell, C., Neuman, M., & Fraga, E. (2016). Combining preschool teacher training with parenting education: A cluster-randomized controlled trial. *Journal of Developmental Economics, 133*, 448–467. https://doi.org/10.1016/j.jdeveco.2018.04.004

Pankhurst, A., Woldehanna, T., Araya, M., Tafere, Y., Rossiter, J., Tiumelissan, A., & Birhanu, K. (2018). *Young Lives Ethiopia: Lessons from longitudinal research with the children of the millennium*. Young Lives.

Parasuram, K. (2006). Variables that affect teachers' attitudes towards disability and inclusive education in Mumbai, India. *Disability and Society, 21*(3), 231–242. https://doi.org/10.1080/09687590600617352

Piper, B., & Miksic, E. (2011). Mother tongue and reading: Using early grade reading assessments to investigate language-of-instruction policy in East Africa. *The early grade reading assessment: Applications and interventions to improve basic literacy* (pp. 139–182). RTI Press. https://doi.org/10.3768/rtipress.2011.bk.0007.1109.1

Piper, B., Zuilkowski, S. S., & Ong'ele, S. (2016). Implementing mother tongue instruction in the real world: Results from a medium-scale randomized controlled trial in Kenya. *Comparative Education Review, 60*(4), 776–807.

Psacharopoulos, G., & Patrinos, G.H. (2018). *Returns to investment in education: A decennial review of the global literature* (Policy Research Working Paper No. 8402). Washington, DC: World Bank.

Psaki, S. R., McCarthy, K. J., & Mensch, B. S. (2018). Measuring gender equality in education: Lessons from trends in 43 countries. *Population and Development Review, 44*(1), 117–142. https://doi.org/10.1111/padr.12121

Rose, P., & Alcott, B. (2015). *How can education systems become equitable by 2030?* Health and Education Advice and Resource Team (HEART). www.heart-resources.org

Rose, P., Sabates, R., Alcott, B., & Ilie, S. (2017). *Overcoming inequalities within countries to achieve global convergence in learning* (Background Paper). REAL Centre, Faculty of Education, University of Cambridge. https://www.repository.cam.ac.uk/bitstream/handle/1810/262418/Overcoming-Inequalities-within-Countries%282%29.pdf?sequence=1&isAllowed=y

Save the Children. (2017). *Windows into early learning and development*. Washington, DC: Save the Children International.

Save the Children. (2018). *Beyond access: Exploring equity in early childhood learning and development*. Washington, DC: Save the Children International. www.idela-network.org/resource/beyond-access/

Save the Children. (2020). *Save our education: Protect every child's right to learn in the COVID-19 response and recovery*. Washington, DC: Save the Children International. https://resourcecentre.savethechildren.net/node/17871/pdf/save_our_education_0.pdf

Sharma, U., & Nuttal, A. (2016). The impact of training on pre-service teacher attitudes, concerns, and efficacy towards inclusion. *Asia-Pacific Journal of Teacher Education, 44*(2), 142–155. https://doi.org/10.1080/1359866X.2015.1081672

Singal, N. (2009). Education of children with disabilities in India. *Prospects, 46*, 171–183. https://doi.org/10.1007/s11125-016-9383-4

Singal, N. (2016). Schooling children with disabilities: Parental perceptions and experiences. *International Journal of Educational Development, 50*, 33–40.

Singal, N. (2019a). Challenges and opportunities in efforts towards inclusive education: Reflections from India. *International Journal of Inclusive Education, 23*, 827–840. https://doi.org/10.1080/13603116.2019.1624845

Singal, N. (2019b). What works? The case of inclusive education. *IIEP Learning Portal*. Paris: UNESCO. https://learningportal.iiep.unesco.org/en/blog/what-works-the-case-of-inclusive-education

Singal, N., & Jain, A. (2012) Repositioning youth with disabilities: Focusing on their social and work lives. *Comparative Education, 48*(2), 167–180. https://doi.org/10.1080/03050068.2011.608895

Singal, N., Jeffery, R., Jain, A., & Sood, N. (2011). The enabling role of education in the lives of young people with disabilities in India: Achieved and desired outcomes. *International Journal of Inclusive Education, 15*(10), 1205–1218. https://doi.org/10.1080/13603116.2011.555076

Sommer, M., Caruso, B. A., Sahin, M., Calderon, T., Cavill, S., Mahon, T., & Phillips-Howard, P. A. (2016). A time for global action: Addressing girls' menstrual hygiene management needs in schools. *PLOS Medicine, 13*(2), e1001962. https://doi.org/10.1371/journal.pmed.1001962

Trudell, B. (2004). *The power of the local: Education choices and language maintenance among the Bafut, Kom and Nso' communities of Northwest Cameroon* (Doctoral thesis). University of Edinburgh.

Trudell, B. (2007). Local community perspectives and language of education in sub-Saharan African communities. *International Journal of Educational Development, 27*(5), 552–563. https://doi.org/10.1016/j.ijedudev.2007.02.002

Trudell, B., & Piper, B. (2014). Whatever the law says: Language policy implementation and early-grade literacy achievement in Kenya. *Current Issues in Language Planning, 15*(1), 4–21. https://doi.org/10.1080/14664208.2013.856985

United Nations Convention on the Rights of Persons with Disabilities. (2007). *United Nations, Treaty Series, No.* (p. 3). https://treaties.un.org/doc/Publication/UNTS/Volume%202515/v2515.pdf

UNESCO Institute for Statistics. (2018). *One in five children, adolescents and youth is out of school* (Fact Sheet No. 48, UIS/FS/2018/ED/48). http://uis.unesco.org/sites/default/files/documents/fs48-one-five-children-adolescents-youth-out-school-2018-en.pdf

UNESCO. (2015a). *Global monitoring report. Education for All 2000–2015: Achievements and challenges.* http://unesdoc.unesco.org/images/0023/002322/232205e.pdf

UNESCO. (2015b). *The Millennium Development Goals report 2015.* http://www.un.org/millenniumgoals/2015_MDG_Report/pdf/MDG 2015 rev (July 1).pdf

UNESCO. (2019). *N for nose: State of the education report for India 2019: Children with disabilities.* http://www.unesco.org/new/en/newdelhi/home

UNESCO. (2020). *Global education monitoring report 2020: Inclusion and education: All means all*. Paris.

UNICEF. (2017). *UNICEF annual report 2017: Ethiopia*.

UNICEF. (2019). *A world ready to learn: Prioritizing quality early childhood education*. New York.

UNICEF. (2020). *Addressing the learning crisis: An urgent need to better finance education for the poorest children*. New York.

Uwezo. (2015). *Are our children learning? The state of education in Kenya in 2015 and beyond*. Nairobi.

Uwezo. (2016). *Are our children learning? Uwezo Kenya sixth learning assessment report*. Nairobi.

Wagner, D. A. (2018). *Learning as development: Rethinking international education in a changing world*. New York: Routledge.

Wagner, D. A., Wolf, S., & Boruch, R. F. (Eds.) (2018). *Learning at the bottom of the pyramid: Science, measurement, and policy in low-income countries*. Paris: UNESCO-IIEP.

Wolf, S., Lawrence Aber, J., Behrman, J. R., & Tsinigo, E. (2019). Experimental impacts of the 'quality preschool for Ghana' interventions on teacher professional well-being, classroom quality, and children's school readiness. *Journal of Research on Educational Effectiveness*, 12(1), 10–37. https://doi.org/10.1080/19345747.2018.1517199

World Bank. (2007). *People with disabilities in India: From commitments to outcomes*. New Delhi: Human Development Unit, South Asia Region.

World Bank. (2018). *World Development Report 2018: Learning to realize education's promise*. Washington, DC. https://doi.org/doi:10.1596/978-1-4648-1096-1

World Bank. (2019). *Every learner matters: Unpacking the learning crisis for children with disabilities*. Washington, DC.

World Bank. (2020). *Simulating the potential impacts of the COVID-19 school closures on schooling and learning outcomes: A set of global estimates*. Washington, DC. https://www.worldbank.org/en/topic/education/publication/simulating-potential-impacts-of-covid-19-school-closures-learning-outcomes-a-set-of-global-estimates

World Economic Forum. (2020). *What impact is COVID-19 having on child marriage?* https://www.weforum.org/agenda/2020/05/coronavirus-early-child-marriage-covid19-pandemic/

Yoshikawa, H., Wuermli, A. J., Rebello Britto, P., Dreyer, B., Leckman, J. F., Lye, S. J., Ponguta, L. P., Richter, L. M., & Stein, A. (2020). Effects of the global coronavirus disease-2019 pandemic on early childhood development: Short- and long-term risks and mitigating program and policy actions. *The Journal of Pediatrics*, 223, 188–193. https://doi.org/10.1016/j.jpeds.2020.05.020

2. Education on the Move

How Migration Affects Learning Outcomes

Jo Kelcey, Ozen Guven, and Dana Burde

Introduction

Education is a right regardless of one's migratory status. Moreover, access to quality education can help migrants navigate the uncertainties of geographical displacement and contribute to the social and economic development of their host states (Dryden-Peterson, 2017; OECD, 2018b; UNESCO, 2019). Of the estimated 7.4 million school-aged refugees registered with UNHCR, only 61 percent are enrolled in primary school, compared to a global average enrollment rate of 92 percent (UNHCR, 2018a). Yet refugees comprise a relatively small proportion of the world's migrants. More numerous, but largely overlooked in the literature, are internally displaced people (IDPs) and the large number of people who migrate for other reasons, including economic need or climate change (United Nations, 2019). Much migration is mixed—people move beyond and within national borders for various and often overlapping reasons, including conflict, violence, poor governance, poverty, and—increasingly—environmental and climate-related pressures (Mixed Migration Centre, n.d.). Although refugees' education has received increased attention in recent years, there is still a paucity of research on how education relates to these other types and causes of migration.

In this chapter, we examine the relationship between education and migration in the Global South.[1] Approximately 82 million South-South migrants account for roughly 36 percent of all migrants globally. Migration plays an important role in the economic and social development of many developing countries (Organization for Economic Cooperation and Development (OECD), n.d.), and providing migrants with access to good-quality education can unlock this potential. Thus, understanding the education provisions for migrants in these contexts and how migrants fare in terms of learning outcomes is critical. We review available literature to understand how policies towards migrants affect their learning outcomes. We also consider case studies from Lebanon and Ecuador, which host large numbers of migrants from Syria and Venezuela respectively.[2] Formal education provisions for migrants vary considerably between these countries, reflecting their different geographies, histories, and domestic policies. These contrasts offer rich insights for policymakers.

Data on this topic are limited and only infrequently disaggregated. However, there is evidence to suggest that migrants in the Global South perform lower on standardized tests than non-migrants. Underscoring this problem are discrepancies between global norms, national provisions, and local resources, which impede the provision of quality education for migrants. In spite of global proclamations regarding migrants' right to education (United Nations General Assembly (UNGA), 2018; 2016), we found that migrants remain legally and socioeconomically vulnerable within host states. Moreover, migrants' learning outcomes

---

1   In this paper we use the term "Global South" to refer to the regions of Asia, Africa, Latin America, and Oceania. Countries in the Global South are generally characterized as lower-income than countries in Europe and North America and are often politically or culturally marginalized within geo-politics. While terminologies and categorizations of large numbers of countries and nations are never without limitations and necessarily over-simplify complex phenomena, we opt to use the term "Global South" owing to its emphasis on geo-political relations of power, rather than levels of development or cultural difference. As Dados and Connell (2012, p. 13) write, the term Global South "references an entire history of colonialism, neo-imperialism, and differential economic and social change through which large inequalities in living standards, life expectancy, and access to resources are maintained".

2   Over six million Syrians have been forcibly displaced within Syria and beyond its borders, making them the largest refugee population in the world at the time of writing. Lebanon hosts the highest number of Syrian refugees per capita as well as a significant Palestinian refugee population. Venezuelans are the largest migrant population in Latin America and the Caribbean, numbering 4.5 million persons (UNHCR, n.d.-b). Ecuador also hosts a large Columbian refugee population.

cannot be understood apart from existing inequities in host states. In other words, existing weaknesses within host-state education systems tend to be reproduced through policies and practices towards migrants. To address these challenges, we argue that policymakers need to adopt a systemic approach to migrant education that addresses inequities within host-state education systems. This achievement requires national and cross-national data on learning outcomes that is disaggregated by factors including migration status and country of origin. There is also a need for historical and qualitative research that examines whether and how different migration regimes (e.g., for refugees, internally displaced people, or guest workers) support access to quality education. Lastly, it is necessary to understand how the learning needs of migrants vary by geographical context and across time (e.g., newly arrived migrants compared to protracted refugees), as well as by other demographic characteristics (not least, gender).

Migration and education: A global priority

We use the following definition of a migrant: "any person who is moving or has moved across an international border or within a State away from his/her habitual place of residence, regardless of (1) the person's legal status; (2) whether the movement is voluntary or involuntary; (3) what the causes for the movement are; or (4) what the length of the stay is" (United Nations, n.d.). This broad definition includes voluntary or economic migrants who select their destinations as well as forced migrants fleeing violence and oppression (i.e., refugees, asylum seekers, IDPs).

The Sustainable Development Goals (SDGs), New York Declaration for Refugees and Migrants (UNGA, 2016) and the Global Compact for Migration (UNGA, 2018), when considered together, highlight the role of migration in sustainable development, and the importance of examining and managing different forms of migration. Policy literature also underscores the complex and bi-directional relationship between migration and education, and the fact that education can influence decisions to migrate. Education plays a key role in supporting the integration of migrants into host societies, and migration can create benefits as well as pose challenges for education systems (UNESCO,

2019). Thus, access to quality education is a prominent feature of global declarations and strategies related to migration.

In recent years, education has also emerged as a tool to govern migration and refugee situations (Buckner, Spencer, & Cha, 2018; Root, 2019). In keeping with UNHCR's most recent education strategies, many countries now include school-aged migrant children in national education systems (UNHCR, 2019b; UNHCR, 2012). Although this approach has been the norm in the Global North for decades, its adoption in the Global South is more recent and less uniform (see Bellino & Dryden-Peterson, 2019; Dryden-Peterson, Adelman, Bellino, & Chopra, 2019). More generally, the education of migrants in the Global South is shaped by the concept of "responsibility sharing" (UNGA, 2018). Responsibility sharing recognizes the strains that large-scale migration places on low- and middle-income states and seeks to manage migration through collective and cooperative efforts that involve a wide range of state and non-state actors.

Our examination of education and migration focuses on learning, which we define as "a change—such as in knowledge, skills, attitudes, and values—based on experiences of some kind" (Schmelkes, 2018, p. 11). We limit our analysis to academic learning outcomes in the context of formal schooling. While we recognize the broader contexts within which learning takes place (including through the non-formal sector) and the importance of diverse education outcomes for migrants (such as protection and social and emotional skills) our focus reflects the current global approach to migrant education: the inclusion of migrants into host-state education systems, which is justified, recognized, and accredited through migrants' performance on standardized national tests (OECD, 2018b; UNHCR, 2019b).

Methods

To understand the relationship between migration and learning outcomes, we drew on peer-reviewed literature, policy reports, and available datasets. We identified peer-reviewed literature by searching for keywords related to education and migration in academic databases. We complemented this review with a focused examination of the policy environments and learning outcomes for migrants in Lebanon and Ecuador. We selected these countries because: (1) they represent two ends of a policy continuum (restrictive vs. progressive policies), and (2) they capture two prominent large-scale migration situations in the world today (Syrians and Venezuelans).

Lebanon has experienced significant out-migration and large-scale internal displacement; it also hosts large numbers of Palestinian and Syrian refugees, and a significant population of economic migrants. However, the country has not signed the 1951 Refugee Convention, and domestic labor laws do not apply to migrant workers. Consequently, there are few legal protections for migrants. Education provision is insufficient, fragmented across different service providers, and often threatened by political currents within the region. Like Lebanon, Ecuador has also historically been a recipient and sender of many migrants, and today hosts a large number of Venezuelan migrants.[3] However, unlike Lebanon, Ecuador has progressive policies towards migrants, who are granted the same rights as nationals, including the right to education and work. These case studies highlight the diverse and dynamic nature of policies and provisions for migrants. They also show how national histories of migration shape contemporary responses. Based on our literature review and these case studies, we argue that migrants' learning needs should not be addressed through piecemeal, project-based efforts that prioritize the needs of some migrant groups over others. Instead, we argue for system-wide approaches that address inequities within host states' education systems, which ultimately benefit all vulnerable learners, including migrants.

Migration, education, and learning: Linkages and discontinuities

Trends in the literature

Though there are numerous studies that examine the education of migrant populations in the Global North (e.g., the US and Australia), far less has been written about the educational experiences of migrants

---

3   Although Colombia hosts the largest number of Venezuelan migrants, Ecuador has emerged as an important host country. In 2018, Ecuador declared a state of emergency over the large numbers of Venezuelans entering the country (UNHCR, 2018b).

in the Global South. Literature on migrants in the Global North highlights challenges related to the language of instruction, as well as the possibilities and limitations of migrants' inclusion in host-state education systems. Although these barriers resonate with research from the Global South, especially with respect to refugees (see, for example, Bellino & Dryden-Peterson, 2019; Dryden-Peterson et al., 2019; Dryden-Peterson, Dahya, & Adelman, 2017), distinctive challenges facing host states in the Global South limit the applicability of recommendations from studies conducted in the Global North.

Of the literature that does relate to migrants' education in the Global South, three important trends emerged from our review. First, pre-existing inequalities in host-state education systems affect migrants' educational opportunities. Migrants often face challenges stemming from socioeconomic vulnerability, the availability and accessibility of schools, teacher preparation, and school-level resources (see, for example, Bellino & Dryden-Peterson, 2019; Burde, Guven, Kelcey, Lahmann, & Al-Abbadi, 2015; Dryden-Peterson et al., 2019; Mendenhall et al., 2017). Moreover, whereas migrants who move within the Global North or who reach the Global North can often access pathways to resettlement or legal status, these options are less common elsewhere. In short, the learning outcomes of migrants in the Global South cannot be addressed without considering the systematic and structural challenges facing migrants and education systems in their host states.

Second, despite the recent increase in research on migrant education, much of this work focuses on refugees. IDPs and economic migrants are often overlooked, even though they are more numerous than refugees. Thus, while global strategies underscore the importance of adopting a holistic approach to migration (UNGA, 2018; 2016), research on migration and education continues to be fragmented along the lines of migrant status. Within the scholarship on refugees, certain populations and geographies are better represented than others. Syrian refugees in Turkey, Lebanon, and Jordan—as well as refugees in Kenya and Uganda—account for a sizeable portion of research on education and migration (see, for example, Akar & Erdoğdu, 2018; Assaad, Ginn & Saleh, 2018; Bellino & Dryden-Peterson, 2019; Buckner et al., 2018; Karam, Monaghan & Yoder, 2017; McCarthy, 2018; Mendenhall et al., 2017).

These trends are likely due to the high number of Syrian refugees in the Middle East, the large number of refugees in Kenya, Uganda's progressive refugee policies, and the relative accessibility of these host states to researchers. However, it is essential to bring other migrants into view in order to "bridge the gap between refugee studies and broader social scientific theories of social transformation and human mobility" (Bakewell, 2008, p. 432). Further, the diverse education experiences of migrants in countries of first asylum are conceptually and practically relevant to understanding post-resettlement experiences, including in the Global North (Dryden-Peterson, 2016). In short, it is important to conduct research about geographically and nationally diverse migrant populations and their learning outcomes, as well as research that captures the different phases of migration and the implications of this for learning.

Third, existing research mostly focuses on access to education. Far less has been written about learning outcomes, despite the focus of global policy actors on the importance of learning for development (World Bank, 2018). A bias towards access is partly caused by the short-term framing of the humanitarian approach to education, which has dominated the responses of international agencies to situations of conflict and displacement (Burde, 2005; 2014). Addressing the analytical separation of access and quality also requires more comprehensive and disaggregated data on learning outcomes for migrants. The majority of studies we reviewed were qualitative and most were conducted at a small scale (at the level of a single school or classroom). Such studies are valuable since they offer rich and in-depth insights into the factors that support student learning. However, to more fully understand migrants' learning outcomes, data on student performance—disaggregated by migration status—is also needed.

Data considerations

To understand whether and how migration shapes learning outcomes, we looked at the factors that shape data collection. Globally, data on migration is weak (UNHCR, 2019a). This is also true of education data related to migration. In 2015 and 2018, for example, tests conducted by the Program for International Student Assessment (PISA) sought to examine the education outcomes of students from immigrant backgrounds.[4] However, even in OECD countries that collect education data systematically, many countries do not gather information on students' countries of origin, thus limiting analysis to the generic category of "immigrant background" (OECD, 2018b).

Data challenges are more prevalent and significant in the Global South, where many countries do not disaggregate enrollment or performance data by migrant background.[5] In Lebanon, for example, Palestinian refugees who learn in schools operated by the United Nations Relief and Works Agency for Palestine refugees (UNRWA) were only included in national statistics in the 1990s—five decades after their arrival in the country—while the majority of Syrian refugees who attend Lebanese public schools are not included in national statistics at all (see Lebanon case study). Although international agencies— including the World Bank, UNHCR, UNICEF, and UNESCO—are working to address data gaps, important methodological challenges remain. Migrant communities can be difficult to access, especially if their migratory status is not legally recognized by host states, and sampling strategies may differ across organizations, limiting the generalizability and comparability of data that is collected.

Migration is also a dynamic, politically contested, and often unstable phenomenon. Countries categorize migrants in inconsistent and different ways, which has important implications for data collection (Rodríguez-Gómez, 2018). Time lags and significant onward migration can render time-specific data on migrants quickly obsolete. Additionally, much of the research examines education outcomes at the level of the nation-state, and this methodological framing has limitations in the case of migrants, who are by definition transnational and increasingly subject to sub-national and local policies and norms within host states (OECD, 2017). Comparative analyses that consider how migrant communities fare across national contexts—and within them—are needed to capture these dynamics.

---

4   "Students with an immigrant background" were defined as students whose mother and father were both born in a country other than that where the student sat the PISA test. This includes first- and second-generation students.

5   Migration status may also be politically sensitive, especially in host countries that have experienced conflict themselves. In Lebanon, for example, tensions ascribed to sectarian identity mean that a national census has not occurred since the 1930s. Consequently, even if substantive data were collected from migrants in the country, the ability to compare this to the Lebanese population would be limited.

Learning outcomes for migrants

Irregular migration makes it difficult to know how many school-aged migrants are out of school. However, enrollment rates for refugees fall far below global averages for primary, secondary, and tertiary education, suggesting that access to education for migrants is a pervasive challenge. For example, recent UNHCR statistics suggest that 63 percent of school-aged refugees are enrolled in primary school compared to a global average of 91 percent. These differences are exacerbated at the level of secondary education, where 24 percent of refugees are enrolled compared to a global average of 84 percent. The discrepancy for higher education is just as stark: only 3 percent of refugees are enrolled compared to 37 percent globally (UNHCR, 2019c). These troubling statistics are an indication of the problem facing migrant children. Compounding the problem, many countries deny education to asylum-seeking children in detention, and bureaucratic barriers such as residency requirements prevent many migrants from accessing education (UNESCO, 2019). This suggests that large numbers of migrants in the Global South are unable to access formal accredited education.

Evidence on student performance is even more sparse, but data from the Global North is probably indicative of similar trends in the Global South. Analysis of data from the OECD PISA tests and the European Social Survey shows, for example, that on average students from a migrant background performed less well than students from a non-migrant background (OECD, 2018b). In 2015, OECD's PISA program sought to understand the resiliency of students from an immigrant background. They measured resiliency through a combination of baseline academic proficiency, along with self-reported feelings of belonging at school and general life satisfaction. First-generation migrant students scored on average 17 points lower than non-migrant students, indicating that migrant students were less resilient than their non-migrant peers (OECD, 2018b).[6] Interestingly, learning disadvantages were less pronounced among second-generation immigrants and more pronounced for first-generation late arrivals (children who migrated after the age of 12) (OECD, 2018b, pp. 56–57). Four important patterns emerged from these

---

6   Similar findings are echoed in qualitative research that examines the resilience of Syrian refugees in Lebanon (Abu-Amsha & Armstrong, 2018).

tests: (1) academic outcomes are linked to migrants' overall wellbeing; (2) students with recent experiences of migration tend to perform less well than their non-migrant or second-generation peers; (3) the age at which migration occurs influences performance (older migrant children do less well); and (4) post-migration academic adjustment needs time.

We also found evidence to suggest a similar learning gap between migrant and non-migrant students in the Global South. For example, UNESCO's Third Regional Comparative and Explanatory Study (TERCE), which was conducted in Latin America and the Caribbean in 2013, demonstrated that third- and sixth-grade migrant students scored lower in reading and math compared to their non-migrant peers (see Ecuador case study). However, we also identified one study that found that refugees outperformed their non-refugee peers. Using data from the PISA and TIMSS tests conducted in 2007, classroom observations, and interviews with students, the World Bank examined how Palestinian refugees attending UNRWA schools performed compared to their peers in public schools in Jordan, Gaza, and the West Bank (Abdul-Hamid, Patrinos, Reyes, Kelcey, & Diaz Varela, 2016). Findings showed that refugee students outperformed non-refugees by the equivalent of one year of schooling. The authors argued that refugee students' better performance was likely related to a rigorous and comprehensive teacher training program, a world-class assessment system, and a supportive culture of learning within the Palestinian community.

In addition, there are barriers both within and outside of schools that contribute to migrants' learning outcomes. In schools, barriers include difficulties with the language of instruction, challenges adapting to a new curriculum, a lack of well-qualified or adequately supported teachers, insufficient educational infrastructure, a lack of administrative capacity, and discrimination against migrant students (Dryden-Peterson, 2011; Dryden-Peterson, Dahya, & Adelman, 2017; Karam et al., 2017; Mendenhall et al., 2017; Rodríguez-Gómez, 2019; UNHCR, 2018a). Outside of schools, barriers include the denial of migrants' right to work (or restrictions on their right to work), precarious legal status, and societal discrimination against migrants, all of which deter and demotivate migrant students. We expand on these barriers in our case studies.

Case study: Lebanon

Migration context

Lebanon has a long history of internal displacement and outward migration related to economic struggles and conflict. The country has also provided asylum for several refugee populations including Armenians (early twentieth century), Palestinians (post 1948), Iraqis and Sudanese (post 2000), and Syrians (post 2011). Currently, Lebanon hosts the largest number of refugees per capita in the world.

Lebanon's complex history of migration has shaped its contemporary policy environment. In 1993, three years after the country's long civil war (1975–1990), the government of Lebanon set up a Ministry of the Displaced and a Central Fund of the Displaced. The stated goal of these institutions was to provide the millions of IDPs in the country with compensation and support to return to their communities within 10 years (i.e., by 2003). However, only a small fraction of Lebanese IDPs received reparations and restitutions, and by 2000 only an estimated 25 percent of IDPs had returned to their communities of origin. Reported reasons include government corruption and inefficiency, inter-communal mistrust, the fact that many of the places IDPs are from have been resettled (resulting in significant resistance to return), and insufficient social services in communities of origin (Migration Network, n.d.). Despite the frequency and scale of migration in Lebanon, the country lacks effective mechanisms to manage internal displacement. Instead, support for IDPs tends to be community-driven or dependent on humanitarian aid agencies and sub-national political actors.

These shortcomings are mirrored in the country's restrictive and discriminatory policies towards refugees. Lebanon has not signed the 1951 Refugee Convention. Nor is there an active regional refugee regime in the Middle East (unlike in Africa and Latin America).[7] The policy environment is weakly legalized (Buckner et al., 2018) and domestic responses to migration are highly susceptible to shifting political currents (Kelcey & Chatila, 2020). Lebanese politicians frequently

---

7 In 1965, the League of Arab States passed the Protocol for the Treatment of Palestinians in Arab States, known as the Casablanca Protocol. Lebanon signed the protocol with reservations. However, this protocol has been largely disregarded by the Government of Lebanon.

invoke the protracted Palestinian case as a justification for the lack of legal protections for migrants, and refugees in particular (Janmyr, 2017). Popular attitudes towards refugees are also shaped by historically fractious relationships between the Lebanese on the one hand, and Palestinian and Syrian political actors on the other.

Education provisions for migrants in Lebanon

Internally displaced Lebanese people are able to access free compulsory education from ages 6 to 15 through the Lebanese public education system. However, public education is under-funded and accounts for only 32 percent of student enrollment in the country; 65 percent of Lebanese students are enrolled in private or state-subsidized private schools and just over 3 percent in UNRWA schools (Government of Lebanon Ministry of Education and Higher Education, 2020). Three institutions oversee the status of foreign migrants in Lebanon, with related implications for their access to quality education opportunities.

1. **UNRWA:** Over 470,000 Palestinian refugees fall under the mandate of UNRWA. UNRWA operates its own schools (currently 65), which provide free compulsory education to school-aged Palestinian refugees who are registered with the agency. UNRWA also operates a limited number of secondary schools and vocational training centers; however, supply is not enough to meet demand (UNRWA, n.d.). UNRWA schools are staffed by Palestinian refugee teachers and teach the Lebanese curriculum (and national examinations). Unlike refugees registered with UNHCR, the majority of compulsory school-aged Palestinian refugees are enrolled in education.

2. **UNHCR:** UNHCR serves all other refugee populations in Lebanon, including over one million Syrian refugees. UNHCR promotes the inclusion of refugees in host-state public schools and the Lebanese government allows Syrians to attend public schools through a double-shift scheme. Double shifting means that two schools are operated out of one school building (one school in the morning and another in the afternoon) (see, for example, Dryden-Peterson et al., 2018). Double shifting facilitates the rapid expansion

of access to education while minimizing unit costs (Bray, 2008). The majority of Syrian students who attend Lebanese public schools attend an afternoon shift where they learn the same curriculum and sit the same examinations as Lebanese students. This ensures their education is accredited by the Lebanese Ministry of Education and Higher Education. However, significant barriers to education remain for school-aged Syrian children in Lebanon, more than half of whom remain out of school (UNHCR, n.d.-a). Barriers include poverty and child labor, bureaucratic constraints, discrimination, inaccessible schools, and problems with the language of instruction (Dryden-Peterson et al., 2018; Human Rights Watch, 2016).

3. **Work sponsorship:** Lebanon also operates a work sponsorship program for around 250,000 migrant domestic workers. Most of these workers are women from African and Asian countries. These migrants are excluded from the provisions of Lebanese Labor Law and are at risk of experiencing exploitative working conditions (Amnesty International, 2019). Prior to 2014 (when the number of Syrians seeking asylum in Lebanon rapidly increased), migrant workers (like refugees) were able to enroll their children in public schools and extend their residency in Lebanon based on their children's school enrollment. Since 2014, the government of Lebanon has increased restrictions on migrants' ability to enroll their children in public schools, even if they legally reside in the country. Some migrants have also been denied residency and deported, interrupting their children's education (Human Rights Watch, 2017; Insan Association, 2015).

Although all migrant children whose status is officially recognized by the Lebanese government can enroll in private schools, fees are often prohibitively high. Thus, although official policies make provisions for migrants within the Lebanese public system, in practice significant barriers remain.

Learning outcomes for migrants in Lebanon

Data on learning outcomes says little about students' migration status

The Centre for Educational Research and Development (CERD) at the Lebanese Ministry of Education and Higher Education compiles data on enrollment rates and performance in standardized tests. However, these data are disaggregated by service provider (e.g., Lebanese government, private actors, UNRWA) rather than by student nationality. The most recent data on student performance in the Lebanese national examination taken in Grade 9 (the Brevet) showed high failure rates for Palestinians who attend UNRWA schools. However, government statistics do not include data on the learning outcomes of Syrians who attend the second shift in Lebanese public schools. Although UNHCR publishes data on enrollment rates for Syrian refugees, it does not publish data on their performance. Except for Palestinian refugees who attend UNRWA schools, it is very difficult to get a nationally representative or comprehensive picture of education outcomes for Lebanon's migrant populations.

Data suggests that migrants perform less well than their Lebanese peers on standardized tests

PISA test results published in 2018 shed light on learning outcomes for Lebanese nationals and migrants. These tests reveal that on average, students in Lebanon scored lower than the OECD average (see Table 1).

Table 1. Mean scores for Lebanese students compared to OECD average (OECD, 2018a, p. 1).

	Mean PISA scores for Lebanese students	OECD average (mean) PISA score
Reading	353	487
Mathematics	393	489
Science	384	489

As in other countries, socioeconomic status was an important predictor of education outcomes. In other words, socioeconomically advantaged students (who are more likely to attend private schools in Lebanon) outperformed socioeconomically disadvantaged students (who are more likely to attend Lebanese public schools).

Since the PISA test included a sub-category of students from immigrant backgrounds, this dataset also sheds light on how migrants in Lebanon compare to their Lebanese peers. Six percent of students who participated in Lebanon had an immigrant background and one in three of these students was socioeconomically disadvantaged (OECD, 2018a, p. 6).[8] Non-immigrants in the Lebanese sample (i.e., Lebanese nationals) scored higher on average than immigrant students, even after accounting for socioeconomic differences between the two groups (OECD, 2018a, p. 6). Immigrant students in Lebanon also performed less well on the PISA reading tests than immigrant students within the OECD (only 15 percent of immigrants in Lebanon scored in the top quarter of reading performance, compared to 17 percent in the OECD) (OECD, 2018a, p. 6). In other words, not only were learning outcomes in Lebanon on average lower than in OECD countries, but migrants in Lebanon were more likely to underperform on these tests than (1) Lebanese nationals, and (2) immigrants in OECD countries. The OECD's report on these findings did not, however, offer possible explanations for these differences.

Structural and systemic barriers lead to comparatively lower learning outcomes in Lebanon

Studies that examine dropout rates among Palestinian refugees find that students and teachers are demotivated by the Lebanese curriculum, which is considered out of date and irrelevant (Al-Hroub, 2015; Shuayb, 2014). Other significant barriers to access and learning are the severe restrictions placed on the participation of Palestinian and Syrian refugees in the Lebanese labor market. Refugees can only

---

8 The low percentage of students who have an immigrant background strongly suggests that Syrian students who learn in second shifts in Lebanese public schools were not included in the sample. Overall, 5,614 students—attending 320 schools in Lebanon—completed the assessment (OECD, 2018a, p. 11).

work in a limited number of professions (and in the case of Syrians registered with UNHCR, they are not allowed to work at all). This forces refugees into the low-paid and informal job markets which, along with high unemployment rates, disincentivize their continuation in formal education (Insan Association, 2015; Shuayb, 2014). Concerns have also been raised regarding the quality of education available to Syrians who learn in the second shift in Lebanese public schools. These shifts are under-resourced and are often staffed by over-stretched and poorly-supported temporary contract teachers (Buckner et al., 2018; Dryden-Peterson et al., 2018; Mendenhall et al., 2017).

More generally, the learning outcomes of migrants in Lebanon cannot be understood apart from pre-existing concerns related to the overall quality of education in Lebanon (Dryden-Peterson et al., 2019). Public education in Lebanon is perceived as low quality, and few provisions are made for students from disadvantaged backgrounds (including migrants) (Shuayb, 2016). Indicative of the systemic problems with the Lebanese education system, in 2013 (the last year for which data is available) only 2.5 percent of Lebanese GDP was spent on education.[9] Although two consecutive strategies were developed to help expand access to education for Syrian refugees (Reaching All Children with Education (RACE) I and II) these strategies focus predominantly on access, and pay less attention to quality-related concerns. Studies show that there is a pressing need for curriculum reform, reduced reliance on teacher-centered approaches and student memorization, and a need to better enforce policy (Buckner et al., 2018; Dryden-Peterson et al., 2019; Kelcey & Chatila, 2020; Mendenhall et al., 2017). This literature suggests that unless more attention is paid to the systemic problems facing Lebanese public schools, it will be difficult to raise learning outcomes among migrants (and vulnerable Lebanese).

However, current prospects for transforming these inequities are low. Since October 2019, Lebanon has experienced a trifecta of political, economic, and health crises. The rapid devaluation of the Lebanese Lira against the US dollar has eroded the salaries of teachers and the ability of many parents to pay school fees or cover education related costs. This

---

9   By comparison, El Salvador, Oman, and Norway—countries with similar-sized populations—spent 3.8 percent, 5 percent, and 7.5 percent of their respective GDP on education.

has reportedly led to large numbers of students leaving the private sector and enrolling in public schools, which are already under-resourced and over-stretched (Babin, 2020; Rahhal, 2020). Widespread political protests which began in October 2019 resulted in significant school closures at the beginning of the 2019/20 academic year. Additional closures owing to the COVID-19 pandemic have since prevented access to school for more than half of this academic year (Save the Children, 2020). School closures have increased the economic burden on already struggling families—including many migrant families—who now have to adapt to, and support, distance learning for their children (Inter-Agency Coordination Lebanon, 2020). Moreover, virtual learning solutions are unavailable to many families owing to the country's irregular electricity supply, and the prohibitive costs of ICT equipment and private electricity generators.

In Beirut, these pressures were compounded by the devasting explosion that occurred in August 2020. The explosion killed over 200 people, injured 6,500, left 300,000 homeless and damaged or destroyed 178 public and private schools in the city (UNOCHA, 2020; see also France 24, 2020). Migrants were especially vulnerable in the aftermath of the explosion since they often lacked the resources to reconstruct damaged shelters and because they live in densely populated neighborhoods with often inadequate access to basic services (UNOCHA, 2020). Ongoing school closures, coupled with the seemingly slim prospects for political reform in Lebanon, risk exacerbating learning inequities between socioeconomic groups and for migrants whose economic situation was strained even before these latest crises.

Case study: Ecuador

Migration context

Ecuador also has a long history of migration. Millions of Ecuadorians migrated to the United States and Europe, although in recent decades there has also been a significant return migration back to Ecuador (Jokisch, 2014). The country has also experienced significant internal migration, especially among young people moving from rural to urban areas for employment (Cazzuffi & Fernández, 2018). Ecuador currently hosts a longstanding refugee population from Colombia and a more recent population of displaced people from Venezuela. According to UNHCR data for 2018 the total number of "persons of concern" in Ecuador was 374,879. This figure includes refugees, people in refugee-like situations, asylum seekers, and migrants. The majority of these persons of concern (almost 70 percent) are Venezuelan (UNHCR, n.d.-b).[10]

Ecuador has progressive immigration laws and policies. The country has signed the 1951 Refugee Convention and its 1967 Protocol, as well as the regional 1984 Cartagena Declaration on Refugees, which adopts a broad and inclusive definition of a refugee. These international commitments have also been fully integrated into Ecuador's domestic legislation. The Ecuadorian Constitution of 2008 recognizes the needs and vulnerabilities of migrants and upholds the principle of "universal citizenship", meaning that migrants in the country should enjoy the same rights as citizens (Comparative Constitutions Project, n.d.; Ortiz, 2011). Alongside a Human Mobility Law passed in 2017, this means that migrants officially enjoy the same rights to education, work, healthcare, and freedom of movement as Ecuadorians.

However, the implementation of these laws has faltered. Reasons for this include bureaucratic barriers, decentralized decision-making, low levels of institutional capacity, discrimination and xenophobia, and security concerns (Benítez & Rivera, 2019; Beyers, 2016; Ruprecht, 2019). The gaps between official policies and the realities facing many migrants have become more pronounced upon the arrival of large numbers of Venezuelan migrants. Ecuador's institutions were unprepared for the arrival of such a large number of migrants in a relatively short period of time, and its approach towards them has become increasingly restrictive in spite of its progressive legal framework (Miller & Panayotatos, 2019).

The most common ways migrants in Ecuador regularize their legal status are through refugee visas, MERCOSUR work visas, and dependent visas (Beyers, 2016). Because many asylum applications are denied, Ecuador also hosts a large population of undocumented migrants (Beyers, 2016). Ecuador considers all non-Ecuadorians within

---

10   UNHCR data indicates that approximately 380,000 Venezuelans have migrated to Ecuador; however, not all of these people are classified as "persons of concern" by UNHCR (UNHCR, n.d.-b).

its borders "migrants" or "non-citizens" (Donger, Fuller, Bhabha, & Leaning, 2017). Consequently, data on the situation of migrants in the country is generally not disaggregated by migrants' status (e.g., refugees, asylum seekers, failed asylum seekers, or economic migrants) (Donger et al., 2017).

Education provisions for migrants in Ecuador

Ecuador's Constitution, its Organic Law on Intercultural Education (LOEI), and its General Education Regulations guarantee universal access to school regardless of migratory status (Mendenhall et al., 2017). These policies mean that all migrant children and youth can, in theory, access primary and secondary public schools. Presentation of any identity document—not necessarily documentary proof of migration status—is sufficient for access (Donger et al., 2017; Rodríguez-Gómez, 2019). Under this framework, the main responsibility for migrants' education lies with national and local government actors. UN agencies and NGOs support the Ecuadorian authorities by providing non-formal education services (Mendenhall et al., 2017).

In 2017, UNICEF estimated that around 240,000 children and youth were excluded from education in Ecuador (UNICEF, 2017). However, it is unclear how many of these out-of-school children and youths were from migrant communities. This makes it very difficult to ascertain the relationship between Ecuador's progressive education laws towards migrants and migrants' access to formal education. There is some evidence to suggest that refugees and asylum seekers face minimal barriers to accessing education (see Benítez & Rivera, 2019; Donger et al., 2017, who document this in the areas of Cuenca and Lago Agrio). However, these findings are countered by a larger body of research that documents persistent barriers to migrants' access to formal education. Barriers include lack of legal status, schools' ability to manage migrant students, bureaucratic hurdles, lack of understanding of legal provisions among local officials, child labor, and discrimination on the part of teachers, peers, and host communities (Bartlett, Rodríguez-Gómez & Oliveira, 2015; Donger et al., 2017; Mendenhall et al., 2017, Rodríguez-Gómez, 2019). On balance, available evidence indicates that important discrepancies exist between official policies and the implementation of these policies.

Nevertheless, Ecuador's government continues to actively uphold the rights of non-nationals to access education. In response to the arrival of large numbers of Venezuelan migrants, the Ministry of Education worked with international partners to quickly enroll out-of-school Venezuelan children into public schools (Response for Venezuelans, 2019). Some accounts indicate that local schools had registered at least 12,000 Venezuelan students by the end of 2018 (US Committee for Refugees and Immigrants, n.d.). As such, Ecuador remains a powerful counter-example to current trends that often exclude migrant children.

Learning outcomes for migrants in Ecuador

The failure to distinguish migrants by their migration status creates policy and practice blind spots, and has far-reaching implications

Although migrants in Ecuador participate in national or cross-national tests, performance data is not disaggregated by migratory status. This makes it very difficult to compare migrants' learning outcomes to the learning outcomes of nationals, and to develop policies and approaches to address learning inequities. The lack of focus on students' migration status also means that education administrators, teachers, and students have a limited understanding of students' migration status and their related administrative and pedagogical needs (Rodríguez-Gómez, 2019; Mendenhall et al., 2017). This may be especially harmful for migrants who do not have a legally recognized status in Ecuador. A study of the refugee youth in Quito and Lago Agrio found that those who had a recognized legal status were significantly more likely to attend school than those who lacked documentation (Donger et al., 2017).[11] This suggests that migrants with a precarious or unrecognized legal status require more targeted support and outreach.

---

11   This issue is especially significant for older children and youths because graduation from secondary school or applications to attend university require a recognized legal status (Donger et al., 2017).

The Ecuadorian education system has increased its focus on learning outcomes; however it is unclear whether or how this benefits migrants

In the mid-2000s, Ecuador undertook a significant reform of its basic education system. Improving learning outcomes was a central goal of this reform, and improving teacher quality was a key strategy to achieve this goal. This was complemented by increased educational assessments and efforts to monitor system-level progress (Bruns, Akmal, & Birdsall, 2019). The Government of Ecuador also increased education spending from one percent of GDP in 2000 to more than five percent in 2014 (Bruns et al., 2019), surpassing the median public expenditure on education globally, which was 4.7 percent of GDP in 2015 (OECD, 2018c). This resulted in impressive gains in learning. Of note, the performance of third- and sixth-graders on the Regional Comparative and Explanatory Studies between 2006 and 2013 showed improvements in reading and math scores that were the equivalent of one extra year of schooling (UNESCO, 2014).[12] These were the largest learning gains in the region (Bruns et al., 2019). Nevertheless, Ecuador's reading, math, and writing scores in the TERCE examination were all average (UNESCO, 2015), indicating that there is still much room for improvement. Similarly, on the PISA for Development (PISA-D) test conducted in 2015, Ecuador performed far below minimum proficiency in reading and math (OECD, 2018c).[13] Forty-nine percent of its test-takers reached minimum proficiency in reading, and only 29 percent achieved minimum proficiency in math.

Evidence from TERCE 2013 is also suggestive of migrants' learning outcomes. Although Ecuador was not included in this particular analysis, regional results indicate that migrant students scored lower on average than non-migrant students in Latin America and the

---

12 This is based on a 40-point difference between the results obtained in the Second Regional Comparative and Explanatory Studies (SERCE) conducted in 2006 and the Third Regional Comparative and Explanatory Studies (TERCE) conducted in 2013.

13 PISA-D is a version of the PISA test specifically advanced for low-to-middle-income countries. Participating countries included Cambodia, Ecuador, Guatemala, Honduras, Paraguay, Senegal, and Zambia. Minimum proficiency corresponds with a PISA Level 2 that all children should reach by the end of lower-secondary school to "participate effectively and productively in life as continuing students, workers and citizens" (OECD, 2018c, p. 5).

Caribbean (LAC) (UNESCO, 2016).[14] We posit that these differences are also likely to exist in Ecuador owing to the similarity of education systems and migration patterns in the region (see Bruns et al., 2019; Schneider, Cevallos Estarellas, & Bruns, 2019, for a detailed discussion of Ecuadorian education system vis-à-vis the other members of the LAC region). Interestingly, in the regional analysis, migration status alone did not explain the learning gap between migrants and nationals. Rather it was the relationship between migration status and other variables, including parents' socioeconomic and educational levels, that was associated with the lower levels of performance among migrant students (UNESCO, 2016). In short, migration status became salient when it occurred alongside other factors that are known to relate to inequities in academic performance.

In spite of progressive national policies, discrimination against migrants undermines the learning process

Qualitative research reveals significant discrimination against migrant students. A study of the schooling experiences of Colombian refugees found that they experienced school-level discrimination and suffered from social stigma, which affected their peer relationships, as well as their relationships with educators (Rodríguez-Gómez, 2017). In fact, community- and school-level discrimination against migrants in Ecuador was identified across several of the studies we reviewed (Donger et al., 2017; Mendenhall et al., 2017; Schmitz-Pranghe, 2018; Shedlin, Decena, Noboa, & Betancourt, 2014). This is concerning because experiences of discrimination are known to have negative impacts on migrants' academic achievement and psychological wellbeing (Brown, 2015).

Given such challenges, the COVID-19 pandemic is likely to have negative ramifications for migrant students' learning outcomes in

---

14　TERCE evaluates student performance on four levels, with Level I being the lowest and Level IV the highest. In third grade, 57 percent of migrant students and 73 percent of non-migrant students in LAC achieved at Levels I and II on the reading test while 64 percent of migrant students and 74 percent of non-migrant students achieved at the same levels in math (UNESCO, 2016). This trend was repeated in sixth grade reading and math.

Ecuador. For example, school closures and unequal access to distance education modalities appear to be exacerbating the educational gaps in Latin American countries, including Ecuador (Basto-Aguirre, Cerutti, & Nieto-Parra, 2020). Students from lower socioeconomic backgrounds, such as migrant households, are at risk of falling behind in learning due to three main reasons: (1) Socioeconomically disadvantaged schools are not adequately equipped for digital learning; (2) Poor households often do not have access to digital devices—for instance, in Ecuador, less than 15 percent of poor students (those living on less than 5.5 dollars per day) in primary education have an internet-connected computer at home compared to more than 50 percent of affluent students (those living on more than 70 dollars per day); and (3) Parents of disadvantaged children are less likely to have the knowledge and digital skills needed to support their children's distance learning (Basto-Aguirre, Cerutti, & Nieto-Parra, 2020).

The impact of COVID-19 on Ecuador's economy also has implications for migrant students' access to education and learning outcomes. Researchers at the Inter-American Development Bank have found that parents who have lost their income as a result of the pandemic have already moved their children from private to public schools (Olsen & Prado, 2020). In June 2020, when the school year had already started in the coastal areas, enrollment in public schools increased by 120,000 students (6.5 percent) (Olsen & Prado, 2020). The transition is anticipated to be more prominent and challenging in larger cities when schools open in September-October 2020, as the majority of the private schools (88 percent) are located in these cities, and there are also fewer spots available in public schools (Olsen & Prado, 2020). Because there are not more teachers to meet the educational needs of the increased number of students in public schools, crowded classrooms are projected to adversely affect the quality of instruction and learning (Olsen & Prado, 2020). No data yet show the effects of the reported private-to-public school transition, or of the pandemic more generally, on students' learning outcomes in Ecuador. However, migrant students are likely to be among the most negatively impacted by the pandemic given the distinct socioeconomic barriers they face because of their migration status.

Conclusion and recommendations

The relationship between education and migration is bi-directional and multi-faceted. Migration affects access to quality education, and education shapes experiences of migration. Through a review of the available literature and two case studies that examine national-level responses to migrant education, we sought to shed light on the particular relationship between migration and learning, which we defined as academic outcomes in the context of formal schooling. In this section we highlight three main findings and discuss their implications for education policy and practice.

The first finding is that data on migrants' learning outcomes is inadequate, patchy, and collected in inconsistent ways. This limits our understanding of the relationship between migration and learning outcomes, and undermines the ability of policymakers to address learning inequities between migrants and nationals. Moreover, some categories of migrants are better represented in existing research than others. Of note, the recent upsurge in literature on the education of refugees has not been matched by literature on other migrant communities, in spite of the diversity of factors that propel migration and the need to understand the relationship between different types of migration and learning. We also found that there is considerably more focus on migrants' access to education than on their learning outcomes. Our case studies revealed the limitations that occur due to these data gaps and silos. We found that national level responses to migrants' education are shaped by complex histories of migration that are not limited to the category of refugees. These case studies also underscore that access to education is not synonymous with learning, and thus data on migrants' access to education may conceal important learning inequities between migrants and nationals. As a result, we recommend collecting more comprehensive and disaggregated data on the learning processes and outcomes of migrants. This data should not be limited to large-scale learning assessments, however. Research that entangles the historical complexities of policies towards migrants as well as ethnographic studies that explore the learning experiences of migrants and host-state nationals—across and within different national contexts—are equally important to understanding the complex relationship between migration and learning.

A second finding relates to the dominant approach to include migrant students in host state education systems. To adequately address migrants' learning needs, it is essential to understand the existing strengths and weaknesses of host-state education systems, and to address these issues in a systemic way. We found some evidence to suggest that migrants underperform their host state peers on standardized tests. Migrants in the Global South are often economically vulnerable, and many have a precarious legal status—factors that are likely to contribute to their marginalization within host states. This means that if the structural issues facing host-state education systems are not addressed, then existing policies are likely to reproduce and entrench existing education inequities towards migrants. This suggests that policymakers should not develop separate plans for migrants, but should instead consider how to strengthen existing policies, in order to offer integrated approaches that address underlying systemic inequities within host states while making specific provisions for the particular needs of migrants.

Third, we highlight the need for a multi-dimensional approach to supporting migrants' education. In particular there is a need to better support and resource local education actors—teachers, school principals, and administrators. In the cases of Lebanon and Ecuador, we found that official policies differ or are interpreted differently at the sub-national level. These differences reflect a lack of information among local-level policy actors regarding migrants and their education needs, different perceptions of migration and migrants within host-state populations, and the fact that local-level actors may not have the necessary resources to uphold migrants' education effectively. This finding highlights the need to ensure that education policies include adequate provisions to manage the local dimensions of migration. It also points to the value of research that examines how migrants' learning processes relate to their school environments, as well as the ways in which student wellbeing and sense of belonging relate to academic outcomes.

References

Abdul-Hamid, H., Patrinos, H. A., Reyes, J., Kelcey, J., & Diaz Varela, A. (2016). *Learning in the face of adversity. The UNRWA education program for Palestine refugees.* Washington, DC.: World Bank. http://documents.worldbank.org/curated/en/683861468000250621/pdf/100532-PUB-Box393232B-OUO-6-PUBDATE-11-11-15-DOI-10-1596978-1-4648-0706-0-EPI-146480706X.pdf

Abu-Amsha, O., & Armstrong, J. (2018). Pathways to resilience in risk-laden environments: A case study of Syrian refugee education in Lebanon. *Journal on Education in Emergencies, 4*(1), 45–73. https://doi.org/10.17609/s563-0t15

Akar, S., & Erdoğdu, M. M. (2018). Syrian refugees in Turkey and integration problem ahead. *Journal of International Migration and Integration, 20,* 925–940. https://doi.org/10.1007/s12134-018-0639-0

Al-Hroub, A. (2015). Tracking drop-out students in Palestinian refugee camps in Lebanon. *Educational Research Quarterly, 38*(3), 52–79.

Amnesty International. (2019). *Their house is my prison. Exploitation of migrant domestic workers in Lebanon.* London, UK: Amnesty International, https://www.amnesty.org/en/wp-content/uploads/2021/05/MDE1800222019ENGLISH.pdf

Assaad, R., Ginn, T., & Saleh, M. (2018). *Impact of Syrian refugees in Jordan on education outcomes for Jordanian youth* (Working Paper Series No. 1214). Economic Research Forum. https://erf.org.eg/publications/impact-of-syrian-refugees-in-jordan-on-education-outcomes-for-jordanian-youth/

Babin, J. (2020). *The economic crisis has pushed 40,000 students to join public schools.* Le commerce du levant. https://www.lecommercedulevant.com/article/29627-the-economic-crisis-has-pushed-40000-students-to-join-public-schools

Bakewell, O. (2008). Research beyond the categories: The importance of policy irrelevant research into forced migration. *Journal of Refugee Studies, 21*(4), 432–453. https://doi.org/10.1093/jrs/fen042

Bartlett, L., Rodríguez-Gómez, D., & Oliveira, G. (2015). Migration and education: Sociocultural perspectives. *Educação e Pesquisa, 41*(special edition), 1153–1171. https://doi.org/10.1590/S1517-9702201508144891

Basto-Aguirre, N., Cerutti, P., & Nieto-Parra, S. (2020). Is COVID-19 widening educational gaps in Latin America? Three lessons for urgent policy action. *OECD Development Matters.* https://oecd-development-matters.org/2020/06/04/is-covid-19-widening-educational-gaps-in-latin-america-three-lessons-for-urgent-policy-action/#_ftnref2

Bellino, M. J., & Dryden-Peterson, S. (2019). Inclusion and exclusion within a policy of national integration: Refugee education in Kenya's Kakuma refugee camp. *British Journal of Sociology of Education, 40*(2), 222–238. https://doi.org/10.1080/01425692.2018.1523707

Benítez, E. H., & Rivera, M. J. (2019). The Ecuadorian legal framework and humanitarian immigration of Colombians in Cuenca: Where is the gap? *The International Journal of Human Rights, 23*(9), 1422–1446. https://doi.org/10.1080/13642987.2019.1613381

Beyers, C. (2016). Preliminary reflections on irregular migration and assistance policy in Ecuador. *Espacios Transnacionales: Revista Latinoamericana-Europea de Pensamiento y Acción Social, 4*(7), 86–97.

Bray, M. (2008). Double-shift schooling: Design and operation for cost-effectiveness. *Fundamentals of Educational Planning, 90*. Paris: UNESCO-IIEP.

Brown, C. S. (2015). *The educational, psychological, and social impact of discrimination on the immigrant child*. Washington DC: Migration Policy Institute. https://www.issuelab.org/resources/22382/22382.pdf

Bruns, B., Akmal, M., & Birdsall, N. (2019). *The political economy of testing in Latin America and sub-Saharan Africa* (Center for Global Development, Working Paper No. 515). https://www.cgdev.org/publication/political-economy-testing-latin-america-and-sub-saharan-africa

Buckner, E., Spencer, D., & Cha, J. (2018). Between policy and practice: The education of Syrian refugees in Lebanon. *Journal of Refugee Studies, 31*(4), 444–465. https://doi.org/10.1093/jrs/fex027

Burde, D. (2005). *Education in crisis situations: Mapping the field*. Washington DC: Creative Associates International. http://www.columbia.edu/~dsb33/Assests/BurdeEdCrisis11-11-05%5B2%5D.pdf

Burde, D. (2014). *Schools for conflict or for peace in Afghanistan*. New York: Columbia University Press.

Burde, D., Guven, O., Kelcey, J., Lahmann, H., & Al-Abbadi, K. (2015). *What works to promote children's educational access, quality of learning, and wellbeing in crisis-affected contexts*. Education Rigorous Literature Review. UK Department for International Development. https://www.gov.uk/government/uploads/system/uploads/attachment_data/file/470773/Education-emergencies-rigorousreview2.pdf

Cazzuffi, C., & Fernández, J. (2018). *Rural youth and migration in Ecuador, Mexico and Peru* (Working Paper Series No. 235). https://www.rimisp.org/wp-content/files_mf/1539440301DocumentoTrabajoenproceso_RuralYouthMigration_Cazzuffi_Fernandez_2018.pdf

Comparative Constitutions Project. (n.d.). *Ecuador's constitution of 2008*. https://www.constituteproject.org/constitution/Ecuador_2008.pdf

Dados, N., & Connell, R. (2012). The Global South: Key concepts in social research. *Contexts, 11*(1), 12–13. https://journals.sagepub.com/doi/pdf/10.1177/1536504212436479

Donger, A. E., Fuller, A., Bhabha, J., & Leaning, J. (2017). *Protecting refugee youth in Ecuador: An evaluation of health and wellbeing*. UNHCR and Harvard FXB Center for Health and Human Rights. https://cdn1.sph.harvard.edu/wp-content/uploads/sites/2464/2018/05/UNHCR-ECUADOR-Report1.pdf

Dryden-Peterson, S. (2011). *Refugee education: A global review*. Geneva: UNHCR. https://www.unhcr.org/research/evalreports/4fe317589/refugee-education-global-review-sarah-dryden-peterson-november-2011.html

Dryden-Peterson, S. (2016). Refugee education in countries of first asylum: Breaking open the black box of pre-resettlement experiences. *Theory and Research in Education, 14*(2), 131–148. https://doi.org/10.1177/1477878515622703

Dryden-Peterson, S. (2017). Refugee education: Education for an unknowable future. *Curriculum Inquiry, 47*(1), 14–24. https://doi.org/10.1080/03626784.2016.1255935

Dryden-Peterson, S., Dahya, N., & Adelman, E. (2017). Pathways to educational success among refugees: Connecting locally and globally situated resources. *American Educational Research Journal, 54*(6), 1011–1047. https://doi.org/10.3102/0002831217714321

Dryden-Peterson, S., Adelman, E., Alvarado, S., Anderson, K., Bellino, M. J., Brooks, R., ... & Suzuki, E. (2018). *Inclusion of refugees in national education systems* (Background paper prepared for the 2019 Global Education Monitoring Report). Paris: UNESCO. https://unesdoc.unesco.org/ark:/48223/pf0000266054

Dryden-Peterson, S., Adelman, E., Bellino, M. J., & Chopra, V. (2019). The purposes of refugee education: Policy and practice of including refugees in national education systems. *Sociology of Education, 92*(4), 346–366. https://doi.org/10.1177/0038040719863054

France 24. (2020). *Dozens of Beirut schools damaged by port blast won't reopen this autumn*. France 24. https://www.france24.com/en/20200828-dozens-of-beirut-schools-damaged-by-port-blast-won-t-reopen-this-autumn

Human Rights Watch. (2016). *Growing up without an education: Barriers to education for Syrian refugee children in Lebanon* (Vol. 33). https://doi.org/10.1093/rsq/hdu002

Human Rights Watch. (2017). *Lebanon: Migrant domestic workers with children deported*. Human Rights Watch. https://www.hrw.org/news/2017/04/25/lebanon-migrant-domestic-workers-children-deported

Insan Association. (2015). *Shattered dreams: Children of migrants in Lebanon*. https://www.insanassociation.org/en/images/Shattered%20Dreams-%20children%20of%20migrants%20in%20Lebanon.pdf

Inter-Agency Coordination Lebanon. (2020). *Education sector short-term response to Covid-19: Lebanon* (Guiding framework). https://data2.unhcr.org/en/documents/details/76675

Janmyr, M. (2017). No country of asylum: "Legitimizing" Lebanon's rejection of the 1951 refugee convention. *International Journal of Refugee Law, 29*(3), 438–465. https://doi.org/10.1093/ijrl/eex026

Jokisch, B. D. (2014). *Ecuador: From mass emigration to return migration?* Migration Policy Institute. https://www.migrationpolicy.org/article/ecuador-mass-emigration-return-migration

Karam, F. J., Monaghan, C., & Yoder, P. J. (2017). 'The students do not know why they are here': Education decision-making for Syrian refugees. *Globalisation, Societies and Education, 15*(4), 448–463. https://doi.org/10.1080/14767724.2016.1222895

Kelcey, J., & Chatila, S. (2020). Increasing inclusion or expanding exclusion? How the global strategy to include refugees in national education systems has been implemented in Lebanon. *Refuge, 36*(2), 9–19. https://doi.org/10.25071/1920-7336.40713

McCarthy, A. T. (2018) Politics of refugee education: Educational administration of the Syrian refugee crisis in Turkey, *Journal of Educational Administration and History, 50*(3), 223–238. https://doi.org/10.1080/00220620.2018.1440541

Mendenhall, M., Russell, S. G., Buckner, E., Peter Bjorklund, B., Cha, J., Falk, D., ... & Spencer, D. (2017). *Urban refugee education: Strengthening policies and practices for access, quality and inclusion.* New York, NY: Teachers College, Columbia University. http://www.tc.columbia.edu/media/centers/refugee-education-research-and-projects/Urban-Refugees-Full-Report.pdf

Migration Network. (n.d.). *The Lebanese government and IDPs.* http://www.lnf.org.lb/migrationnetwork/lebgov.html

Miller, S., & Panayotatos, D. (2019). *A fragile welcome: Ecuador's response to the influx of Venezuelan refugees and migrants* (Report). Refugees International. https://www.refugeesinternational.org/reports/2019/6/17/a-fragile-welcome

Ministry of Education and Higher Education, Lebanon, Centre for Educational Research and Development (MEHE-CERD). (2020). *Statistical bulletin of scholastic year 2019–2020.* https://www.crdp.org/sites/default/files/2021-03/Stat_Nashra_Inside_2020_V_4.pdf

Mixed Migration Centre. (n.d.). *MMC's understanding and use of the term mixed migration.* http://www.mixedmigration.org/wp-content/uploads/2019/10/terminology_MMC.pdf

OECD. (n.d.). *South-south migration.* https://www.oecd.org/dev/migration-development/south-south-migration.htm

OECD. (2017). *Localising the response* (The Commitments into Action Series). https://www.oecd.org/development/humanitarian-donors/docs/Localisingtheresponse.pdf

OECD. (2018a). *Lebanon: What 15-year-old students in Lebanon know and can do.* http://www.oecd.org/pisa/publications/PISA2018_CN_LBN.pdf

OECD. (2018b). *The resilience of students with an immigrant background. Factors that shape well-being.* https://doi.org/10.1787/9789264292093-en

OECD. (2018c). *PISA for development: Results in focus.* https://www.oecd-ilibrary.org/education/pisa-for-development_c094b186-en#:~:text=

Olsen, A. S., & Prado, J. (2020). *COVID-19 and the transition from private to public education in Ecuador.* https://blogs.iadb.org/educacion/en/covid-19-and-the-transition-from-private-to-public-education-in-ecuador/

Ortiz, G. (2011). *Ecuador: "Universal citizenship" clashes with reality.* IPS News. http://www.ipsnews.net/2011/02/ecuador-universal-citizenship-clashes-with-reality/

Rahhal, N. (2020). *The impact of Lebanon's economic woes on schools and parents: Putting a price tag on education.* Executive Magazine. https://www.executive-magazine.com/economics-policy/the-impact-of-lebanons-economic-woes-on-schools-and-parents

Response for Venezuelans. (2019). *Ecuador, working group on refugees and migrants (GTRM)* (Situation Report, April 2019).

Rodríguez-Gómez, D. (2017). When war enters the classroom: A case study on the experiences of youth on the Ecuador–Colombia border. In J. Williams, & M. Bellino (Eds.), *(Re)constructing memory: Education, identity, and conflict* (pp. 269–289). Rotterdam: Sense Publishers.

Rodríguez-Gómez, D. (2018). "That word is not used here": Challenges of qualitative research in areas affected by armed conflict. In M. Mendenhall (Ed.), *Data collection and evidence building to support education in emergencies* (pp. 49–52). https://resources.norrag.org/storage/documents/nqvqcvRU7rlA4hf1KvTI9WKwTVYD2HnhoSa57QsX.pdf

Rodríguez-Gómez, D. (2019). Bureaucratic encounters and the quest for educational access among Colombian refugees in Ecuador. *Journal on Education in Emergencies, 5*(1), 62–93.

Root, R. (2019). *Why education stole the show at the Global Refugee Forum.* Devex. https://www.devex.com/news/why-education-stole-the-show-at-the-global-refugee-forum-96246

Ruprecht, M. N. (2019). Colombia's armed conflict and its refugees: International legal protection versus interregional state interests. *Colombia Internacional, 100*, 67–90. https://doi.org/10.7440/colombiaint100.2019.04

Save the Children. (2020). *Lebanon: Students miss half the school year due to double impact of economic and coronavirus crisis.* Save the Children. https://www.savethechildren.net/news/lebanon-students-miss-half-school-year-due-double-impact-economic-and-coronavirus-crisis#

Schmelkes, S. (2018). What is 'learning' in the case of marginalized populations in low-income countries? In D. A. Wagner, W. Sharon, & R. F. Boruch (Eds.), *Learning at the bottom of the pyramid: Science, measurement, and policy in low-income countries* (pp. 11–23). https://unesdoc.unesco.org/ark:/48223/pf0000265581

Schmitz-Pranghe, C. (2018). *Protection, reconciliation and access to rights for DPs in Ecuador: Requirements for the integration of displaced persons (DPs) from Colombia and Venezuela in Ecuador* (BICC Policy Brief, 9/2018). Bonn International Center for Conversion (BICC). https://nbn-resolving.org/urn:nbn:de:0168-ssoar-62621-8

Schneider, B. R., Cevallos Estarellas, P., & Bruns, B. (2019). The politics of transforming education in Ecuador: Confrontation and continuity, 2006–2017. *Comparative Education Review 63*(2), 259–280. https://doi.org/10.1086/702609

Shedlin, M. G., Decena, C. U., Noboa, H., & Betancourt, Ó. (2014). Sending-country violence and receiving-country discrimination: Effects on the health of Colombian refugees in Ecuador. *Journal of Immigrant and Minority Health, 16*(1), 119–124. https://doi.org/10.1007/s10903-013-9777-9

Shuayb, M. (2014). The art of inclusive exclusions: Educating the Palestinian refugee students in Lebanon. *Refugee Survey Quarterly, 33*(2), 20–37. https://doi.org/10.1093/rsq/hdu002

Shuayb, M. (2016). Education for social cohesion attempts in Lebanon: Reflections on the 1994 and 2010 education reforms. *Education as Change, 20*(3), 225–242. https://doi.org/10.17159/1947-9417/2016/1531

United Nations. (n.d.). *Migration*. https://www.un.org/en/sections/issues-depth/migration/index.html

United Nations. (2019). *International migration 2019*. https://www.un.org/en/development/desa/population/migration/publications/wallchart/docs/MigrationStock2019_Wallchart.pdf

UNESCO. (2014). *Comparison of results between the second and the third regional comparative and explanatory studies: SERCE and TERCE, 2006–2013*. UNESCO Santiago Office. https://unesdoc.unesco.org/ark:/48223/pf0000244239_eng

UNESCO. (2015). *TERCE executive summary: Learning achievements*. UNESCO Santiago Office. https://unesdoc.unesco.org/ark:/48223/pf0000243983_eng

UNESCO. (2016). *TERCE in sight: What affects learning achievements among migrant children?* UNESCO Santiago Office. https://unesdoc.unesco.org/ark:/48223/pf0000245060_eng?posInSet=1&queryId=cfe53c9d-2a31-47ca-8b98-14998497e51d

UNESCO. (2019). *Migration, displacement and education. Building bridges not walls* (Global Education Monitoring Report). Paris: UNESCO. https://unesdoc.unesco.org/ark:/48223/pf0000366946/PDF/366946eng.pdf.multi

UNHCR. (n.d.-a). *Education*. https://www.unhcr.org/lb/education

UNHCR. (n.d.-b). *Ecuador*. http://reporting.unhcr.org/node/2543

UNHCR. (2018a). *Turn the tide. Refugee education in crisis.* Geneva: UNHCR. https://www.unhcr.org/publications/brochures/5b852f8e4/turn-tide-refugee-education-crisis.html

UNHCR. (2018b). *UNHCR ramps up response as Ecuador declares emergency.* UNHCR. https://www.unhcr.org/news/briefing/2018/8/5b6d4f554/unhcr-ramps-response-ecuador-declares-emergency.html

UNHCR. (2019a). *Global trends: Forced displacement in 2018.* Geneva: UNHCR. https://www.unhcr.org/5d08d7ee7.pdf

UNHCR. (2019b). *Refugee education 2030: A strategy for refugee inclusion.* Geneva: UNHCR. https://www.unhcr.org/publications/education/5d651da88d7/education-2030-strategy-refugee-education.html

UNHCR. (2019c). *Stepping up. Refugee education in crisis.* Geneva: UNHCR. https://www.unhcr.org/steppingup/wp-content/uploads/sites/76/2019/09/Education-Report-2019-Final-web-9.pdf

UNICEF. (2017). *Annual report 2017: Ecuador.* https://www.unicef.org/about/annualreport/files/Ecuador_2017_COAR.pdf

UNGA. (2016). *New York declaration for refugees and migrants* (Pub. L. No. A/RES/71/1). https://www.un.org/en/development/desa/population/migration/generalassembly/docs/globalcompact/A_RES_71_1.pdf

UNGA. (2018). *Global compact for safe, orderly and regular migration.* Marrakesh: United Nations. https://refugeesmigrants.un.org/sites/default/files/180711_final_draft_0.pdf

UNOCHA. (2020). *Lebanon: Beirut port explosions* (Situation Report No. 7). https://reliefweb.int/report/lebanon/lebanon-beirut-port-explosions-situation-report-no-7-25-august-2020-enar

UNRWA. (n.d.). *Where we work.* https://www.unrwa.org/where-we-work/lebanon

US Committee for Refugees and Immigrants. (n.d.). *Venezuelan refugees: The Ecuador-Colombia border. Findings and recommendations.* https://reliefweb.int/sites/reliefweb.int/files/resources/FINAL-Ecuador-Venezuela-Report.pdf

World Bank. (2018). *Learning to realize education's promise* (World Development Report 2018). Washington, DC.

3. Teaching at the Bottom of the Pyramid

Teacher Education in Poor and Marginalized Communities

Kwame Akyeampong

Introduction

Achieving SDG4—inclusive and quality education for all—requires every child to have access to quality teachers. However, in many low-income countries (LICs) and lower-middle-income countries (LMICs) large numbers of children, especially in poor and marginalized communities, lack access to well-trained teachers (UNESCO, 2013/14). As a result, many of these disadvantaged children fail to meet the expected minimum learning outcomes for their grade, causing many to drop out of school in the early years. UNESCO Institute of Statistics (UIS), for example, estimates that six out of 10, or 617 million, children and adolescents in LICs and LMICs are not achieving minimum proficiency levels in reading and mathematics (UIS, 2017). The crisis is more acute in sub-Saharan Africa, where about 85 percent of children are not reaching minimum proficiency levels despite being in school (Luschei & Fagioli, 2016; Luschei & Carnoy, 2010; World Development Report, 2018).

However, the crisis is not simply about the inadequate number of teachers, but also about the fact that few trained teachers know how to meet the learning needs of poor and marginalized children. These children are in school but not learning—described as the "silently excluded" (Lewin, 2011). For many of these children, the schools they have access to are so low quality that any hope of education providing a route out of poverty is unrealistic (Lewin, 2011). As Dyer (2013) points out, "the schooling available to the poorest is itself often so poor that it is likely to perpetuate cycles of deprivation as it is to interrupt them" (p. 221). Ultimately, this learning crisis points to a lack of programs that can help teachers meet the needs of children at the bottom of the learning pyramid. However, some promising research shows the possibilities of effective classroom practices and teacher education reform, some of which are discussed in this chapter.

The chapter is organized into three sections. First, it discusses the teacher training and supply crisis, outlining the factors that impact teachers' abilities to meet the learning needs of children who are being left behind. The second section presents case studies of inclusive pedagogies that report positive impact on learning for children who have dropped out of school. The third and final section concludes with a discussion of the implications for reforms that can improve teacher education and close the learning achievement gap between advantaged and disadvantaged children.

The learning crisis and teachers: Mapping the Global South evidence and challenges

Improving access to quality education over the past two decades has not produced improvements in learning outcomes for children in poor and marginalized communities (Bashir et al., 2018). The challenge is not only about closing the learning achievement gap between disadvantaged and advantaged children, but also ensuring that the gap does not widen as they progress through their education. Studies suggest that when learning achievement gaps emerge in the early primary school grades, they continue to widen in later grades. For example, data from the National School Effectiveness Study (NSES) in South Africa found that only the top 16% of Grade 3 children are performing at an appropriate Grade 3 level, and that the learning gap between the poorest 60 percent of students and the wealthiest 20 percent of students amounts to approximately three grade levels in Grade 3, growing to four grade levels by Grade 9 (Spaull & Kotze, 2015).

Evidence also shows that the learning crisis is linked to where a child lives and attends school (UNESCO, 2013/14; Rose & Alcott, 2015). In Ethiopia, urban 8-year-olds are over five times more likely than rural 8-year-olds to be able to read sentences (Rolleston, 2014). Children from poor and marginalized communities experience higher dropout rates and poorer learning outcomes (UNESCO 2013/14). Results from the OECD's PISA for Development (PISA-D)[1] show that students attending urban schools outperform those in rural schools in reading, achieving an average performance difference of 42 score points, equivalent to more than a year of schooling. The PISA-D data also show that socioeconomically advantaged students (i.e., students from the top 25 percent) are, on average, five times more likely than disadvantaged students (those in the bottom 25 percent) to attain the minimum level of proficiency in mathematics. In fact, according to the PISA-D analysis, very few disadvantaged students in rural areas are able to achieve minimum levels of proficiency, and even fewer score among the best in their countries, with many making so little progress in learning that they risk dropping out of school (Ward, 2018).

In South Asia, the situation is similar. Based on over ten years of data from the Annual Status of Education Report (ASER)[2], evidence shows unacceptably low learning levels at every grade, with data from India showing that only about "half of all children enrolled in Std V can read at least at Std II level" (p. 68). Although more recent data show some improvements in lower grades, it is not enough to bring children up to expected levels. The ASER data reveal that overall progress in learning trajectories has remained flat, an indication that foundational skills in the early grades are so low this is likely to impede progress in later grades (ASER, 2013).

A longitudinal study in Andhra Pradesh, India, tracking a cohort of students over a school cycle, found that only 2.4 percent of Grade 1 students achieved the Grade 1 standard. By Grade 5, only 60 percent of these students achieved the Grade 1 level, and only 8 percent achieved the Grade 5 level. The study finds that the gap between the top-performing and bottom-performing students widens in later grades,

---

1   PISA for Development (PISA-D) countries include Cambodia, Ecuador, Guatemala, Honduras, Panama, Paraguay, Senegal, and Zambia.
2   ASER is a nationwide household survey that reaches a representative sample of children in every rural district in India.

and that most learning happens in Grades 1 and 2. The argument is that, if instruction is better aligned to learning goals in early grades, then by Grade 3, children should be expected to "read to learn". Those unable to achieve this goal are then left further behind. In many school systems, as it happens, only the top 10 percent of students are able to keep pace with the early grade curriculum. The bottom 10 percent, meanwhile, can spend several years in school with little benefit in terms of their learning (Muralitharan & Zieleniak, 2013).

Studies on learning achievement in LMICs suggest that once children from poor and marginalized communities begin to fall behind in the early grades, they are unable to catch up, and are then more likely to drop out of school (Rose & Alcott, 2015). This presents two main challenges for many LIC and LMIC education systems. The first is ensuring that children from poor and disadvantaged backgrounds have access to trained teachers with skills to improve their learning. The second is ensuring that teacher education programs are incorporating the best practices on what works to improve learning for disadvantaged children. These challenges raise the issue of how we should define teacher quality for the early schooling years, train teachers to meet the standards, and measure their ability reliably.

The teacher quality crisis: Where do children from poor and marginalized communities stand?

Research on teacher quality often defines it as a teacher's ability to improve student learning, measured by increased standardized test scores relative to a baseline score (Pugatch, 2017). Bold et al. (2018) argue that it is important to understand which dimensions of teacher quality matter, and how teachers perform along these dimensions. Typically, in the literature, teacher quality is measured along the dimensions of subject knowledge and the ability to diagnose learning difficulties, provide regular feedback, and use effective questioning techniques to promote effective learning (World Bank, 2018; Bashir et al., 2018). It suggests that possession of a minimum educational qualification is a poor predictor of teacher quality, compared to a teacher who has undergone formal training and demonstrated competence on these dimensions. UIS data suggests that, in many LICs, about 70 percent of teachers who teach at the primary-education level have not received formal training, and that these teachers tend to teach predominantly in schools serving children from poor and marginalized communities (UIS, 2013; UNESCO, 2013/2014).

Teacher quality is also defined by the ability to promote effective learning in the classroom (Bold et al., 2018; Filmer et al., 2015). Based on direct unannounced classroom observation and test data from primary schools in seven sub-Saharan African countries—Kenya, Nigeria, Mozambique, Senegal, Tanzania, Togo, and Uganda—Bold et al. (2018) were able to determine levels of teacher quality by measuring: (a) how much time teachers actually spend teaching; (b) whether they possessed relevant subject-matter knowledge to teach basic and higher-order language and mathematics skills; and (c) whether they had the pedagogical knowledge and skills to transfer what they knew to students. They concluded from the analysis of the data that "… students receive about two hours and fifty minutes of teaching per day—or just over half the scheduled time … largely because teachers, even when in school, are not teaching … Regarding pedagogy, few teachers can assess children's abilities and evaluate their students' progress, and few exhibit practices that are typically associated with good teaching (e.g., regularly checking for students' understanding and giving feedback)" (p. 5).

However, what has been lacking in the literature is teacher quality data disaggregated by geographic location to draw comparisons between those who teach in poor and marginalized communities and those in more urban settings. This data gap notwithstanding, it is reasonable to assume that teacher quality measured in terms of classroom performance will be much worse in disadvantaged areas, since these have schools that are mostly staffed with untrained teachers or underqualified teachers (UNESCO, 2013/4).

Subject content knowledge

Irrespective of the region in which studies have been conducted, the emerging evidence suggests that the level of teachers' subject content knowledge impacts student learning outcomes (Filmer et al., 2015; Glewwe et al., 2015; Ganimian & Murnane 2016; Hanushek et al., 2014; Metzler & Woessmann 2012). In the sub-Saharan Africa region, for example, Altinok's (2013) analysis of SACMEQ data revealed that if weak students had access to teachers with strong subject content knowledge, this improved their learning outcomes. But, generally, primary and lower-secondary teachers in sub-Saharan Africa countries, including those who have received formal training, have weak subject content knowledge (Altinok, Antoninis, & Nguyen-Van, 2017). In some cases, teachers' subject content knowledge has been found to be no better than that of the students they teach. A recent assessment of a sample of primary teachers' English, mathematics, and science subject knowledge by the Teacher Development Programme (TDP) in Nigeria found that most teachers lacked enough subject knowledge to teach effectively all three areas (De et al., 2016). In a similar analysis of teachers' subject knowledge in "14 sub-Saharan Africa countries, the average grade 6 teacher performed no better on reading tests than do the highest-performing students from that grade" (World Bank, 2018, p. 10).

Even where teachers have received training, many still say they feel inadequately prepared to teach basic school subjects. In a survey of teachers in six sub-Saharan Africa (SSA) countries (Ghana, Kenya, Mali, Senegal, Tanzania, and Uganda), newly-trained teachers revealed they experienced considerable difficulty teaching basic literacy and numeracy topics in the primary school curriculum (see Figures 1 and 2).

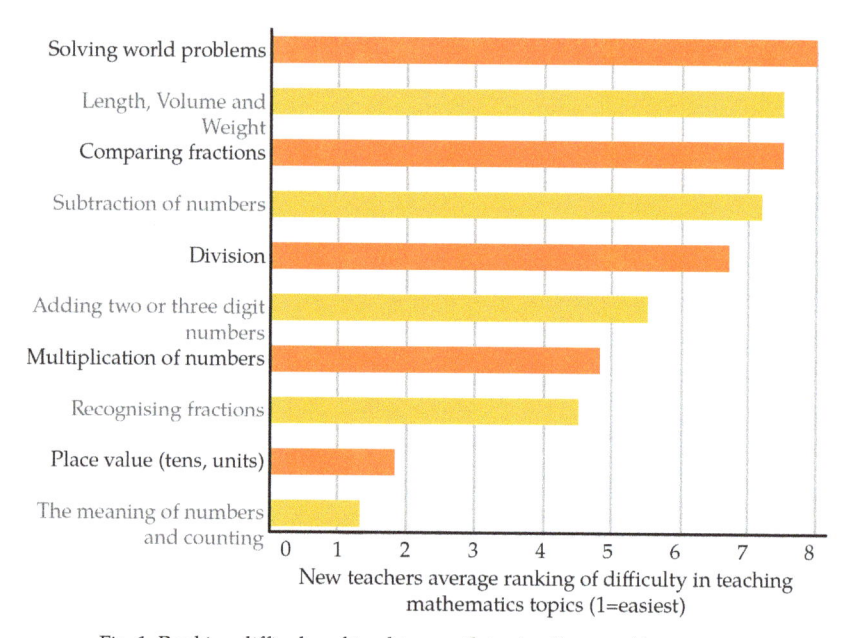

Fig. 1. Ranking difficulty of teaching math topics. Source: Akyeampong et al. (2013).

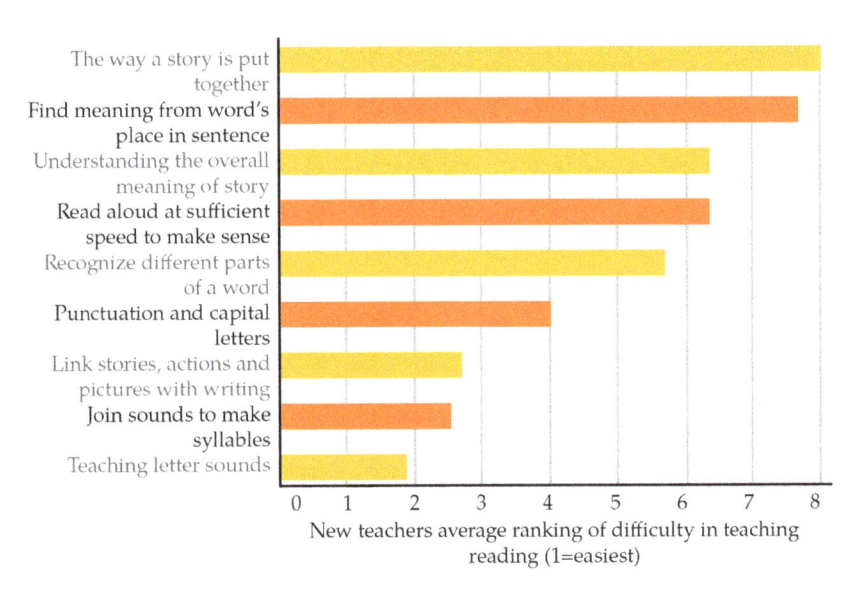

Fig. 2. Ranking difficulty of teaching reading. Source: Akyeampong et al. (2013).

These weaknesses reflect gaps in their teacher-preparation program. Such gaps or weaknesses, especially in subject content knowledge, must be addressed before teachers can adequately improve learning for children at the bottom of the pyramid.

Improving learning depends on Teaching at the Right Level

For teaching to be effective, teachers must have a deep understanding of the subject they teach and the pedagogical skills to convey the concepts meaningfully to students. However, research is establishing that it is equally important for teachers to provide instruction at the right level of the learner they are teaching (Banerjee et al., 2016).

In typical LIC classrooms, many children are not learning at grade level, and therefore a grade-based curriculum often means teachers' instruction is appropriate for some and not others. This factor is rarely considered in teacher education. In sub-Saharan Africa, for example, "the range of children's ages within grades can be wide—5- and 10-year olds can be in grade 1—and the range gets even wider the higher the grade" (Lewin & Akyeampong, 2009, p. 144; Akyeampong et al., 2007). With most national curricula organized on the assumption that children will be learning in a grade appropriate for their age (i.e., monograde), this silences the wide ranges in capability associated with age, whose occurrence is much higher among schools in disadvantaged rural areas and communities (Lewin & Akyeampong, 2009). Grade-based curriculum in wide-age-range classrooms means that, often, teachers' instruction is pitched at a level not appropriate for many.

Teaching at the Right Level (TARL) is particularly important for low-performing students. Instruction should be tailored to meet abilities or learning levels rather than students' ages and grades. Evidence from a series of randomized controlled evaluations in India, Pakistan, Kenya, Ghana, and Zambia indicate that TARL can produce significant gains in learning, especially for low-performing students (Saeed & Jamil, 2018; Banerjee et al., 2016; Duflo et al., 2011). The concept of TARL was pioneered by Pratham to provide education to children in the slums of Mumbai and has grown in both scope and scale, with programs today reaching children and youths across the country (Banerjee et al., 2016). The TARL pedagogy targets each child's learning needs, regardless of their age or grade. Children work in small groups, big groups, and individually to maximize their learning potential. Characteristically, learning is learner-driven and assessment is used to track individual progress. Children are grouped by level rather than by grade for instruction, and move quickly from one group to the next as they progress in their learning (Banerjee et al., 2016).

An RCT study of 530 schools in Pakistan using the TARL methodology and pedagogy found that children in the program outperformed control-group children across three subjects—English, Urdu, and math. This was attributed to the flexibility of TARL as opposed to the traditional structured curriculum that left many children behind (Saeed & Jamil, 2018). In Ghana, public-school teachers trained to use the TARL approach achieved similar results (Duflo, Kiessel, & Lucas, 2018). The teachers split their students by ability levels, rather than grade levels, for one hour daily. Students improved their test scores by 4 percent on average compared to the comparison group. The relatively low impact was attributed to the fact that teachers did not wholeheartedly implement the approach, due to competing goals of completing the core curriculum. However, larger increases in learning relative to the comparison group emerged (6.4 percent in scores for third- and fourth-graders) when teacher community assistants (TCAs) were trained to focus on low-performing students in the classrooms of the regular teachers. The TCAs were also able to impact the development of complex skills. This confirmed the positive impact of TARL on low achievers, but also showed that in traditional classrooms where teachers follow a rigid curriculum, the gains are marginal.

Providing targeted help to children who are falling behind and grouping them based on what they know has also been found to be an effective strategy in Kenya (Duflo et al., 2011). In a study which tracked initial achievement in Kenya, lower-achieving students gained significantly, but overall, all students benefited. The tracking was beneficial because it helped teachers focus their teaching at a level appropriate for most students in the class (Duflo et al., 2011). Unfortunately, for the most part, in the Global South, teaching programs assume a monograde curriculum and discourage teachers from targeting instruction to different ability levels. Thus, although there is robust evidence from RCT and experimental studies that TARL works for low-performing students, national systems that train teachers use approaches that do not reflect this evidence.

Teacher reforms in LICs/LMICs to improve teacher quality analysis

The learning crisis has prompted questions about the competency of teachers, but not so much in terms of teachers' ability to target instruction to improve learning for low achievers. Instead, policies have focused on increasing the supply of qualified teachers and improving their general knowledge of teaching. UNESCO's 2013 Global Monitoring Report singled out the failure to reach marginalized groups of students as a contributory factor to the learning crisis, and put forward a four-part strategy to address the teacher quality crisis (UNESCO 2013/14): (1) attract the best teachers; (2) improve teacher education so all children can learn; (3) get teachers to where they are most needed; and (4) provide incentives to retain the best teachers. However, the report said little about what was required, in terms of the design and content of programs, to prepare teachers to address the learning crisis.

Reforms to improve teacher quality must also address the declining status of teachers, as this influences teacher recruitment, deployment, and retention. In sub-Saharan Africa, for example, public perception of teachers has suffered badly because of the worsening state of teachers' working and living conditions (Razquin, 2009). Economic growth in recent times appears to have done little to offset the poor working and living conditions, large class sizes, and the low motivation of teachers in LMICs (Bennell & Akyeampong, 2007). For well-trained teachers to accept teaching positions in poor and marginalized communities, it would require attractive pay scales that make teaching in poor and marginalized communities economically and professionally rewarding.

However, rarely are the socioeconomic characteristics of students, communities, or regions factored into resource allocation. Instead, allocations are based mainly on student-teacher ratios and student enrollment rates (Fredriksen, 2011). Teachers in poor and rural communities find themselves disproportionately under-resourced in schools and classrooms, which limits their ability to provide quality instruction (UNESCO 2013/14). Policies around resource allocation should allot more resources per capita to poor and marginalized communities so that trained teachers can improve learning for low-achieving children.

Although many countries have developed teacher allocation formula to address the problem of inequitable deployment of teachers, consistent application remains a problem. It is common for wide variations to exist across schools and between districts. In countries that have been more successful in achieving greater equity, such as Mauritius and Zimbabwe, they have utilized criteria-based teacher allocation procedures (Bashir et al., 2018). Sometimes inconsistencies in allocations stem from a lack of input of teacher supply and demand data, preventing the collection of reliable information on teacher gaps (UIS, 2006). Stakeholders can also undermine the efficiency and equity of the teacher allocation process through rent-seeking and exertion of political influence (Quak, 2020; Hedges, 2002). When this happens, schools serving poor and marginalized communities are particularly affected because they exhibit all the conditions that make them unattractive places to teach.

Teacher factors that limit learning for children from disadvantaged backgrounds

Inequitable deployment of quality teachers

Several studies have noted that for LICs/LMICs to close the learning achievement gap, schools serving students from disadvantaged backgrounds should aim for equitable allocation of trained teachers (Luschei & Chudgar, 2015; Hanushek & Rivkin 2012). In the sub-Saharan Africa context, Burundi presents an interesting example of how increasing the supply of trained teachers to rural areas can help close the achievement gap between children from poorer and richer backgrounds. After achieving greater equity in the supply of trained teachers, an international study found that overall numeracy scores of students from poor socioeconomic backgrounds was higher than the average scores of students in relatively richer schools (Bashir et. al., 2018). A large part of the success was attributed to the way in which the country had aligned the teacher education curriculum with the school curriculum and supported teachers with continuous professional development.

Generally, there is a lack of strong evidence on how to achieve equitable allocation of teachers. In many LICs, patronage-based recruitment of teachers undermines the credibility of allocation policies, which disadvantages schools in rural areas. The practice of posting newly-qualified teachers to poor and disadvantaged communities can also become counterproductive if teachers view the posting system as unfair and open to manipulation. In Ghana, research by Hedges (2002) found that teachers viewed teaching in rural areas as limiting of their professional aspirations and opportunities compared to teaching in urban towns and cities. Incentives to attract teachers to underserved communities, like stipends in exchange for agreed postings in remote areas, may encourage teachers to take a different view (UNESCO 2013/14).

In a four-country study—Guinea, India, Mexico, and Tanzania—Luschei and Chudgar (2015) showed how equitable teacher deployment could possibly be achieved, if education systems can meet five conditions: commitment to equity, collaboration of key stakeholders, cost-consciousness, careful design, and attention to context. Another example of a successful initiative is the Rainbow Spectrum initiative from the Philippines, which focused on making disparities in teacher deployment more visible for action to be taken. Districts were color-coded according to their pupil/teacher ratios, with blue indicating a ratio below 24:1, red a ratio over 50:1, and black a complete teacher shortage. This simple device was then used to raise awareness about teacher deployment issues by making information readily available and easily understandable. Between 2009 and 2011, a study found that over 60 percent of new teacher allocation went to black and red areas (Albert, 2012). The Philippines initiative demonstrates the importance of providing specific and context-relevant information in order for appropriate action to be taken.

Teacher absenteeism

Improving teacher supply and allocation to disadvantaged schools is not enough to improve learning outcomes if teacher attendance is poor, and worse still if teachers spend little time actually teaching on the days they are in school. In LICs and LMICs, teacher absenteeism hits disadvantaged students and schools in rural areas the hardest—teacher absenteeism can range from 11 percent to 30 percent (Guerrero et al., 2012). In Ecuador, unexcused absences have been reported to be as high as 53 percent. Quite apart from the damage this does to learning, it is also very costly, accounting for the loss of up to one-quarter of primary school spending—$16 million annually in Ecuador and $2 billion a year in India (Patrinos, Velez & Wang, 2013).

The impact of teacher absenteeism is more serious when viewed in terms of the time teachers spend in classrooms teaching. In sub-Saharan Africa, teacher absenteeism from class can sometimes exceed absenteeism from school by "at least 20 percent and as much as 300–400 percent" (Bashir et al., 2018, p. 264). However, in some cases, absenteeism is due to illness, attendance at in-service training organized outside the school, or due to teachers staying away from school to collect their salaries (Bennell & Akyeampong, 2007). Unauthorized absences are also sometimes due to low levels of teacher pay, poor housing and transportation for teachers, or simply low expectations of teacher performance across the board (Guerrero et al., 2012). Many LICs and

LMICs have inaccurate or insufficient data on teacher absenteeism, which makes tackling the problem (Rogers & Vegas, 2009) or knowing the extent of the problem difficult (UNESCO, 2017).

Interventions that have proved successful in reducing teacher absenteeism include acknowledging and rewarding teachers who attend school regularly (e.g., Knoster, 2016) and improving economic incentives for attendance (e.g., Chapman, 1994). According to Rogers and Vegas (2009), countries must be willing to try different approaches to improve attendance and effort, and evaluate them for their impact before widespread adoption. In other words, there are no magic-bullet solutions to the problem of teacher absenteeism. Three of the most promising policies that Rogers and Vegas (2009) recommend are:

1. Make teacher salaries and promotions dependent in part on performance, not just on qualifications and experience;
2. Introduce mechanisms for accountability by involving the community and school management;
3. Increase the intrinsic and non-pecuniary rewards for good attendance by turning schools into pleasant learning environments that offer adequate support for teachers.

Addressing the problem of teacher absenteeism effectively should also involve key actors (teachers, heads, institutions, education managers, and community members), and place emphasis on improving teachers' living and working conditions in disadvantaged communities.

Teacher incentives

There is debate in the literature on whether monetary incentives are an effective tool for tackling the problem of teacher absenteeism or encouraging trained teachers to accept postings to poor and marginalized communities (see Duflo et al., 2015). In Zambia and Mozambique, hardship allowance was used to make deployment to rural areas more attractive. In Mozambique, allowances calculated on a sliding scale based on distance from the nearest tarred road was introduced. Up to 20 percent salary increases for traveling to hard-to-reach areas were also introduced for qualified teachers in Uganda (Mulkeen & Chen, 2008). However, it appears that monetary incentives may not be enough to make teachers accept rural postings (UNESCO, 2010) or improve their school attendance or teaching performance (Rogers & Vegas, 2009). Although paying teachers based on child performance or attendance has been shown to work in India (Muralidharan & Sundararaman, 2011), in the longer-term such incentives fail because they are hard to design well, as evidenced in the case of Pakistan (Barrera-Osorio & Raju, 2015), or their effects erode with time (Glewwe et al., 2010).

To achieve more equitable teacher deployment, some countries have tried to use non-monetary incentives. For example, Ecuador grants early tenure to teachers willing to work in difficult areas. Mexico's Carrera Magisterial teacher incentive program offered participating teachers working in marginalized areas opportunities to advance more rapidly through the promotion system than teachers in wealthier areas (Luschei & Chudgar, 2015). There is a sense in which non-monetary incentives that promise professional rewards would be appealing to teachers who choose the profession because of high intrinsic motivation, but this has to be accompanied with improved working conditions to achieve improved performance from teachers (Bennell & Akyeampong, 2007).

Contract teachers

Contract teachers are often unqualified or underqualified, and recruited to meet the increasing demand for teachers in rural schools. The recruitment of contract teachers is seen as a short- or in some cases long-term solution to teacher supply and deployment challenges in LICs, especially in rural areas. In systems struggling to train enough teachers or deploy teachers to poor and rural communities, contract teachers become an attractive option (ILO, 2016; Razquin, 2009). However, are contract teachers able to improve learning outcomes in schools in poor and marginalized communities? Two studies provide some insights.

In the World Bank's Service Delivery Indicators (SDI) survey, the content and pedagogical knowledge of contract teachers in primary schools in Africa was found to be comparable with regular trained teachers. They were also more likely to be present in the classroom (Bold et al., 2018). Evidence from randomized control trial (RCT) studies in some LICs shows that contract teachers can help to lower the student-teacher ratio, and overall, contribute to the improvement of student learning outcomes (Kremer, Brannen, & Glennerster, 2013). However, a study in China—which used a dataset from rural primary schools in western China to estimate the causal effect of contract teachers on student achievement—found that gains in student scores on standardized examinations in mathematics and Chinese were lower in classes taught by contract teachers than in classes taught by trained teachers (Lei et. al., 2018). Another study of contract teachers, using data from five francophone countries for Grades 2 and 5, produced inconclusive results (Chudgar, 2015). The study concluded that their impact varies depending on the *"country context, and the attributes of teacher demographics, working conditions ..."* (Chudgar, 2015, p. 261 emphasis added). Countries that have recruited contract teachers who meet minimum qualification standards and offered them training to achieve trained teacher status have been able to maximise their impact on student learning and achievement, e.g., Ghana, Madagascar, and Mali (Dembélé, Chudgar, & Ndow 2016; Duflo, Dupas, & Kremer, 2015).

Contract teachers may offer a solution to schools in poor and marginalized communities struggling to recruit trained teachers, but the inconclusive nature of evidence on learning outcomes suggest that, just like trained teachers, they also need professional development if they are to improve learning for the most disadvantaged children.

Teacher beliefs and attitudes

Evidence from LIC and LMIC contexts suggests that targeted instructional support can maximize the learning potential of students from diverse backgrounds (Westbrook et al., 2013). However, teacher beliefs about what students can do can inform the learning opportunities they provide. They also become the lens through which teachers make sense of their everyday classroom experience (Akyeampong & Stephens, 2002) and the instructional strategies they adopt (Pajares, 1992). This suggests that if teachers, in the course of their initial training or through professional development activities, are not provided with training to improve their attitudes and perceptions of students with different abilities and backgrounds, they may not develop strategies to improve learning for these students.

A teacher's own belief in their competence to address learning needs of weak students does not simply emerge because they have received formal teacher training. For example, a survey of newly qualified teachers in Ghana found that about 59 percent believed they could improve the academic performance of slow learners, but also quite a sizeable proportion (41 percent) did not share this view. In that study, head teachers often indicated "that newly qualified teachers had difficulty selecting appropriate content and instructional strategies to meet pupils' ability level and background characteristics" (Akyeampong & Lewin, 2002, p. 347). Part of the problem seems to lie with unfamiliarity with the learning needs of children from disadvantaged backgrounds, and with how to target instruction to improve learning for this group.

A study of teacher education in six sub-Saharan African countries found that newly-trained primary school teachers did not know enough about the backgrounds of the children in their class to be able to create tailored learning opportunities (Akyeampong et al., 2013). They may deny students from minority or disadvantaged backgrounds equal learning opportunities out of false assumptions or insufficient knowledge about their difficulties in learning. Besides, positive attitudes towards students, irrespective of their background or learning difficulties, matter. In a systematic review of evidence from developing countries, Westbrook et al. (2013) revealed that, "teachers who had positive attitudes towards girls, overage students, those marginalized by class and caste, and students with disabilities were more likely to be socially responsive towards them in their practice" (p. 51).

Pedagogies that improve learning for disadvantaged children

Mother-tongue instruction in the early grades

Children's identities are affirmed and their academic achievement improves when their local languages and cultural knowledge are respected. Since language is both a source of identity and a key means by which people can either gain access to power or be excluded from it, mother-tongue instruction is central to empowering poor and disadvantaged students to become successful learners (Cummins, 2000). For many children in poor and marginalized communities, their first encounter with formal education is through a language they do not speak at home. This becomes the first barrier to overcome if they are to succeed in school and continue their education (Brock-Utne, 2001; 2010).

Studies have demonstrated the benefits of mother-tongue instruction in the early years of education (e.g., Piper et al., 2016a; 2016b). Increasingly, evidence from studies in sub-Saharan Africa suggests that matching the students' home language to the language of instruction in the lower grades of primary school improves learning in later grades (Akyeampong et al., 2018; Ball, 2011; Carter et al., 2020a; Piper et al., 2016a; Sailors et al., 2010). In Ghana, for example, a study found that out-of-school children who were enrolled in an accelerated literacy and numeracy program and taught using their mother-tongue outperformed a comparative control group of public-school students who were not taught using mother-tongue instruction (Carter et al., 2020a). Mother-tongue instruction was also instrumental in successful transition to government public schools. However, the study found that, in the case of both low-performing boys and girls, some continued to disengage from learning, and show social withdrawal, anxiety, and frustration after transition. The lack of attention given to this group by teachers seems to explain this pattern (Carter et al., 2020a; Akyeampong et al., 2018). The study also found that not having access to mother-tongue instruction was linked to lower progress in numeracy. As reviewed elsewhere, it is critically important that teachers be competent in the mother-tongues that the students speak (Wagner, 2018).

A study in Ethiopia, which explored the impact of mother-tongue instruction in early grades on the performance of students later after they switch to English instruction found that, "learning first in the mother tongue in the early grades improves maths test scores later (in grade 5) … suggesting students taught first in their mother tongue learn in English better after they switch to English-instruction classrooms" (Seid, 2019, p. 577). Further analysis of data from the Ghana study by Carter et. al. (2020a) revealed that instructing children from poor and disadvantaged backgrounds in their mother-tongue also improves their chances of sustaining gains in literacy in multilingual learning environments in the government school system, even if initially these children experience some difficulties at the point of transition.

One of the reasons given for why many children in poor countries drop out of school is because they are instructed in a language they are unfamiliar with and find hard to understand. DeGraff (2016) explored the power of "Kreyol" in learning to read and in reading to learn in Haiti, and found that a large proportion of school dropout happened at an early age and language was a contributory factor in their academic failure (p. 436).

Accelerated learning pedagogies

To achieve SDG4 by 2030, it is imperative to provide children who are out of school with access to quality education. This population is comprised of many children who once attended school, but failed to make progress in their early years. Children and youth in SSA, for example, make up about 35 percent of the world's out-of-school child and youth population (UNESCO Institute for Statistics (UIS), 2017; World Bank, 2018). According to UIS statistics, there are about 25.7 million out-of-school adolescents of lower-secondary-school age and about 34.4 million in the upper-secondary-school age in SSA. This translates to out-of-school rates of 34 percent for the 12–14 age group, and 58 percent for the 15–17 age group (UIS, 2017). This is a large population of children who are unlikely to access dignified and fulfilling employment and escape intergenerational poverty (Dyer, 2013). For this population, accelerated education promises rapid acquisition of basic knowledge and skills to enable resumption of formal education. Accelerated education programs have therefore emerged as a viable response to the educational needs of out-of-school children who either dropped out or never attended formal school due to poverty, conflict, and crisis. Accelerated education is described as a flexible, age-appropriate program that promotes access to education in an accelerated timeframe (Shah, 2015; Myers & Pinnoc, 2017). The timeframe is important because out-of-school children need to catch up quickly on the foundational knowledge and skills they lost before they can continue successfully in their education and gain dignified employment in the future.

Several studies present evidence of the efficacy and efficiency of accelerated learning instruction in South Africa (Taole, 2018), Ethiopia (Akyeampong et al., 2017), and Ghana (Akyeampong et al., 2018). Each of these studies suggest that it is possible to bridge the learning gap of predominantly out-of-school children through pedagogies that are different from those used in mainstream education systems. Two of these studies will be described in more detail to understand why and how accelerated learning pedagogies are able to achieve this effect.

The Speed School program in Ethiopia[3]

The Speed School program in Ethiopia provides out-of-school children between the ages of 8 and 14 with an opportunity to be reintegrated into government schools after ten months of accelerated learning instruction. The program aims to improve this group's learning by seeking not only faster learning but also deeper and more effective learning than they had experienced before dropping out of formal education. An impact evaluation study in 2014 found that after one year in government schools, children who had gone through this program, dubbed "Speed Schools", made faster progress in learning than other non-Speed-School students who served as the control group. A longitudinal evaluation study which tracked Speed School students to measure the impacts of the program on primary school completion, learning outcomes, and attitudes towards learning found that the program had long-term impact. It was able to sustain cognitive gains in literacy and numeracy, enabling Speed School students to transition smoothly into the mainstream public education system.

As in many accelerated education programs, the program incorporated emotional, social, relational, and cultural aspects of learning rooted in the learner's context (Tobbell et al., 2010). Basically, the pedagogy affirmed and extended the students' identities and enabled them to develop skills in collaborative critical inquiry. They were able to repurpose their previously unsuccessful learning experiences to achieve more meaningful and lasting learning outcomes. The basic elements of the Speed School pedagogy are: its emphasis on developing reading skills (four times as many hours than in government public schools); extensive use of formative assessment; use of local languages to access and construct knowledge—and, in the process, to develop critical consciousness and cognitive competence—and finally, practical applications that invite the learners to draw on their cultural knowledge and experiences (Akyeampong et al., 2018). The pedagogy

---

3   Akyeampong et al., 2014; Akyeampong et al., 2018.

was inclusive in that it provided every child the opportunity to express their knowledge and receive collective support from their peers and teachers. Each contribution was equally valued, and the responsibility for learning and developing understanding became a shared one.

Working mainly in groups, teachers formulated questions that allowed students to think deeply about problems, which they discussed and summarized in group responses before presenting their ideas and solutions to the whole class. This format was used to encourage knowledge to be shared, debated, reconstructed, and retained meaningfully. Other salient features of the pedagogy included:

- Multilingual teaching, using both Amharic and English, but above all, Amharic to ensure all students understood;
- Constant repetition and frequent revision until understanding was achieved by all;
- The incorporation of visual aids, group- and pair-work, songs, and craftwork into everyday classroom teaching and learning.

This approach was successful, in that it motivated out-of-school children to become successful learners. Curriculum content that related to their everyday experience, combined with mother-tongue instruction and a supportive, friendly learning environment, built their confidence and self-esteem. Group activities became a vehicle for students to talk about their learning, which encouraged teachers to eschew viewing teaching as the mere transmission of knowledge. Instead, it allowed them to engage learners in a collaborative process that supports the development of cognitive and other personal and social skills. This approach seems to have benefited learners who otherwise would have been left behind in traditional classrooms, where teachers' classroom instruction is pitched at the level of high achievers or children from advantaged backgrounds.

The Complementary Basic Education (CBE) program in Ghana[4]

The CBE program in Ghana attempted to provide a second chance at education for out-of-school children in predominantly rural areas of Northern Ghana. An evaluation study designed to examine evidence

---

4 Akyeampong et al., 2018.

of impact on learning outcomes and progression into public schools revealed that, in less than a year, it had improved the abilities of children who had either dropped out of school or never attended, to levels similar to— and for some, better—than children who already had at least three years of primary education. But, unlike the Speed School program in Ethiopia, it adopted a pedagogy that was more closely aligned to instructional practices in mainstream government schools. The expectation was that this would smoothen transitions. For example, the structure of teachers' instructional approach used in the CBE classroom was similar to what was commonly used in public schools—a short introduction using question and answer techniques to recall previous knowledge, followed by a main lesson which comprised teacher-led instruction, finally ending with a summary of the lesson using questions and answers. Two "new" elements of the CBE accelerated learning pedagogy were the use of:

- The syllabic and phonetic methods of learning local language;
- Collaborative learning and connecting learning with the everyday life experiences of learners to make it more meaningful and enjoyable.

What was lacking was attention to the learning needs of low performers who were increasingly silently excluded from classroom discourse. Unlike the Ethiopia case, the CBE pedagogy lacked the strong collaborative culture that produced a greater sense of shared responsibility for learning and incorporated the needs of low-performing students.

In summary, accelerated learning pedagogies, of the kind used by the Speed Schools in Ethiopia and the CBE program in Ghana, provide insights into how the learning needs of children at the bottom of the learning pyramid could be met. What both programs show, particularly the Speed Schools, is that pedagogies that position teachers as facilitators of learning—and provide every child, irrespective of their ability, equal access to learning activities and the production of knowledge—have the potential to enhance low-achieving children's ability to learn and progress. Teachers are able to visualize and experience knowledge production as a co-construction activity. Where this is done more efficiently, as in the Ethiopia case, teachers orchestrate lessons with significant input from every child. In the case of Ghana, where the pedagogy was more teacher-led, the level of participation from low achievers was reduced, resulting in slower progress (Sabates et al., 2020; Akyeampong, 2018).

Inclusive pedagogies

According to James & Pollard (2011, p. 280), "'pedagogy' expresses the contingent relationship between teaching and learning ... and does not treat teaching as something that can be considered separately from an understanding of how learners learn". Inclusive instructional strategies use social and emotional supports to both scaffold learning and foster motivation. In this way, inclusive pedagogy creates space for all learners to contribute to knowledge production (Molbaek, 2018). Such pedagogies recognize that effective learning requires every child to participate, making it less likely for low achievers to be silently excluded. Stentiford and Koutsouris (2020) point out that the concept of inclusion must also extend beyond participation, and address diverse learning needs of students. However, studies suggest that teachers generally struggle to consistently create and sustain inclusive classrooms (Molbaek, 2018; Husbands & Pearce, 2012; Florian et al., 2010).

It could be argued that inclusive classroom concepts underpin the Speed School pedagogy in Ethiopia, and to some extent, the CBE program in Ghana. Particularly with the Speed School, all learners engage in peer-tutoring, group learning, and role play, with teachers using scaffolds to facilitate student learning. But it required restructuring the classroom seating arrangements so that students could face each other, in order to encourage cooperation and collaboration. A study in Kenya that explored primary teachers' inclusive practices also found that, when teachers reorganized their classrooms into a horseshoe format, this created a sense of community and enhanced participation for all students (Elder et al., 2016). However, traditional classrooms in LICs often lack the space and facilities to create this kind of classroom environment.

A survey and qualitative research study of experienced teachers from around the world aimed to understand important qualities needed for teaching disadvantaged students, including low achievers. An important quality was identified by the experienced teachers: an ability to build strong relationships with disadvantaged students (Akyeampong et al., 2018b). According to the experienced teachers, it was important for teachers to know which students were disadvantaged, or why they did not engage in learning, to empathize with their difficulties and give them regular attention during classroom instruction.

The challenge is for teacher preparation programs to develop such qualities and capabilities in the teachers they produce. The difficulties that students experience must be reframed as dilemmas for teaching rather than problems within students (Florian et al., 2010). However, as Florian and Black-Hawkins (2011) point out, "meeting this challenge sets a high standard for inclusive practice because extending what is ordinarily available to all learners is a complex pedagogical endeavor. It requires a shift in teaching and learning from an approach that works for most learners ... towards one that involves the development of a rich learning community characterised by learning opportunities that are sufficiently made available for everyone, so that all learners are able to participate in classroom life" (p. 814).

Meeting learning needs of disadvantaged children through teacher professional development

Teacher education programs in many LICs and LMICs often pay little attention to improving the ability of teachers to help minority or disadvantaged students learn. In Ghana, for example, studies have found that teacher education programs are largely ineffective at producing teachers with the skills to improve learning for most students. Teacher education programs in many LICs have decontextualized teaching, reducing it to a set of homogenized strategies which then make it difficult for teachers to pick out and respond to the learning needs of disadvantaged students with the appropriate instruction (Lewin & Stuart, 2003). Another limiting factor, found in teacher education systems in developing countries, is misalignment between teacher training and teaching methods with the school curriculum (Westbrook et al., 2013).

Another challenge is that school settings and policies may hinder teachers who wish to reorganize their classrooms to support a more inclusive pedagogy. For example, "a school's policy on setting may make it difficult for a teacher to use alternative grouping strategies in some lessons" (Florian & Black-Hawkins, 2011, p. 819). Education systems and school policies may not sufficiently highlight the importance of tracking under-achieving students for remedial action, which makes it less likely for teachers to give this focused attention.

In the study of the qualities of experienced teachers who teach disadvantaged children, the teachers were asked how much their education had contributed to their ability to help disadvantaged children learn. Most responded that, overall, it had done very little to prepare them to meet the learning needs of the silently excluded child. They had developed their capacity to address the learning needs of these children through the occasional professional development course, and through trial and error from classroom practice (Akyeampong, et al., 2018b). To make a difference, the teachers felt that teacher education had to improve in three areas:

- **Amend the selection process for entry to initial teacher education programs to include interpersonal skills and qualities in addition to academic qualifications.** This would draw attention to the importance of empathy and communication/relational skills as qualities that teachers must possess and promote.

- **Consider ways in which the pool of teacher candidates can become more diverse, attracting candidates with knowledge and experience of disadvantaged communities.** Teacher candidates should ideally reflect student demographics in the country. To achieve this, other teacher recruitment practices may have to be considered—for example, recruiting student teachers from poor and disadvantaged areas who may lack the initial entry qualifications for formal teacher training. These teachers may require a mixture of on-the-job training and institution-based training where they, for example, are trained to use scripted lessons to teach. Studies have found that low-skilled teachers can be trained to use scripted lessons and scaffolding on how to improve low-performing student learning outcomes (Murnane & Ganimian, 2014).

- **Help teachers gain hands-on practical experience using skills and strategies which support the learning of all students.**

Education programs should increase school-based teacher training elements and expose student teachers to learners from diverse backgrounds, in order to move away from generic teaching methods that leave low achievers or disadvantaged students behind. For assumptions and procedures that favor advantaged students to be replaced by new ways of thinking and working that support every student, irrespective of their socioeconomic background or learning difficulties, prospective teachers would have to experience what works to improve learning in different classroom environments composed of students from different backgrounds and communities.

Recommendations

The evidence reviewed in this chapter points to the importance of helping teachers develop the capacity to create inclusive classrooms. The following are key recommendations that emerge from the review of evidence in this paper.

Teacher policy

- Many practicing teachers in LICs and LMICs have not mastered the school subjects they teach. Their basic pedagogical knowledge can also be weak. Often, many of these underqualified teachers end up teaching in schools that serve poor and marginalized communities, and they are unable to provide quality instruction to improve learning. It is not enough to simply increase the supply of trained teachers. Equally important is ensuring that teacher training develops strong foundational knowledge in school subjects, either through continuous professional development or in-service training.

- There must also be policies aimed at reducing high teacher absenteeism rates, especially in schools in rural areas. As the evidence reviewed suggests, addressing this problem requires policies that improve weak governance and poor teacher management, and incentivize teaching in disadvantaged communities.

Teacher professional development policy

- Many teacher professional development programs do not sufficiently focus on how to address the learning needs of disadvantaged children, or how to implement an inclusive curriculum. Teacher professional development curriculum policy should emphasize identification of the "silently excluded" child and promote inclusive instructional strategies, such as those used in accelerated learning programs. All programs must pass key inclusive practices criteria, such as: (a) to what extent does the professional training equip the teacher to address different learning needs and challenges; (b) to what extent are strategies sensitive to learning needs of students at the bottom of the learning pyramid; and (c) to what extent does the program "create (a rich learning community) rather than using teaching and learning strategies that are suitable for most" (Florian & Black-Hawkins, 2011, p. 818).

- Recruitment policy should also target teachers from diverse backgrounds, and make the attitudes and dispositions that are important for meeting diverse learning needs important in teacher selection criteria. If teacher candidates have strengths in other important areas but not in this area, they should, in the early stages of their career, take professional development courses that address this gap. This training should aim to make them see "difficulties in learning as professional challenges for teachers, rather than deficits in learners, that encourage the development of new ways of working" (Florian & Black-Hawkins, 2011, p. 819).

- This chapter has also identified the importance of teaching at the right level of the child, so no child is left behind. But it has also pointed out that current classroom instructional practice in LICs and LMICs lacks sensitivity to this approach. Teacher education curriculum specialists should design programs that prepare teachers to teach at the right level of each child, and skills for teaching in multi-grade classroom environments.

- Lessons from successful accelerated learning pedagogies suggest that mother-tongue instruction is critical for inclusive education to have impact, especially at the early stages of education. It is important for early-grade teachers in LICs and LMICs to master mother-tongue instructional languages and pedagogies. Programs should be designed to teach mother-tongue language instruction or incorporate aspects of it in early-grade teacher training.

Teacher and teacher education research

- There is a paucity of research that examines the kinds of inclusive pedagogical practices that help to close the learning gap between low-achieving students and their more advantaged counterparts in LICs and LMICs. Further study of what works to improve learning for low-achieving students from disadvantaged backgrounds in actual classroom settings is also needed.

- Inclusive pedagogical strategies from accelerated learning programmes (ALPs) suggest that they can address diverse learning needs. More research in this area is needed to develop a better understanding of how the different types of ALPs improve learning for disadvantaged students in the early years of schooling (e.g., Grades 1 to 3), but also how they can be effectively and efficiently mainstreamed into public school classrooms to improve learning for all.

- Research is also needed to understand how pre-service teachers and classroom teachers can establish better connections between students' lives and the school curriculum, and how teachers can develop supportive relationships with disadvantaged students to advance their learning. There is also the need for studies which explore how pre-service teachers learn to teach in contexts of increasing student diversity (as well as mother-tongue languages), including teaching students with very different learning needs in the same classroom space.

Conclusion

SDG4 is an ambitious goal, achievement of which will require greater investment in teachers' abilities to address the learning needs of poor and vulnerable groups in LICs and LMICs. For many of these children, school attendance is not synonymous with learning, because they are silently excluded from everyday classroom activities. Even for those who survive and continue beyond the early years of primary education, they continue to make slow progress compared with children from advantaged backgrounds. We need to understand and implement effective techniques and teaching programs that improve learning outcomes for children at the bottom of the learning pyramid. While the research shows some promising interventions, this chapter argues that we need to start from the initial preparation and in-service training of teachers. Given the scale of the challenge, inclusion must be a high priority for teacher education systems in LICs and LMICs.

References

Albert, J. R. G. (2012). *Improving teacher deployment practices in the Philippines* (Policy notes). Philippine Institute for Development Studies.

Altinok, N., Antoninis, M., & Nguyen-Van P. (2017). *Smart teachers, smarter pupils? Some new evidence from sub-Saharan Africa* (Working Papers of BETA). Bureau d'Economie Théorique et Appliquée, UDS, Strasbourg.

Altinok, N. (2013). *The impact of teacher knowledge on student achievement in 14 sub-Saharan African countries* (Paper commissioned for Education for All (EFA) Global Monitoring Report 2013/14, Teaching and Learning: Achieving Quality for All). Paris: UNESCO.

Akyeampong, K. (2017). Reconceptualising teacher education for equitable learning outcomes: Towards a comprehensive approach. In B. Hudson (Ed.), *Overcoming fragmentation in teacher education policy and practice*, (pp. 231–248). Cambridge University Press. https://www.worldcat.org/title/overcoming-fragmentation-in-teacher-education-policy-and-practice/oclc/1041442361

Akyeampong, K., Lussier, K., Pryor, J., & Westbrook, J. (2013). Improving teaching and learning of basic maths and reading in Africa: Does teacher preparation count? *International Journal of Educational Development, 33,* 272–282.

Akyeampong, K., Djangmah, J., Oduro, A., Seidu, A., & Hunt, F. (2007). *Access to basic education in Ghana: The evidence and the issues* (CREATE country analytic report). Centre for International Education, Department of Education, University of Sussex.

Akyeampong, K. (2006). Extending basic education to out-of-school children in Northern Ghana: What can multi-grade schooling teach us? In A. W. Little (Ed.), *Education for all and multi-grade teaching: Challenges and opportunities*. Dordrecht: Springer Netherlands. https://www.worldcat.org/title/education-for-all-and-multigrade-teaching-challenges-and-opportunities/oclc/873384691

Akyeampong, K. (2018). *Understanding CBE in Ghana: An analysis of the CBE pedagogy in Ghana* (Paper prepared for the UK Department for International Development (DFID)). REAL Centre, University of Cambridge.

Akyeampong, K., & Stephens, D. (2002). Exploring the backgrounds and shaping factors of beginning student teachers in Ghana: Towards greater contextualization of teacher education. *International Journal of Educational Development, 22,*(3/4), 261–274.

Akyeampong, K., & Lewin, K. (2002). From student teachers to newly qualified teachers in Ghana: Insights into becoming a teacher. *International Journal of Educational Development, 22*(3/4), 339–352.

Akyeampong, K., Higgins, S., Sabates, R., Rose, P., & Carter, E. (2018). *Understanding complementary basic education (CBE) in Ghana*. Glasgow: DFID Crown.

Akyeampong, K., Vegas, E., Wolfenden, F., Salhanha, K., Al-Attia, H. D., Oduro, E., & Weinstein, J. (2017). *Qualities of effective teachers who teach disadvantaged students: Insights from the Varkey Teacher Ambassador Community*. Global Education and Skills Forum (GESF), Alliances Varkey Foundation.

Akyeampong, K., Delprato, M., Sabates, R., James, Z., Pryor, J., Westbrook, J., Humphreys, S., & Tsegay, A. (2018). *Tracking the progress of Speed School children in Ethiopia: A longitudinal study*. Centre for International Education, University of Sussex and Geneva Global Inc. USA.

ASER. (2013). *Annual status of education report (rural)*. ASER Centre, New Delhi.

Ball, J. (2011). *Enhancing learning of children from diverse language backgrounds: Mother tongue-based bilingual or multilingual education in the early years*. Paris, France: UNESCO. http://unesdoc.unesco.org/images/0021/002122/212270e.pdf

Banerjee, A., Banerji, R., Berry, J., Duflo, E., Kannan, H., Mukherji, S., Shotland, M., & Walton, M. (2016). *Mainstreaming an effective intervention: Evidence from randomized evaluations of "Teaching at the Right Level" in India* (Working Paper No. w22746). National Bureau of Economic Research.

Barrera-Osorio, F., & Raju, D. (2014). *Teacher performance pay: Experimental evidence from Pakistan*. Washington, DC: World Bank.

Bashir, S., Lockheed, M., Nihan, E., & Jee-Peng, T. (2018). *Facing forward: Schooling for learning in Africa*. Washington, DC: World Bank.

Bennell, P., & Akyeampong, K. (2007). *Teacher motivation and incentives in sub-Sahara Africa and South Asia*. London: DFID.

Bold, T., Filmer, D., Martin, G., Molina, E., Rockmore, C., Stacy, B., Svensson, J., & Wane, W. (2018). *What do teachers know and do? Does it matter? Evidence from primary schools in Africa* (Background Paper to the 2018 World Development Report). Washington, DC: World Bank.

Brock-Utne, B. (2001). Education for all: In whose language? *Oxford Review of Education, 27*(1), 115–134. https://doi.org/10.1080/03054980125577

Brock-Utne, B. (2010). Research and policy on the language of instruction issue in Africa. *Int. J. Educ. Dev., 30*, 636–645. https://doi.org/10.1016/j.ijedudev.2010.03.004

Carter, E., Rose, P., Sabates, R., & Akyeampong, K. (2020a). Trapped in low performance? Tracking the learning trajectory of disadvantaged girls and boys in the Complementary Basic Education Programme in Ghana. *International Journal of Educational Research, 100*, 1–11.

Chapman, D. W. (1994). *Reducing teacher absenteeism and attrition: Causes, consequences and responses*. Paris: UNESCO, International Institute for Educational Planning.

Chudgar, A. (2015). Association between contract teachers and student learning in five francophone African countries. *Comparative Education Review, 59*(2), 261–288.

Cummins, J. (2000). *Language, power, and pedagogy: Bilingual children in the crossfire*. Clevedon: Multilingual Matters.

De, S., Pettersson, G., Morris, R., & Cameron, S. (2016). *Teacher development programme (TDP) impact evaluation of Output 1: In-service training* (Final Baseline Technical Report: Results and Discussion). Education Data, Research and Evaluation in Nigeria (EDOREN) & UKAid.

DeGraff, M. (2016). Mother-tongue books in Haiti: The power of Kreyòl in learning to read and in reading to learn. *Prospects, 46*(3–4), 435–464.

Dembélé, M., Chudgar, A., & Ndow, I. (2016, December 3–7). *The use of contract teachers in sub-Saharan Africa: A review of the situation in 24 countries* (Conference presentation). 9th International Policy Dialogue Forum, Secretariat of the International Task Force on Teachers for Education 2030, Siem Reap, Cambodia.

Duflo, E., Dupas, P., & Kremer, M. (2011). Peer effects, teacher incentives, and the impact of tracking: Evidence from a randomized evaluation in Kenya. *American Economic Review, 101*(5), 1739–1774.

Duflo, E., Pascaline, D., & Kremer, M. (2015). School governance, teacher incentives, and pupil-teacher ratios: Experimental evidence from Kenyan primary schools. *Journal of Public Economics, 123*, 92–110.

Dyer, C. (2013). Educating the poorest and ideas of poverty. *International Journal of Educational Development, 33*, 221–224.

Elder, B. C., Damiani, M. L., & Oswago, B. O. (2016). From attitudes to practice: Utilising inclusive teaching strategies in Kenyan primary schools. *International Journal of Inclusive Education, 20*(4), 413–434. https://doi.org/10.1080/13603116.2015.1082648

Filmer, D., Ezequiel, M., & Stacy, B. (2015). *What goes on inside the classroom in Africa? Assessing the relationship between what teachers know, what happened in the classroom, and student performance* (Paper for the Service Delivery Indicators initiative). Washington, DC: World Bank.

Florian, L. (2009). Preparing teachers to work in 'schools for all'. *Teaching and Teacher Education, 25*(4), 533–534.

Florian L., Young, K., & Rouse, M. (2010). Preparing teachers for inclusive and diverse educational environments: studying curricular reform in an initial teacher education course. *International Journal of Inclusive Education, 14*(7), 709–722. https://doi.org/10.1080/13603111003778536

Florian L., & Black-Hawkins, K. (2011). Exploring inclusive pedagogy. *British Educational Research Journal, 37*(5), 813–828.

Fredriksen, B. (2011). *Education resource mobilization and use in developing countries: Scope for efficiency gains through more strategic use of education aid.* Washington, DC: Results for Development Institute.

Ganimian, A. J., & Murnane, R. J. (2016). Improving education in developing countries: Lessons from rigorous impact evaluations. *Review of Educational Research 86*(3), 719–755.

Glewwe, P., & Muralidharan, K. (2015). Improving school education outcomes in developing countries: Evidence, knowledge, gaps, and policy implications. In E. A. Hanushek, S. Machin, & L. Woessman (Eds.), *Handbook of the economics of education, Volume 5* (pp. 653–743). Elsevier.

Glewwe, P., Ilias, N., & Kremer, M. (2010). Teacher incentives. *American Economic Journal: Applied Economics, 2*(3), 205–227.

Guerrero, G., Leon, J., Zapata, M., Sugimaru, C., & Cueto, S. (2012). *What works to improve teacher attendance in developing countries? A systematic review.* London: EPPI-Centre, Social Science Research Unit, Institute of Education, University of London.

Hanushek, E., Piopiunik, M., & Wiederhold, S. (2014). *The value of smarter teachers: International evidence on teacher cognitive skills and student performance.* Hoover Institution, Stanford University, CESifo, and NBER.

Hanushek, E. A., & Rivkin, S. G. (2012). The distribution of teacher quality and the implications of teacher policy. *Annual Review of Economics, 4*, 131–157. https://doi.org/10.1146/annurev-economics-080511-111001

Hedges, J. (2002). The importance of posting and interaction with the education bureaucracy in becoming a teacher in Ghana. *International Journal of Educational Development, 22*, 353–366.

Husbands C., & Pearce, J. (2012). *What makes great pedagogy? Nine claims from research.* National College for School Leadership. https://assets.publishing.service.gov.uk/government/uploads/system/uploads/attachment_data/file/329746/what-makes-great-pedagogy-nine-claims-from-research.pdf

International Labour Organisation (ILO). (2016). *Rural teachers in Africa.* Geneva: ILO.

Innovations for Poverty Action. (2018). *Evaluating the teacher community assistant initiative.* https://www.poverty-action.org/study/evaluating-teacher-community-assistant-initiative-ghana

James, M., & Pollard, A. (2011). TLRP's ten principles for effective pedagogy: Rationale, development, evidence, argument and impact. *Research Papers in Education, 26*(3), 275–328.

Knoster, K. C. (2016). *Strategies for addressing student and teacher absenteeism: A literature review.* Washington, DC: US Department of Education, North Central Comprehensive Centre.

Kremer, M., Brannen, C., & Glennerster, R. (2013). The challenge of education and learning in the developing world. *Science, 340*(6130), 297–300.

Lei, H., Cui, Y., & Zhou, W. (2018). Relationships between student engagement and academic achievement: A meta-analysis. *Social Behaviour and Personality: An International Journal, 46*(3), 517–528.

Lewin, K., & Akyeampong, K. (2009). Education in sub-Saharan Africa: Researching access, transitions and equity. *Comparative Education, 45*(2), 143–150.

Lewin K. (2011). *Making rights realities: Researching educational access, transition and equity.* CREATE University of Sussex/DFID London. https://assets.publishing.service.gov.uk/media/57a08aede5274a31e0000866/Making-Rights-Realities-Keith-Lewin-September-2011.pdf

Little, A. W. (2007). *Education for all and multi-grade teaching: Challenges and opportunities.* Berlin: Springer Science & Business Media.

Luschei T. F., & Fagioli L. P. (2016). A vanishing rural school advantage? Changing urban/rural student achievement differences in Latin America and the Caribbean. *Comparative Education Review, 60*(4).

Luschei, T. F., & Chudgar A. (2015). *Teacher distribution in developing countries: Teachers of marginalized students in India, Mexico and Tanzania.* Palgrave Macmillan.

Luschei, T. F., & Carnoy, M. (2010). Educational production and the distribution of teachers in Uruguay. *International Journal of Educational Development, 30*(2), 169–181.

Metzler, J., & Woessmann, L. (2012). The impact of teacher subject knowledge on student achievement: Evidence from within-teacher within-student variation. *Journal of Development Economics, 99*(2), 486–496.

Molbaek, M. (2018). Inclusive teaching strategies: Dimensions and agendas. *International Journal of Inclusive Education, 22*(10), 1048–1061.

Mulkeen, A., & Chen, D. (2008). *Teachers for rural schools: Experiences in Lesotho, Malawi, Mozambique, Tanzania & Uganda* (Africa Human Development Series). Washington, DC: World Bank.

Muralidharan, K., & Sundararaman V. (2011). Teacher performance pay: Experimental evidence from India. *Journal of Political Economy, 119*(1), 39–77.

Myers, J., & Pinnock, H. (2017). *Guide to accelerated education principles.* UNHCR.

Pugatch, T. (2017). *Is teacher certification an effective tool for developing countries?* IZA World of Labour.

Pajares, M. F. (1992). Teachers' beliefs and educational research: Cleaning up a messy construct. *Review of Educational Research, 62*(3).

Patrinos, H. A, Velez, E., & Wang, C. Y. (2013). *Framework for the reform of education systems and planning for quality* (Policy Research Working Paper, No. 6701). Washington, DC: World Bank. https://openknowledge.worldbank.org/handle/10986/16910

Piper, B., Zuilkowski, S., & Ong'ele, S. (2016a). Implementing mother tongue instruction in the real world: Results from a medium scale randomized controlled trial in Kenya. *Comparative Education Review, 60*(4), 776–807. https://doi-org.ezp.lib.cam.ac.uk/10.1086/688493

Piper, B., Schroeder, L., & Trudell, B. (2016b). Oral reading fluency and comprehension in Kenya: Reading acquisition in a multilingual environment. *Journal of Research in Reading, 39*(2), 133–152.

Quak, E. (2020). *The political economy of the primary education system in Tanzania* (K4D Helpdesk Report No. 710). Brighton, UK: Institute of Development Studies.

Rogers, F. H., & Vegas, E. (2009). *No more cutting class? Reducing teacher absence and providing incentives for performance* (Policy Research Working Paper 4847). World Bank, Human Development Research Group. https://openknowledge.worldbank.org/bitstream/handle/10986/4043/WPS4847.pdf;jsessionid=35D7638C3DC36323093287128482B611?sequence=1

Rolleston, C. (2014). Learning profiles and the 'skills gap' in four developing countries: A comparative analysis of schooling and skills development. *Oxford Review of Education, 40*(1), 132–150.

Rose, P., & Alcott, B. (2015). *How can education systems become equitable by 2030?* (DFID think pieces: Learning and equity). Heart & Education Advice & Resource Team (HEART).

Razquin, P. (2009). Global trends in teaching employment: Challenges for teacher education and development in developing countries. In M. T. Tatto & M. Mincu (Eds.), *Reforming teaching and learning: Comparative perspectives in a global era* (pp. 75–96). Sense Publishers.

Sabates, R., Carter., E., & Stern, J. (2020). *Using educational transitions to estimate learning loss due to Covid-19 school closures: The case of Complementary Basic Education in Ghana.* REAL Centre, University of Cambridge. https://doi.org/10.5281/zenodo.3888219

Saeed, S., & Jamil, B. (2018, 27–29 June). *Ins and outs of rolling out Teaching at the Right Level (TARL) in Pakistan* (Conference presentation). The 14th Annual Conference of the British Education Studies Association (BESA).

Sailors, M., Pearson, P. D., & Beretvas, S. N. (2010). *Bilingual Research Journal, 3391*, 21–41.

Seid, Y. (2019). The impact of learning first in mother tongue: Evidence from a natural experiment in Ethiopia. *Applied Economics, 51*(6), 577–593.

Shah, R. (2015). *Norwegian Refugee Council's accelerated education responses: A meta evaluation.* Norwegian Refugee Council. https://www.nrc.no/globalassets/pdf/evaluations/meta-evaluation-of-nrcs-accelerated-education-programme.pdf

Spaull, N., & Kotze, J. (2015). Starting behind and staying behind in South Africa: The case of insurmountable learning deficits in mathematics. *International Journal of Educational Development, 41,* 13–24.

Stentiford, L., & Koutsouris, G. (2020). *What are inclusive pedagogies in higher education? A systematic scoping review* (Studies in Higher Education). https://doi.org/10.1080/03075079.2020.1716322

Taole, M. J. (2018, 12–14 November). *Exploring teachers' practices in giving feedback in rural South African multi-grade classrooms* (Conference presentation). 11th Annual International Conference of Education, Research and Innovation, Seville, Spain. https://doi.org/10.21125/iceri.2018.0196

Tobbell, J., O'Donnell, V., & Zammit, M. (2010). Exploring transition to postgraduate study: Shifting identities in interaction with communities, practice and participation. *British Educational Research Journal, 36*(2), 261–278.

Tayyaba, S. (2012). Rural-urban gaps in academic achievement, schooling conditions, student, and teachers' characteristics in Pakistan. *International Journal of Educational Management, 26*(1), 6–26.

UNESCO. (2013/14). *Teaching and learning: Achieving quality for all* (EFA Global Monitoring Report). Paris: UNESCO

UIS (UNESCO Institute for Statistics). (2006). *Teachers and educational quality: Monitoring global needs for 2015*. Montreal: UNESCO Institute for Statistics.

UIS (UNESCO Institute for Statistics). (2017). *More than one-half of children and adolescents are not learning worldwide* (Fact Sheet No. 46). Paris: UNESCO Institute for Statistics.

Wagner, D. A. (2018). *Learning as development: Rethinking international education in a changing world*. New York: Routledge.

Ward, M. (2018). PISA for development: Results in focus. *PISA in Focus, 91*. Paris: OECD Publishing. https://doi.org/10.1787/c094b186-en

Westbrook, J., Durrani, N., Brown, R., Orr, D., Pryor, J., Boddy, J., & Salvi, F. (2013). *Pedagogy, curriculum, teaching practices and teacher education in developing countries* (Final Report, Education Rigorous Literature Review). Department for International Development.

World Development Report. (2018). *Learning to realize education's promise*. Washington, DC: World Bank. https://doi.org/10.1596/978-1-4648-1096-1

4. Improving the Impact of Educational Technologies on Learning Within Low-Income Contexts

Nathan M. Castillo, Taskeen Adam, and Björn Haßler

Introduction

Achieving the Sustainable Development Goal for education (SDG4) requires tackling long-standing inequalities in education systems (United Nations, 2015; Sriprakash et al., 2019; Jansen, 2019). Quality and inclusive learning that emphasizes inquiry-based pedagogies has been shown to have emancipatory powers for marginalized groups (Freire, 1970). However, material constraints such as overcrowded classrooms, limited materials, and under-resourced teachers create barriers to foundational skill development. For instance, recent estimates reveal that 50 percent of children worldwide are not achieving minimum proficiency levels in reading and mathematics after four years of schooling (Stone et al., 2019). Additionally, out-of-school learners make up one in five (262 million) children globally (UNESCO-UIS, n.d.). School closures brought on by the COVID-19 pandemic have only increased this number, and generated fear that some learners may not return to schools once they are reopened (UNESCO-IIEP, 2020). The goal of studying learning at the "bottom of the pyramid" (LBOP) is to address these educational barriers that have historically prevented poor and marginalized students from achieving their full potential (Wagner & Castillo, 2014).

Information and communication technology (ICT) can play a crucial role in enhancing teaching and learning quality. It can provide more efficient data analysis methods, and improve the implementation of interventions. However, ICT can only be supportive of learning if it aligns with local contexts and human capacities. ICT can help teachers be more effective, for example, but only if they have adequate digital literacy skills to make use of it. Similarly, ICT interventions can help enhance the monitoring of educational inputs, such as teacher attendance, but only if the broader educational ecosystem supports it (World Bank, 2016).

To reach our global development goals for learning, we need to disrupt the traditional learning model through experimentation with dynamic and responsive interventions. However, it is important to note that disruption as it relates to education has a different connotation than it does in other industries. For example, in commerce, disruption could take the form of replacing older practices with newer, more efficient ones (through automation, outsourcing, etc.). However, within the field of education, the goal of "disruption" is not to replace older practices (i.e., teachers) with new technologies. On the contrary, teachers are critical stakeholders who need to be included in the design and implementation of EdTech solutions. In this sense, pedagogical disruption refers to a shift towards more constructive teaching and learning, either directly through teacher involvement, or by reducing tasks that prevent them from focusing on their principal role as learning facilitators (Bada & Olusegun, 2015; Dede, 1995; Li, 2001).

In this chapter, we first provide an overview of educational technology interventions, with a special consideration for designing within LBOP contexts. We then examine relevant research on EdTech implementation and learning outcomes. The second half of the chapter contrasts constraints of educational programming with opportunities for technology to improve progress in key domains. We conclude with a discussion of new directions for EdTech research and their implications for low-income contexts.

Overview of educational technologies and educational technology interventions

ICT in education is often referred to as "educational technology", or EdTech. Here we use the term "EdTech" to mean any digital or electronic technologies that support teaching and learning, both broadcast (e.g., radio and TV) and digital (e.g., feature and smartphones, mp3 players, tablets, laptops, and smartboards) (Power et al., 2014). Access to these technologies—and their supporting infrastructure—vary across contexts, and it is important to design EdTech programs with this in mind.[1] Figure 1 illustrates the different levels of access for different population groups. Of note, low-income populations tend to have greater access to broadcast technologies and phones than to other connected devices (see Figure 1).

However, the success of an EdTech intervention depends on far more than the technology itself. Contextualized design, stakeholder engagement, community buy-in, support structures for teachers and learners, and the ability of communities to independently maintain equipment and facilities are all elements of successful implementation and planning. Programs are most effective when they take a problem-first approach rather than a techno-solutionist approach, i.e., when they focus on addressing barriers to improved learning outcomes rather than merely digitizing the learning environment (Government Digital Services, 2019; Schurr, 2013; Centre for International Development, 2018).

EdTech programs vary in both the amount and complexity of technology used. They include broadcasting content over radio; the use of audio and video resources in a classroom setting; digital resources that support teachers' professional development; e-readers, tablets, or laptops distributed to each learner; virtual learning environments (offline, intermittently online, and fully online) and virtual reality classrooms (Power et al., 2014; Adam, McBurnie, & Haßler., 2020).

---

1 These technologies depend on enabling infrastructure such as electricity, connectivity, and safe storage facilities. Here, "electricity" and "connectivity" means a range of different things. For example, electricity could come from grid-connected power, off-grid solar power, or home diesel generators; these may also vary in their supply reliability. Connectivity could be internet connection—GSM/SMS, GPRS/3G/4G, broadband—or be a local connection over WiFi without internet. In COVID-19, key infrastructure also includes hand-washing facilities for safe, shared use.

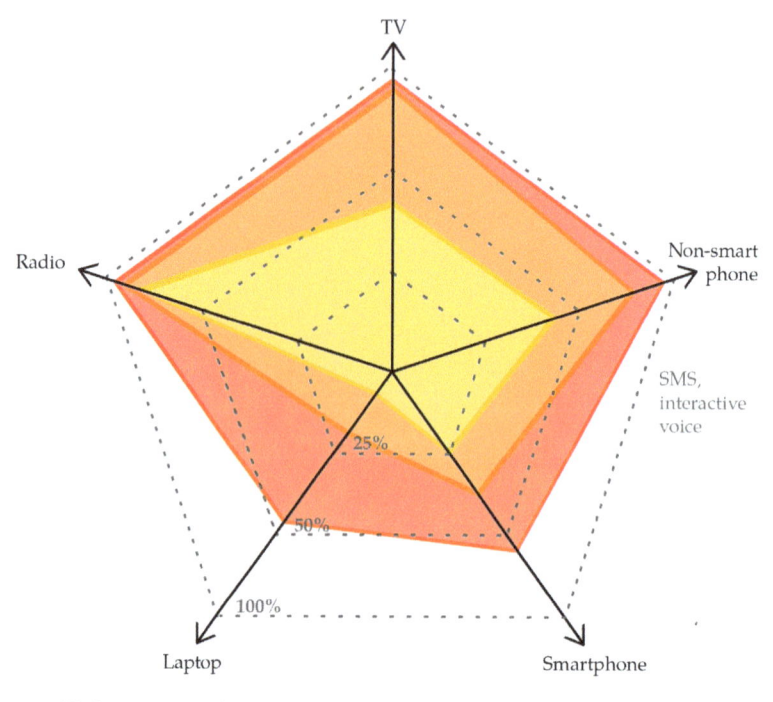

Fig. 1. Differing levels of access to devices for low-, middle-, and high-income populations. Source: Haßler, Khalayleh, & McBurnie, 2020.

Despite the variations in technology-enhanced programming, effective practices generally:

1. Address a distinct curricular focus (e.g., improving numeracy or literacy);

2. Use relevant and appropriate learning materials and modalities (e.g., use visual aids as needed);

3. For programs implemented at a school- or system-level, focus on the teachers' professional development and use of (digital) pedagogies (e.g., when and how to effectively integrate technology);

4. Focus on evaluation of program impact (e.g., was there an improvement in learning outcomes and their correlated components?);

5. Are rolled out incrementally and iteratively (e.g., small pilot programs are tested and evaluated before bringing to scale at a greater investment);

6. Use technology to monitor and evaluate factors within the education system (e.g., they monitor teacher and learner attendance, or determine schools' geolocations and their ease of access) (Power et al., 2014; Adam, McBurnie, & Haßler, 2020).

In addition to the principles above, designing for the most marginalized learners will necessarily require additional considerations. LBOP EdTech programs should prioritize cost-effectiveness, contextualized content, and alignment with existing infrastructure if they are to truly reach and support those most in need. These considerations are further elaborated below.

Further considerations when designing for LBOP

A central goal of SDG4 is to improve learning quality overall while reducing disparities in learning outcomes across populations. To improve learning outcomes for LBOP populations, solutions must take into account the multiple contextual factors and stakeholders that interact with learning within poor and marginalized contexts.

Language. Language of instruction (LOI) is a key factor in designing EdTech for learners at the bottom of the pyramid. A considerable constraint on these learners is that they often have little or no exposure to the dominant language of instruction in their schools, making their transition to school even more complicated (Ball et al., 2014). Digital solutions that deploy learning content in home languages can create better opportunities for a successful transition to a country's dominant LoI.

Local(ized) content, skills, and resources. Central to successful EdTech design for BOP settings is relevance to users' needs, digital skills, and motivation for learning (UNESCO, 2018). Additionally, leveraging home-grown technologies and innovations rather than importing foreign ICT interventions can have a positive impact on sustainability (DeBoer, 2009).

Basic infrastructure. Understanding the local infrastructure—both physical and digital—is important. Every new intervention should begin with a needs assessment and community mapping exercise to understand what possibilities currently exist for leveraging existing infrastructure (see, for instance, Highet et al., 2018). While infrastructure is a pre-determinant to access, other sociocultural factors can also lead to unequal access to resources, such as sex, age, employment status, educational background, or household income (Rohs & Ganz, 2015). Within the COVID-19 era, needs assessments are crucial to prevent governments from investing massively in interventions from which their populations cannot access or benefit (Adam, McBurnie, & Haßler, 2020; Haßler, Khalayleh, & McBurnie, 2020).

The role of connectivity. As of 2020, only 39.3 percent of Africans have internet access, compared to 87.7 percent of Europe and 95 percent of North Americans (Internet World Stats, 2020). The UN Broadband Commission for Sustainable Development is attempting to close this connectivity gap by 2025 with universal access by 2030 (ITU & UNESCO, 2019). Similar to internet access, the cost of data varies considerably. For instance, data costs on islands such as St. Helena are approximately $52.50 per gig in comparison to $0.09 in India (Cable.co.uk, 2020). "Internet-in-a-box" programs offer a solution for low-bandwidth communities by providing localized digital learning environments in a pre-packaged, offline suite of teaching and learning materials (Adam, McBurnie, & Haßler, 2020).

Competencies. End-user competencies include comfort with digital resources, but also more foundational competencies such as functional literacy and language ability. Digital and foundational competencies should ideally influence user interface design. A recent series of case studies showed that successful designs include attention to end-user competencies when building out a platform's user interface (Vosloo, 2018). For instance, using images instead of text-heavy menus and making button actions more intuitive led to improved utilization of the software. As learning shifts online during and post COVID-19, critical digital literacy is needed by teachers and learners to deal with the floods of information available online, as well as misinformation and online predators (Adam, 2020c; Bali, 2019).

Equity, inclusion, and ethical considerations. Importantly, EdTech solutions should strive to prevent reproducing inequalities across student groups (sociocultural minorities, struggling learners, etc.). Previous interventions using technology have produced greater benefits for higher-achieving students than for their lower-achieving peers (Kam, 2013; Warschauer, 2003). Inequalities also persist with regard to representation within digital content as well as contribution to design features (Graham et al., 2015). While equitable access is an important goal, inequality in authorship, narratives, contributions, and epistemic diversity (Graham et al., 2015; Adam, 2020b)—termed "existential inequality"(Czerniewicz, 2018)—should be considered in the design process.

Stakeholder engagement. In addition to contextual considerations for EdTech design, stakeholder engagement is essential. Stakeholders may include students, parents, teachers, school administrators, the private sector, mobile network operators, donors, and national and regional governments. Each stakeholder contributes unique needs, perspectives, and interests. For example, teachers voice important challenges related to using technological tools in the classroom, and know what aspects of their job technology could best support. Learners can provide important information about the user experience. Adding to the complexity, it may also be necessary to engage multiple government departments and NGOs within the same context. For instance, South Africa has a department of basic education, a separate department of government communication and information systems, and yet another department for higher education, science, and technology (GoSA, 2020). Each of these departments could potentially contribute to the coordination of an EdTech program, but it would require careful communication across groups so as not to unintentionally undermine or duplicate efforts.

Participatory approaches that center on social justice can be used to ensure that marginalized voices are not silenced in the process (Mertens, 2007). This means elevating the voice and needs of the various stakeholders in a tangible way that contributes to the programmatic design. Communication with stakeholders should be ongoing throughout the life of the program, allowing for collaboration at various points in the design and implementation process. This feedback is particularly important in the design of software and graphical user interfaces, where different stakeholders may require different design features.

Finally, it is important to follow ethical procedures and explain to stakeholders the risks that may be associated with an intervention and/or study, such as data collection and the creation of digital footprints that users may not have previously had. This is particularly important with the implementation of "free" software that requires registration and collects user data.

Lessons learnt from EdTech interventions

For about half a century, experimentation with educational technologies has led to mixed results for improving the quality of learning overall (Power et al., 2014; Wagner, 2018; Hinostroza et al., 2014). The next section reviews lessons learned from EdTech interventions by contrasting two prominent cases and discussing trends from recent examples.

The case of Interactive Radio Instruction

One of the earliest EdTech interventions was developed by Stanford researchers, and involved the use of Interactive Radio Instruction for math education (Searle et al., 1976). Interactive Radio Instruction combined radio broadcasts with active learning strategies and delivered specially-designed curriculum to areas where access to quality education is limited (World Bank, 2005).

Building on early success from the Stanford project (implemented originally in Nicaragua), Interactive Radio Instruction rapidly expanded to other countries and subjects (Potter & Naidoo, 2006). The approach was designed around four key principles: (1) guided support to under-trained teachers through scripted instruction, (2) development of content in local languages by curriculum experts; (3) an engaging and interactive learning environment that differed from traditional, rote-learning practices; and (4) delivery of quality learning materials to remote schools (virtually) (Ho & Thukral, 2011).

Interactive Radio Instruction has been an effective model for EdTech interventions in developing countries, and has successfully improved education quality at scale (Naslund Hadley, Parker, & Hernandez-Agramonte, 2014; Damani & Mitchell, 2020; Trucano, 2010; Anzalone & Bosch, 2005). However, there have also been challenges in some contexts. While radio broadcast has the ability to reach remote locations, radio transmission of learning content eliminates the facilitator's ability to pause or review the content. Recent versions of this approach have attempted to provide an on-demand experience by moving to pre-recorded audio, but the additional resources required (stereo, speakers, power, etc.) may still be limiting factors in some contexts. Poor supply of basic conditions to promote clear and consistent broadcasts, loosely incorporated language and cultural relevance, and limited integration into classroom practice have also been noted as barriers to success for IRI implementation (Alaro, 2007).

In response to the COVID-19 pandemic, many countries around the world revitalized their interest in delivery of educational content through technology-supported means. However, for low-income contexts, broadcast is still a prominent means of content delivery. In fact, a recent survey of 110 countries revealed that radio-based instruction accounts for 80 percent of remote learning policies, whereas internet-based instruction accounts for less than half of the learning policies deployed during school closures (Figure 2; UNICEF, 2020).

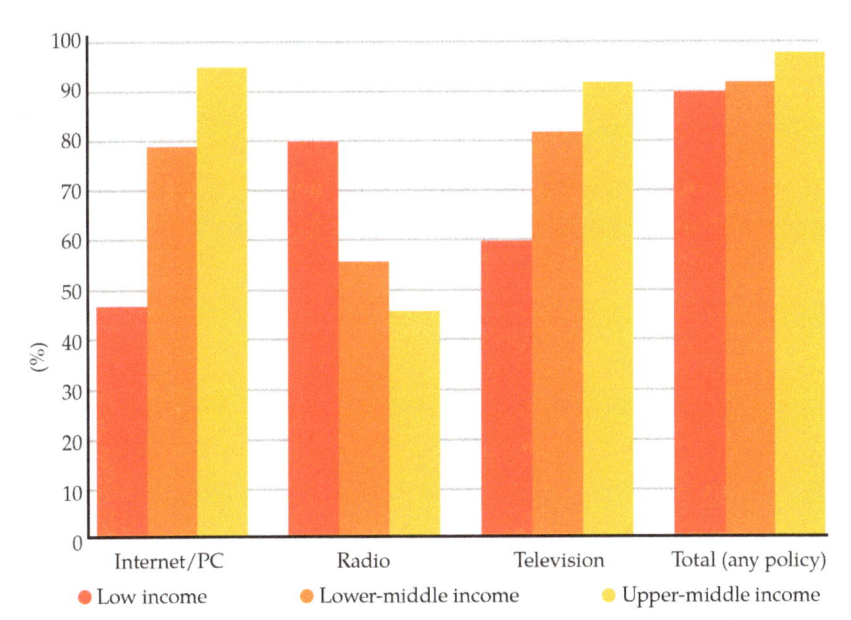

Fig. 2. Share of countries implementing remote learning policies at the pre-primary to upper-secondary levels of education, by technology and country income group, during COVID-19. Sources: UNESCO-UNICEF-World Bank Survey on National Education Responses to COVID-19 School Closures (2020) and UNICEF country offices (2020). Note: Figures are estimated using simple averages across countries.

The case of the One Laptop Per Child Initiative

Another widely-known EdTech experiment is the One Laptop Per Child Initiative. This project has provided laptops (and software) to roughly 2 million children across 42 countries (OLPC, n.d.). Learning outcomes have been mixed. A large-scale randomized evaluation in Peru concluded that One Laptop Per Child dramatically increased access to technology and digital learning content, but showed a limited effect on academic achievement (Beuermann et al., 2015). Limitations associated with the early One Laptop Per Child model in Rwanda were: (1) insufficient attention to teachers' professional development to properly integrate the devices into classroom practices; (2) lack of training in device maintenance; (3) mixed visions between international partners and local implementers; and (4) the decontextualization of the digital content pre-loaded onto the devices (Adam et al., 2016). Uruguay and Nepal are two other well-known implementations of One Laptop Per Child at scale. Both interventions similarly had a non-significant impact on academic achievement, which was attributed to improper use of the devices and limitations associated with maintenance (de Melo et al., 2014; Sharma, 2012).

Both Interactive Radio Instruction and One Laptop Per Child present important considerations for the design and implementation of technology-enhanced programs. The contextualized content and integrated instructional support provided, through IRI, improved learning outcomes across subjects and age groups, despite its use of relatively low-tech devices. Conversely, One Laptop Per Child's limited emphasis on teacher development and classroom integration has led to little impact on academic achievement in a variety of contexts. Such mixed outcomes from technology implementation—and the significant opportunity costs—have led to skepticism about the role of EdTech in low-income contexts.

Recent trends and examples

Recent experimentation with EdTech has focused on promoting inclusivity among sociolinguistic minorities (Castillo & Wagner, 2019), providing teacher support through professional development and coaching (Piper & Kwayumba, 2014; Haßler, 2020), and generating evidence-based management approaches to improve data collection and utilization for policy planning (Castillo & Vosloo, 2018).

Technology is becoming cheaper and more powerful each year, with access expanding to nearly every sector. Particularly, mobile phones are outpacing every other form of technology—even in low-income contexts (ITU & UNESCO, 2019). For school-based learning, this phenomenon opens up opportunities to move away from "traditional" teaching materials (textbooks, chalkboards, notebooks) towards technology-enhanced instructional supports. These new developments allow children to access learning materials in their home languages, offer tailored lesson plans that reinforce skills at the student's own pace, and support teachers' ability to track their students' progress, so that they can provide faster and more accurate feedback.

Despite decades of research illustrating the advantages and limitations of using EdTech to improve learning outcomes (Kimmel & Deek, 1996), particularly in light of the digital divide (Selwyn, 2002), the recent pivot to online and broadcast learning in the COVID-19 era has neglected to acknowledge previous findings (Burns, 2020). For instance, while 90 percent of governments enacted digital or broadcast policies for remote learning in response to school shutdowns, 31 percent (463 million learners globally) are not accessing remote learning programs, while in Africa the proportion increases to about 50 percent (UNICEF, 2020).

Early failures with digital learning interventions were often predictable due to poor planning. In 2015, an international group of informed stakeholders put forward a set of recommendations for the planning and design of digital resources, specifically for international development, referred to as the Principles for Digital Development (PDD, n.d.). Each principle is complemented with additional resources and case studies to plan, design, deploy, and monitor the use of technology for development programming.[2] Increased attention to the PDD and similar frameworks will help circumvent earlier failures of EdTech design and implementation.

---

2 The principles include: design with the user, understand the existing ecosystem, design for scale, build for sustainability, be data-driven, use open standards, reuse and improve existing research, address privacy and security, and be collaborative. For further detail see www.digitalprinciples.org/principles.

Constraints and opportunities for LBOP

This section contrasts some pervasive constraints of education interventions with opportunities for emerging applications of technology to support LBOP. The scope of the review considers teaching and learning, data collection, and implementation and evaluation practices.

Teaching and learning

Teachers play a pivotal role in student achievement and wellbeing (Evans & Popova, 2016; Popova et al., 2018). However, recruiting strong educators and sufficiently supporting their efforts has not been a straightforward task in many parts of the world.

Constraints

Limited personnel. There is a dearth of skilled teachers necessary to reach the expanding global student population. In 2015, an estimated 1.6 million additional primary-level teachers were needed in sub-Saharan Africa alone (UNESCO, 2014). Teachers working in low-income contexts are often underpaid and undervalued in society, which leads to a lack of motivation and escalated teacher absenteeism (Haßler, Khalayleh, & McBurnie, 2020). At the policy level, there is often a lack of long-term vision for education (Andrews et al., 2017). Therefore, national curricula are constantly being revised, usually aligned with changes in political powers. With each revision, teachers are expected to learn additional content and modify their methods with little attention to the costs and impacts of such extensive training campaigns (Botha, 2002; Chisholm et al., 2000).

Lack of teacher support in diverse contexts. Teaching quality in low-resource contexts is impacted by several systematic problems. In many cases, teachers are not adequately prepared, schools are under-resourced, and classrooms are overcrowded with students representing a variety of language and learning skills (Bennell & Akyeampong, 2007; Education Commission, 2019). For instance, less than two-thirds of primary school teachers in sub-Saharan Africa are trained (United Nations, 2019). Such circumstances inhibit teachers from adequately responding to the magnitude of complexity in learning spaces and individual student needs. Differences in economic circumstances, home environments, and other sociolinguistic characteristics further complicate teachers' ability to create quality learning environments.

Opportunities through EdTech

The constraints presented above can, in some ways, be addressed through appropriate integration of educational technologies. As with all tech-based solutions, the primary objective should be improving learning outcomes. Technological interventions for teachers can provide the most benefit when they support overall classroom function by automating routine tasks (data capture and marking, skills classification, etc.) so teachers can focus on broader pedagogical tasks (Power et al., 2014).

Tech-supported professional development. The effectiveness of EdTech for teachers in low-income contexts has varied. Limiting factors include device access and usage, costs, attitudinal factors, technical challenges, and pressures that teachers face in other areas of their jobs (Allier-Gagneur et al., 2020; Boitshwarelo, 2009; McAleavy et al., 2018; Haßler, Hennessy, & Hofmann, 2018). Effective use of EdTech in teacher education programs should empower teachers to be reflective practitioners, and structure teacher professional development around cycles of continuous practice, reflection, and iterative improvement (Allier-Gagneur et al., 2020; Lawrie et al., 2015).

Some technology-supported professional development programs include the use of platforms that teachers are already familiar with for communication and exchange of ideas. For instance, WhatsApp and Facebook have been used to build virtual communities within and between schools (Mendenhall, 2017); provide open educational resources (OER) to reduce the costs of teaching and learning materials (Haßler, 2020); and transfer video recordings of lessons to enable teachers to critically reflect on concrete examples of effective practices (Borko et al., 2008).

Cost effectiveness of teacher education with technology is an important consideration to monitor. One-tablet-per-school models implemented in Zambia and Zimbabwe through OER4Schools demonstrated the potential to reach marginalized communities at a very low cost while preparing the ground for more complex interventions (Haßler, Khalayleh, & McBurnie, 2020). Mobile applications that can be downloaded to smartphones or tablets are also relevant for ongoing teacher professional development. iAct, developed by the Roger Federer Foundation, delivers participatory teaching modules for untrained teacher volunteers in Zambian primary schools.[3]

Rethinking pedagogies. One of the greatest opportunities that EdTech provides is the possibility to rethink pedagogies and practices in teaching. When used effectively, technology-supported teaching has encouraged a shift from uni-directional, instructivist pedagogies to collaborative, constructivist ones that emphasize learner-centered classrooms (Bada & Olusegun, 2015; Dede, 1995; Li, 2001; Sims, 2006). In fact, Bulman and Fairlie (2015) found positive effects of ICT interventions in developing countries due to their ability to substitute it for lower-quality traditional instruction. Consequently, the diversity of learner needs can be better supported than with the traditional curricular model (Banerjee et al., 2016). The Universal Design for Learning (UDL) is one example of a learner-centered model that is often coupled with EdTech (CAST, 2018). The UDL framework emphasizes the importance of individual differences for effective instructional design (Morin, 2020). Other relevant frameworks have documented strategies for effective digital learning design (Conole, 2015; Conole & Weller, 2008; Schurr, 2013; Wagner et al., 2014).

Multilingual content. Language of instruction plays a prominent role in foundational skill development, especially within multilingual settings. Evidence shows that, in many developing country contexts, there is a misalignment of the language spoken at home and the official language of instruction in formal school settings (Ball, 2010; UNESCO, 2020). Research promoting the benefit of learning in home languages has prompted support of full proficiency in home language skill development before learning in a first additional language (Pinnock, 2009; Cummins, 1981; see also Cortina, 2014).

However, moving from policy to practice has proven more elusive for many school systems around the world. A considerable advantage of EdTech solutions is the ability for content to be deployed in multiple languages based on learner preference (Castillo & Wagner, 2019). Same-language captions of video content and downloadable audio transcripts can provide additional support to learners who are hard of hearing and

---

3   iAct stands for "interactive learning and teaching". See http://iact.info/ for more information.

those who are learning in a second language (Adam, 2020a; Kothari & Bandyopadhyay, 2020).

Printed and digital OER. Learners at the bottom of the pyramid often come from homes with limited parental involvement in their reading practices as well as limited exposure to written text (Wagner et al., 2016). Investment in OER provides an opportunity to address the lack of teaching and learning materials at home and in school (Hodgkinson-Williams et al., 2017).

Increased attention to OER content has already produced a vast online repository, albeit overwhelmingly representative of Global North contexts (Santos-Hermosa et al., 2017; Adam, 2020b). As such, the resources often need to be adapted in order for them to be culturally appropriate. For instance, the African Storybook Initiative aims to address the shortage of books for early grade reading in the languages and contexts of Africa. To date, the initiative has produced over 1500 user-generated books in more than 200 languages.[4]

While OER are often used in their digital form, they may have a greater impact in low-income contexts in printed form. Use of OER material—as opposed to costly proprietary content—offers a considerable reduction in the cost of printed educational material.

E-learning platforms. Given that learners have diverse needs, a tailored approach has the potential to reach each learner at their respective level. E-learning platforms offer a range of functionalities (Adam, McBurnie, & Haßler, 2020), such as:

- curated educational resources in different formats (text, audio, or video);
- scaffolding and the ability to schedule learning;
- facilitating communication between students, parents, and teachers;
- facilitating discussion between users in discussion forums;
- administering exercises and quizzes;
- conducting formative and summative assessments;
- monitoring student progress;

---

4   See https://www.africanstorybook.org/ for information.

- providing infrastructure for synchronous virtual lessons.

These functionalities can allow for learning to happen at a student's own pace, and be tailored to their specific needs. Moreover, since virtual learning environments can assist in marking assignments and tests, they can give teachers more time to focus on areas where learners are struggling. Through data analysis and dashboards, teachers are able to more easily see where students need support.

In LBOP contexts, e-learning platforms should be designed to function without continuous connectivity. Presently, a variety of offline e-learning platforms are emerging, such as Kolibri, eGranary, Rachel Plus, Kiwix, Bibliothèques Sans Frontières, and Internet-in-a-Box. These platforms work over a local area network, and thus no internet connection is needed. Traditionally online virtual learning environments like Moodle are also developing better offline capabilities. Other platforms such as Coursera, a Massive Open Online Course provider, have mobile apps that work offline and synchronize answers when there is connectivity. A key feature of offline virtual learning environments is being able to adapt and curate the content provided. The Kolibri platform, for instance, offers a user-friendly content curation studio.

Data to improve education

The ability to assess and make claims about learning impact is perhaps one of the more important outcomes that has resulted from the increased scrutiny of educational inputs and funding. However, the push for more accountability in terms of meeting SDG4 faces certain constraints. Aspects of data planning and its utilization for both policy and teaching present barriers to making timely, evidence-based decisions to improve education.

Constraints

Data for decision-making in policy. Policymakers must make important decisions about the types and amount of data to collect, and how it will be stored. One challenge surrounding this process is predicting the "right size" of data to collect within a program's scope of resources (Braun & Kanjee, 2006). Similarly, data collection efforts within international education projects are limited by funding availability for monitoring and evaluation activities. For instance, the United States Agency for International Development (USAID) allocates approximately three percent of total program dollars to fund external performance and impact evaluation of funded projects (USAID, 2017). Consequently, data management systems do not exist universally in all school systems. For instance, as seen in Figure 3, by 2013 just over 70 percent of developing countries reported data across select global development indicators for education (Abdul-Hamid, 2014). Other findings point to even greater "data deprivation" along key development indicators (Serajuddin et al., 2015).

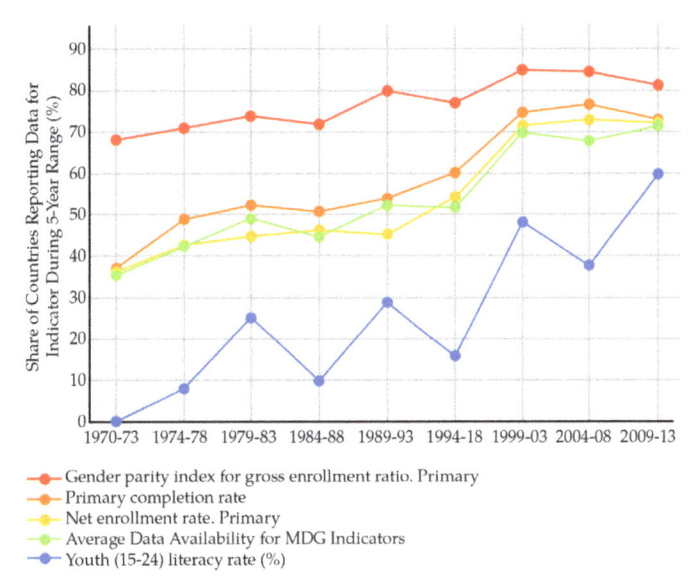

Fig. 3. Percent of countries reporting data for select education indicators at five-year increments, 1970–2013. Source: World Bank EdStats calculations based on UNESCO Institute for Statistics data, in Abdul-Hamid (2014).

Another challenge for policymakers is data access. When data is collected, it is often scattered, decentralized, or collected without regard for disaggregated analysis. One effort to improve data-driven decision-making was the promotion of Education Management Information Systems (EMIS), led by the World Bank. While EMIS activities have increased considerably, a recent review found that roughly 50 percent of projects had been rated less than satisfactory, due in part to operational challenges and limited data utilization (Abdul-Hamid, Saraogi, &

Mintz, 2017). EMIS can be challenging to implement due to the level of complexity that the system requires to produce results. In its current format, an EMIS requires multiple stages of development over a variety of management units, with an average project cycle of four to seven years (2017). While EMIS has produced important contributions to the data revolution for education development, a more feasible approach may be to shorten the distance between data scientists and classroom practice.

Data to support teaching. As noted above, teachers in low-income contexts face several challenges that impact their ability to promote quality learning environments. Large class sizes, lack of contextualized content, and limited training are among these challenges. However, an implicit constraint related to teaching is how classroom assessments are conducted. Around the developing world, teachers engage primarily in summative assessment of their students' ability to grasp curricular content. These assessments generally take the form of annual exams that require hand-grading, with delayed feedback that is rarely incorporated into pedagogical change to support individual skill development. Oftentimes, outcomes are unknown until too late in the school year, and in some cases, reports are not provided until students have already moved along to the next level in the schooling cycle. If pedagogical agility is expected for improved learning outcomes, data processing and utilization must be improved to support better classroom practices.

Opportunities through EdTech

Data for policy decisions. Perhaps the easiest way that data can support policy decisions is through real-time input monitoring. Technology is creating new opportunities to capture, disseminate, and increasingly, automatically analyze data to this end.

For example, the Sierra Leone Education Attendance Monitoring System (SLEAMS) is a pilot project led by the Teaching Service Commission (TSC) that monitors teacher attendance in schools.[5] The 2020 pilot was implemented in over 40 schools across five districts using mobile devices. Data were validated using daily self-reporting by school administrators, combined with teacher fingerprint data and monthly visits from district deputy-directors. The data were then uploaded to a

---
5   https://sleams.org/.

server for monitoring by the central government as well as a public data dashboard that parents and other stakeholders could view. A future iteration of the software plans to incorporate data capture for students, as well as COVID-19 indicators. Sierra Leone's Department of Science and Technology has also built an education data hub and digital census, which mapped the location of all schools, along with other factors (Namit & Thanh, 2019).

In Peru, the EduTrac program sought to improve teacher and student attendance, increase the availability of educational material, and improve the use of local funding to maintain education infrastructure in two remote regions of the country.[6] Each week, community volunteers traveled to project schools to record observation data based on a set of input monitoring prompts via text messaging on feature phones. Data processed from a central server was used to generate routine reports and distributed among community members for tracking progress along project indicators through monthly planning meetings. This effort helped mobilize parental participation, citizen monitoring, and local decision-making in a cost-effective way via technology (R4D, 2016).

Emerging applications of learning analytics are revolutionizing data practices, with some exciting possibilities on the horizon (see 'New Directions' section below). Learning analytics gather and interpret data from environments with built-in modes of assessments (like intelligent tutors, adaptive quizzes/assessments, or peer review) to help measure students' progress over time (Cope & Kalantzis, 2015a; 2015b). Technology-mediated learning environments can also provide fine-grained insight into learner activities and offer a better understanding of progress in skill acquisition for teachers, parents, and other stakeholders (DiCerbo & Behrens, 2014). Learning analytics do not focus only on the cognitive effects of learning, but help shift attention to actual representations of knowledge and the knowledge processes that learning causes (Cope & Kalantzis, 2015b). Several EdTech applications are supported through learning analytics in order to produce data to support policy and practice in low-income contexts.

Brazilian startup *Letrus* is applying learning analytics to improve writing and literacy by combining an artificial-intelligence-to-human

---

6   https://www.educationinnovations.org/p/edutrac-peru.

feedback loop with linguistic knowledge and teacher support.[7] Students write essays on the platform where the AI identifies writing patterns and provides immediate feedback on their writing. Upon automated feedback, the writing samples go to an interface where teachers make additional comments and assign grades in real-time. An evaluation of the innovation across 178 secondary schools is currently underway (J-PAL, n.d.; Bruno, Lima, & Riva, 2021).

Peer assessment applications of EdTech have also proven feasible within low-resourced classrooms with high learner-to-teacher ratios. In South Africa, findings showed support for a hybrid natural language processing (NLP) peer-assessment system using mobile phones for second-language learning among high-school students in an urban setting (Molapo et al., 2019).

Learning analytics can also help with understanding students' patterns of engagement. This technique involves collecting user metadata to assess use patterns on the platform and other conditions that affect proper use (software crashes, students lingering on a particular part of the platform, etc.). Data can also help identify patterns of "wheel spinning" that could indicate difficulties in understanding the educational content. Importantly, developers can use this data to refine and iterate the platform to improve the overall user experience.

Implementation and evaluation

Early efforts to bring technology into the classroom were grounded in the assumption that the devices would stimulate motivation and improve learning outcomes. Another assumption was that implementation would neatly reflect program planning. However, in some cases, school administrators were more concerned with keeping their devices in "like new" condition and kept them stored to avoid damage or theft. Consequently, they were under-utilized. These parallel assumptions have led to what some have referred to as the "last mile problem" (Banerjee & Duflo, 2012). The term refers to the fact that good designs may fail due to poor implementation, rather than the idea behind the intervention itself.

Implementation involves other programmatic components as well. Decisions concerning where data are stored, who manages the data,

---

7   https://www.letrus.com.br/.

and how content is updated according to evolving needs are all key to a sound implementation framework. Learning design and measurement requires care and technical skill, as well as knowledge of the sociocultural context within participating communities (Wagner, 2018). Combining each of these skill sets has been challenging for social science research to date.

Constraints

<u>Lack of cultural and contextual awareness</u>. A major factor that affects success or failure at the last mile is how much (or little) consideration is given to the socioeconomic, cultural, sociotechnological, political, and geopolitical contexts. Similar to digital design considerations for LBOP, poor implementation designs fail to account for programmatic characteristics grounded in cultural awareness, such as local language needs, end-user competencies, and infrastructure to name a few.

<u>Complex rollouts and distribution activities</u>. Another implementation challenge is rolling out interventions to hard-to-reach areas, as well as updating content and distributing new materials as program needs change. Generally, distribution tasks are bottlenecked within a particular project unit and are accompanied by costly training workshops to teach teachers and administrators about updated content. These should be integrated into the revised implementation plan. Delays in distribution have direct and adverse implications for last-mile service delivery, especially for marginalized learning sites.

<u>Limitations in program oversight and research</u>. Proper oversight through routine implementation monitoring poses an additional challenge for BOP contexts. Cost and safety implications of physical travel to project sites often result in unequal program support, where remote and otherwise hard-to-reach communities are most adversely affected (Ho & Thukral, 2011). Without proper implementation monitoring, it becomes difficult to assess progress along intended objectives, and what improvements or adaptations need to be made.

A popular approach of analyzing the impact of educational inputs at scale is the application of randomized controlled trials (RCTs), which require advanced methodological expertise and abundant operating costs (see Castillo & Wagner, 2014 for a review of cases; also Pritchett, 2020). Meanwhile, the rigor with which RCTs are deployed often leads to marginal or inconclusive impacts for the amount of money invested (Lortie-Forgues & Inglis, 2019). Where RCTs have shown an impact, replication studies have produced an alarming amount of null findings (OSC, 2015; Kerwin & Thornton, 2020). Thus, deep consideration needs to be given to whether an RCT is the most effective way to evaluate a project. Other simpler, less expensive methods that produce faster results should be explored.

Opportunities through EdTech

<u>Taking a problem-first approach</u>. A common source of failure in EdTech interventions is that a problem is often defined as lack of some other, more preferred solution, e.g., poor learning due to a lack of tablets at school (Adam et al., 2020). Shifting from a solution-driven approach to a problem-focused approach could help offset implementation failure. One widely used problem-focused approach is the Problem Driven Iterative Adaptation (PDIA) method designed for governments to unpack complex problems (Centre for International Development et al., 2018).

Before jumping to a particular solution, PDIA guides implementers to fully understand the problems that need to be addressed. This is crucial to ensure that technology is not being added without purpose. The PDIA framework is a step-by-step approach that helps break down problems into their root causes, identify entry points, search for possible solutions, take action, reflect upon what has been learned, adapt, and then act again (Centre for International Development et al., 2018). PDIA is a dynamic process with tight feedback loops that allow program developers the ability to build a solution that fits the local context.

<u>Agile development</u>. Implementation at scale can be challenging for some education systems. Rapidly evolving technologies and processes that are contextually dependent limit static distribution strategies. However, EdTech can allow systems to operate within a dynamic delivery model that responds to local needs.

Historically, the education development approach has operated within a paradigm that seeks to reach a desired end goal—such as a certain level of literacy after six years of schooling. An overemphasis on the end goal creates a static deployment approach that may limit the ability to iterate and optimize *en route* to the end goal.

Agile development, by contrast, deploys an iterative, flexible, and adaptable approach. Rather than building the parts of the whole, agile development creates a sequence of "minimal viable products". A minimal viable product is the most basic version of the product needed to provide feedback for further development. It helps to assess and evaluate whether the intervention is developing in the right direction, towards a product that will be as useful and impactful as possible (Adam, McBurnie, & Haßler, 2020).

The agile development process emphasizes a strong discovery phase where the problem and its assumptions are thoroughly investigated. Further, it emphasizes reflection and redesign after each iteration. The different phases of development of a product or service are sometimes labeled as based on their deployment maturity levels from a baseline discovery phase where the problem is fully unpacked, to an advanced, live phase where the product is supported at scale (Government Digital Service, n.d.).

Design Based Implementation Research (DBIR) is another common approach to agile development. DBIR is a collaborative, iterative, systematic method for refining interventions for large-scale roll-out that follows a method of grounded systematic enquiry, and acknowledges that while an intervention may work in one setting, successful implementation may not be transferable to another (LearnDBIR, n.d.). Through a tight connection between research and practice, DBIR assists interventions to be more effective, sustainable, and scalable (Fishman et al., 2013).

New directions for learning with EdTech

While the need for radical changes in schooling has been discussed for decades (Illich, 1971), COVID-19 has ushered in renewed global efforts to reconfigure formal education. It has required stakeholders to reconsider how to provide equitable support to learners, and has accelerated experimentation with technology. In many parts of the world, formal schooling has been delivered with relatively little modification since its inception (Winthrop & McGivney, 2015). One outcome of the crisis is that it has changed how children, teachers, and parents interact. However, this disruption also has the potential to widen the learning gap between the rich and the poor, and deepen educational divides along access to digital resources (Vegas, 2020). Therefore, to support education in the face of the pandemic is as critical as the adoption of the SDGs for improving learning quality. This shift in thinking must consider pedagogies, evidence-based practices for remote learning, as well as new approaches through emerging technologies.

For instance, ever-increasing computing power makes technologies such as machine learning (ML) and artificial intelligence (AI) feasible for day-to-day applications. In fact, over 80 percent of the targets within the society grouping of the SDGs (including education) could potentially benefit from ML/AI integration (Vinuesa et al., 2020). However, there are major drawbacks to consider. One is the massive computational resources required and the subsequent negative environmental impact (as discussed in Unwin, 2020). Also, more advanced technology could require the already-stretched teacher workforce to upgrade their job skills. While experimentation with emerging technologies is nascent and the benefit for BOP learners is far from clear, some recent applications for education are encouraging. (Kharas & Cohen, 2018; Paul et al., 2019; Pedro et al., 2019).

Processing power combined with ML techniques allows computers to analyze multiple datasets simultaneously and identify complex patterns within the data. Similarly, deep-learning approaches use artificial neural networks (as in brain science) to evaluate characteristics in multiple layers of data and iterate on historical trends. Within international development, data-processing methods that incorporate neural networks have been used to combine nighttime satellite imagery with national survey data to improve forecasting along poverty and mortality indicators, and even extend predictions to areas not covered through existing survey data (Jean et al., 2016). Applying a similar approach to the field of education development could have important implications. Satellites mapping school placement combined with ministry data on student enrollment can help allocate resources to schools to address digital connectivity gaps, as was recently done in Kyrgyzstan (Kumenova, 2019). This example is part of UNICEF's broader Innovation initiative to use satellite imagery to map every school in the world.[8]

Cloud storage services and analytic systems are another emerging application of technology. Cloud services have been driving commerce, higher education, and governance activity in countries across the Global South (Kshetri, 2011). An attractive component of cloud services is the ability to overcome IT infrastructure barriers and integrate with ubiquitous devices for enhanced information flow (Kshetri, 2017). Within a locally connected environment, EdTech solutions can leverage cloud services to push software updates across school sites, eliminating costly distribution campaigns and delayed delivery to remote communities. The Internet of Things, combining connected devices and cloud services, can now play a greater role in a school system's ability to provide continuous oversight and make use of data for policy decisions.

Although emerging technologies can expand analysis across robust amounts of information, it is important to consider ethical concerns associated with their implementation. Profiling of students leading to discrimination (O'Neil, 2016), compromised privacy, and the institutionalization of social inequality mechanisms are some issues that require further attention when engaging in analysis with big data (Cope & Kalantzis, 2015b).

Reports from The Institute for Ethical AI in Education highlight important considerations for ethical AI use (2020a; 2020b). Some considerations include ensuring no limitation of human agency and autonomy, technological robustness and safety, non-discrimination and fairness, privacy and data governance, transparency, societal and environmental wellbeing, and accountability. Similarly, UNICEF considers ethical issues to be an integral part of program design with emerging technologies through their multi-stakeholder Generation AI initiative (Kochi et al., 2018).

Deploying emerging technologies in low-income contexts requires serious groundwork to determine a design's appropriateness and feasibility along multiple contextual parameters (network availability, technical literacy, community buy-in, etc.). Ultimately, the focus should be on enhancing data processing and utilization while increasing

---

8   https://www.unicef.org/innovation/.

access to inclusive, high-quality content that addresses student needs along the full spectrum of the achievement distribution. This perspective is in contrast to the broadly implemented one-size-fits-all approach. Central to the implementation of emerging technologies is a reciprocal model whereby student input helps optimize the model and the model, in turn, helps optimize user skills through continuous, formative analysis.

Conclusion

This chapter has presented new perspectives for improving progress toward SDG4 targets that focus on the use of data and digital solutions to improve pedagogical practices and policy planning within complex low-income contexts. LBOP EdTech design should acknowledge the intersecting characteristics that interact with learning. Understanding local needs and realities related to language, cultural relevance, digital and physical infrastructure, and local competencies will help inform more appropriate design features and increased chance of sustainable success. Central to a learning-equity approach is moving beyond a single-curricular approach and creating policies that focus on bottom of the pyramid populations. Therefore, the best use of educational technologies can be mapped out along the following areas:

- Providing resources to teachers and students to improve pedagogical practices and personalized learning opportunities through continuous feedback.

- Supporting data collection and analysis with formative assessment and better resources for data reporting and utilization.

- Creating dynamic implementation ecosystems that adapt to local contexts and facilitate distribution and oversight efforts, especially for the hardest-to-reach schools.

Global megatrends such as climate change, migration, or pandemics like COVID-19 are altering how we think about education. If we are to truly accomplish the targets set forth by SDG4, we must redirect our focus toward solutions for BOP populations and leverage emerging applications of technology to improve those efforts.

References

Abdul-Hamid, H. (2014). *SABER: What matters most for education management information systems—A framework paper* (Text/HTML SABER Working Paper Series No. 7). Washington, DC: World Bank. https://documents.worldbank.org/en/publication/documents-reports/documentdetail

Abdul-Hamid, H., Saraogi, N., & Mintz, S. (2017). *Lessons learned from World Bank Education Management Information System Operations.* Washington, DC: World Bank. https://openknowledge.worldbank.org/bitstream/handle/10986/26330/9781464810565.pdf?sequence=2&isAllowed=y

Adam, T. (2020a). *Between social justice and decolonisation: Exploring South African MOOC designers' conceptualisations and approaches to addressing injustices* (Conference presentation O-143). OER20 Conference: The Care in Openness. https://oer20.oerconf.org/sessions/o-143/

Adam, T. (2020b). Open educational practices of MOOC designers: Embodiment and epistemic location. *Distance Education, 41*(2), 171–185. https://doi.org/10.1080/01587919.2020.1757405

Adam, T. (2020c). *Addressing injustices through MOOCs: A study among peri-urban, marginalised, South African youth* (Thesis). University of Cambridge. https://doi.org/10.17863/CAM.56608

Adam, T., Agyapong, S., Asare, S., Heady, L., Wacharia, W., Mjomba, R., Mugo, J., Mukuria, F., & Munday, G. (2020). *Unlocking data to tell the story of education in Africa: Webinar summary & synthesis.* ESSA, Zizi Afrique, EdTech Hub.

Adam, T., Haßler, B., & Cruickshank, H. (2016, 24–26 April). One laptop per child Rwanda: Enabling factors and barriers. In U. I. Ogbonnaya & S. Simelane-Mnisi (Eds.), *Empowering the 21st century learner: Proceedings of the South Africa International Conference on Educational Technologies* (pp. 184–195). Pretoria, South Africa: African Academic Research Forum. https://eprints.lancs.ac.uk/id/eprint/78812/5/SAICET_2016_Proceedings.pdf

Adam, T., McBurnie, C., & Haßler, B. (2020). *Rolling out a national virtual learning environment* (EdTech Hub Helpdesk Request No. 22). EdTech Hub. https://doi.org/10.5281/zenodo.3406132

Alaro, M. (2007). *A study on the implementation of English Interactive Radio Instruction (IRI) in selected government primary schools in Addis Ababa* (Thesis). Addis Ababa University. http://etd.aau.edu.et/handle/123456789/2227

Anzalone, S., & Bosch, A. (2005). *Improving educational quality with interactive radio instruction: A toolkit for policymakers and planners* (Working Paper No. 35742; pp. 1–140). Washington, DC: World Bank. http://documents.worldbank.org/curated/en/288791468035958279/Improving-educational-quality-with-interactive-radio-instruction-a-toolkit-for-policymakers-and-planners

Bali, M. (2019). Reimagining digital literacies from a feminist perspective in a postcolonial context. *Media and Communication, 7*(2), 69–81. https://doi.org/10.17645/mac.v7i2.1935

Ball, J. (2010). *Enhancing learning of children from diverse language backgrounds: Home language-based bilingual or multilingual education in the early years.* Paris: UNESCO. http://unesdoc.unesco.org/images/0021/002122/212270e.pdf

Ball, J., Paris, S. G., & Govinda, R. (2014). Literacy and numeracy skills among children in developing countries. In D. W. Wagner (Ed.), *Learning and education in developing countries: Research and policy for the post-2015 UN development goals* (pp. 26–41). Scopus. https://doi.org/10.1057/9781137455970

Banerjee, A., Banerji, R., Berry, J., Duflo, E., Kannan, H., Mukerji, S., Shotland, M., & Walton, M. (2016). *Mainstreaming an effective intervention: Evidence from randomized evaluations of "Teaching at the Right Level" in India* (NBER Working Paper No. 22746; p. 39). NBER. https://www.povertyactionlab.org/sites/default/files/research-paper/TaRL_Paper_August2016.pdf

Banerjee, A. V., & Duflo, E. (2012). *Poor economics: A radical rethinking of the way to fight global poverty* (Illustrated edition). PublicAffairs.

Beuermann, D. W., Cristia, J., Cueto, S., Malamud, O., & Cruz-Aguayo, Y. (2015). One laptop per child at home: Short-term impacts from a randomized experiment in Peru. *American Economic Journal: Applied Economics, 7*(2), 53–80.

Braun, H., & Kanjee, A. (2006). Using assessment to improve education in developing nations. In J. E. Cohen, D. E. Bloom, & M. Malin (Eds.), *Improving education through assessment, innovation, and evaluation* (pp. 1–46). Cambridge, MA: American Academy of the Arts and Sciences.

Bruno, F., Lima, L. & Riva, F. (2021). Artificial intelligence, teacher tasks, and individualized pedagogy. Working paper. https://drive.google.com/file/d/1xcY4uSU2rWzGx5R60gU7VcveXZ4RRael/view

Burns, R. (2020). A COVID-19 panacea in digital technologies? Challenges for democracy and higher education. *Dialogues in Human Geography, 10*(2), 246–249. https://doi.org/10.1177/2043820620930832

Cable.co.uk. (2020). *Worldwide mobile data pricing league: Cost of 1 GB in 230 countries.* Cable. https://www.cable.co.uk/mobiles/worldwide-data-pricing/

CAST. (2018). *Universal design for learning guidelines version 2.2.* CAST: Research evidence. http://udlguidelines.cast.org/more/research-evidence

Castillo, N. M., & Vosloo, S. (2018). *UNESCO-Pearson initiative for literacy: Improved lives in a digital world.* UNESCO. https://en.unesco.org/themes/literacy-all/pearson-initiative/case-studies

Castillo, N. M., & Wagner, D. A. (2019). Early-grade reading support in rural South Africa: A language-centred technology approach. *International Review of Education, 65*(3), 389–408. https://doi.org/10.1007/s11159-019-09779-0

Castillo, N. M., & Wagner, D. A. (2014). Gold standard? The use of RCTs for international education. *Comparative Education Review, 58*(1), 166–173.

Centre for International Development. (2018). *PDIA toolkit: A DIY approach to solving complex problems*. Harvard University. https://bsc.cid.harvard.edu/files/bsc/files/pdiatoolkit_ver_1_oct_2018.pdf

Conole, G. (2015). The 7Cs of learning design. In J. Dalziel (Ed.), *Learning design: Conceptualizing a framework for teaching and learning online* (pp. 129–157). Routledge.

Conole, G., & Weller, M. (2008). Using learning design as a framework for supporting the design and reuse of OER. *Journal of Interactive Media in Education, 2008*(1), Art. 5. https://doi.org/10.5334/2008-5

Cope, B. & Kalantzis, M. (2015a). Interpreting evidence-of-learning: Educational research in the era of big data. *Open Review of Educational Research, 2*(1), 218–239. https://doi.org/10.1080/23265507.2015.1074870

Cope, B. & Kalantzis, M. (2015b). Sources of evidence-of-learning: Learning and assessment in the era of big data. *Open Review of Educational Research, 2*(1), 194–217. https://doi.org/10.1080/23265507.2015.1074869

Cortina, R. (Ed.) (2014). *The education of indigenous citizens in Latin America*. Clevedon, UK: Multilingual Matters.

Cummins, J. (1981). The role of primary language development in promoting educational success for language minority students. In *Schooling and language minority students: A theoretical framework*. Los Angeles: California State University: Evaluation, Dissemination, and Assessment Center.

Czerniewicz, L. (2018). Inequality as higher education goes online. In N. Bonderup Dohn, S. Cranmer, J. A. Sime, M. de Laat, & T. Ryberg (Eds.), *Networked learning* (pp. 95–106). Springer, Cham. https://doi.org/10.1007/978-3-319-74857-3_6

Damani, K., & Mitchell, J. (2020). *Rapid evidence review: Radio* (EdTech Hub Rapid Evidence Review). https://edtechhub.org/wp-content/uploads/2020/07/Rapid-Evidence-Review_-Radio-1.pdf

Dede, C. (1995). The evolution of constructivist learning environments: Immersion in distributed, virtual worlds. *Educational Technology, 35*(5), 46–52.

DiCerbo, K. E., & Behrens, J. T. (2014). *Impacts of the digital ocean on education*. London: Pearson.

Fishman, B. J., Penuel, W. R., Allen, A.-R., Cheng, B. H., & Sabelli, N. (2013). Design-based implementation research: An emerging model for transforming the relationship of research and practice. *Yearbook of the National Society for the Study of Education, 112*(2), 136–156.

Freire, P. (1970). *Pedagogy of the oppressed*. The Continuum International Publishing Group Inc.

GoSA. (2020). *National departments*. GOV.ZA. https://www.gov.za/about-government/government-system/national-departments

Government Digital Services. (2019). *Agile delivery: How the discovery phase works*. GOV.UK. https://www.gov.uk/service-manual/agile-delivery/how-the-discovery-phase-works

Graham, M., De Sabbata, S., & Zook, M. A. (2015). Towards a study of information geographies: (Im)mutable augmentations and a mapping of the geographies of information: Towards a study of information geographies. *Geo: Geography and Environment*, 2(1), 88–105. https://doi.org/10.1002/geo2.8

Haßler, B., Hennessy, S., & Hofmann, R. (2018). Sustaining and scaling pedagogic innovation in Sub-Saharan Africa: Grounded insights for teacher professional development. *Journal of Learning for Development*, 5(1), 58–78.

Haßler, B. (2020). *Teacher professional development and coaching in low-income contexts: Overarching considerations for the use of technology* (EdTech Hub Helpdesk Response No. 2). EdTech Hub. https://doi.org/10.5281/zenodo.3631747

Haßler, B., Khalayleh, A., & McBurnie, C. (2020). *A five-part education response to the COVID-19 pandemic* (EdTech Hub Helpdesk Response No. 5). EdTech Hub. https://doi.org/10.5281/zenodo.3756012

Highet, C., Skelly, H., & Tyers, A. (2018). *Gender and information communication technology (ICT) survey toolkit*. Washington, DC: USAID.

Hinostroza, J. E., Isaacs, S., & Bougroum, M. (2014). Information and communications technologies for improving learning opportunities and outcomes in developing countries. In D. A. Wagner (Ed.), *Learning and education in developing countries* (pp. 42–57). New York: Palgrave Macmillan.

Ho, J., & Thukral, H. (2011). *Tuned into success: Assessing the impact of Interactive Radio Instruction for the hardest to reach*. Education Development Center. http://idd.edc.org/sites/idd.edc.org/files/EDC%20Tuned%20in%20to%20Student%20Success%20Report.pdf

Illich, I. (1971). *Deschooling society*. Marion Boyars.

Internet World Stats. (2020). *Internet world stats: Usage and population statistics*. https://www.internetworldstats.com/

ITU & UNESCO. (2019). *State of broadband report 2019*. Geneva: ITU & UNESCO. https://www.itu.int/en/ITU-D/Statistics/Documents/facts/ICTFactsFigures2013-e.pdf

J-PAL. (n.d.). *The impact of automated writing evaluation on learning and access to college in Brazil*. The Abdul Latif Jameel Poverty Action Lab (J-PAL). https://www.povertyactionlab.org/evaluation/impact-automated-writing-evaluation-learning-and-access-college-brazil

Jansen, J. D. (Ed.). (2019). *Decolonisation in universities: The politics of knowledge*. Wits University Press. https://doi.org/10.18772/22019083351

Kam, M. (2013). Mobile learning games for low-income children in India: Lessons from 2004–2009. In Z. Berge & L. Muilenburg (Eds.), *Handbook of mobile learning*. New York: Routledge.

Kimmel, H., & Deek, F. (1996). Instructional technology: A tool or a panacea? *Journal of Science Education and Technology, 5*(1), 87–92. JSTOR. https://doi.org/10.1007/BF01575474

Kerwin, J. T., & Thornton, R. L. (2020). Making the grade: The sensitivity of education program effectiveness to input choices and outcome measures. *The Review of Economics and Statistics, 103*(2), 1–45. https://doi.org/10.1162/rest_a_00911

Kharas, H., & Cohen, J. L. (2018). *Using big data and artificial intelligence to accelerate global development*. Brookings. https://www.brookings.edu/research/using-big-data-and-artificial-intelligence-to-accelerate-global-development/

Kochi, E., Bernstein, J., & Ghei, T. (2018). *Generation AI*. UNICEF. https://www.unicef.org/innovation/stories/generation-ai

Kothari, B., & Bandyopadhyay, T. (2020). Lifelong reading for a billion people. *Stanford Social Innovation Review, 18*(3), 34–41.

Kshetri, N. (2011). Cloud computing in the Global South: Drivers, effects and policy measures. *Third World Quarterly, 32*(6), 997–1014. https://doi.org/10.1080/01436597.2011.586225

Kshetri, N. (2017). The economics of the Internet of Things in the Global South. *Third World Quarterly, 38*(2), 311–339. https://doi.org/10.1080/01436597.2016.1191942

Kumenova, C. (2019). *School connectivity in the Kyrgyz Republic*. UNICEF. https://www.unicef.org/innovation/Magicbox/school-connectivity-kyrgyz-republic

LearnDBIR. (n.d.). *Design based implementation research*. http://learndbir.org/

Li, W. (2001). Constructivist learning systems: A new paradigm. *Proceedings of the IEEE International Conference on Advanced Learning Technologies* (pp. 433–434). https://doi.org/10.1109/ICALT.2001.943967

Lortie-Forgues, H., & Inglis, M. (2019). Rigorous large-scale educational RCTs are often uninformative: Should we be concerned? *Educational Researcher, 48*(3), 158–166.

de Melo, G., Machado, A., & Miranda, A. (2014). *The impact of a one laptop per child program on learning: Evidence from Uruguay*. Banco de México. https://doi.org/10.36095/banxico/di.2014.22

Mertens, D. M. (2007). Transformative paradigm: Mixed methods and social justice. *Journal of Mixed Methods Research, 1*(3), 212–225. https://doi.org/10.1177/1558689807302811

Molapo, M., Moodley, C. S., Akhalwaya, I. Y., Kurien, T., Kloppenberg, J., & Young, R. (2019). Designing digital peer assessment for second language learning in low resource learning settings. *Proceedings of the Sixth (2019) ACM Conference on Learning @ Scale*, 1–13. https://doi.org/10.1145/3330430.3333626

Morin, A. (2020). *What is Universal Design for Learning (UDL)?* Understood. https://www.understood.org/en/learning-thinking-differences/treatments-approaches/educational-strategies/universal-design-for-learning-what-it-is-and-how-it-works

Namit, K., & Thanh, T. M. (2019). *Digital school census in 10 weeks? How it was done in Sierra Leone.* World Bank. https://blogs.worldbank.org/education/digital-school-census-10-weeks-how-it-was-done-sierra-leone

Naslund Hadley, E., Parker, S. W., & Hernandez-Agramonte, J. M. (2014). Fostering early math comprehension: Experimental evidence from Paraguay. *Global Education Review, 1*(4), 135–154.

OLPC. (n.d.). *Countries: One laptop per child.* http://one.laptop.org/about/countries

O'Neil, C. (2016). *Weapons of math destruction: How big data increases inequality and threatens democracy* (1st edition). Crown Publishers.

Open Science Collaboration (OSC). (2015). Estimating the reproducibility of psychological science. *Science, 349*(6249). https://science-sciencemag-org.proxy2.library.illinois.edu/content/sci/349/6251/aac4716.full.pdf

Paul, A., Jolley, C., & Anthony, A. (2019). *Reflecting the past, shaping the future: Making AI work for international development.* USAID. https://www.usaid.gov/digital-development/machine-learning/ai-ml-in-development

Pedro, F., Subosa, M., Rivas, A., & Valverde, P. (2019). *Artificial intelligence in education: Challenges and opportunities for sustainable development.* UNESCO. http://repositorio.minedu.gob.pe/handle/MINEDU/6533

Piper, B., & Kwayumba, D. (2014). *USAID/Kenya primary math and reading initiative: Kisumu information and communication technology (ICT) intervention* (Endline Report). Research Triangle International. https://www.eddataglobal.org/reading/index.cfm?fuseaction=pubDetail&ID=664

Pritchett, L. (2020). Randomizing development: Method or madness? In F. Bédécarrats, I. Guérin, & F. Roubaud (Eds.), *Randomized control trials in the field of development: A critical perspective.* Oxford University Press.

Pinnock, H. (2009). *Language and education: The missing link: How the language used in schools threatens the achievement of Education for All.* CfBT & Save the Children Alliance.

Potter, C., & Naidoo, G. (2006). Using interactive radio to enhance classroom learning and reach schools, classrooms, teachers, and learners. *Distance Education, 27*, 63–86. https://doi.org/10.1080/01587910600653280

Power, T., Gater, R., Grant, C., & Winters, N. (2014). *Educational technology topic guide*. Health and Education Advice Resource Team (HEART). http://oro.open.ac.uk/41070/

Principles for Digital Development (PDD). (n. d.). https://digitalprinciples.org

R4D. (2016). *Journeys to scale: Accompanying the finalists of the innovations in education initiative*. Results for Development. https://r4d.org/resources/journeys-scale-accompanying-finalists-innovations-education-initiative/

Rohs, M., & Ganz, M. (2015). MOOCs and the claim of education for all: A disillusion by empirical data. *International Review of Research in Open and Distance Learning*, 16(6). http://search.proquest.com/docview/1770070648/abstract/28DB32F24ED7450FPQ/1

Santos-Hermosa, G., Ferran-Ferrer, N., & Abadal, E. (2017). Repositories of open educational resources: An assessment of reuse and educational aspects. *The International Review of Research in Open and Distributed Learning*, 18(5), 84–120. https://doi.org/10.19173/irrodl.v18i5.3063

Schurr, M. (2013). *Design thinking for educators* (261495: HPJKGN4A). https://designthinkingforeducators.com/design-thinking/

Searle, B., Friend, J., Parness, B., & Suppes, P. (1976) *The Radio Mathematics project: Nicaragua 1974–1975 Stanford*. California Institute for Mathematical Studies in the Social Sciences, Stanford University.

Selwyn, N. (2002). *Defining the digital divide: Developing a theoretical understanding of inequalities in the Information Age*. Cardiff University, School of Social Sciences.

Serajuddin, U., Uematsu, H., Wieser, C., Yoshida, N., & Dabalen, A. (2015). *Data deprivation: Another deprivation to end*. Washington, DC: World Bank. https://doi.org/10.1596/1813-9450-7252

Sharma, U. (2012). *Essays on the economics of education in developing countries* (Thesis). University of Minnesota. http://www.proquest.com/en-US/products/dissertations/individuals.shtml

Sims, R. (2006). Beyond instructional design: Making learning design a reality. *Journal of Learning Design*, 1(2), 1–9.

Sriprakash, A., Tikly, L., & Walker, S. (2019). The erasures of racism in education and international development: Re-reading the 'global learning crisis'. *Compare: A Journal of Comparative and International Education*, 50(5), 676–692. https://doi.org/10.1080/03057925.2018.1559040

Stone, R., de Hoop, T., & Nakamura, P. (2019). *What works to improve early grade literacy in Latin America and the Caribbean? A systematic review and meta-analysis* (p. 112). Campbell Collaboration. https://onlinelibrary.wiley.com/doi/full/10.1002/cl2.1067

The Institute for Ethical AI in Education. (2020a). *Developing a shared vision of ethical AI in education: An invitation to participate*. The University of Buckingham.

https://www.buckingham.ac.uk/wp-content/uploads/2020/09/Developing-a-Shared-Vision-of-Ethical-AI-in-Education-An-Invitation-to-Participate.pdf

The Institute for Ethical AI in Education. (2020b). *Interim report: Towards a shared vision of ethical AI in education.* University of Buckingham. https://www.buckingham.ac.uk/wp-content/uploads/2020/02/The-Institute-for-Ethical-AI-in-Educations-Interim-Report-Towards-a-Shared-Vision-of-Ethical-AI-in-Education.pdf

Trucano, M. (2010). *Interactive Radio Instruction: A successful permanent pilot project?* World Bank. https://blogs.worldbank.org/edutech/iri

UNESCO. (2014). *Teaching and learning: Achieving quality for all.* UNESCO-GMR. https://en.unesco.org/gem-report/report/2014/teaching-and-learning-achieving-quality-all

UNESCO. (2018). *Accountability in education: Meeting our commitments* (Global Education Monitoring Report). UNESCO-GEM. https://unesdoc.unesco.org/ark:/48223/pf0000259338

UNESCO. (2020). *Inclusion and education: All means all* (Global Education Monitoring Report). UNESCO-GEM. https://unesdoc.unesco.org/ark:/48223/pf0000373718

UNESCO-IIEP. (2020). *Reopening schools: How to get education back on track after COVID-19.* IIEP-UNESCO. http://www.iiep.unesco.org/en/reopening-schools-how-get-education-back-track-after-covid-19-13424

UNESCO-UIS. (n.d.). *UIS statistics.* UIS-UNESCO. http://data.uis.unesco.org/#

United Nations. (2015). *Transforming our world: The 2030 agenda for sustainable development.* Springer Publishing Company. https://doi.org/10.1891/9780826190123.ap02

United Nations. (2019). *The sustainable development goals report: 2019.* United Nations Statistics Division. https://unstats.un.org/sdgs/report/2019/

UNICEF. (2020). *COVID-19: Are children able to continue learning during school closures?* UNICEF. https://data.unicef.org/resources/remote-learning-reachability-factsheet/

Unwin, T. (2020). *Digital technologies are part of the climate change problem.* ICTworks. https://www.ictworks.org/digital-technologies-climate-change-problem/

USAID. (2017). *Evaluation: Learning from experience—USAID evaluation policy.* USAID. https://www.usaid.gov/evaluation/policy

United Nations Children's Fund (UNICEF). (2020). *Covid-19: Are children able to continue learning during school closures? A global analysis of the potential reach of remote learning policies using data from 100 countries* (Factsheet). New York: UNICEF. https://data.unicef.org/resources/remote-learning-reachability-factsheet/

Vegas, E. (2020). *School closures, government responses, and learning inequality around the world during COVID-19*. Brookings-CUE. https://www.brookings.edu/research/school-closures-government-responses-and-learning-inequality-around-the-world-during-covid-19/

Vinuesa, R., Azizpour, H., Leite, I., Balaam, M., Dignum, V., Domisch, S., Felländer, A., Langhans, S. D., Tegmark, M., & Fuso Nerini, F. (2020). The role of artificial intelligence in achieving the Sustainable Development Goals. *Nature Communications, 11*(1), 233. https://doi.org/10.1038/s41467-019-14108-y

Vosloo, S. (2018). *Designing inclusive digital solutions and developing digital skills: Guidelines*. UNESCO Digital Library. https://unesdoc.unesco.org/ark:/48223/pf0000265537

Wagner, D. A. (2018). *Learning as development: Rethinking international education in a changing world*. New York: Routledge.

Wagner, D. A., & Castillo, N. M. (2014). Learning at the bottom of the pyramid: Constraints, comparability and policy in developing countries. *Prospects, 44*(4), 627–638. https://doi.org/10.1007/s11125-014-9328-8

Wagner, D. A., Castillo, N. M., Murphy, K. M., Crofton, M., & Zahra, F. T. (2014). Mobiles for literacy in developing countries: An effectiveness framework. *Prospects, 44*(1), 119–132. https://doi.org/10.1007/s11125-014-9298-x

Wagner, D. A., Zahra, F. T., & Lee, J. (2016). Literacy development: Global research and policy perspectives. In U. P. Gielen & J. L. Roopnarine (Eds.), *Childhood and adolescence: Cross-cultural perspectives and applications* (pp. 97–117). Prayer.

Warschauer, M. (2003). *Technology and social inclusion: Rethinking the digital divide*. MIT Press.

Winthrop, R., & McGivney, E. (2015). *Why wait 100 years? Bridging the gap in global education*. Brookings-CUE. https://www.brookings.edu/research/why-wait-100-years-bridging-the-gap-in-global-education/

World Bank. (2005). *Improving educational quality through Interactive Radio Instruction: A toolkit for policy makers and planners* (Africa Region Human Development Working Paper Series). Washington, DC: World Bank.

World Bank. (2016). *World development report 2016: Digital dividends* (p. 391). Washington, DC: World Bank. https://www.worldbank.org/en/publication/wdr2016

5. Reducing Inequality in Education Using "Smaller, Quicker, Cheaper" Assessments

Luis Crouch and Timothy S. Slade

Introduction

With the advent of the Sustainable Development Goals (SDGs), and especially SDG4, several important trends have developed within the global education community, particularly in low-income and lower-middle-income countries. Some of the trends pre-date the SDGs, but the SDGs certainly increased focus on them.

First, the world is moving towards the concurrent measurement of access to education *and* learning, not just access (or a learning proxy such as primary-school completion), as was the emphasis under the Millennium Development Goals. In addition, it is moving away from tracking average performance, and is instead focusing on equity and equality. Second, there has been a mushrooming of efforts and data sources that are intended to measure equity and inequality. International and regional assessments continue to grow and adapt by honing their ability to discriminate at the bottom of the learning scale.[1] In particular, there has been an enormous growth in the sorts of "smaller, quicker, cheaper" (SQC) measurements Wagner called for in

---

1   E.g., PISA for Development (https://www.oecd.org/pisa/pisa-for-development/) and IEA's LANA (https://www.iea.nl/publications/presentations/ga56introducing-ieas-lana-developing-countries).

© 2022 Luis Crouch and Timothy S. Slade, CC BY-NC 4.0   https://doi.org/10.11647/OBP.0256.05

an influential 2003 paper, and further discussed in Wagner's books in 2011 and 2018. Measures like PAL and EGRA have now been used in hundreds of country/language/script contexts.[2] Third, in part because of the dramatic evidence provided by the SQC data, there has been a wave of interest in using the measurements to improve outcomes, precisely as Wagner intended. In one of the latest signs of that interest, the World Bank is seeking to cut the proportion of 10-year-old non-readers in lower-middle-income countries by half, from around 50 percent to around 25 percent, by 2030 (World Bank, 2019). Fourth, there is evidence that countries are beginning to make significant measured progress on some of these fronts, at least at the pilot level (Graham & Kelly, 2019). These efforts have made micro data on pre- and-post treatment-and-control sets available that have typically not been available previously.

This chapter responds to these trends, and will show how they can be potentiated to tackle the issue of learning inequality. It will focus on two issues: (1) whether and how inequality measures can be applied to different sorts of assessment data, especially SQC data, and (2) how different kinds of assessment data, and their corresponding inequality measures, can be used to actually address inequality, along with average performance levels. The focus will be largely empirical, based on data and qualitative observations, and children at the "bottom of the pyramid", as defined in the research by Wagner and others (Wagner, Wolf, & Boruch, 2018). In this chapter, the "bottom of the pyramid" will be represented by the percentage of children who achieve a score of zero on an oral reading fluency exam.

The chapter is structured as follows. After this introduction, a literature review sets out what we could find on the relationship between variations in averages and variations in inequality or (a very different concept) "percent below a learning floor". A subsequent section briefly notes how this chapter differs from that literature, and thus hopes to make an original contribution. The most substantial

---

2   People's Action for Learning Network assessments, informally known as Citizen-Led assessments, as at https://palnetwork.org/the-pal-network-case-citizen-led-assessments-to-improve-learning/, Early Grade Reading Assessments as at https://www.sciencedirect.com/science/article/pii/S0738059314001126 and described by Dubeck and Gove (2015).

section of the chapter then uses micro data to test various hypotheses about the measurability of inequality and "percent below a learning floor" and, much more importantly, how these two things co-vary with improvements in the average levels of learning. We do this via reference to two cases (from the same country and modeled on each other) and their corresponding micro data. We give primacy to a set of data from Kenya because of foreknowledge that the data were clean, detailed, and plentiful. The next section describes the substantive literature from the cases. Then, we provide policy implications as to why the data look the way they look, and what the data are telling us about whether and how things change (or don't) for the bottom of the pyramid as averages improve (or don't). Finally, we reprise the finding and provide new research directions in this area.

Literature review

To the best of our knowledge, the application of inequality indices to education—of the sort usually applied by economists to monetary income, wealth, or physical assets such as land—dates to a decade or two after the World Bank first launched significant operations in education. In the early 2000s, Thomas, Wang, and Fan (2001; 2003) published papers calling for the application of the Gini coefficient to educational attainment (years of schooling). At around the same time, the World Bank's World Development Report (2006) was the first major publication by an international agency to provide a systematic compilation of such measures for a relatively large set of countries (28), with a good mix of countries from the low-, middle-, and high-income groupings. The coefficients were based on years of education already received by the adult population, not the current expected years of education. Thus, the concept was analogous, in some sense, to financial or physical wealth.

Strikingly but not surprisingly, these coefficients varied from around 0.2 for countries in Europe and an entity called "C Europe" to around 0.6 for sub-Saharan Africa—the same as what similar tables for income show. While they do not say so explicitly, one can infer from Thomas, Wang, and Fan (2001) that the median value for this education Gini (applied to years of schooling rather than learning outcomes) was about 0.4, which is similar to the current median global income Gini of 0.38. They establish certain interesting facts, such as that the Gini coefficient for years of educational attainment shows quickly-reducing inequality as average years of schooling increase. This is sensible, since individuals are unlikely to pile Ph.D. upon Ph.D. the way they might pile on income.

Both "years of education" and scores on learning assessments could have reasonable upper limits (and certainly do in most international assessments), and therefore the higher the average, the lower the inequality, as high values would be censored from above.[3] However, in those assessments, only a tiny (a few percent at most) of children "top out" at the constructed maximum, and the learning measures used in this chapter do not even have a theoretical or constructed maximum.[4] As noted above, recent calls for this kind of analysis have been associated with the work of Dan Wagner and various colleagues such as in Wagner, Wolf, and Boruch (2018), but their focus has been more on the notion of the "bottom of the pyramid" which is more of a "poverty of learning" concept than a strictly distributionist one.

In addition, other research has asked whether increases in average performance are associated with decreases in inequality or in "percent below a learning floor". These include two existing lines of research (though they typically do not use SQC measurements). One associates differences in cross-sectional data, especially in assessments such as PISA, TIMSS, and PIRLS, to the hypothesized dynamics of increases in average performance; that is, this research looks at whether variations in mean levels of performance are systematically associated with variations in either the *distribution* of performance or the *percent of children below some minimum* ("percent below a learning floor"). Other research looks at these variables as actual changes, over time, in countries that have participated in assessments multiple times.

Papers that compare differences in mean scores cross-sectionally with differences in inequality include Freeman, Machin, and Viarengo

---

3 While oral reading fluency, the primary measure discussed in the analysis section, lacks a theoretical upper limit, for all practical purposes it rarely exceeds 200 correct words per minute, especially in the early grades.
4 The previous five or six sentences borrowed liberally from Crouch and Gustafsson (2018).

(2011), Oppedisano and Turani (2015), Micklewright and Schnepf (2006), Bruckauf and Chzhen (2016), and Sahn and Younger (2007). They also attempt to dig into some of the possible determinants (e.g., Ferreira & Giroux, 2011). A paper by Crouch and Rolleston (2017) as part of the RISE program looked at many of these issues, bringing in evidence from regional learning assessments and special longitudinal studies that measure learning in the same group of children as they grow older (SACMEQ & Young Lives). Little research seems to have explored the long-term changes in the inequality coefficients. One exception was Crouch, Gove, and Gustafsson (2009). Using household surveys from Latin America, we asked about respondents' years of education and their recall of their parents' years of education; the Gini coefficient for years of education improved from 0.58 to 0.36—quite a significant change.

These studies typically focus on one assessment for a specific (sometimes relatively distant) year. Crouch and Gustafsson (2018), on the other hand, systematically look at data from all of the known assessments within a certain period of time and attempt to explore the same issues. Two or three conclusions are relevant here. First, looking at cross-sectional data from most recent assessments, the correlation between differences in average learning levels and differences in the within-country *distribution* of scores is ambiguous: for some, there is a positive association, for some there is a negative association. Somewhat worryingly, the study found that the associations depended on the assessment organization, suggesting that some of the association, positive or negative, could have been due to methodological issues. Second, the paper unambiguously concludes that, in all of the used assessments, differences in average scores between the low scorers and the medium scorers are very strongly associated with reductions in the percent of children below a certain level of proficiency (both in the correlation sense and in the effect-size sense, though these are more or less equivalent in two-factor correlations). The World Bank (2019) calls this percentage the "learning poor", which is analogous with Wagner's concept of the "bottom of the pyramid".[5] Thirdly, the

---

5   In this context we will eschew the term "learning poverty" because it connotes, to non-economists, that below that floor there is no learning. But, of course, children do learn even if they are not in school. We know that is not what economists mean,

paper concludes that when time-series *are* available, they confirm the impression from the cross-section analysis: improvements in overall levels are at first strongly associated with reductions in the percentage of children below a learning floor. A methodological point in Crouch and Gustafsson (2018) is that it is hard to study inequality using Item Response Theory (IRT)[6] scores, since they are not a completely natural metric.[7]

The learning metric used in this chapter, oral reading fluency, is also a "natural" metric. However, it is important to clarify that we are not talking about the distribution of knowledge or skill. After all, regardless of whether one is using IRT or classical scores, increases in scores do not necessarily mean the same thing, regardless of the starting value.[8] Studies of the issue by IEA confirm this (Mullis, Martin, & Loveless, 2016), and their results are amplified by Crouch and Gustafsson (2018, p. 29):

> ...An analysis by Mullis et al. (2016: 58), ... examine(s) the improvements amongst TIMSS Grade 4 countries, between 1995 (but in some cases 2003) and 2015, focusing on improvements at the 10th and 90th percentiles. They conclude that national gains are driven more by the desired change at the bottom end of the performance spectrum than the top. Of eighteen countries, all but four saw larger—and often much larger— improvements at the 10th than the 90th percentile. The present analysis...establishes that the movement is towards less 'percent below a learning floor.' Just six SACMEQ countries were considered to have made significant improvements in their national mathematics score

---

    but to prevent communications barriers we will use another term, namely "percent below a learning floor".
6   The more "modern" technique for scoring learning assessments, which has many advantages, but has one disadvantage in that the scores are not easy to interpret as a "percent correct answer" in a more classical scoring method.
7   That paper tends to use classical (percent correct) scores, even for the international assessments. It shows that the correlation between classical and IRT scores is so high that one may as well work with the more natural "percent correct" measure.
8   It is difficult to say, for instance, that a child whose score improved from 50 to 60 improved their knowledge as much as one moving from 60 to 70. Perhaps the questions answered in moving from 60 to 70 were harder. Many economists recognize that the ultimate goal of policy should be utility or happiness, not income. But they tend to talk about the distribution of income, not the distribution of happiness. This is probably by accident, not by wisdom. But it would do for us to talk about the distribution of scores, not of learning.

between 2000 and 2007. ...Generally, the six SACMEQ countries did see larger reductions at the bottom than gains at the top.

We draw three distinctions in the rest of this chapter. First, we distinguish between *inequality*—especially as a measure of pure dispersion, most often not in association with other putatively causative factors such as gender or socioeconomic status—and *percent below a learning floor* (a measure similar to income poverty). Second, we distinguish between what one may call *pure inequality*—namely "pure" variance or something like it—and variance associated with other factors. *Inequality* and *percent below a learning floor* are clearly not the same thing, and this distinction has proven to be analytically useful in the literature on economic development and, to some degree, education. Only the notion of *percent below a learning floor* is directly relevant to the calls for attention to the issue from the World Bank (2019) and Wagner et al. (2018). Third, the notion of "pure" inequality or "percent below a learning floor", as de-linked from gender, social status, etc., is most relevant to measurement-based standards and practices related to teaching and learning. Measures associated with other factors like gender or income suggest targeting school support based on those factors, whereas measures associated with "pure" inequality suggest targeting support based on learning outcomes.

Points of departure of the present study from the reviewed literature

The research reviewed above uses aggregated data, either reflecting cross-sectional variation or changes over time for the few countries that have participated in given assessments for multiple years. None of it looks at micro data from the same students, or at least the same teachers or classes at different points in time, while controlling for whether a bona fide pedagogical intervention has taken place, if possible.

We focus almost entirely on issues surrounding measurement: do the measures "behave well", do they seem robust, and are they interpretable? We also delve briefly into the pedagogical issues that relate to the changes in measures, but more as a way of showing what one can learn for educational programs and policies, rather than to come to any firm and generalizable conclusions. If the measures do not seem to have any actionable implications for policymakers, they would be of little use.

At the same time, though the evidence from the literature review seems to show that countries can improve their average performance (at least from low to middling levels) by paying attention to the left tail of their score distributions, how precisely they do so is not clear. In this chapter, we focus more on whether micro evidence of improvement in averages also addresses either cognitive inequality or percent below a learning floor (or both). However, the data themselves and some of the qualitative write-ups on improvement efforts do provide some tantalizing early suggestions.

Data and methods

Measures used

Though the most recent calls for a "Gini coefficient" analysis of education and learning inequality (sometimes implicitly) call for that specific measure, it seemed prudent to assess the behavior and utility of several others as well. We chose the following measures for the reasons noted in Table 1.[9]

---

9 A good primer on measures of poverty and income inequality is to be found at Haughton and Khandker (2009), available at: https://openknowledge.worldbank.org/bitstream/handle/10986/11985/9780821376133.pdf.

5. Reducing Inequality in Education 157

Table 1. Inequality measures.

Measure	Explanation of the measure	Reason for using it
Gini coefficient	A coefficient ranging from 0 to 1, where 0 represents a hypothetical situation where everyone in society owns an equal amount of the good in question (income, wealth, years of education learning as measured by a test score), and 1 represents a situation where one individual in society owns all of the good in question. Note that this is a measure of relative inequality. If, for instance, everyone's incomes or test scores were to increase by the same absolute amount, the Gini coefficient would decrease, even if the absolute distance between the income (score) of the highest earner (scorer) and the lowest is the same as before. In the rest of this chapter, whenever we use the term "Gini coefficient" we will mean the Gini coefficient as applied to just one measure of learning, namely oral reading fluency, unless we explicitly say otherwise in order to refer to income or wealth or some other underlying concept.	It is best known to both economists and non-economists, and has a one-to-one correspondence with a well-known graphical interface, the Lorenz curve.[10] The Lorenz curve can be used to visualize where in the distribution the inequality comes from, and can be linked to concepts of absolute poverty or "percent below a learning floor". (These concepts are used in the chapter, and the Lorenz curves are shown.) It has also been the most used measure in education (but mostly for years of schooling).

---

10 For a comparison between the Lorenz curves for the learning outcomes shown here and some income distributions from very equal and very unequal countries, see the section called "Lorenz curves for learning and for income" below.

Measure	Explanation of the measure	Reason for using it
Coefficient of variation	Standard deviation over the mean. Zero lower bound, no theoretical upper bound. As with the Gini coefficient, an equal absolute increase in income or test scores, for everyone, would make the measure decrease.	It is easy to calculate even with common software such as Excel. No specialized substantive or computational knowledge is required.
Ratio of Px to Py, typically 90th to 10th or 75th to 25th	Ratio of a measure (e.g., income, score on a test) characteristic of the person at the xth percentile of a distribution compared to the same characteristic at the yth percentile of the distribution. Lower bound of 1, no upper bound. A relative measure in the same way as the others.	It is intuitively appealing and often used, analogous to the popular economic and political literature around "percent of wealth possessed by the one-percenters".
Generalized Entropy [GE()] index with	Generalized entropy indices are a class of income inequality measures. The parameter governs the weight given to the distances between two incomes along the distribution; smaller values of increase sensitivity to changes at the lower end, while larger values of increase sensitivity to changes at the upper end.[11] GE(0) and GE(1) are undefined for incomes of 0, and are therefore an ill fit for our data, which feature large proportions of zero scores. We use GE(2).	Though they are the least known outside the economics profession, they have a few advantages. One is that there are various measures and they can be relatively more or less sensitive to inequality in certain portions of the distribution (e.g., more sensitive to the inequality amongst the poor than amongst the rich). A second is that they are easily decomposable in a manner similar to analysis of variance: e.g., inequality within schools and between schools, adding up to total inequality.

---

11 World Bank Institute. (2005). *Introduction to Poverty Analysis*.

Measure	Explanation of the measure	Reason for using it
Percent scoring zero	This is a measure akin to what the World Bank is calling "learning poverty", what we are calling *percent below a learning floor*. It is similar to income poverty, which is measured as the percent of people below a certain income threshold. In our case we have chosen zero—the inability to read a single word—as a dramatic cut point, and one whose improvement would seem to be able to easily draw attention and bureaucratic effort.[12]	Very easy to interpret and possibly act upon.

---

12 For the notion and use of "learning poverty" see World Bank (2019), where they define as "learning poor" any child not in school or not able to read and understand a simple paragraph by age 10. This is a more advanced age and level than the specific definition of "percent below a floor" we use in this chapter, which is the percent of children unable to read even one word.

Data and methods, PRIMR and Tusome in Kenya

Over the last decade, the Early Grade Reading Assessment (EGRA) has been used in more than 70 countries and 120 languages to estimate the reading abilities of primary school learners, using a variety of reading and pre-reading metrics (RTI International, 2015). EGRA is comprised of tasks designed to measure skills such as phonological awareness, decoding, listening comprehension, and others. But policymakers frequently focus on learners' results on the oral reading fluency (ORF) metric, as it is the closest analogue to the common "educated layperson's" understanding of what "being able to read" means—independent reading of narrative text.[13]

From the earliest days of EGRA, and using various classical analyses of EGRA results, it was the skill that had the highest item-test and item-rest correlation, and is the one that weighs most heavily in factor analyses attempting to discern whether there is a latent construct that can be called "early grade reading skill". These correlations or associations are all highly statistically significant and, substantively, follow the patterns one would hope (e.g., the principal-components analysis has a big first-factor weight, a big drop-off between the first and second factor, and the sub-skills load reasonably evenly onto that first factor). For the two EGRA applications in PRIMR and Tusome, described below, the Cronbach's alpha measures 0.81 and 0.86 respectively.

In the data that comprise the source for this chapter, the child is presented with a simple story of approximately 60 words in length and is asked to read aloud as much of it as they can within one minute. If the child is unable to complete the text within the minute, the exercise is stopped and the last word they attempted to read is noted. If the child reads the entirety of the text before the minute elapses, the assessor stops the timer and notes the amount of time remaining. In either case, the assessor tracks the child's progress and marks any words that the child reads incorrectly.

ORF is reported in *correct words per minute* (cwpm). For children who do not complete the passage, their cwpm score is simply the number of words they read correctly. For children who complete the passage with time remaining, the number of words they read correctly is transformed into a cwpm score according to the formula as follows:

---

13   Silent reading skill as an addendum to EGRA tasks is being piloted.

$$items\_per\_minute = \frac{items\_correct}{(time\_for\_task - time\_remaining) * 60}$$

The result is a continuous measure bounded from below at 0.[14] Children who are unable to read a single word correctly obtain a *zero score*. The inequality analyses presented in this chapter depend upon a continuous measure and are therefore appropriate for use with EGRA data. Note that there are many other tasks in a typical EGRA application, from more phonemic ones to others aimed at comprehension.

The ORF data used in these analyses were collected under the United States Agency for International Development (USAID) Primary Math and Reading Initiative (PRIMR) and Tusome Early Grade Reading Activity ("Tusome").

PRIMR was a partnership between USAID and Kenya's Ministry of Education, Science, and Technology (MoEST), meant to identify mechanisms to improve reading outcomes in Kiswahili and English (RTI International, 2014). It was implemented from 2012–2014 in 547 government primary schools and low-cost private schools (LCPS) in four Kenyan counties: Nairobi, Murang'a, Kiambu, and Nakuru. PRIMR used a three-cohort design: Cohort 1 received the intervention from 2012–2013, Cohort 2 from 2013–2014, and Cohort 3 was retained as a control until after the endline data collection had concluded. Kiswahili and English reading outcomes among Grade 1 and Grade 2 children were assessed using EGRA at baseline, midline, and endline, and using comparison groups.[15]

Tusome was a partnership between USAID and Kenya's MoEST that brought the most promising interventions from PRIMR to *all* public primary schools in the country and 1,500 LCPS. While the intervention was ultimately extended to Grade 3, the external impact evaluation only assessed the Kiswahili and English reading performance of Grade

---

14   There is no fixed theoretical maximum, as it depends on the total items in the task and the time allotted. Practically speaking, it is extremely rare to find ORF scores exceeding 200 cwpm. Adults with many years of education and who read for a living, but without training in speed reading, can read (aloud) about 200–220 cwpm at an unforced pace.

15   The current analyses do not include data from PRIMR's "ICT Pilot" in Kisumu County.

1 and Grade 2 children. Given the universality of Tusome, there was no control group. The analyses shown in this chapter incorporate data from Tusome's baseline and midline EGRAs, conducted in July 2015 and September through October 2017 respectively. The data were collected from 204 schools (of which 174 were public and 30 LCPS) according to a three-stage cluster sampling approach designed to yield nationally representative estimates.

Results

Results are presented separately for PRIMR and Tusome. Initial analyses focused on whether specific measures of inequality could be computed, and if so, whether they appeared to behave in ways that would be consistent with theory. Separate analyses for Kiswahili and English are presented for key subpopulations defined by grade (Grade 1 vs. Grade 2) and round of assessment (baseline, midline, or endline). For the PRIMR data, additional breakdowns are provided by cohort, which capture treatment status and duration of intervention (see Table 2). As Tusome was a nationwide intervention in all public primary schools, the results are from treatment schools. We focus exclusively on the oral reading fluency score, as it is our best available proxy for reading ability.[16]

Basic results, behavior, and interpretation of the measures

The following section first shows basic results that help us decide whether the measures are "well-behaved".[17] We then draw out some of the substantive interpretations. Table 2 and Table 3 below report estimates

---

16   Reading comprehension measures better represent the actual goal of reading. However, EGRA's reading comprehension measures have very few (five) items and are categorical in nature, making them ill-suited for this analysis.

17   We do not mean "well-behaved" in a particularly rigorous manner. In general we are looking for "good behavior" in the sense of ratios that do not become infinite or undefined, indicators that move more or less with each other (so that the Gini coefficient does not decrease significantly while the coefficient of variation goes up, say), or numerical results whose directional movement ends up making intuitive sense and lines up with some reasonable substantive narrative that fits the observed facts. In some sense, this notion of "good behavior" is meant to answer questions such as "does it seem possible to measure learning inequality in these ways", and "does that measurement make sense for the context and situations noted?"

for several inequality measures: the Gini coefficient, the Generalized Entropy Index with $(GE(2))$, the ratio of the 90th percentile score to the 10th percentile score (*ratio_p90p10*), the ratio of the 75th percentile score to the 25th percentile score (*ratio p75p25*), and percent scoring zero (*pct_zero*). The tables also include estimates for the mean fluency and associated coefficient of variation (CV) for each subpopulation. The mean is presented not as a measure of inequality (which it is not, of course) but because without it, it is harder to interpret the measures of inequality that are presented (see Table 2).

In terms of being "well-behaved", several patterns emerge.

1. **Ratio of Px to Py**. In nearly every subpopulation, *ratio_p90p10* cannot be calculated because more than 10 percent of the children assessed recorded a score of zero. While *ratio_p70p25* can be calculated more frequently, it is available for fewer than 50 percent of the subpopulations, and far less frequently for Kiswahili than English. We know from the work of other colleagues that this ratio, applied to other datasets, also tends to break down (e.g., Dowd, 2018). It may be that, in spite of the intuitiveness of the ratio and its easy use in income and wealth analysis, it is the least usable of all the measures assessed. In fact, the measure is so ill-behaved that we find it difficult to say anything substantive based on it. However, for the sake of illustration, in some 30 rich countries, Gromada et al. (2018) found a median ratio of only 1.41 (for p90/p10) for education (reading, primary school), considerably lower than the 5.0 (estimating across all our measures) that we observe.[18] In a variety of US household surveys from the 1990s, Hao and Naiman (2010) show this ratio to be around 25 on average, for income.

2. **Gini coefficient**. The Gini coefficient for learning seems to consistently behave well. The values observed are in line with what one observes from comparative studies or simple

---

18 The 1.38 for the Gromada et al. (2018) study is our interpretation. Given that they use a metric without a valid zero, we projected "zero" as our projected score of the child at 1st percentile, subtracted that from scores at all the key percentiles, and then calculated the p75/p25 ratio.

Table 2. Range of inequality measure results, PRIMR.

Language	Grade	Cohort	Round	mean	CV	ratio_p90p10	ratio_p75p25	Gini	GE(2)	pct_zero
Kiswahili	Gr 1	1 (Full Tx)	Baseline	4.8	15.1	•	•	0.826	2.29	71.0
			Midline†	21.6	4.5	•	11.3	0.484	0.37	23.0
			Endline†	19.1	5.6	•	•	0.527	0.49	28.4
		2 (Delayed Tx)	Baseline	4.9	7.7	•	•	0.771	1.51	64.4
			Midline	19.6	3.8	•	5.6	0.451	0.32	17.8
			Endline†	20.8	4.2	•	3.8	0.455	0.34	22.3
		3 (Control)	Baseline	3.3	9.4	•	•	0.848	2.60	73.8
			Midline	15.4	4.8	•	•	0.522	0.45	28.6
			Endline	13.4	5.7	•	•	0.517	0.44	28.7
English		1 (Full Tx)	Baseline	6.8	18.4	•	•	0.823	2.45	66.3
			Midline†	30.6	5.9	•	16.6	0.534	0.48	24.0
			Endline†	29.9	5.6	•	12.8	0.543	0.51	22.7
		2 (Delayed Tx)	Baseline	7.5	8.1	•	•	0.750	1.46	54.0
			Midline	29.4	5.0	•	7.7	0.505	0.43	20.1
			Endline†	33.7	4.1	•	4.4	0.469	0.36	18.3
		3 (Control)	Baseline	4.4	10.0	•	•	0.852	2.75	72.4
			Midline	19.6	6.3	•	•	0.620	0.73	31.4
			Endline	20.1	7.0	•	36.0	0.569	0.57	26.3
Kiswahili	Gr 2	1 (Full Tx)	Baseline	17.0	7.7	•	•	0.542	0.49	33.6
			Midline†	32.4	3.5	•	•	0.369	0.22	10.7
			Endline†	32.0	3.4	•	•	0.362	0.21	10.4
		2 (Delayed Tx)	Baseline	19.7	4.1	•	•	0.479	0.36	25.5
			Midline	32.5	3.5	•	14.2	0.344	0.19	9.1
			Endline†	34.4	3.2	•	5.5	0.309	0.16	7.2
		3 (Control)	Baseline	15.1	5.1	•	•	0.578	0.58	36.5
			Midline	26.6	3.7	•	•	0.358	0.20	12.4
			Endline	26.9	3.7	•	•	0.352	019	10.5
English		1 (Full Tx)	Baseline	25.3	9.5	•	•	0.553	0.52	30.1
			Midline†	48.6	4.4	•	3.7	0.424	0.29	11.5
			Endline†	56.0	3.2	26.6	2.9	0.382	0.23	9.3
		2 (Delayed Tx)	Baseline	28.3	4.6	•	9.0	0.496	0.40	19.0
			Midline	53.7	3.8	16.7	2.6	0.372	0.22	8.6
			Endline†	60.6	3.3	7.1	2.2	0.318	0.16	5.5
		3 (Control)	Baseline	18.8	5.6	•	•	0.626	0.73	33.0
			Midline	36.8	4.3	•	4.1	0.439	0.32	10.7
			Endline	42.8	4.3	•	3.0	0.402	0.26	13.1

† = had received the intervention in the period preceding the assessment.

• = could not be calculated.

databases of income and wealth inequality.[19] In recent years, according to World Bank estimates, the most income-unequal countries (taking together all countries' unique measurement points in the last five years), were South Africa and Namibia, with income inequality Ginis around 0.6, and the most equal were some of the ex-Soviet countries such as Ukraine and Belarus, with Ginis for income around 0.25, similar to many of the Nordic countries. Below we can see the Ginis for learning consistently (but not invariably) decrease from baseline to endline, and are similar to the income Ginis for unequal societies. At a glance, the Gini appears to be roughly comparable across languages, and tends to be smaller in Grade 2 than in Grade 1. This is also intuitive: we would expect Grade 2 scores to have less variation, as longer exposure to the school system begins to smooth out the effects of household-level factors.

3. **Coefficient of variation**. This indicator also behaves well. The correlation coefficient between the CV and the Gini is 0.84 (across all cohorts); these two measures of inequality move together well and tell more or less the same story. It does have the disadvantage of not having a theoretical upper bound, and it can be more influenced by outliers than the Gini coefficient.

4. **Percent scoring zero**. The "percent scoring zero" also behaves well. Analysts working on fluency have been analyzing these data for some time, and do not report major issues with this measure, so one would expect this.[20] Note that this indicator is more akin to the concept of "percent below a learning floor" than inequality and, as noted in Crouch and Rolleston (2017) and Crouch and Gustafsson (2018), this indicator may matter more. The correlation with the Gini coefficient across the observed data points is 0.97. As will be noted below, this measure influences the Gini coefficient in a very understandable and reasonable way.

---

19   The data referenced here are from a download of the World Bank's World Development Indicators, that can be found at https://datacatalog.worldbank.org/dataset/world-development-indicators.
20   See examples from many countries at https://earlygradereadingbarometer.org/.

5. **GE(2) index.** The GE(2) index appears to behave well, too. Values generally but not uniformly decrease over time, both from baseline to endline and from Grade 1 to Grade 2. Any differences between the GE(2) values for English vs. Kiswahili within a given cohort and round of assessment appear slight and may not be meaningful. For all subpopulations in both languages, the GE(2) was substantially reduced by midline relative to the baseline; changes between midline and endline were comparatively modest, and sometimes reversed course. In general the GE(2) measures seem more sensitive than the Gini coefficient: they show bigger changes between baseline and midline. Whether that would continue to be the case with other datasets is unknown for now.

Table 3. Range of inequality measure results, Tusome.

Language	Grade	Round	mean	CV	ratio_p90p10	ratio_p75p25	Gini	GE(2)	pct_zero
Kiswahili	Gr 1	Baseline	4.9	11.8	•	•	0.819	2.02	69.9
		Midline	12.2	6.1	•	•	0.634	0.75	43.0
	Gr 2	Baseline	13.5	6.8	•	•	0.617	0.68	43.3
		Midline	24.5	4.2	•	2.73	0.401	0.25	18.4
English	Gr 1	Baseline	10.6	10.6	•	•	0.741	1.36	52.8
		Midline	22.3	6.2	•	12.3	0.572	0.58	20.9
	Gr 2	Baseline	23.8	7.3	•	•	0.615	0.68	37.9
		Midline	43.6	4.7	32.6	3.0	0.397	0.24	10.7

• = could not be calculated.

The general patterns we observed in the PRIMR data—which contained more schools, but were from a narrower representative sample—are reflected in the Tusome data as well. The *ratio_p90p10* can rarely be calculated, and while *ratio_p75p25* is available slightly more often, it is not consistently so. The Gini coefficient appears roughly comparable across languages and tends to diminish both over time, both from baseline to midline and from Grade 1 to Grade 2. The coefficient of variation in both languages narrows from baseline to midline and from Grade 1 to Grade 2, while the mean scores increase. Likewise, the percent scoring zero and GE(2) diminish substantially from baseline to midline and Grade 1 to Grade 2 for both languages.

Selected graphical analyses and interpretation

The tabulations above suggest the *ratio_p90p10* and *ratio_p75p25* are unlikely to present fruitful avenues of exploration and the GE(2) is unfamiliar to non-economists. So, we set them aside in favor of further exploring the Gini coefficient, the CV, and the percent scoring zero.

Fig. 1. Comparison of Gini measures at t0 and t1 to chart improvement. presents the Gini coefficients separately for each language for various subpopulations at t_0 and t_1, where t_0 is a reference point and t_1 represents a subsequent round of data collection. For Tusome, all t_0 are baseline and all t_1 are midline. For PRIMR, a given t_0–t_1 pairing may be any of baseline–midline, baseline–endline, or midline–endline.[21]

The reference line is the line of equality (but only in the definitional, mathematical sense, not the Lorenz curves sense—see below). If the Gini coefficient for a given comparison were the same at both time periods, the dot would be plotted on the line of equality. If it has diminished from t_0 to t_1, the dot will move farther below the line. If it has increased from t_0 to t_1, the dot will move up toward the line.

Fig. 1. Comparison of Gini measures at t0 and t1 to chart improvement. also shows the Gini coefficient for each subpopulation at baseline, and at the next period. Perhaps the most interesting and immediately visible point is that the results are strongly patterned. One does not have to know which subpopulation each dot represents to see the pattern.

---

21 We acknowledge that this approach results in some duplication of data. Removing internal points (e.g., midline for PRIMR Cohorts 1 and 3) would eliminate some of that duplication, but risk introducing either varying durations for the t0–t1 period (baseline-endline for Cohorts 1 and 3, but midline-endline for Cohort 2) or preserving the durations but muddying the treatment/control status (as for PRIMR Cohort 2, which was a control group from baseline to midline before receiving treatment between midline and endline).

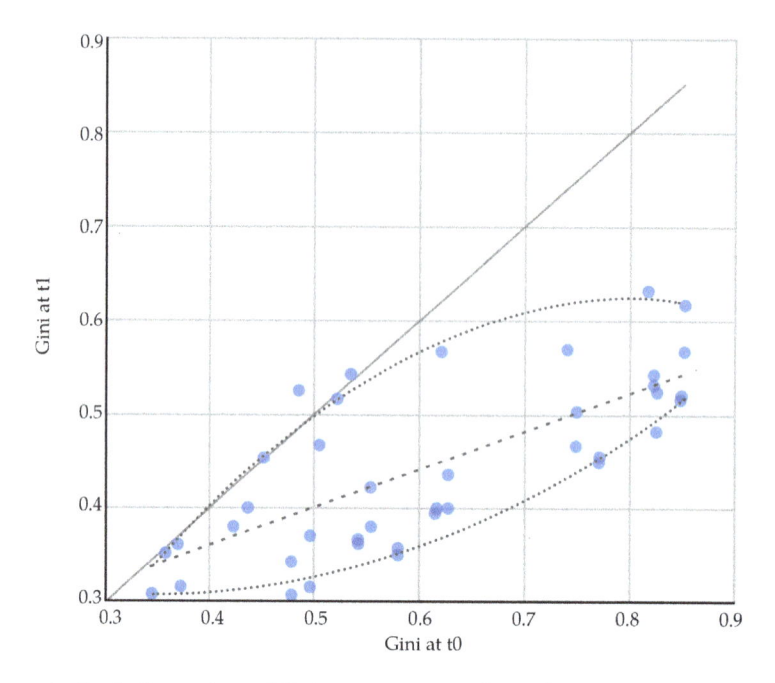

Fig. 1. Comparison of Gini measures at t_0 and t_1 to chart improvement.

The gray line on the graph represents the 45-degree line of equality as noted above. The fact that almost all points are below it tells us that, in almost all cases, the Gini improved.

In addition to the 45-degree line of equality, we have overlaid three other lines. The first one (middle line, dashed) is a simple linear regression. It obviously has a slope less than 1, as can be seen when comparing it to the 45-degree line of equality. The other two dotted lines are "quantile regressions" that provide the best (non-linear, in this case) fit through the scatter at the 15th and 85th percentile on the vertical axis for every point on the horizontal axis.

We interpret these overlays as follows. First, using the 45-degree line of equality, we can see that, as noted, the Gini coefficient nearly always either diminishes from t_0 to t_1 or stays the same, but rarely gets worse. The interventions nearly always improve equality.

Second, we truncated both the horizontal and vertical axes at 0.3, which is more or less the smallest value for both the t_1 and t_0 Ginis. This just helps us concentrate better on the more meaningful parts of the graphical analysis. Note that the regression through the points has a slope much smaller than 1. This is telling us that at low values of inequality in the baseline (t_0), it is harder to further reduce the value by t_1—at around 0.3 for t_0, we end up at about 0.3 for t_1. But at 0.8 for t_0, things have improved all the way to 0.53 or so for t_1. This makes sense given the concept of diminishing returns—but it is interesting how strong it is. Thirdly and finally, the "buttonhole" shape created by the lines at the 15th and 85th percentiles means that at both extremes (low-starting and high-starting inequality, or a low- and high-starting Gini at t_0), the shift in Gini by t_1 is more *predictable*—not bigger or smaller (we have already noted that the bigger it is at baseline the more it improves), but rather, we are saying that for low- or high- starting Ginis the change is more *reliable*. With Ginis of 0.3 and 0.8 at t_0, the range of improvement is about 0.05 and .15 respectively, but with a Gini of 0.6 at t_0, the range of improvement is about 0.22, a positive outcome.[22]

In Fig. 2. Non-readers at t0 and t1., the percentage of non-readers, or "percent scoring zero", shows the same pattern as the Gini measures. Comparison of the dots to the grey line of equality shows that the percentage of non-readers nearly always improves, and the dashed regression line shows that the worse the value is at baseline (i.e., the more children reading at 0), the more it improves—by a lot.

Improvements in mean reading fluency in Fig. 3. Mean reading fluency at t0 and t1. show the same pattern as the inequality measures, but, as one would hope, in reverse: almost all the points are above the 45-degree line, showing that skills almost always improved. The dashed regression line through the observations does not have a slope very different from the 45-degree line. It is slightly flatter than the line of equality, which suggests that at low levels of fluency it is slightly easier to make gains—again as one would hope, if not expect, given all the foregoing (see Figure 3).

---

22 It is possible that we are seeing some regression towards the mean in these results. However, it seems doubtful, given that the observations are not related to schools, but to skill types and levels. Also, there is actually no regression: "good" values in one period do not regress. It also seems less likely with measures of inequality than with point measures. A simple principle more likely at work is something akin to the law of diminishing returns: when one starts at a relatively good place, it may be harder to move forward. On the other hand, while laws of diminishing return make a lot of sense in fairly simple production processes (the returns of 100 kg more fertilizer on a field of corn are not the same at high existing levels of fertilization than at low), it is not as obvious that they would operate similarly in complex social and managerial situations, such as school improvement.

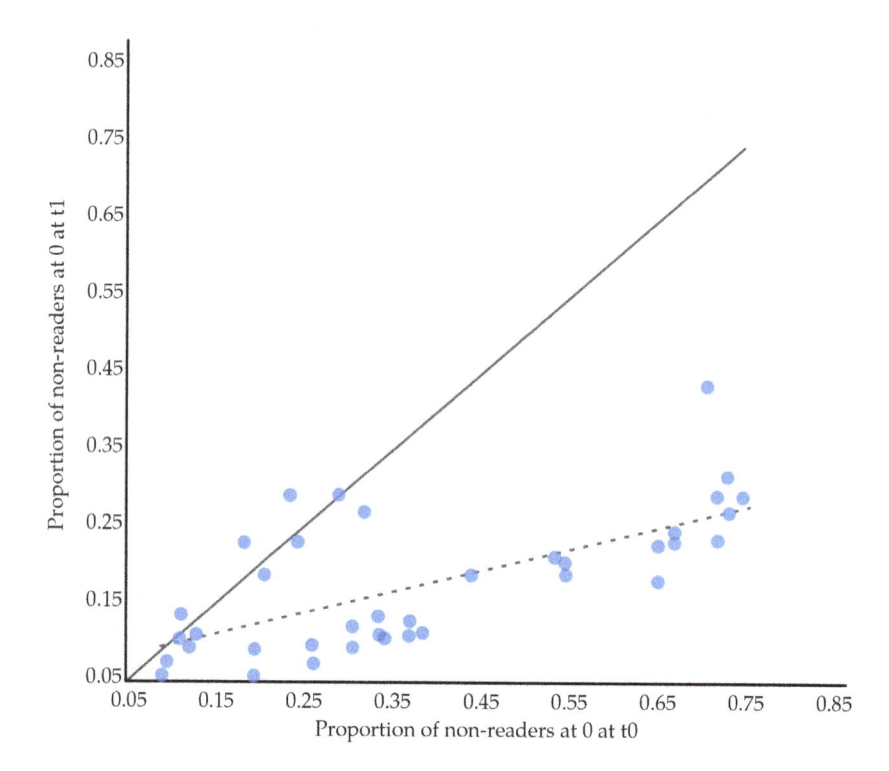

Fig. 2. Non-readers at t_0 and t_1.

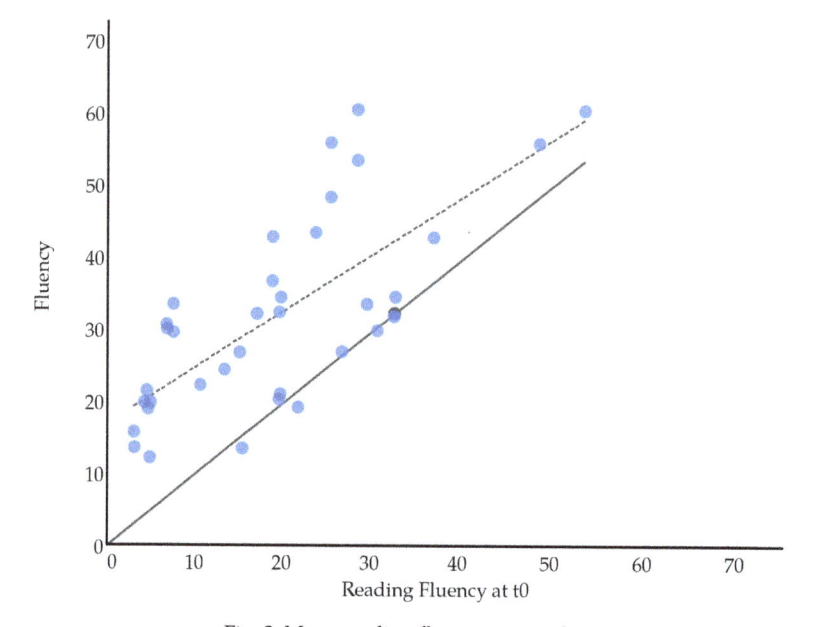

Fig. 3. Mean reading fluency at t_0 and t_1.

5. Reducing Inequality in Education

The graphical and statistical analysis done thus far shows that the measures of inequality (Gini and CV) or percent below a learning floor (percent scoring zero) and the means for reading fluency all behave as expected, and in ways that are eminently interpretable—at least in data from a couple of successful and related projects.

But the most interesting and important question is whether the improvements in means from t_0 to t_1, cohort by cohort (as shown in Table 1 and Table 2), were correlated with reductions in inequality for the same cohorts between t_0 and t_1. Fig. 4. Changes in the mean and changes in inequality. shows the correlation between improvements in mean reading fluency and reductions in the Gini of reading fluency (and not for any of the other inequality measures). The dark dashed line is the standard regression and the dotted lines are the quantile regressions. First, the correlation, at -0.65, is strong. The slope is also fairly strong: with fluency improvements of around 10, the Gini improves by -0.15, but with fluency improvements around 25, the Gini is improved by about -0.25. This is notable, given that the starting Ginis were pretty high. So, we can strongly conclude that in this case, the bigger the improvement in the means, the greater the reduction in inequality in oral reading fluency. We believe that this is a very important result.

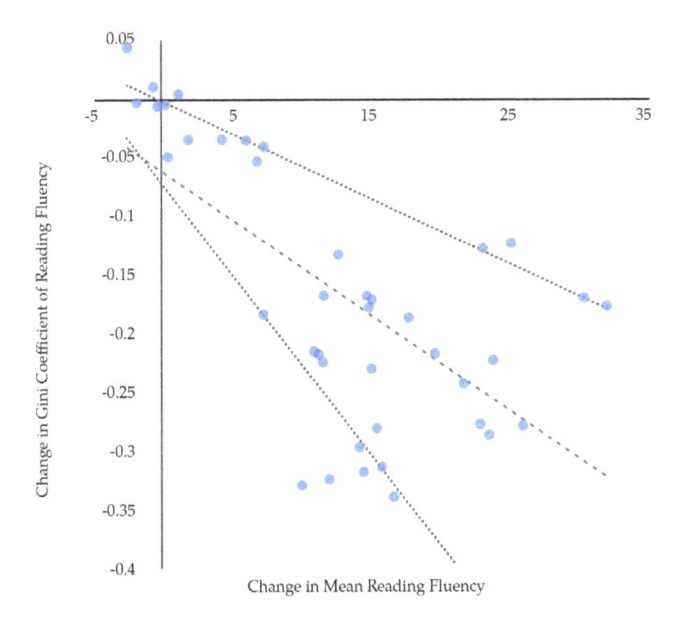

Fig. 4. Changes in the mean and changes in inequality.

Graphical link between the Gini measures and the percent scoring zero measures

One advantage of the Gini coefficient, aside from it being a widely used measure of inequality, is that it has a graphical equivalent in the Lorenz curve. It also seems to work well with the Gini coefficient for learning, with the measures as used in this chapter. In this section we first explore what the Lorenz curves tell us, then explain a link between them (and the Ginis they represent), and the "percent scoring zero" measure of percent below a learning floor.

Fig. 5. Shifts in Lorenz curves in response to successful interventions. provides another way of reasoning about the distribution of oral reading fluency within a subpopulation. It displays the Lorenz curves for Grades 1 and 2 with respect to oral reading fluency, assessed in English and Kiswahili. In this instance, a point on the Lorenz curve can be interpreted as "the bottom X percent of children possess Y percent of the total fluency". The reference line is the line of equality: if fluency skills were equally distributed among the population, for instance, the bottom 20 percent of the children would have 20 percent of the fluency skill. The gap between the reference line and the actual curve represents the inequality of distribution; as the actual curve approaches the line of equality, fluency is distributed more equally, and the gap between the fluency *haves* and *have nots* is closing. The more bowed towards the right-hand bottom corner, the more inequality the curve represents. The dashed lines around each Lorenz curve are the confidence intervals for the curves.[23] The link between the Lorenz curves and the Gini coefficient is simple: the Gini represents double the area between the line of equality and the Lorenz curve. It is important to keep this in mind when using the Lorenz curves to analyze the inequality.

Consider the top left panel in the figure, representing the distribution of English-language ORF among Grade 1 children assessed under PRIMR. At baseline (represented by the yellow line), the bottom 80 percent of children together represent roughly 20 percent of the total English-language ORF observed. As children at the lower end of the

---

23   We do not dwell further on the issue of statistical significance as it is generally extremely high, and it is not the issue of interest—but it is good to just establish that the differences are generally very significant.

skill distribution improve their performance, the inequality diminishes and the gap between the *haves* and *have nots* begins to close: by endline (represented by the red line), the same 20 percent of English-language fluency is held by "only" the bottom 60 percent of the children. The bottom 80 percent of children, who formerly held only 20 percent of the fluency, now hold nearly 50 percent of it.[24]

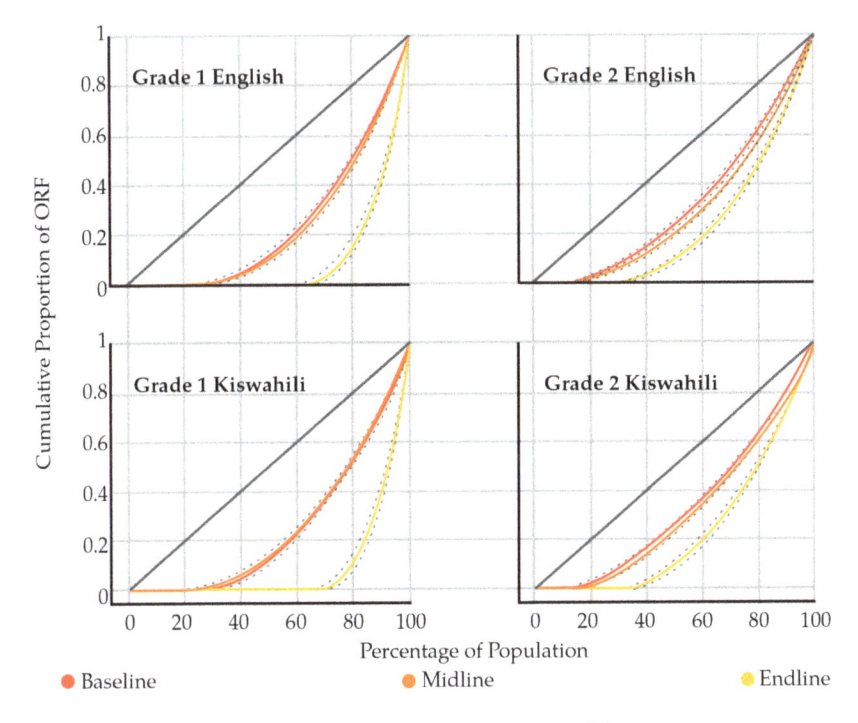

Fig. 5. Shifts in Lorenz curves in response to successful interventions.

Note that the interesting comparisons are not only across the grades and languages, but also between the baselines, midlines, and endlines. Fluency is unequally distributed in all cases. However, it is more unequally distributed in Grade 1 than in Grade 2, as would be expected due to unequal access to resources at the household level. While Kiswahili fluency is slightly more unequally distributed than English in

---

24 Recall that these Lorenz curves are analogizing from income, thus the percent of fluency is "held" by a given percentage of the children, exactly as one would say for income or wealth.

Grade 1 at baseline, by midline and endline (and throughout Grade 2) it is *less* unequally distributed.

In each subpopulation, an initially enormous gap between the *haves* and *have nots* has been substantially reduced by endline. In the case being analyzed in this chapter, the vast majority of that gap is closed between baseline and midline, with very little change in any subpopulation between midline and endline. This is especially interesting because the time elapsed from baseline to midline (10 months) and from midline to endline (12 months) is approximately the same. This aligns with what would be expected in the context of an intervention like PRIMR, which explicitly prioritized the teaching of basic literacy skills (such as letter recognition and decoding) before addressing higher-order literacy skills (such as reading with automaticity for comprehension).

We can now explore the link between the Lorenz curves and the "percent scoring zero"—a measure of percent below a learning floor. From the graphics, it is clear that these Lorenz curves all have a flat portion at the left, essentially the same as the horizontal axis, and then bump up a bit further to the right as the curve departs from the horizontal axis. The length of the flat line to the left of the bump represents the percentage of the population "scoring zero". The interpretation is clear: since the children to the left of that bump read at zero, they will cumulatively "possess" zero percent of the cumulative proportion or distribution of fluency—the variable represented on the vertical axis—thus the line is flat and is the same as the horizontal axis. It is particularly interesting that it is the shifting of that bump that accounts for much of the decrease in how "bowed out" the curve is towards the right-hand lower corner of the graphics. That is to say, the reduction in percent below a learning floor (percent scoring zero) accounts for a great deal of the improvement in inequality.[25]

Policy implications

This chapter focused on answering several simple questions: do inequality measures typically used in socioeconomic analysis work for learning, and do they detect levels and changes (in response to

---

25 This is evident visually, and we do not quantify it here, but it would be possible to do so.

interventions) that are interpretable and meaningful? Do various measures of inequality (such as the Gini coefficient) and measures of percent-below-a-minimum correlate and reinforce each other, again, in ways that are interpretable and meaningful? The results of the data analysis carried out for the chapter strongly suggest that the answer to these questions is "yes".

But what accounts for the changes we observed? From a policy or pedagogical standpoint, how do the indicators help us formulate actions that could improve performance at the bottom of the pyramid? The data from the implementations and pilots reported here were not designed explicitly to deal with these questions. However, the results are strongly suggestive.

There are strong indications as to the possible causal mechanisms in some of the scholarly literature coming from PRIMR and Tusome. Piper, Jepkemei, and Kibukho (2015) note:

> Although the project [PRIMR] did not explicitly target the [income] poor, the basic strategies in teaching literacy and numeracy skills have proven to be effective in supporting pupils at risk for reading difficulties. PRIMR is organized in ways that align with how best to support those at risk (p. 72).

In that paper, the authors compare the positive impact of PRIMR to the negative impact of simply being poor (as measured by socioeconomic status) and conclude that the PRIMR effect is considerably larger than the poverty effect (see p. 78). This does not mean that the project definitely improved the learning of the poor, as there was no specific targeting of school support to specifically poorer regions, nor did the project work in a set of randomized poor schools and a set of randomized wealthy schools. It does mean, however, that the project's impact was enough to overcome the impact of being poor, as measured using the same dataset. At the same time, the project was able to distinguish formal from non-formal schools. The latter are more frequented by the poor, and PRIMR's impact on non-formal schools was much higher, in general, than its impact on formal schools. Effect sizes (in terms of proportions of a standard deviation) were twice as high among the non-formal schools (p. 77). But note that the effect size, in this context, is a close cousin of the coefficient of variation (the difference being that one is the inverse of the other, and in one the change in means is used as opposed to the mean itself).

We have seen above that PRIMR typically improved the coefficient of variation. This measure of "pure" inequality is thus associated with having a larger effect size among the schools more frequented by the poor.[26] Thus, the finding from Piper et al. (2015) is not necessarily inconsistent with a reduction in "pure" inequality, even if what was being reported was not the impact on pure inequality but the impact on the poor. As emphasized by a report where the impacts of various treatments are assessed, the interventions in PRIMR and Tusome were heavily focused on the basics, and also stressed fidelity of implementation (Piper, Zuilkowski, Dubeck, Jepkemei, & King, 2018). Perhaps just as importantly, both PRIMR and Tusome were fairly zealous about ensuring that the main "vectors" whereby children are helped to learn—namely the yearly scope-and-sequence of lessons, the actual lessons themselves, the books, and the formative and summative assessment—are tightly integrated with each other.[27] Indeed, Piper et al. (2018) conclude that to get the best impact you have to go "all the way", with a combination of teacher professional development, instructional support and coaching, quality student books at a 1:1 ratio, and structured, scripted lesson plans.

There are important policy, planning, and managerial implications here. Generally, if inequality is strongly driven by factors like poverty, gender, or rurality, then targeting support to schools based on those factors makes the most sense. And, after all, there are other complementary reasons to direct resources, in general, to poorer communities, as shown by the literature on income transfers. However, if there is a high degree of inequality amongst the poor themselves (and also, perhaps, inequality amongst the non-poor), then an approach that targets the basics might

---

26 When the PRIMR dummy variable interacts with the poverty variable, oral reading fluency being the dependent variable, the program seems to have had greater absolute impact among the non-poor. Yet, this difference was small compared to the average (much improved) absolute level of fluency, especially in the non-formal schools. It may also be that, as noted or implied in other papers as well (e.g., Crouch & Rolleston, 2017; Crouch & Gustafsson, 2018), "pure" inequality could be reduced nonetheless, because inequality was reduced both amongst the poor and amongst the wealthier.

27 Often, efforts to improve "quality" are more nebulous, and involve the use of "thin" inputs, such as ensuring teachers are certified, or that there is a 1:1 pupil:book ratio, without much consideration of actual teaching skill, or how relevant a book's content is.

be best—one that is integrated and executed with considerable (but not obsessive) fidelity, and (perhaps in addition) helps schools (and individual children) based on results rather than location, poverty, or gender.

Conclusions

This paper tests a variety of measures of inequality and a measure of "percent below a floor" (or, in a loose sense, "learning at the bottom of the pyramid") to see whether they are "well-behaved" with the sorts of data that are typically produced with SQC assessments. The measures, used in Kenya, include the Gini coefficient, the ratios of performance at the 90th and 75th percentiles to performance at the 10th and 25th percentiles, the coefficient of variation, the GE(2) generalized entropy measure, and the percentage of children not reading at all. These measures of inequality, and above all, changes in the measures, are then compared to average performance on the assessment and improvements in the averages.

We used the concept of "pure" inequality or dispersion to study change over time, which is assumed to be produced at least in part by random variation in teaching (where some children might be in luck and get a fairly good teacher, and others are out of luck). In some sense, this approach to inequality is one that corresponds most closely to issues such as having systems stick to standards of outcome-oriented quality assurance.

Our findings showed that the utilized measures were what we term "well-behaved". The Gini coefficient for learning, for instance, corresponded to similar numbers for income. Generally, changes (or very large or small values) in one measure correspond to changes (or the corresponding large or small values) in the other measures. Thus, there is internal coherence among all the measures and they all help to tell more or less the same story. In other words, an important conclusion from the use of the measures for assessing change over time is that the changes are strongly and consistently patterned. In addition, while it is true that, when inequality was high to start with, the reduction was greatest, it is also the case that that reduction was statistically less predictable. In the obverse, where inequality was relatively low to start with, reductions were harder to produce, but they were somewhat more certain.

In sum, we found that when one correlates improvements in the average levels (of reading fluency in this case) to changes in inequality, the larger improvements in the average almost always correspond to larger reductions in inequality. Though it is impossible to determine precisely why these inequality reductions are achieved, it seems safe to conclude that children with low initial learning (reading) results benefit disproportionately from programs that are (a) aimed at the very basics and the mechanics of learning to read; (b) contain at least the minimum necessary set of "inputs" or "vectors" of quality (e.g., teacher coaching, development of guided lesson plans, and corresponding books for children to read, at the right ratio); and (c) provide tight integration between vectors (so that lesson plans match the books' content quite rigorously, and so on for all other inputs) and are implemented with considerable fidelity. Our findings support the hypothesis that consistent measures of low-end performance can improve learning among children at the bottom of the pyramid.

References

Bruckauf, Z., & Chzhen, Y. (2016). *Education for all? Measuring inequality of educational outcomes among 15-year-olds across 39 industrialized nations* (Innocenti Working Paper 2016–08). Florence: UNICEF Office of Research.

Crouch, L., Gove, A., & Gustafsson, M. (2009). Educación y cohesión cocial. In S. Scharzman & C. Cox (Eds.), *Políticas educativas y cohesión social en Américan Latina*. Santiago de Chile: Uqbar Editores.

Crouch, L., & Gustafsson, M. (2018). *Worldwide inequality and poverty in cognitive results: Cross-sectional evidence and time-based trends* (Research on Improving Systems of Education (RISE) Programme Working Paper, RISE-WP-18/019).

Crouch, L., & Rolleston, C. (2017). *Raising the floor on learning levels: Equitable improvement starts with the tail* (An insight note from the RISE Programme). https://riseprogramme.org/sites/default/files/publications/RISE%20Equity%20Insight%20UPDATE.pdf

Dowd, A. J. (2018, March 8–13). *Visualizing learning equity: New options for communicating about learning gaps and gains* (Conference presentation). Comparative and International Education Society Annual Conference, San Francisco.

Dubeck, M., & Gove, A. (2015). The early grade reading assessment (EGRA): Its theoretical foundation, purpose, and limitations. *International Journal of Educational Development, 40*, 315–322.

Ferreira, F. H., & Giroux, J. (2011.) *The measurement of educational inequality: Achievement and opportunity* (IZA Discussion Paper, No. 6161). http://ftp.iza.org/dp6161.pdf

Freeman, R. B., Machin, S. J. & Viarengo, M. G. (2011). Inequality of educational outcomes: International evidence from PISA. *Regional and Sectoral Economic Studies, 11*(3), 5–20.

Graham, J., & Kelly, S. (2019). How effective are early grade reading interventions? A review of the evidence. *Educational Research Review, 27*, 155–175.

Gromada, A., Rees, G., Chzhen, Y., Cuesta, J., & Bruckhauf, Z. (2018). *Measuring inequality in children's education in rich countries* (Innocenti Working Paper 2018–18). Florence: UNICEF Office of Research.

Hao, L., & Naiman, D. (2010). *Assessing inequality*. Thousand Oaks: Sage Publications.

Haughton, J., & Khandker, S. (2009). *Handbook on poverty and inequality*. Washington, DC: World Bank. https://openknowledge.worldbank.org/bitstream/handle/10986/11985/9780821376133.pdf

Micklewright, J., & Schnepf, S. (2006). *Inequality of learning in industrialised countries* (IZA Discussion Paper Series, No. 2517). https://www.researchgate.net/publication/5136840_Inequality_of_Learning_in_Industrialised_Countries

Mullis, I. V. S., Martin, M. O., & Loveless, T. (2016). *20 years of TIMSS: International trends in mathematics and science achievement, curriculum and instruction*. Chestnut Hill: Boston College. http://timssandpirls.bc.edu/timss2015/international-results/timss2015/wp-content/uploads/2016/T15-20-years-of-TIMSS.pdf

Oppedisano, V., & Turati, G. (2015). What are the causes of educational inequality and its evolution over time in Europe? Evidence from PISA. *Education Economics, 23*(1), 3–24.

Piper, B., Jepkemeib, E., & Kibukhob, K. (2015). Pro-poor primr: Improving early literacy skills for children from low income families in Kenya. *Africa Education Review, 12*(1), 67–87. https://doi.org/10.1080/18146627.2015.1036566

Piper, B., Simmons Zuiliwski S., Dubeck, M., Jepkemei, E., & King, S. (2018). Identifying the essential ingredients to literacy and numeracy improvement: Teacher professional development and coaching, student textbooks, and structured teachers' guides. *World Development, 106*, 324–336.

RTI International. (2014). *The primary math and reading (PRIMR) initiative: Endline impact evaluation: Revised edition* (United States Agency for International

Development (USAID) Working Paper Series). https://pdf.usaid.gov/pdf_docs/PA00K27S.pdf

RTI International. (2015). *Early Grade Reading Assessment (EGRA) toolkit, second edition*. Washington, DC: United States Agency for International Development.

Sahn, D. E. & Younger, S. D. (2007). *Decomposing world education inequality*. Ithaca: Cornell University. http://www.cfnpp.cornell.edu/images/wp187.pdf

Thomas, V., Wang, Y., & Fan, X. (2001). *Measuring education inequality: Gini coefficients of education* (Policy Research Working Paper, No. 2525). Washington, DC: World Bank.

Thomas, V., Wang, Y., & Fan, X. (2003). Measuring education inequality: Gini coefficients of education for 140 countries, 1960–2000. *Journal of Education Planning and Administration, 17*(1), 5–33.

Wagner, D. A. (2003). Smaller, quicker, cheaper: Alternative strategies for literacy assessment in the UN Literacy Decade. *International Journal of Educational Research, 39*(3), 293–309. http://authors.elsevier.com/sd/article/S088303550400031X

Wagner, D. A. (2011). *Smaller, quicker, cheaper: Improving learning indicators for developing countries*. Washington/Paris: FTI/UNESCO-IIEP. http://unesdoc.unesco.org/images/0021/002136/213663e.pdf

Wagner, D. A. (2018). *Learning as development: Rethinking international education in a changing world*. New York: Routledge.

Wagner, D., Wolf, S., & Boruch, R. (2018). *Learning at the bottom of the pyramid: Science, measurement, and policy in low-income countries*. UNESCO, IIEP.

World Bank. (2019). *Ending learning poverty: What will it take?* Washington, DC: World Bank. https://openknowledge.worldbank.org/bitstream/handle/10986/32553/142659.pdf?sequence=6&isAllowed=y

6. Not All Pyramids Are the Same

Relative Learning Exclusion and Its Evolution Over Time

Dirk Van Damme, Tijana Prokic-Breuer, and Stan Vermeulen

Introduction

We can achieve a better understanding of the learning opportunities and outcomes of poor and marginalized populations at "the bottom of the pyramid" (Wagner & Castillo, 2014; Wagner, Wolf, & Boruch, 2018) through two different approaches. The first approach is an "absolute" assessment of the learning of a population, performed by calculating how many learners meet a certain benchmark performance. This is the approach taken, for example, by the World Bank in measuring "learning poverty": "Learning poverty means being unable to read and understand a simple text by age 10".[1] According to that definition, 53 percent of children in low- and middle-income countries are "learning poor". Other examples of absolute learning benchmarks include the usage of Level 2 as the minimal threshold level in OECD's PISA assessment framework. According to the most recent PISA survey of 2018, 77.4 percent of 15-year-olds in OECD countries have a reading proficiency of Level 2 or above, but in middle- and low-income non-OECD countries participating in PISA, this figure can drop to around 20 percent, as is the case for the Philippines or the Dominican Republic (OECD, 2019).

---

[1] https://www.worldbank.org/en/topic/education/brief/learning-poverty

These benchmark-oriented measures are important for understanding the global learning crisis relative to the achievement of SDG4. It is important to know the size of the population of learners "at the bottom of the pyramid". However, SDG4 also speaks about ensuring "inclusive and equitable quality education". An absolute approach to learning poverty does not say much about the inclusiveness of education, nor in itself about the equity in learning opportunities and outcomes. Inclusiveness and equity refer to the specific context in which learning happens and how learners at the bottom of the pyramid relate to other learners in their social environment. In other words, not all pyramids are the same. A certain level of proficiency can provide access to the resources that ensure a good life in a specific context, but can be dramatically insufficient in another context.

As a second, alternative approach, this paper advances the concept of "learning exclusion" as a relative measure to better understand the relationship between learners at the bottom with those in the rest of the pyramid. We define "learning exclusion" as the relative distance in learning outcomes between the lowest 10 percent of performers and the median in a country's population. A higher gap suggests that learners at the bottom are relatively more excluded from what a nation's population considers to be the norm. A smaller gap suggests that learners at the bottom are more integrated into the skill profile of a nation's population. The level of "learning exclusion" is independent from the absolute learning threshold. The performance of the lowest 10 percent can indeed be quite high in comparative terms, suggesting a relatively low level of learning poverty. But at the same time, the lowest 10 percent can still experience a high degree of exclusion within their social environment. And in a country with a relatively low median, a relatively small gap between the median and the lowest 10 percent can still point to a comparatively low degree of exclusion of the learners at the bottom.

This approach of "learning exclusion" is inspired by relative definitions of poverty (Eskelinen, 2011). This relative definition is based on the assumption that whether a person or household is considered poor depends on their income share *relative* to the income shares of other people who are living in the same society. We apply the same reasoning to learning. The exclusion of an individual or group in terms of skills depends not so much on the absolute level of proficiency, but on the relative gap with what a given society considers to be the median level of proficiency. As in sociology, relative scarcity or poverty has a major impact on an individual's perception of self-worth (Lamont, 2019).

The concept of "learning exclusion" should be distinguished from learning inequality, although there are connections between the two. Measuring educational inequality has been the purpose, for example, of attempts to measure the Gini coefficient of education (Thomas et al., 2001). Societies with wider variation in learning outcomes tend to be societies with higher levels of learning exclusion. Yet it all depends on where in the learning distribution the variance is located. A society with a large gap between the median and 90th percentile and a relatively milder gap between the median and 10th percentile has a lower level of learning exclusion than a society where the gap is concentrated in the bottom half of the distribution, even if both societies have a similar level of overall inequality. For learners at the bottom of the pyramid, it all depends on how the distribution of learning opportunities and outcomes in their society is shaped.

This distinction has important policy implications. From an inequality perspective, a compressed distribution of learning outcomes looks desirable. But is it desirable for countries to have the upper part of the distribution situated at a relatively low level? Countries also benefit from high levels of learning excellence, which potentially permeate the whole of society. On the other hand, a learning distribution with a relatively high upper part and a relatively high median—but with a long tail of low-performing learners—is far from being inclusive. For inclusive learning, the shape of the pyramid matters.

Measuring learning exclusion

In this study, we used the OECD PISA database for the six rounds of PISA scores between 2000 and 2018. We measured learning exclusion as the relative distance between the median and 10th percentile. In Figure 1, we have mapped countries in a two-dimensional chart according to their average learning exclusion in the PISA cycles 2009 to 2018 compared to the median learning exclusion (X-axis) and their average median score in these cycles relative to the overall median PISA score in reading for all countries (Y-axis).

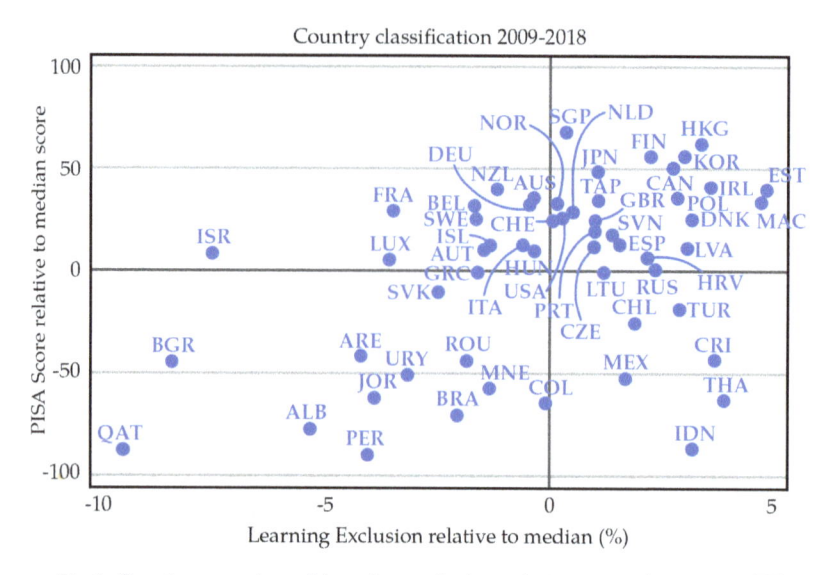

184   Learning, Marginalization, and Improving the Quality of Education

Country classification 2009-2018

Fig. 1. Country mapping of learning exclusion relative to median score (PISA database). Note: Countries depicted are those that are present for all PISA cycles between 2009–2018. Median PISA scores are calculated by averaging the median score over all four cycles. Learning exclusion is operationalized as the percentage difference between the median score and 10th percentile for each country.

The median level of learning exclusion over the four PISA cycles studied is -27 percent. This implies that students at the 10th percentile of the PISA reading score distribution score 73 percent as high as the students at the median of the score distribution. Negative values on the X-axis represent higher levels of learning exclusion. For example, the learning exclusion level of Bulgaria is 8 percent higher than the PISA average at -35 percent, and their students at the 10th percentile of the distribution score 65 percent as high as their median-performing students.

The first observation is that the degree of learning exclusion is largely unrelated to the median PISA score itself. While fitting a regression line reveals a slightly positive relationship between relative PISA score and lower levels of learning exclusion, there are countries represented in each of the four quadrants, and countries with fairly similar median PISA scores can differ widely on their levels of learning exclusion. Countries in the top-right quadrant are those with a relatively high median PISA score and a relatively low level of learning exclusion, while countries in the bottom-left quadrant combine relatively low median PISA scores with relatively high levels of learning exclusion.

Evolution of learning exclusion over time

After exploring the more static view on learning exclusion, we can now turn to the more dynamic perspective by looking at the evolution of learning exclusion over time. In Figure 2 we show the evolution of a select number of countries' median scores and their level of learning exclusion between the 2012 and 2018 waves.

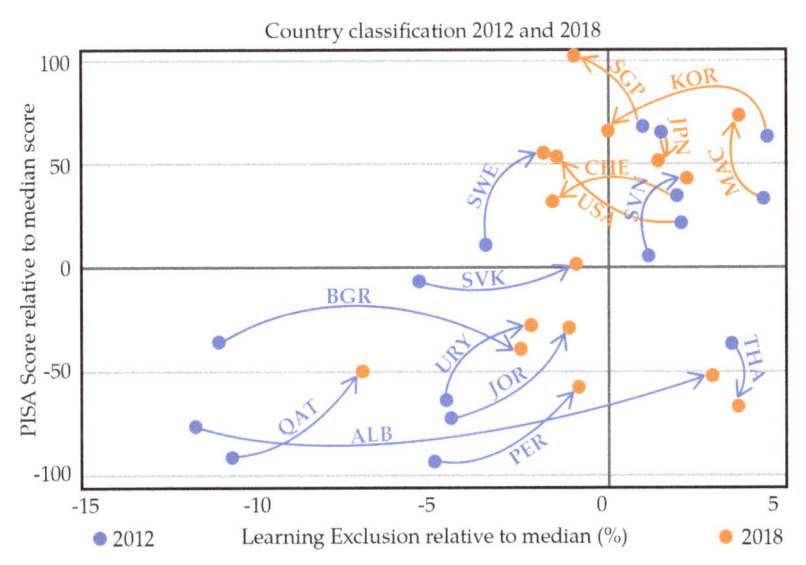

Fig. 2. Development of learning exclusion relative to median score between 2012 and 2018 – selected countries (PISA database). Note: For legibility, the only countries included were those above or below a specific threshold in terms of their development in relative median PISA scores or learning exclusion between the 2012 and 2018 PISA waves. The results for all other countries are available upon request.

As shown in Figure 2, learning exclusion is by no means an immutable characteristic of a country's educational system. Some countries that scored fairly poorly in terms of learning exclusion in 2012 have shown remarkable progress over time. For example, in 2012 Albania had one of the highest levels of learning exclusion: around 12 percentage points below the PISA average. This implies that the Albanian students at the 10th percentile of the PISA reading score distribution scored only 61 percent as high as the median Albanian student (PISA average: 73 percent). Yet, in the 2018 wave, their learning exclusion dropped below the PISA average: Albanian students at the 10th percentile of the 2018

PISA reading score distribution scored 75 percent as high as the median Albanian student. Similar developments can be seen for other countries such as Qatar, Peru, Jordan, Uruguay, Bulgaria, the Slovak Republic, Slovenia, and Sweden. The progress of these countries is indicated in blue arrows. It is interesting to see that most of those countries (Bulgaria is an exception) not only improved their learning exclusion, but also their median score.

By contrast, some countries' median scores showed overall improvement between 2012 and 2018, while their level of learning exclusion remained relatively similar (e.g., Macao) or even increased (e.g., Singapore, the US). The US and Singapore seem to have improved their overall performance at the expense of those at the bottom of the pyramid. In other countries, learning exclusion even increased while median scores remained stagnant (Korea, Switzerland). Countries with a worsening degree of learning exclusion are indicated with red arrows.

While these patterns might represent some form of regression to the mean (countries with extreme values in one period will naturally revert to less extreme values in other periods), they could also be the result of deliberate policy interventions by governments that aimed to increase educational performance at a certain part of the ability distribution. In this case, it could be that the increased policy attention and resources expended at the bottom of the ability distribution has come at the expense of students' performance at the top of the distribution (see also the discussion by Al Samerrai and Benveniste, this volume).

Evolution of learning exclusion in some specific countries

In this section, we illustrate the different paths of PISA development in terms of learning exclusion and the shape of the "pyramid" by plotting three sets of countries on different trajectories over all of their available PISA cycles in terms of their reading performance (see Figure 3).

What is interesting about different countries' trajectories is that the countries that improved the most in terms of learning exclusion seem to have compressed their pyramid somewhat. The performance of the students at the 90th percentile in Albania and Bulgaria decreased relative to the median performance. Some countries, however, appear to have been able to reduce their learning exclusion without it being at the expense of their top performers, such as Qatar and Uruguay.

Countries that strongly improved in terms of learning exclusion

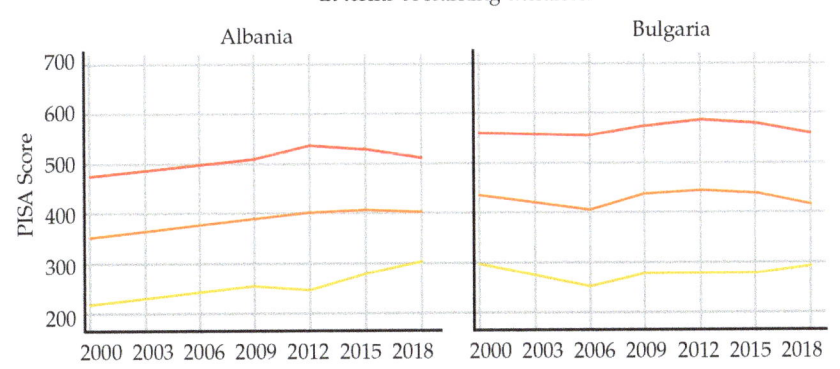

Albania
Bulgaria

Countries that improved in terms of learning exclusion and in terms of median performance

Qatar
Uruguay

— 90th percentile — Median — 10th percentile

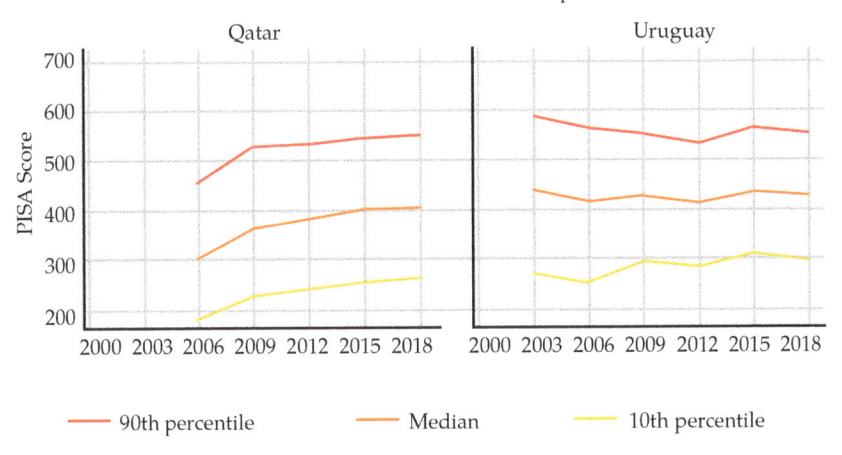

Fig. 3. (Continued on following page)

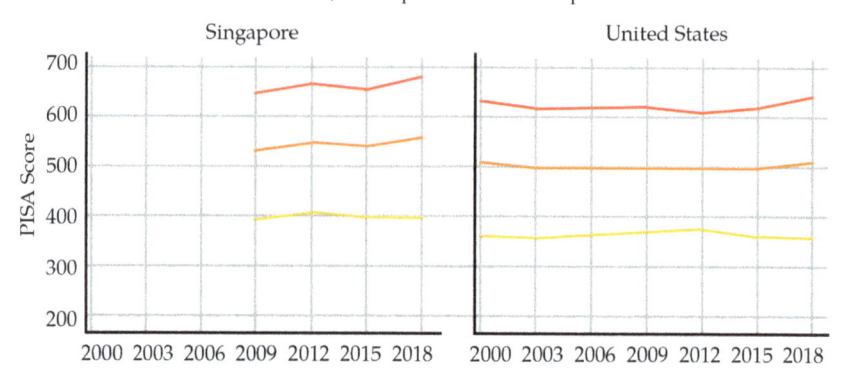

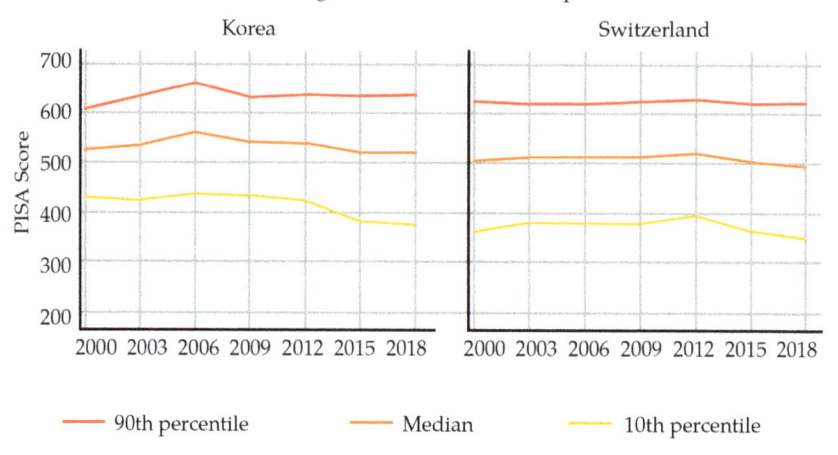

Fig. 3. Development of the pyramid between 2000 and 2018—selected countries (PISA database).

In contrast, countries such as Singapore and the US have seen increases in the performance of their median- and top-performing students, but the performance of the students at the lower end of the ability distribution has remained stagnant over time. These countries illustrate the importance of the learning exclusion indicator: evaluating these countries' educational systems based on average performance would perhaps find positive results, but taking into account their increasing levels of learning exclusion would paint a different and more disturbing picture.

Finally, in some countries, median performance is relatively stable or even decreasing, with an even stronger decrease in the scores at the 10th percentile. Korea and Switzerland, for example, while maintaining the strong performance of their students at the 90th percentile, appear to be deteriorating in terms of both their median score and measure of learning exclusion.

Conclusion

In this paper, we investigated the evolution of learning exclusion over time in a number of countries, on the basis of PISA data (2000–2018). We defined learning exclusion as the relative gap in learning outcomes, measured as the distance on the PISA scale between the median and percentile 10. This metric differs from similar approaches, such as the concept of "learning poverty" as defined by the World Bank, which is an absolute measure of low performance, or attempts to calculate the "education Gini" or other measures of educational inequality, which are metrics of variation in the entire distribution.

To measure the exclusion produced by relative low performance, inequalities between the median and the top of the distribution are largely irrelevant. Measuring the relative distance in learning outcomes between the median performance in a population and the performance of the *lowest 10 percent* gives an indication of the relative exclusion of the bottom end of the learning distribution in a society. Thus, we tracked the evolution of learning exclusion over successive PISA surveys. We identified trajectories in the measurement of learning exclusion in order to find patterns that can be related to the overall evolution of social inequality and social segregation. We also tried to identify different categories of countries according to the evolution of their political tolerance to learning exclusion. One important caveat in our research is the limitation of data to only a small handful of countries that are in low-income countries—further research will be needed to make a direct application of our methodology to the much poorer works in LICs.

In a functional sense, however, the exclusion of a learner is not primarily defined by his or her absolute performance in a global perspective or by his or her distance to the top performers, but by the deviation from what a society considers to be the norm, which is defined here as the median level of performance. People are excluded when their proficiency level is very much below the norm which a society considers to be functional. We found that this norm is not the same across countries.

Educational policy interventions aimed at reducing learning exclusion are not necessarily identical to policies aimed at reducing overall inequality in learning. Trying to compress the overall learning distribution can be achieved by decreasing the performance at the top of the distribution, while the learning exclusion at the bottom remains unchanged. This can hardly be seen as educational progress. Policies that lift the bottom of the distribution, thereby reducing learning exclusion, make a lot more sense from an equity and fairness point of view.

References

Crouch, L., & Slade, T. S. (2021). *Reducing inequality in education using "smaller, quicker, cheaper" assessments.* In this volume.

Eskelinen, T. (2011). Relative poverty. In D. K. Chatterjee (Ed.), *Encyclopedia of global justice.* Dordrecht: Springer. https://doi.org/10.1007/978-1-4020-9160-5_182

Lamont, M. (2019). From 'having' to 'being': Self-worth and the current crisis of American society. *The British Journal of Sociology, 70*(3), 660–707.

OECD. (2019). *PISA 2018 results (Volume I): What students know and can do.* Paris: PISA, OECD Publishing. https://doi.org/10.1787/5f07c754-en

Thomas, V., Wang, Y., & Fan, X. (2001). *Measuring education inequality: Gini coefficients of education* (Policy Research Working Papers). Washington, DC: World Bank. https://doi.org/10.1596/1813-9450-2525

Van Damme, D. (2018). Is it sustainable to leave the bottom behind in the process of educational development? In D. A. Wagner, S. Wolf, & R. F. Boruch (Eds.), *Learning at the bottom of the pyramid: Science, measurement, and policy in low-income countries* (pp. 235–249). Paris: UNESCO & IIEP.

Wagner, D. A., & Castillo, N. M. (2014). Learning at the bottom of the pyramid: Constraints, comparability and policy in developing countries. *Prospects, 44,* 627–638.

Wagner, D. A., Wolf, S., & Boruch, R. F. (Eds.) (2018). *Learning at the bottom of the pyramid: Science, measurement, and policy in low-income countries.* Paris: UNESCO & IIEP.

7. Financing Education at the Bottom of the Pyramid

Samer Al-Samarrai and Luis Benveniste

Introduction

Global public spending on education has more than doubled in real terms since the early 2000s. In most countries, the bulk of the increased spending has come from increases in overall government revenues brought about by healthy economic growth. Increased education spending has also supported a large increase in educational access over the same period. Children (particularly poor children) start school earlier and stay in school longer (World Bank, 2018). Yet these impressive achievements pale in comparison to need. Estimates show that the total share of national income devoted to education in low-income countries would need to double to achieve goals similar to the SDGs by 2030. And while access to education has improved, 90 percent of 10-year-olds in low-income countries are unable to read a short, age-appropriate text with comprehension (World Bank, 2019). Moreover, the COVID-19 pandemic has impacted public finances dramatically, and the outlook for maintaining recent increases in education funding is not encouraging.

Mobilizing additional resources is only part of the challenge. Research shows that recent increases in public education spending are associated with relatively small changes in education outcomes. The reasons why education systems struggle to use resources effectively are many. Overall, levels of spending and the use of funds may not be aligned with learning objectives, spending may not be allocated equitably, funds may not reach schools or may not be used for their intended purposes, and government agencies may lack the capacity to use funds efficiently. Strengthening public financial management systems, introducing allocation mechanisms that adjust for need, and building effective systems to monitor the use of funds can improve the use of education funding and support efforts to achieve learning for all.

This chapter explores these issues, with a focus on populations at the bottom of the pyramid (Wagner et al., 2018). The next section looks briefly at education spending inequalities between countries and the issues associated with narrowing these gaps. The following sections then focus on spending disparities within countries, and how available funding can be used more effectively to provide quality learning opportunities for all children, particularly those at the bottom of the pyramid.

Global spending inequalities

Between 1998 and 2017, government education spending increased by 80 percent, from $2.9 to $5.3 trillion in real terms (Figure 1). Spending growth has been most rapid in low- and lower-middle-income countries. For example, since the 1990s, real education spending in low-income countries almost tripled (Figure 1). Despite these faster rates of spending growth, low- and lower-middle-income countries account for less than 20 percent of total education spending, even though 60 percent of children between the ages of 5 and 24 live in these countries (see Figure 1).

Global spending inequalities translate into large disparities in government education spending per child. Low-income countries spend considerably less per child than middle-income countries. For example, in 2014–18, low-income countries spent, on average, purchasing power parity (PPP) $188 per primary school aged child, compared to PPP $894 in lower-middle-income countries (Figure 2). While public spending per child has increased among all income groups, the gap between the poorest and wealthiest nations has not closed, and in some cases has widened. For example, in 1998–2001, lower-middle-income countries spent nearly 11 times as much per primary school child than low-income countries (PPP $1,226 compared to PPP $109). By 2014–17 they spent

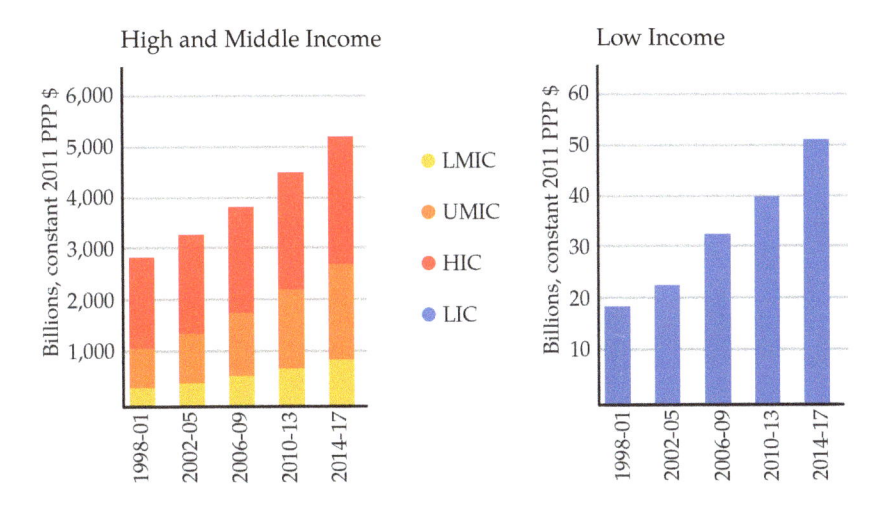

Fig. 1. Public education spending estimates, constant 2011 PPP dollars (billions), 1999–2017. Source: World Bank calculations based on World Development Indicators, UIS, and IMF online databases. Note: Total spending is estimated using income group averages of GDP and public education spending as a share of GDP.

almost 13 times as much as low-income countries (PPP $2,488 compared to PPP $188).

Looking over a child's whole school career reveals stark differences between how much rich and poor countries invest in education. By the age of 18, a child growing up in a low-income country will have attended school for 8 years compared to 13 years in a high-income country. Overall, their government will have invested about $1,300 on educating them, with almost all of that money ($900) spent on salaries. In contrast, a high-income country will have devoted $111,000 (100 times more), with a significant share devoted to other learning resources beyond salary spending.

Lower levels of public spending put a greater burden on lower-income households to contribute to education expenses. Comparable information on household education spending at the country level is relatively scarce. However, Al-Samarrai et al. (2019) find that households in low-income countries provided 41 percent of all education spending compared to only about 13 percent in high-income countries. Evidence from many countries shows that the direct costs of schooling are a major barrier to school attendance, and reforms that have lowered them have resulted in improvements in education outcomes (Fredriksen & Craissati, 2009).

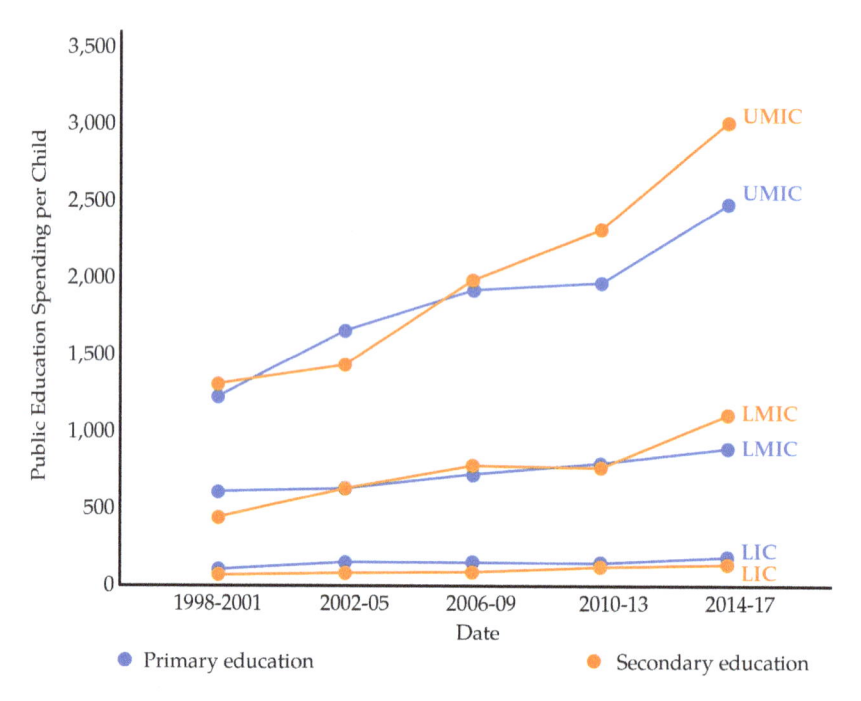

Fig. 2. Public education spending per child (constant 2015 PPP $), 1998–2001 to 2014–17. Real spending per child has generally risen in low-income and middle-income countries, but the gap between income groups has widened. Source: World Bank calculations using UIS and IMF online databases. Note: LIC = low-income country, LMIC = lower-middle-income country, and UMIC = upper-middle-income country.

The ongoing COVID-19 pandemic risks exacerbating education spending inequalities between low- and lower-middle-income countries. While the impacts on education financing are still uncertain at this stage, the pandemic is having a negative effect on all sources of education funding (Al-Samarrai, 2020). Yet there is a need for additional funding to support learners while schools are closed, to reopen schools safely, and to make up for the learning losses that have occurred during lockdowns (Azevedo et al., 2020; Rogers & Sabarwal, 2020). The ability of low-income countries to both protect existing levels of education funding and respond to the additional COVID-19-related needs is more limited compared to that of wealthier countries. Without efforts to protect public education spending, there is a risk that the pandemic will widen the gaps in both education spending and outcomes between low- and high-income countries.

Mobilizing more resources for education

Ensuring that all children have access to good-quality education will require unprecedented increases in public funding in many countries. Recent global estimates undertaken by UNESCO, the Education Commission, and the IMF all point to very large financing gaps associated with achieving the Sustainable Development Goals (UNESCO, 2015; Education Commission, 2016; Gaspar et al., 2019). For instance, the Education Commission estimates that public spending (including development assistance) as a percentage of GDP for pre-tertiary education would need to increase from 3 percent to 8 percent in LICs between 2015 and 2030 to achieve SDG-like goals (equivalent to an increase from $27 billion to $102 billion). This kind of increase is unprecedented. No low- or lower-middle-income country has been able to achieve an increase of this kind over the last 15 years. Only Senegal came close, increasing public education spending from three to seven percent of GDP between 1998 and 2014.

Over the next 15 years, rapid population growth will have a big impact on the ability of LICs and LMICs to mobilize the resources they need. Between 2020 and 2035, the school-aged population in low-income countries and sub-Saharan Africa is projected to increase by approximately a third, from 0.9 to 1.2 billion (Figure 3). Providing sufficient school spaces, teachers, and other resources for this growing population will put significant strain on already stretched government budgets. Population growth rates in the fastest growing low-income countries will mean that the school-aged population will increase by around 40 percent over the next 15 years. In these countries, government education spending, in real terms, would need to increase at a similar rate just to maintain existing levels of access and quality. While low-income countries have managed to increase annual education spending at a much faster rate in recent years, population growth rates will restrict the funding available to expand education access to more children and improve learning outcomes.

While development assistance will remain important in low-income countries, the bulk of the additional funding will need to come from domestic sources. Overall, levels of official development assistance (ODA) to education have been declining over the last 15 years. However, ODA made up about 21 percent of total public education spending in low-income countries or just under 1 percent of GDP (Al-Samarrai et al., 2019). However, there is a lot of variation around the average, with aid to education in Malawi in 2017 representing about 2.4 percent of GDP compared to only 0.7 percent in Madagascar.

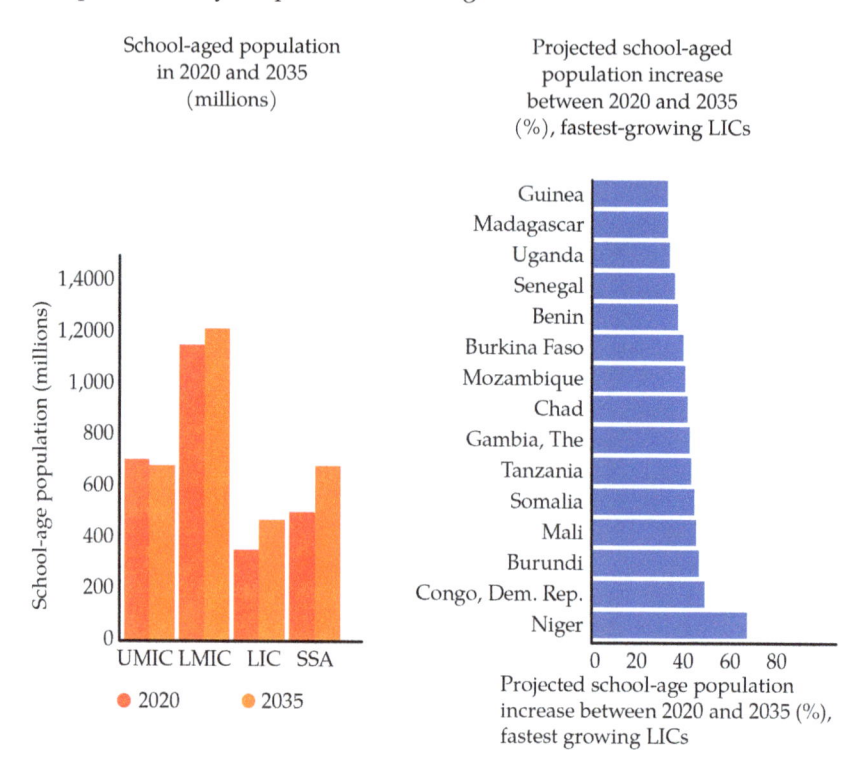

Fig. 3. Rapid population growth will put significant pressure on government education budgets. Source: United Nations Population Division (2019). Note: School-aged population includes children between 5 and 24 years of age. World Bank income group classifications are used to group countries and are as follows: LIC=low-income country, LMIC = lower-middle-income country, UMIC = upper-middle-income country. SSA = sub-Saharan Africa.

The fiscal space available for education differs considerably across countries, but falls short of the projected needs to universalize good-quality basic education. While definitions of fiscal space differ, it refers to the financing available to pursue national objectives, which arises from enacting a set of feasible and sustainable policies to increase resource availability while at the same time maintaining macroeconomic stability. It can include the space created by increasing government revenues (including development assistance) or by borrowing to fund differences between revenues and spending. At the sectoral level, it includes the potential to obtain a greater share of the overall government budget as well as improved spending efficiency. Low- and lower-middle-income countries vary considerably in the fiscal space they have to mobilize more funding for education. Figure 4 provides information on two key indicators of fiscal space in education for LICs and LMICs. The horizontal and vertical lines indicate the lower-middle-income average for education spending as a share of total government spending, and total government spending as a share of national income, respectively. They represent plausible levels of spending that low- and lower-middle-income countries could be expected to reach over time. Based on these benchmarks, countries in the lower-left quadrant, for example, Uganda and Lao, have significant fiscal space since total government spending and education's share are below the averages for lower-middle-income countries. In contrast, total government spending and the share going to education in countries like Senegal and Moldova exceed lower-middle-income averages and suggest that fiscal space may be more constrained in these countries. The dashed line in Figure 4 plots the combinations of total government spending and the share going to education, which are equivalent to public spending on education of six percent of GDP. Afghanistan and Moldova are close to this line, but other countries would need to go far beyond existing average levels to achieve this level of public education spending and move closer to the eight percent of GDP required to achieve quality universal basic education (see Figure 4).

While mobilizing the required resources for education is challenging, many countries have the potential to mobilize more domestic resources. At present, developing countries currently take in approximately half the tax dollars per GDP than advanced economies do. Besley and Persson (2014) note that many factors get in the way of adequate levels of taxation in developing countries today, including tax exemptions,

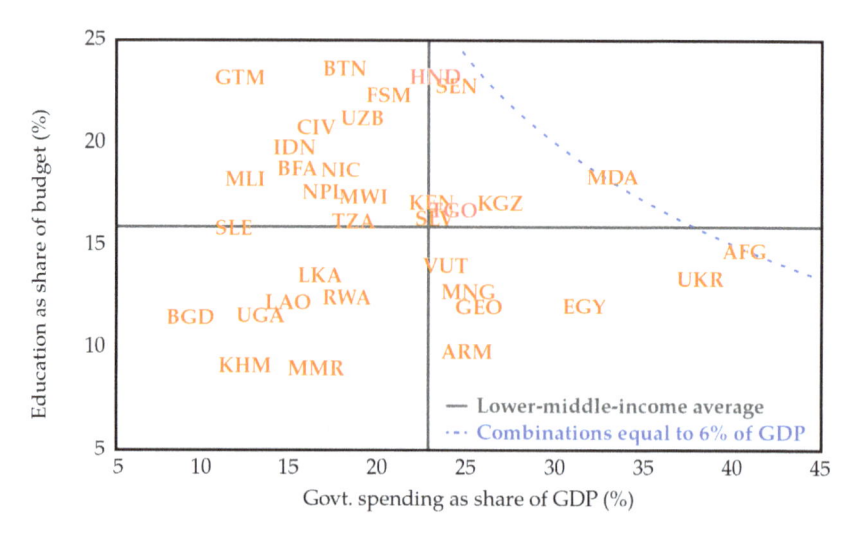

Fig. 4. Education as a share of total government budget, and government spending as a share of GDP in low- and lower-middle-income countries (%), 2014–17. Fiscal space for mobilizing greater funding for education varies considerably. Source: World Bank calculations based on World Development Indicators, UIS, and IMF online databases.

poor tax administration, an underdeveloped private sector, and informality, to name a few. Weak institutions and corruption can lead to both poor tax administration and a lack of trust in government, which itself undermines tax compliance. Also, many developing countries have failed to accomplish the level of state building required to broaden their tax base, such as the ability to withhold tax directly from income. Developing countries can raise revenues through a range of actions including deploying various forms of taxation, raising tax compliance, and strengthening tax administration. In addition, taxes on activities that directly harm people's health remain an option in many countries. Countries will also need to explore a variety of non-tax revenue sources, including the appropriate management of natural resource wealth.

Moreover, many countries could shift public funding from other sectors to education. Many countries invest in costly energy or other subsidies that are often a drain on public coffers, and frequently regressive. In Saudi Arabia, spending on energy subsidies is 4.6 percent of GDP, while in Zambia, it is 7.1 percent. While Saudi Arabia spends a similar amount on education, Zambia spends only 1 percent of GDP on education. Many subsidies not only have high costs, they can also disproportionately benefit the wealthy and lead to distortions in the economy by incentivizing the use of cheap energy. An analysis of the unequal benefits of energy subsidies across 32 countries showed that the richest 20 percent of households receive about six times more in subsidies than the poorest 20 percent (Coady et al., 2015). Gasoline subsidies have the most regressive distribution, with more than 83 percent of benefits going to the richest 40 percent of households. These subsidies can be politically difficult to dislodge, particularly when there is public concern about the outcomes for people. When the government of Nigeria attempted to repeal its fuel subsidies in 2012 it encountered heavy public resistance and was eventually forced to backtrack, despite its plans to direct the additional resources to maternal and child health services.

The COVID-19 pandemic is having a significant negative impact on funding for education, which will make achieving national goals even harder. The economic shock associated with the COVID-19 pandemic is likely to be significantly larger than anything seen since the financial crisis of 2008/09. It will have a negative effect on the three main sources of education financing. First, government revenues have declined sharply as a result of lockdowns aimed at reducing the spread of the virus. For example, between 2019 and 2020, government revenue as a share of GDP is expected to fall from 17.2 to 16.4 percent in sub-Saharan Africa (IMF, 2020). While in the short-term, governments are expected to maintain or even increase overall levels of spending, there is expected to be a significant slowdown in the growth of government spending on education in low-income countries and, in the worst-hit countries, forecasts suggest that spending might fall (Al-Samarrai, 2020). Second, household education spending, which makes up 29 percent of total education spending in low-income countries, is also expected to fall. Poorer households are expected to suffer significant economic hardships. COVID-19 could push between 71–100 million people into extreme poverty in 2020 and increase the extreme-poverty rate for the first time since 1998. South Asia will account for almost half and sub-Saharan Africa more than a third of the projected rise in poverty numbers (World Bank, 2020a). Finally, aid to education, another key source of funding, particularly for low-income countries, only recently recovered from the drops experienced after the financial crisis in 2008 and 2009.[1] Estimates suggest that aid to education may drop by as much as $2 billion by 2022 due to the massive drops in national income in high-income countries (UNESCO, 2020b). Collectively, these effects on education funding will significantly widen the financing gap associated with achieving national education goals. For example, updated global estimates of achieving the education SDGs estimate a $30–45 billion increase in the global financing gap due to the additional needs associated with COVID-19 and the declines in domestic financing (UNESCO, 2020a).

Improving spending equity

Public spending on education can also be highly unequal within countries, with wealthier groups often capturing a greater share of the available resources. Using a benefit-incidence approach, it is possible to get a sense of how public funding for education is distributed across different income groups within a country. Analysis of this kind generally shows that total public education spending tends to be unequally distributed, particularly in low-income countries (Figure 5). These results are largely due to differences in participation rates by level of education between income groups. For example, it is common for the poorest and wealthiest quintiles to have similar enrollment rates in public primary schooling, but a far greater proportion of children in the wealthiest quintile are enrolled in public tertiary institutions. Since per-student expenditure is much higher in tertiary institutions, this tends to skew the distribution of public education funding in favor of wealthier quintiles. These differences in enrollment patterns by income quintile tend to be most pronounced in low-income countries, and result in significant inequalities in public education funding across the income distribution (see Figure 5).

Analysis of this kind masks large regional disparities in education spending that often reinforce existing patterns of inequality. Benefit-incidence studies often do not factor into their calculations the significant differences in how much governments spend on each student in different parts of a country. It is very common for a child living in one part of

---

[1] Aid to education made up approximately 12.5 percent of total education spending in low-income countries in recent years (UNESCO, 2019).

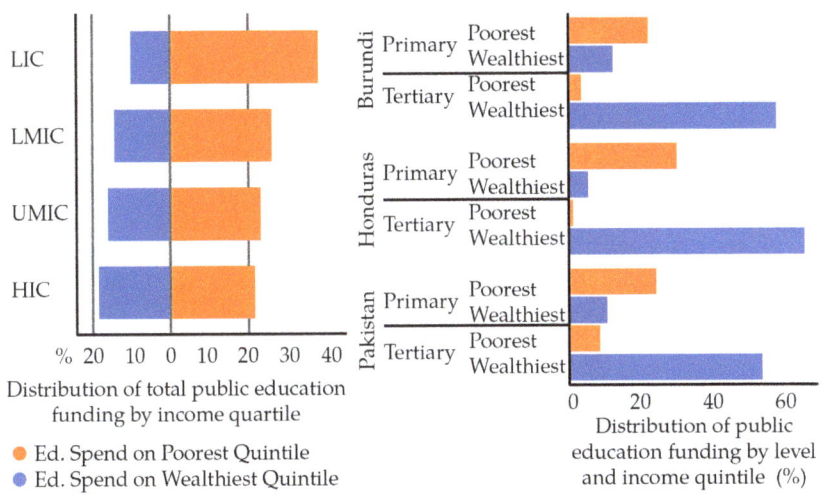

7. Financing Education at the Bottom of the Pyramid

Fig. 5. Differences in education participation imply that public funding for education is distributed unequally. Source: Left-hand panel: UNICEF (2020). Right-hand panel: Burundi: Tsimpo & Wodon (2014). Pakistan: Asghar & Zahra (2012).

a country to go to a school that has several times more funding than a school in another part of the same country (Figure 6). For example, in Sudan, spending per child is approximately six times higher in the highest-spending region compared to the lowest-spending region. Subnational public spending differences tend to reinforce existing patterns of poverty and disadvantage. It might be expected that poorer regions in a country receive more education funding, since providing services in remote regions can be more expensive and children from more disadvantaged backgrounds need more support. However, in many countries, per-capita education spending is significantly lower in poorer regions than in wealthier regions. For example, in Uganda, the relationship between district per-capita spending on education and levels of poverty is negative and statistically significant (see Figure 6).

Subnational spending inequalities are often the result of public funding allocation mechanisms. In decentralized countries, differences in education spending are driven by the overall revenues a subnational administration has and, where they have autonomy, their preferences for education compared with other priorities. Since many subnational governments rely on transfers from the central government to fund basic education, the way these mechanisms allocate funding across

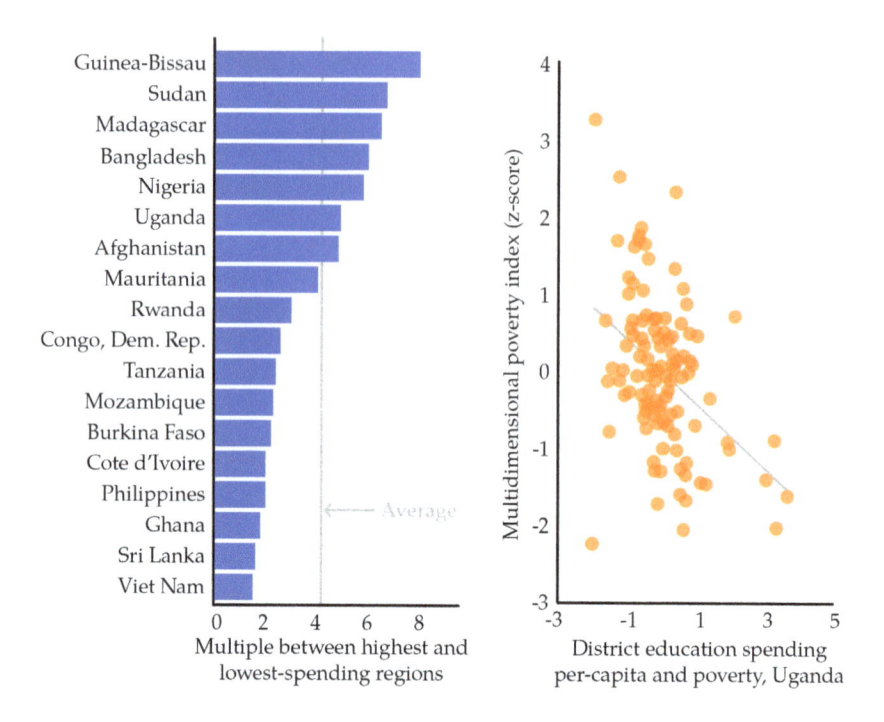

Fig. 6. Education spending inequalities are large and can reinforce existing patterns of poverty and disadvantage. Source: Left-hand panel: Manuel et al. (2019) and various World Bank Public Expenditure Reviews. Right-hand panel: Manuel et al. (2019).

regions has implications for the levels and distribution of education funding. For example, in Indonesia a general transfer from the central government accounts for over 60 percent of subnational revenue (World Bank, 2020b). However, these transfers are allocated very unequally, since they are allocated on a district rather than per-capita basis. The district with the highest per-capita transfer has 40 times more revenue than the district with the lowest per-capita transfer, even accounting for differences in the costs of service delivery between districts (Al-Samarrai & Lewis, 2021). This can lead to major disparities in the quality of education offered in different parts of a country (see Box 1).

Reforming allocation mechanisms can reduce inequalities in spending and education outcomes across regions. Many countries use the intergovernmental fiscal transfer system to try and address education spending inequalities between regions. For example, in China, the new

Box 1: Differences in district revenue result in large differences in education spending and quality in Indonesia.

> Education spending in Indonesia differs considerably between districts. Districts rely heavily on fiscal transfers from the central government to fund basic services, including basic education and other delegated responsibilities. For example, in 2018, approximately 85 percent of all district-level spending was funded by a number of fiscal transfers from the central government. The largest transfer is not allocated according to a district's population size, but on a district-level basis. This results in large differences in transfers between districts. The smallest 20 percent of districts, in terms of population size, received per-capita transfers that were approximately five times as large as the largest and most populous 20 percent of districts. These differences in revenue translate into very different levels of spending on education across districts. In 2016, the highest-spending district spent 21 times as much as the lowest-spending district on a per-capita basis, even after controlling for delivery costs.
>
> Large differences in per-capita revenues translate into very different levels of education quality across Indonesia. In some districts, education funding is so low that many schools are unable to achieve a set of minimum service standards. Differences in funding also lead to very different student-teacher ratios, with some districts registering less than 10 students per teacher in primary education, while others had more than 30. It has been estimated that over 17 percent of teachers could be redistributed across districts to make class sizes more equal and still comply with maximum class sizes of 32 in primary education. The quality of teachers that also varies. In 2015, the proportion of teachers with a bachelor's degree in the relatively poor province of West Kalimantan was only 20 percent, compared to 60 percent in Jakarta, a wealthy province including the capital city.

education funding mechanism introduced in 2006 includes specific purpose transfers that provide different levels of funding in recognition of the differences in the ability of provinces and counties to fund their education systems from their own revenues (Al-Samarrai & Lewis, 2021). In Brazil, the Fund for the Development of Primary Education and Appreciation of Teachers (FUNDEB) addresses equity issues by guaranteeing minimum levels of education spending across municipalities (Loureiro et al., 2021). Prior to the introduction of FUNDEB's predecessor in 1996, education spending differences between municipalities were large due to the limited revenues of poorer municipalities. Before the program started, the wealthier south, southeast, and central west regions in Brazil were spending almost twice as much per student as the poorer regions in the north and northeast (Gordon & Vegas, 2005). These spending disparities led to significant differences in education outcomes and exacerbated more general socioeconomic inequalities across regions. FUNDEB and its predecessor FUNDEF aimed to narrow spending inequalities by redistributing a portion of federal, state, and municipal tax revenues to guarantee a minimum level of spending per student across all municipalities. The funds have been successful at narrowing spending inequalities between municipalities and, in particular, increasing the funding of education in the poorest states (Gordon & Vegas, 2005; Cruz & Silva, 2020).

The FUNDEB and FUNDEF transfers not only raised education spending in some of the poorer municipalities in Brazil, it also contributed to narrowing inequalities in education outcomes. There has been considerable research into the effect of these funds on education outcomes. Overall, the findings suggest that these funds increased enrollment in basic education particularly in poorer municipalities, improved education quality, and narrowed achievement gaps (Gordon & Vegas, 2005; Cruz & Rocha, 2018; Cruz, 2018). A recent study exploring the impact of FUNDEB on upper-secondary-school student achievement found that it had increased average achievement in both Portuguese and mathematics, and the gains were larger for the poorer students (Silveira et al., 2017).[2]

School funding formulas have also been used effectively to address spending inequalities and improve the support and outcomes of disadvantaged children. School grants have been used in many countries to help reduce the cost burden on parents, particularly poorer parents. Evaluations show that grants of this kind are successful at improving access to education and increasing attainment (McEwan, 2013; Snilstveit et al., 2015). For example, grants in Niger and Uganda increased the number of children enrolling in primary school, and in Mexico, grants improved student progress and retention (Grogan, 2009; Gertler et al., 2012; Beasley & Huillery, 2013). Funding formulas can also be

---

2 FUNDEB is set to expire at the end of 2020, but is likely to be renewed and improved to strengthen its impact on spending equity. It will also include a performance element, based on the successful experience of the state of Ceara.

designed to account for the different needs of schools serving different populations. For example, many OECD countries include weights or special allocations in their formulas to provide additional targeted funding for students from disadvantaged backgrounds, students with special needs, or refugees (see Box 2 and OECD, 2017). School funding formulas in developing countries also attempt to account for the differences associated with the costs of delivering education to different student groups. For example, some district-level funding formulas in Indonesia include an equity component to address the cost differentials associated with delivering education in different parts of the district (World Bank, 2012). Schools located on small and remote islands are provided with a 20 percent higher per-student amount to cover the higher travel-related costs (Al-Samarrai et al., 2018).

Improving spending effectiveness

Improving the efficiency of public spending is also critical to ensuring universal access to good-quality education, particularly for poor and disadvantaged children. Given the challenge of mobilizing additional resources for education, it is important that funds are used as effectively as possible to improve the education outcomes of all students. However, studies show that many low-income countries could improve the effectiveness of existing spending.

Cross-country evidence points to significant differences in how effectively public spending is translated into education outcomes. For example, Burundi and Togo spend a similar amount per school-aged child, but that spending provides one additional learning-adjusted year of schooling in Togo compared to Burundi (see Figure 7). These comparisons suggest that spending is more inefficient in Burundi than in Togo. Similarly, Côte d'Ivoire spends more than twice as much as Burkina Faso, but its spending delivers a similar amount of learning for each child. Similar patterns between spending and outcomes are also seen at the subnational level, and also suggest that some regions appear to be more efficient than others when it comes to using their education funds.

Box 2: The "pupil premium" in England.

Introduced in 2011, the pupil premium provides government-funded schools in England with additional per-student funding to raise the attainment of disadvantaged pupils and narrow inequalities between them and other students. In 2014/15, schools received an additional £1,300 ($2,031) per primary-aged student and £935 ($1,461) per secondary-aged student. Rough calculations suggest that an average-sized secondary school received approximately £200,000 ($312,500) in additional funding through the pupil premium, which is the equivalent of five full-time teachers.

The main criterion of deprivation used to calculate eligibility is the number of students in the school that have received free school meals over the last six years. Head teachers and school governing bodies are accountable for the use of these funds in two ways. First, tables that outline the performance of disadvantaged students compared to their peers are made available to the public. Second, schools are required to publish details online each year of how they have used the premium and what impact it has had.

Schools typically use the additional resources to hire more teachers and teaching assistants in order to introduce special programs for disadvantaged students. In addition, resources are frequently used to allow eligible students to participate fully in after school activities.

A study of the implementation of the pupil premium found:

- Since the introduction of the premium, an increasing number of schools are targeting the funding more effectively at improving the attainment of disadvantaged students and narrowing learning disparities.
- The best schools combine a series of targeted interventions with robust tracking systems to evaluate effectiveness.
- Governing bodies in these schools take strategic responsibility for ensuring the pupil premium supports eligible pupils. They also hold school leaders accountable for the use of these additional resources and the results obtained.
- Challenges remain in some schools with leaders and governing bodies in the weakest schools failing to ensure the pupil premium is used effectively to narrow attainment gaps.

Sources: OFSTED (2014) and
www.gov.uk/pupil-premium-information-for-schools-and-alternative-provision-settings.

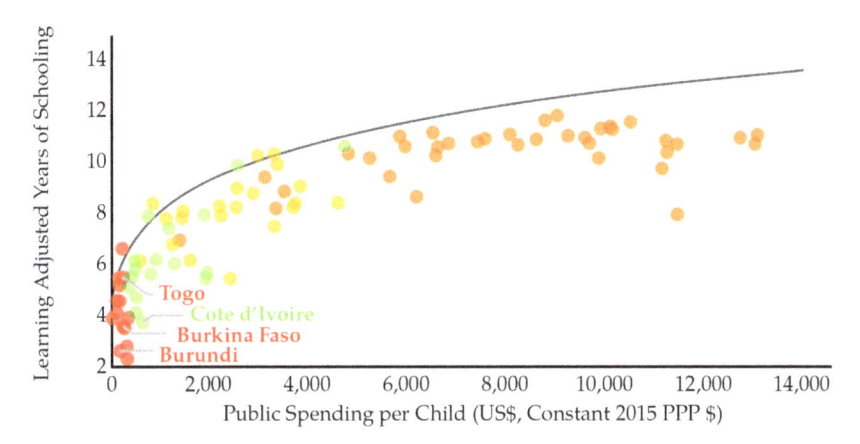

7. *Financing Education at the Bottom of the Pyramid*   209

Fig. 7. Association between spending per child and enrollment-adjusted learning. Source: Expenditure Per Child and Learning-Adjusted Years of Schooling (LAYS), 2015. World Bank calculations based on HCI, UIS, and IMF data. Note: The stochastic frontier is drawn from data and analytical work described in Al-Samarrai et al. (2019).

Looking at the relationship between spending and outcomes over time suggests that recent spending increases have not had a big effect on learning outcomes. Cross-sectional comparisons are only a rough indication of how efficient countries are in translating spending into outcomes. Another way to explore the efficiency of public education spending is to look at changes in spending in countries over time. While data limitations make this difficult, the evidence suggests that, on average, a doubling of spending per child improves outcomes by about a half of a learning-adjusted year of schooling (Al-Samarrai et al., 2019).[3] However, the effect of spending increases in countries that spend relatively little per child and are inefficient are more promising. For most low-income countries, this suggests that spending increases are likely to have a larger effect on outcomes (a finding that complements those of Crouch and Slade on investments among learners at the bottom quintile—see their chapter in this volume).

There are many proximate causes of spending inefficiencies, and their relative importance differs for each country. The previous section highlighted how inequitable spending can lead to an inefficient use

---

3   The size of the effects is similar to those seen in health (Gallet & Doucouliagos, 2017).

of resources. For example, student-teacher ratios in some districts in Indonesia are sub-optimal, and redistributing teachers to districts where student-teacher ratios are very high would likely lead to an efficiency gain (see again Box 1 above). This is important to keep in mind, as improving the efficiency of public spending can also improve equity outcomes through a better distribution of existing resources. There are many sources of inefficiency in the education sector, and estimates of the costs of inefficiency are high. For example, estimates from India suggest that inefficiency may account for as much as 60 percent of public primary-school spending (Pritchett & Aiyar, 2014). In Indonesia, inefficiencies in teacher distribution were estimated to account for approximately 17 percent of the overall teacher wage bill (Chang et al., 2013). While the magnitude and type of inefficiencies will vary across countries, they result from a combination of two main factors: spending decisions that are not aligned with learning equity and outcomes, and the failure of allocated funds to reach schools and be used as they were intended.

Sub-optimal spending decisions

Overall levels of spending and the decisions on how funds are used are often not aligned with sector objectives. Despite most education-sector plans identifying learning as a key objective, few include it as a key performance indicator when making budget decisions. For example, in the Philippines, government strategies and spending documents state that the overarching mission of the Department for Education is to promote the right to quality, equitable, and culture-based basic education (Republic of the Philippines, 2016). Yet the key performance indicators that are part of the budget process for the department focus only on whether students enroll and complete schooling, with no specific indicators included for equity or learning outcomes. And even where equity and learning are key goals, the way governments are organized can often mean that responsibility for key tasks is split between different agencies, with no single agency accountable for the final outcome (World Bank, 2018).

Inefficiencies also arise from spending and policy decisions that fail to make the best use of resources. The internal efficiency of education systems in many low-income countries is low because of high rates of repetition in the lower grades of primary school (Bashir et al., 2018). It is estimated that this repetition in the early grades costs between 5 and 10 percent of the overall education budget each year (Crouch et al., 2019). Addressing the "early-grade bulge" by expanding access to early childhood education or by introducing guidelines to ensure a better intra-school distribution of teachers and resources has the potential to improve efficiency and raise education outcomes using existing funding.

The evidence base for improving policy and decision-making on resource use has grown significantly over the last decade. For example, the number of evaluations of interventions aimed at improving learning outcomes in developing countries increased from 19 to 299 between 2000 and 2016 (World Bank, 2018). This growing evidence base can help policymakers choose the most appropriate interventions to improve learning. It can also help identify the most appropriate mix of inputs and actions required to ensure that resources are used effectively. For example, school funding may be used more effectively when the systems used to govern the use of these funds is also simultaneously strengthened. In Indonesia, a randomized control trial found that the provision of school grants alone did not have an effect on student achievement, but when grants were coupled with efforts to strengthen the link between schools and local village councils, learning outcomes improved (Pradhan et al., 2014). Other evidence suggests that coupling school-level funding with incentives for teachers to utilize these funds to improve student performance can also raise outcomes and improve efficiency (Mbiti et al., 2019).

Understanding the political economy of the education sector is critical in order to successfully apply insights from this evidence base to improve efficiency. Education systems are complex and involve many different actors (e.g., parents, teachers, children, private providers) with different interests that are not always aligned. This can often mean that introducing changes to an entire education system that have been shown to work in a small number of test schools is not so simple. For example, the Kenyan government recently tried to introduce teacher-related reforms that had been introduced successfully by an NGO in a small number of schools. However, scaling up the reforms failed because of a combination of implementation challenges and political economy issues (Bold et al., 2013; Duflo et al., 2015). Experiences like this demonstrate that reforms that aim to improve spending efficiency must be both technically and politically feasible to be effective.

Redirection of education funds

Inefficiencies in education also arise because funds do not get to where they are supposed to go, or are not used for their intended purposes. When funds fail to reach schools or when funds are diverted or unused, the quality of education suffers. Surveys that track the flow of funds within the public financial management system have highlighted many of these issues. For example, in primary and secondary schools in the Philippines, 23 percent of budgeted operational funds were not received (World Bank, 2016). In some cases, schools receive resources, but do not distribute them in the way that central authorities intended. Inefficiencies in textbook distribution systems, for example, prevent many books from actually reaching children (Read, 2015). In Sierra Leone, even when textbooks were successfully distributed, school principals were reluctant to distribute them because they were unsure whether or when they would receive future deliveries (Sabarwal et al., 2014). In other cases, funds allocated to improve education services remain unused because of limited planning capacity and weaknesses in public procurement systems.

Inefficiencies also arise because funds are not available for maintenance, or because staff are unable to carry out their duties due to lack of complementary funding. Weaknesses in planning can result in situations where schools are built, but teachers are not recruited or maintenance funds are not provided, resulting in faster depreciation rates of key infrastructure, books, and other equipment (Read, 2015). Often complementary resources needed for other inputs to be effective are not available. In Bangladesh, district education officers found it challenging to carry out their school quality-assurance duties because travel allowances were not released (FMRP, 2005). These relatively small travel payments reduced the overall efficiency of the much larger salary payments of district education officers.

Spending inefficiencies of this kind can disproportionately affect poorer households and children. When budgets are tight or not released, it is often the poorer and more remote schools that suffer. In the example of school operating expenses in the Philippines, per-student allocations for poorer schools are actually much larger than for schools serving wealthier students. However, schools that serve a greater proportion of poorer children receive a smaller proportion of their allocated funds, which results in similar levels of per-student funding for poor and wealthy students (Figure 8). This further reinforces the inequality in total education spending per student (Figure 8).

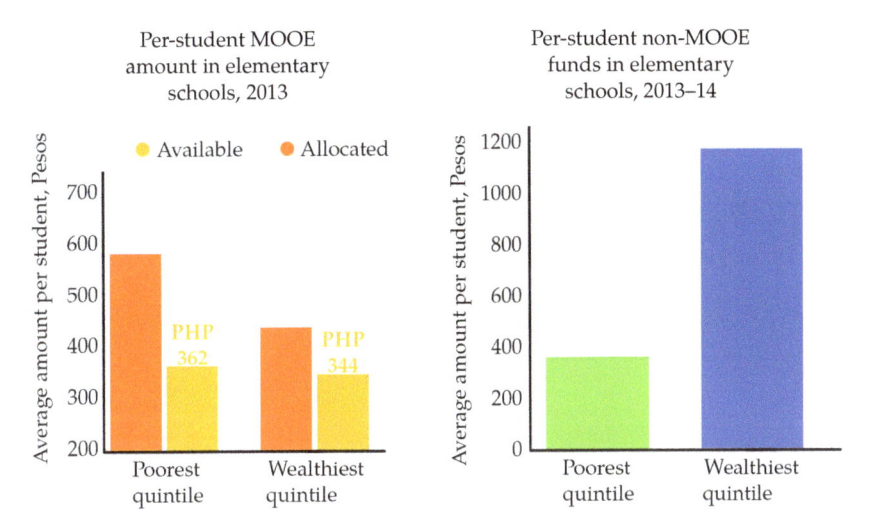

Fig. 8. Elementary school per-student funding by source, 2013 and 2013/14 school year. MOOE refers to maintenance and other operating expenses. Funds that schools receive do not reduce inequalities in overall school funding in the Philippines. Source: World Bank (2016).

Improving efficiency and equity

Tackling many of these identified inefficiencies requires strengthening public financial systems. However, the ability of government agencies to manage public funding is sometimes limited. For example, Public Expenditure and Financial Accountability (PEFA) assessments suggest that many low- and middle-income countries have low levels of capacity in key areas of service delivery (Figure 9). For example, only around a half of the 70 countries assessed had any kind of system in place to check that resources intended for schools, health clinics, and other service delivery units actually reached the frontline and were used as intended. More detailed capacity assessments in education also show that public financial management systems have been slow to change, even when significant investment has been made to strengthen them (World Bank, 2013). There are many aspects to strengthening the way government systems plan, budget, and utilize funding, but the remaining part of this section focuses on three: (1) improving sector financial planning; (2) strengthening the links between spending and outcomes; and (3) procuring better data for monitoring and accountability.

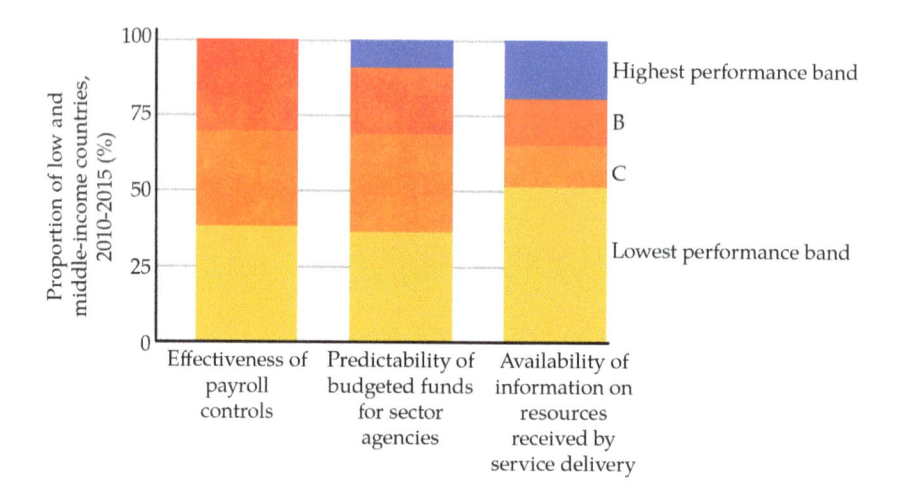

Fig. 9. Government planning and monitoring capacity for service delivery is weak. Proportion of low- and middle-income countries by Public Expenditure and Financial Accountability (PEFA) rating, 2010–2015. Source: Public Expenditure and Financial Accountability database. Notes: A four-point ordinal scale based on specific criteria for each dimension is used to score country performance.

The planning process in many developing countries is ineffective at matching sector needs, with a realistic assessment of the resources available over the medium-term. Aligning education goals with credible estimates of the resources available to the sector is challenging. Most developing countries undertake a five-year sector planning cycle, often supported through Global Partnership for Education (GPE) grants and technical assistance from local education groups. A partial review of recent sector plans shows that after two years of implementation, they have funding shortfalls of between 16 and 20 percent. A recent assessment of GPE support to the development of sector plans also reported significant weaknesses in the standards associated with plan implementation, financial sustainability, feasibility, and monitorability (Universalia, 2019).

Projections of resource availability often lie at the heart of these shortfalls, with plans including overambitious forecasts of economic growth, government revenue collection, and the priority that education will receive in annual budget negotiations. Unrealistic resource mobilization projections can result in major challenges for key government education policies. These shortfalls can leave important policies underfunded, and reduce the accountability for the ways funds are used to support learning. In Tanzania, for example, public education spending has stagnated since 2016, despite large projected increases aimed at supporting the fee-free basic education policy. As a result of the policy, significant increases in enrollment have occurred, but without additional funding, class sizes have increased, and the quality of education has deteriorated. Credible financing strategies are needed in many countries to better inform the sector planning process, align funding more clearly towards learning goals, and ensure that resources are used equitably and efficiently. These strategies need to assess macroeconomic conditions and overall fiscal space in order to accurately estimate resource availability from all sources (domestic, household, and external) over the medium- and long-term, as well as develop monitorable indicators for resource mobilization, spending equity, and efficiency.

A key element of better planning is strengthening the link between public spending and outcomes. In some cases, performance-based funding mechanisms can be used to drive better spending efficiency (Lee & Medina, 2019). For example, evidence in Zambia shows that the introduction of incentives to improve the efficiency of the book supply chain has resulted in more books getting to schools on time (Hong et al., 2020). In other cases, performance-based transfers to local governments and schools have led to improvements in outcomes and better use of public funds (Al-Samarrai et al., 2018; Loureiro et al., 2021). In other cases, shifting the focus of planning and budgeting processes towards intermediate- and higher-level outcomes can also go some way to improving the effectiveness of public education spending. For example, in Colombia, a new information system that can assess different quality dimensions has been developed to ensure that resources are targeted more effectively to schools (Cerdan-Infantes & Zavala Garcia, 2019).

Publicly available information on government budgets, allocations, and utilization of funding in the education sector is often quite limited. In 2016, only half of all countries reported basic information on public education spending to the UNESCO Institute of Statistics. At the country level, it is difficult for schools, parents, and students to assess whether they are receiving the levels of funding that they are entitled to, and in many cases they have little information on how effectively funds are being used. At the global level, efforts to monitor overall levels of government spending and aid have existed for some time, but there has been far less attention on monitoring country-level funding commitments and improving spending efficiency and equity. For example, only one in six countries has an annual education-monitoring report, and even fewer examine education funding (UNESCO, 2019). Improving the transparency of education spending has the potential to strengthen accountability mechanisms as well as help to evaluate whether scarce resources are being used efficiently and equitably.

Conclusion

In many low-income countries, improving education at the bottom of the pyramid will require mobilizing more resources. This chapter has shown that many countries need to spend significantly more on education if they are to provide good-quality education opportunities for all children. The ability to mobilize more resources and the speed at which it can be done differs across countries. The COVID-19 pandemic will undoubtedly make it much harder for many countries to mobilize the required resources. This makes it even more important to ensure that funding is used effectively and is reaching the poorest and most marginalized children. This chapter has shown that there are many areas of education spending that are inequitable and inefficient, but that a growing evidence base points to ways that these problems can be addressed. Using these experiences to generate context-specific approaches that address the twin challenges of mobilizing more funding and using it more effectively will be critical for improving education at the bottom of the pyramid.

References

Al-Samarrai, S. (2020). *The impact of the COVID-19 pandemic on education financing.* Washington, DC: World Bank.

Al-Samarrai, S., Cerdan-Infantes, P., & Lehe, J. D. (2019). *Mobilizing resources for education and improving spending effectiveness: Establishing realistic benchmarks based on past trends* (World Bank Policy Research Working Paper 8773). Washington, DC: World Bank.

Al-Samarrai, S., & Lewis, B. (2021). The Role of Intergovernmental Fiscal Transfers in Improving Education Outcomes. International Development in Focus. Washington, DC: World Bank.

Al-Samarrai, S., Shrestha, U., Hasan, A., Nakajima, N., Santoso, S., & Wijoyo, W. H. A. (2018). Introducing a performance-based component into Jakarta's school grants: What do we know about its impact after three years? *Economics of Education Review, 67,* 110–136.

Asghar, Z., & Zahra, M. (2012). A benefit incidence analysis of public spending on education in Pakistan using PSLM data. *The Lahore Journal of Economics, 17*(2), 111–136.

Azevedo, J. P., Hasan, A., Goldemberg, D., Iqbal, S. A., & Geven, K. (2020). *Simulating the potential impacts of COVID-19 school closures on schooling and learning outcomes: A set of global estimates.* Washington, DC: World Bank.

Bashir, S., Lockheed, M., Ninan, E., & Tan, J. P. (2018). *Facing forward.* Washington, DC: World Bank.

Beasley, E., & Huillery, E. (2013). *Empowering parents in school: What they can (not) do* (Sciences Po Economics Discussion Papers 2013–03). Sciences Po Department of Economics.

Besley, T., & Persson, T. (2014). Why do developing countries tax so little? *Journal of Economic Perspectives, 28*(4), 99–120.

Bold, T., Kimenyi, M., Mwabu, G., Ng'ang'a, A., & Sandefur, J. (2013). *Scaling-up what works: Experimental evidence on external validity in Kenyan education* (CSAE Working Paper Series). Centre for the Study of African Economies, University of Oxford.

Cerdan-Infantes, P., & Zavala Garcia, F. (2019). *Colombia: Can a management and information system improve education quality?* Washington, DC: World Bank.

Chang, M.-C., Shaeffer, S., Al-Samarrai, S., Ragatz, A., De Ree, J., & Stevenson, R. (2013). *Teacher reform in Indonesia: The role of politics and evidence in policy making.* Washington, DC: World Bank.

Coady, D., Parry, I. W., Sears, L., & Shang, B. (2015). *How large are global energy subsidies?* International Monetary Fund.

Crouch, L. A., Merseth, K., Devercelli, A. E., Choi, M. J., Denboba, A. D., & Gurgel, A. (2019). *Over-enrollment in the early grades*. Washington, DC: World Bank.

Cruz, G., & Rocha, R. (2018). Efeitos do FUNDEF/B sobre frequência escolar, fluxo escolar e trabalho infantil: uma análise com base nos Censos de 2000 e 2010. *Estudos Econômicos (São Paulo), 48*(1), 39–75.

Cruz, T. (2018). Teacher hiring decisions: How do governments react to an exogenous redistribution of education funds? *Economics of Education Review, 67*, 58–81.

Cruz, T., & Silva, T. (2020). Minimum spending in education and the flypaper effect. *Economics of Education Review, 77*, 102012.

Duflo, E., Dupas, P., & Kremer, M. (2015). School governance, teacher incentives, and pupil–teacher ratios: Experimental evidence from Kenyan primary schools. *Journal of Public Economics, 123*, 92–110.

Education Commission. (2016). *The learning generation: Investing in education for a changing world*. New York: International Commission on Financing Global Education Opportunity.

FMRP. (2005). *Social sector performance surveys: Secondary education in Bangladesh: Assessing service delivery*. Dhaka, OPM and FMRP.

Fredriksen, B., & Craissati, D. (2009). *Abolishing school fees in Africa: Lessons learned in Ethiopia, Ghana, Kenya and Mozambique*. Washington, DC: World Bank.

Gallet, C. A., & Doucouliagos, H. (2017). The impact of healthcare spending on health outcomes: A meta-regression analysis. *Social Science & Medicine, 179*, 9–17.

Gaspar, V., Amaglobeli, M. D., Garcia-Escribano, M. M., Prady, D., & Soto, M. (2019). *Fiscal policy and development: Human, social, and physical investments for the SDGs*. International Monetary Fund.

Gertler, P. J., Patrinos, H. A., & Rubio-Codina, M. (2012). Empowering parents to improve education: Evidence from rural Mexico. *Journal of Development Economics, 99*(1), 68–79.

Gordon, N., & Vegas, E. (2005). *Educational finance equalisation, spending, teacher quality, and student outcomes: The case of Brazil's FUNDEF* (Incentives to Improve Teaching: Lessons From Latin America Series). Washington, DC: World Bank.

Grogan, L. (2009). Universal primary education and school entry in Uganda. *Journal of African Economies, 18*(2), 183–211.

Hong, S. Y., Cao, X., & Mupuwaliywa, M. (2020). *Impact of financial incentives and the role of information and Communication in last-mile delivery of textbooks in Zambia*. Washington, DC: World Bank.

IMF. (2020). *Fiscal monitor: Policies to support people during the COVID-19 pandemic.* Washington, DC: International Monetary Fund.

Lee, J. D., & Medina, O. (2019). *Results-based financing in education: Learning from what works.* Washington, DC: World Bank.

Loureiro, A., Cruz, L., & Mello, M. (2021). Intergovernmental fiscal transfers and education outcomes in Brazil. In S. Al-Samarrai and B. Lewis (Eds.), *The role of intergovernmental fiscal transfers in improving education outcomes.* Washington, DC: World Bank.

Manuel, M., Coppard, D., Dodd, A., Desai, H., Watts, R., Christensen, Z., & Manea, S. (2019). *Subnational investment in human capital.* ODI. https://odi.org/en/publications/subnational-investment-in-human-capital/

Mbiti, I., Muralidharan, K., Romero, M., Schipper, Y., Manda, C., & Rajani, R. (2019). Inputs, incentives, and complementarities in education: Experimental evidence from Tanzania. *The Quarterly Journal of Economics, 134*(3), 1627–1673.

McEwan, P. (2013). Improving learning in primary schools of developing countries: A meta-analysis of randomized experiments. *Review of Educational Research, 85*(3), 353–394.

OECD. (2017). *The funding of school education: Connecting resources and learning.* Paris: OECD Publishing.

Pradhan, M., Suryadarma, D., Beatty, A., Wong, M., Gaduh, A., Alisjahbana, A., & Artha, R. P. (2014). Improving educational quality through enhancing community participation: Results from a randomized field experiment in Indonesia. *American Economic Journal, Applied Economics, 6*(2), 105.

Pritchett, L., & Aiyar, Y. (2014). *Value subtraction in public sector production: Accounting versus economic cost of primary schooling in India* (HKS Faculty Research Working Paper Series RWP15–027).

Read, T. (2015). *Where have all the textbooks gone Toward sustainable provision of teaching and learning materials in Sub-Saharan Africa.* Washington, DC: World Bank.

Republic of the Philippines. (2016). *Republic Act 10717. General Appropriations Act Volume I: Fiscal year 2016.* Manila: Department of Budget and Management.

Rogers, F. H., & Sabarwal, S. (2020). *The COVID-19 pandemic: Shocks to education and policy responses.* Washington, DC: World Bank.

Sabarwal, S., Evans, D. K., & Marshak, A. (2014). *The permanent input hypothesis: The case of textbooks and (no) student learning in Sierra Leone* (World Bank Policy Research Working Paper No. 7021).

Silveira, I. M. d., Lima, J. E. d., Teixeira, E. C., & Silva, R. G. d. (2017). Avaliação do efeito do Fundeb sobre o desempenho dos alunos do ensino médio no Brasil. *Pesquisa e planejamento econômico, 47*(1), 7–44. https://ppe.ipea.gov.br/index.php/ppe/article/viewFile/1658/1237

Snilstveit, B., Stevenson, J., Phillips, D., Vojtkova, M., Gallagher, E., Schmidt, T., Jobse, H., Geelen, M., & Pastorello, M. (2015). Interventions for improving learning outcomes and access to education in low- and middle-income countries: A systematic review. *Campbell Systematic Reviews, 13,* 1–82. https://doi.org/10.1002/CL2.176

Tsimpo, C., & Wodon, Q. (2014). *Measuring the benefit incidence of public spending for education in Burundi.* UNESCO Institute for Statistics and UNICEF.

UNESCO. (2015). *Pricing the right to education: The cost of reaching new targets by 2030.* Geneva: UNESCO.

UNESCO. (2019). *Global Education Monitoring Report: Migration, displacement and education.* Paris: UNESCO.

UNESCO. (2020a). *Act now: Reduce the impact of COVID-19 on the cost of achieving SDG 4* (Policy Paper). Paris: UNESCO.

UNESCO. (2020b). *COVID-19 is a serious threat to aid to education recovery* (Policy Paper). Paris: UNESCO.

UNICEF. (2020). *Addressing the learning crisis: An urgent need to better finance education for poorest children.* New York: UNICEF.

United Nations Population Division. (2019). *World population prospects 2019.* https://population.un.org/wpp/

Universalia. (2019). *Evaluation of the GPE's support to sector plan development.* https://www.globalpartnership.org/sites/default/files/document/file/2020-06-12-evaluation-gpe-support-sector-plan-development%E2%80%93final-report.pdf

Wagner, D. A., Wolf, S., & Boruch, R. F. (2018). *Learning at the bottom of the pyramid.* Paris: IIEP Publishing.

Wang, X., &. Wu, B. (2021). Intergovernmental fiscal transfers and education outcomes in China. In S. Al-Samarrai and B. Lewis (Eds.). *The role of intergovernmental fiscal transfers in improving education outcomes.* Washington, DC: World Bank.

World Bank. (2012). *The BOSDA improvement program: Enhancing equity and performance through local school grants.* Jakarta: World Bank.

World Bank. (2013). *Local governance and education performance: A survey of the quality of local education governance in 50 Indonesian districts.* Washington, DC: World Bank.

World Bank. (2016). *Assessing basic education service delivery in the Philippines: Public education expenditure tracking and quantitative service delivery study.* Washington, DC: World Bank.

World Bank. (2018). *World Development Report 2018: Learning to realize education's promise.* Washington, DC: World Bank.

World Bank. (2019). *Ending learning poverty: What will it take?* Washington, DC: World Bank.

World Bank. (2020a). *Projected poverty impacts of COVID-19 (coronavirus).* Washington, DC: World Bank.

World Bank. (2020b). *Spending for better results: Indonesia public expenditure review.* Jakarta: World Bank.

8. Mexico

Education and Learning at the Bottom of the Pyramid

Sylvia Schmelkes del Valle, Héctor Robles Vásquez, and Annette Santos del Real

Introduction[1]

Mexico has gradually established the right to free and compulsory education at all stages. The right to education is not limited to children's access to schools with well-trained teachers and adequate teaching materials and infrastructure, nor is it only about ensuring their graduation from compulsory education levels. It also includes, explicitly in the constitutional reform of 2019, the right to learn through "constant integral improvement that promotes the maximum learning achievement of students" (CPEUM, 2019, May 15, Art. 31).[2]

This chapter addresses the populations of children at the bottom of the learning pyramid at the preschool (three grades), primary (six

---

1. The authors would like to thank Luis Degante and Raúl René Rojas for their contributions to this section.
2. The Mexican Constitution (CPEUM) mandated compulsory primary education in 1934, secondary education in 1993, and preschool education in 2002 (Rives Sánchez, 2010). In 2012, upper-secondary education was made compulsory and its gradual universalization will theoretically end in 2021. Recently, in May 2019, initial education and higher education (the latter with conditions) were also made compulsory. Initial education was also added to the category of basic education (CPEUM, 2019, May 15, Art. 3).

grades), and secondary (three grades) levels of education. The typical ages for these three levels are 3–5, 6–11, and 12–14 respectively.[3]

Various sources of information and studies are used to describe the subpopulations of children as thoroughly as possible and with the latest data available. School data are from the 2018–2019 school year.

As of 2018, there are estimated to be 26.7 million children aged 3–14 in Mexico, just over a fifth (21.3 percent) of the total population of 125 million people. Of the total number of children aged 3–14, a quarter of them are aged 3–5 (6.6 million), half are aged 6–11 (13.3 million), and the remaining quarter (6.7 million) are aged 12–14 (CONAPO, 2019).

So far, the Mexican State has not managed to guarantee either universal access to schools, universal completion of compulsory education levels, or, for most who graduate from primary and secondary education, the basic levels of learning that will allow them to develop further. This implies a social debt, especially to children in conditions of social vulnerability. They have the lowest levels of learning, but also the lowest rates of access to schools, of progress between grades and school levels, and of completion of compulsory basic education when compared to their peers in better social conditions (INEE, 2007; 2014a; 2018a; and 2019a; Galeana, 2016).

In this section, we introduce two approaches to the definition of the population of children at the bottom of the learning pyramid. The first criterion is demographic and describes children in conditions of social vulnerability. The second criterion focuses on subpopulations of primary and secondary school students with insufficient achievement levels in comparison with standardized testing outcomes. The two perspectives are complementary. On the one hand, by considering only student information, especially educational achievement, children who are not in school are left out. On the other hand, the Mexican Education System (MES) generally lacks personal and family information about its students that correlate with educational performance. Thus, identifying subpopulations of children in conditions of social vulnerability makes it possible to identify those who are the most disadvantaged in terms of learning.

---

3   These age ranges relate to the ages for each school level, assuming uninterrupted school progress, one grade per school cycle, and starting at three years of age in the first grade of preschool education (DOF, 12 November 2002).

There are children who are part of several dimensions of vulnerability at the same time (for example, indigenous children may live in highly marginalized areas, work long hours, and live in extreme poverty). Because these children are in multiple situations of vulnerability, and the information available is generally not sufficient, the subsets of the population in conditions of vulnerability are generally defined by considering only one condition of social exclusion and, therefore, the subpopulations thus defined have members in common because there is considerable overlap between the categories.

The demographic approach

The subpopulations of children in conditions of social vulnerability are determined by place of residence, poverty, ethnic and linguistic affiliation, and disability. They also include street-children, child laborers, and children in continuous migration as part of agricultural day-laborer households. In what follows, the main subpopulations are described.

Children in rural areas

In 2015, there were 119.5 million people in Mexico, 23 percent of whom lived in rural localities—that is, towns with fewer than 2,500 inhabitants. Almost a quarter of the rural population (7 million people) consisted of children aged 3–14. The number of rural children aged 3–5 and 12–14 years was very similar (1.8 million in each), while the population of 6-to-11-year-olds amounted to 3.5 million. These figures add up to just over a quarter of all Mexican children in each age group.

Rural localities range from hamlets with a couple of homes and very few inhabitants to towns of up to 2,500 people. In 2010, the entire population of Mexico was distributed in 192,247 localities, 98 percent of which were rural. Almost three-quarters of rural localities (139,158) have fewer than 100 inhabitants, are distributed sparsely, and together account for only 9.2 percent of the rural population. That same year, the population census counted 627,350 children aged 3–14 in these small localities, which also amounts to 9 percent of the total rural population of the same age group. The fragmentation and dispersion of the population may be even more acute, given that 15 percent of the rural population of children aged 3–14 lived in localities with fewer than three houses and fewer than 100 inhabitants.

Children in extreme and moderate poverty

In Mexico, the measurement of multidimensional poverty considers factors such as education, health, social security, nutritional food, housing, and its services in addition to income. The population in extreme poverty is defined as those whose income is so low that, even if they were to devote it entirely to the acquisition of food, they would not be able to nourish themselves adequately for a healthy life. Moreover, they are deprived of at least three of the six social rights mentioned above. The population in moderate poverty consists of those whose income does not allow them to acquire the goods and services they require to satisfy their needs (both food- and non-food-related) and who suffer at least one social deprivation, but are not in a situation of extreme poverty. The union of these subpopulations constitutes the population in multidimensional poverty or, briefly, in poverty (CONEVAL, 2019a).

According to these measures, in 2018, 34.5 percent of the population in Mexico (43.1 million people) lived in moderate poverty and 7.4 percent (9.3 million people) in extreme poverty. If both types of poverty are considered, 52.4 million people were in a situation of multidimensional poverty (CONEVAL, 2019b).

Poverty in general, and extreme poverty, is greater in younger children. In 2016, 20.7 million children aged 0–17 lived in poverty; this figure represented almost two-fifths (38.8 percent) of the total number of people living in poverty that year. When considering the incidence of poverty among children in age groups 0–5, 6–11, and 12–14, we can see that 52.5 percent of those aged 0–5 were living in poverty, as well as 52.2 percent of those aged 6–11, and 48.8 percent of those aged 12–17 (see Table 1).

Poverty affects children in rural areas disproportionately more than their urban peers. In 2016, 63.9 percent of children aged 0–17 living in rural areas were living in poverty, as compared to 46.5 percent of their urban peers (CONEVAL, undated).

Table 1. Percentage of children in poverty in Mexico (2018).

Age	Moderate poverty	Extreme poverty	Multidimensional poverty
0–5	42.2	10.2	52.5
6–11	43	9.2	52.2
12–17	41	7.8	48.8

Note: Data obtained from "Pobreza infantil y adolescente en México 2008–2016" by Coneval & UNICEF (s/f), p. 6 (https://www.coneval.org.mx/Medicion/Documents/UNICEF_CONEVAL_POBREZA_INFANTIL.pdf).

Indigenous children

The great cultural heritage and diversity of Mexico comes in part from its native populations, whose languages can be organized into 68 linguistic groups and 364 variants integrated into 11 Indo-American linguistic families (INALI, 2008). In 2018, with data from the National Household Income and Expenditure Survey (ENIGH), 9.6 percent of the population resided in a household where any head of household or any of their ascendant relatives spoke an indigenous language. According to this criterion, out of a total of 125 million people, approximately 12 million were indigenous. Of these, 7 million people (5.9 percent of the population aged 3+) spoke an indigenous language. Of the total number of speakers, 9.2 percent (652,000) exclusively spoke an indigenous language. There were 3.7 million indigenous children aged 3–17, equivalent to 10.9 percent of the total number of children in this age group. 1.6 million children, amounting to 43.7 percent of all indigenous people in this age group, spoke an indigenous language.

If self-identification is considered a criterion of cultural and ethnic affiliation, then 36.5 million people—that is, 30.5 percent of the total population—self-identify as indigenous. For the 3–17 age group, the figure increases to 43.7 percent, amounting to 1.6 million children (INEE-UNICEF, 2019).

In 2018, the places of residence of indigenous populations were almost equally distributed between rural and urban localities, with 49.8 percent residing in localities with fewer than 2,500 inhabitants. It is to be expected that the proportion of speakers living in rural locations will be higher than their urban counterparts. In 2015, 55.4 percent of the indigenous population and 76.7 percent of speakers aged 3–17 resided in rural areas (INEE, 2018b).

Poverty among indigenous people is greater in rural areas, affects younger children disproportionately, and increases among speakers of indigenous languages. In 2014, 31.8 percent of the indigenous population lived in extreme poverty and 41.4 percent in moderate poverty, while for the non-indigenous population, the figures were 7.1 percent and 36.1 percent, respectively. Among the indigenous population living in rural areas, extreme poverty affects 42.2 percent and moderate poverty 38.5 percent of the population; for indigenous people in urban areas with more than 100,000 inhabitants, these figures were 6.9 percent and 44.3 percent, respectively (INEE-UNICEF, 2015).

Among indigenous children aged 3–17, more than one-third (35.5 percent) lived in extreme poverty and 43.2 percent in moderate poverty; among their non-indigenous peers, these figures were 8.4 percent and 42.3 percent, respectively. If the children are speakers of an indigenous language, more than half (54 percent) are in extreme poverty and 36.8 percent in moderate poverty. Thus, 78.7 percent of indigenous children between the ages 3–17, and 90.8 percent of those who speak an indigenous language, live in conditions of poverty (INEE-UNICEF, 2015).

Children with disabilities

In Mexico, disability is measured mostly in the areas of impairments and limitations. In 2016, it was estimated that 2.6 percent of the population aged 3–14 experienced difficulty with walking, moving, climbing, or descending; seeing, even with the use of glasses; speaking, communicating, or conversing; hearing, even with the use of a hearing aid; dressing, bathing, or eating; paying attention or learning simple things; or experiencing a mental impairment. This figure amounted to nearly 700,000 children, 16.8 percent of whom were aged 3–5, 56.5 percent were aged 6–11, and 26.8 percent were 12–14 years old (INEE, 2018b).

Children of internal migrant workers

The migration of day laborers from poor rural areas to developed agricultural regions, following the different production cycles of crops, is a complex structural phenomenon (Rojas, 2017). In this seasonal rural-rural migration, some children migrate alongside their parents, giving rise to a subpopulation of migrant children in conditions of great social vulnerability.

Migrant children often face barriers in access to education, school retention, grade advancement, and school-level progression in order to complete compulsory basic education in a timely manner. These children are in fact excluded from the learning provided by schooling (INEE, 2014b). According to official estimates using the results of the 2009 National Day Laborers' Survey (ENJO, 2009), the migrant day-laborer population amounts to 2,071,483 people. More than a third of this population (36.6 percent) are children aged 0–15, amounting to 758,163 people. In 2014, the INEE reported that only 10 percent of the children of migrant-worker families attended school.[4]

Child laborers

In 2017—excluding all forms of labor that seriously undermine the wellbeing of children, like slavery, forced labor, human trafficking, paramilitary recruitment, commercial sex or pornography, or other illicit activities—one in 10 children aged 5–17 (11 percent), that is, 3.2 million children, worked in unauthorized economic activities or in domestic work under unsuitable conditions. Considering 20 hours a week as the lower limit for defining a long or extended working day, it is estimated that, in 2015, 2.1 percent of children aged 6–11 worked long hours, a figure that rises to 9.3 percent among those aged 12–14. In absolute terms, over 83,000 and 637,000 children in these age ranges, respectively, worked long hours that could put their school attendance, learning, and due rest at risk.[5]

---

4 The only specialized survey on migrant day-laborers in Mexico for which public information is available is the ENJO 2009. The post-2009 estimates of the number of agricultural day-laborers are indirect. They use the ENJO results in combination with the results of household surveys (not specialized in migrant day-laborers). ENJO data are reported here rather than indirect estimates that may underestimate the number of children in migrant worker families.

5 Calculations derived from INEE (2018b).

The schooling and testing approach

In this section, we consider primary and secondary schooling attendance as well as students' learning outcomes according to standardized tests.

Size and structure of preschool, primary, and secondary education in Mexico

The Mexican Educational System (MES) is the third largest in the American Continent (INEE, 2019a). At the beginning of the 2018–2019 school year, the preschool, primary, and secondary education system contained approximately 25 million students served by 1.2 million teachers in 227,000 schools (see Table 2).

Table 2. Students, teachers, and schools in preschool, primary, and secondary education (2018–2019).

Educational service	Students		Teachers		Schools	
	Number	%	Number	%	Number	%
Preschool	4 780 787	19.0	236 509	19.5	90 446	39.9
Primary school	13 972 269	55.4	572 104	47.1	96 508	42.5
Secondary school	6 473 608	25.7	406 084	33.4	39 967	17.6
Total	25 226 664	100.0	1 214 697	100.0	226 921	100.0

Note: Calculations based on the Continuous Statistics from Formato 911 (school year 2018–2019), SEP-DGPPyEE.

The MES has devised different types of educational services aimed at different subpopulations of children. Preschool and primary education is provided through three types of service: general, indigenous, and community education. Secondary education is provided in general, technical, community, and telesecondary schools, as well as in schools for workers.

Children from indigenous communities, settled in rural areas, are assigned to indigenous preschools and primary schools. Ideally, teachers should speak the same language as their students, but this is not the case in one-tenth of schools (INEE-UNICEF, 2019). Indigenous children who attend school in cities do not have teachers who speak their mother-tongue.

Children living in rural localities, particularly in smaller ones, are served through the community service provided by the National Council for the Promotion of Education (CONAFE), which offers the three levels of basic education. Community schools must operate in locations where there is no other type of service and where there is a minimum of 5 and a maximum of 29 students (DOF, 2017). They also serve indigenous children, children of farmworkers and circus performers, and migrant children. Unlike in other educational services, community schools' teachers are not education professionals; they are young people who have completed their high-school studies and have been qualified and trained to implement a multigrade pedagogical model with educational materials designed expressly for their situation. At each educational level, these young people teach students of different ages, learning rates, and educational grades.

General (public) schools serve urban areas or rural localities with more than 30 students. Such schools, typical of urbanized areas, usually have one teacher per grade for preschool and primary education. However, the small number of students makes it impossible for rural schools to follow this system. Educational authorities have allowed the emergence of multigrade general schools, where instructors simultaneously teach students in more than one grade without accompanying the multigrade organization of their work with an appropriate pedagogical model or teaching materials (INEE, 2018a). In the 2017–2018 school year, almost one-third of general schools were multigrade (32.5 percent). Two-thirds (65.8 percent) of indigenous primary schools are in a similar situation.

In secondary education, there are five types of schools: general, technical, telesecondary, community schools, and schools for workers. The first two are mainly intended for urban localities; their organization requires that each subject should be taught by a specialized teacher. Telesecondary schools, conceived to expand secondary education to rural areas, differ in their teaching organization and pedagogical model, as students watch lessons on a television set and are supported by a single teacher per grade who is responsible for answering questions and guiding their learning in all subjects. As in previous levels of education, children from smaller rural locations are assigned to community-based secondary schools.

At the beginning of the 2018–2019 school year, there were about 6 million students enrolled in 124,000 preschools (25.2 percent), primary (24.6 percent), and secondary (20.7 percent) schools in rural areas. In relative terms, rural schools accounted for 23.7 percent of total preschool, primary, and secondary education enrollment, but for more than half of all schools in Mexico (54.5 percent) (see Table 3 below). This means that rural schools are considerably smaller than urban schools. Indigenous preschools and primary schools target rural children subpopulations in localities with a high presence of indigenous populations, and community schools target children in small localities, but the greatest educational coverage in rural areas is provided by general schools (see Table 3 below).

For indigenous and rural children, and more generally for those in poverty, public intervention is necessary to ensure their access to education. In Mexico, 85 percent of preschool students and 90 percent of primary- and secondary-school students go to public schools; almost 100 percent of indigenous, community, and telesecondary schools are public (INEE, 2019b).

Primary- and secondary-school students at the bottom of the learning pyramid according to standardized tests

The National Institute for the Evaluation of Education (INEE), which was in charge of evaluating the quality of the MES until April 2019, administered standardized tests to samples of students in the final grades of preschool, primary, secondary, and upper-secondary education to assess their degree of mastery of key learning objectives in the national curriculum. This section will use the results of the PLANEA tests administered in 2018 to sixth-grade primary-school students and in 2017 to third-grade secondary-school students. The subjects evaluated were language and communication and mathematics.

The results are presented according to the students' distribution in four levels of achievement. In general, at Level I, students are found to have insufficient mastery of key learning objectives, making it difficult for them to continue learning. Students in Level II have a basic mastery of such learning, while students in Levels III and IV show satisfactory and outstanding mastery, respectively (INEE, 2019a). We identify students in Level I as the bottom of the learning pyramid in Mexico. In the description of the results on the PLANEA test, Levels III and IV are grouped together because of the small number of students at the outstanding level in community and indigenous schools (see Table 3).

In 2018, at the national level, almost half of sixth-grade primary-school students (49.1 percent) had insufficient achievement in language and communication (see Table 4 below); among those who study in an indigenous or community primary school, the percentages increase to 79 percent and 70.7 percent, respectively. Being at the insufficient level means, for example, that one cannot relate explicit information segments to each other and establish the meaning of implicit elements in narrative and expository texts. Nor can one use conjunctions and causal links in complex sentences. It is difficult for children at this level to understand the information and recognize the general structure of some expository texts (INEE, 2019a). In math, six out of 10 sixth-grade students (59.1 percent) were found to have insufficient achievement (see Table 4 below), which means, for example, that they cannot solve arithmetic problems with decimal numbers, calculate the perimeter of irregular polygons, or use percentages. More than three-quarters of those who study in indigenous or community primary schools, and 60.9 percent of general school students, experience these same difficulties (INEE, 2019a).

In 2017, the PLANEA test was administered to third-grade secondary-school students. In Table 5 below we can see that one-third (33.8 percent) of students in Mexican schools had insufficient mastery of language and communication skills, which means that they "fail to recognize the plot and conflict in a story or interpret the figurative language of a poem, or to organize relevant and non-relevant information for the purpose of a survey, or to identify the purpose, theme, opinion and evidence of argumentative texts" (INEE, 2018a).

In math, the results are more discouraging, since about two-thirds of the students (64.5 percent) were in Level I and only 13.7 percent reached satisfactory or outstanding levels. Those in Level I are unable to solve problems with rational numbers or those that go beyond arithmetic, such as problems involving square roots, the common divisor, and linear

Table 3. Preschool, primary, and secondary education students and schools by type of service at national level and in rural localities (2018–2019).

Educational level by type of service	Totals by educational level and types of service					Rural						
	Absolute figures		% of educational level			Absolute figures		% of total		% of educational level	
	Students	Schools	Students	Schools		Students	Schools	Students	Schools	Students	Schools
PRESCHOOL	4 780 787	90 446	100	100		1 205 648	47 480	25.2	52.5	100.0	100.0
General	4 229 648	62 541	88.5	69.1		776 717	21 560	18.4	34.5	64.4	45.4
Indigenous	396 755	9 826	8.3	10.9		278 824	8 241	70.3	83.9	23.1	17.4
Community	154 384	18 079	3.2	20.0		150 107	17 679	97.2	97.8	12.5	37.2
PRIMARY SCHOOLS	13 972 269	96 508	100	100		3 437 092	54 269	24.6	56.2	100.0	100.0
General	13 081 359	76 895	93.6	79.7		2 721 770	35 976	20.8	46.8	79.2	66.3
Indigenous	793 566	10 275	5.7	10.6		620 867	9 186	78.2	89.4	18.1	16.9
Community	97 344	9 338	0.7	9.7		94 455	9 107	97.0	97.5	2.7	16.8
SECONDARY SCHOOLS	6 473 608	39 967	100	100		1 340 872	22 004	20.7	55.1	100.0	100.0
General*	3 283 021	12 570	50.7	31.5		172 513	1 152	5.3	9.2	12.9	5.2
Technical	1 748 255	4 732	27.0	11.8		175 913	984	10.1	20.8	13.1	4.5
Telesecondary	1 379 920	18 741	21.3	46.9		948 750	16 215	68.8	86.5	70.8	73.7
for Workers	17 956	210	0.3	0.5				0.0	0.0	0.0	0.0
Community	44 456	3 714	0.7	9.3		43 696	3 653	98.3	98.4	3.3	16.6
TOTAL	25 226 664	226 921				5 983 612	123 753	23.7	54.5		

*Note: The general school system includes 1,557 students, 89 teachers, and 58 schools in the migrant program, located in Baja California, Baja California Sur, Coahuila, Colima, Michoacán, Morelos, San Luis Potosí, Sinaloa, Sonora, and Zacatecas.

Calculations based on the Continuous Statistics of the Formato 911 (school year 2018–2019), SEP-DGPPyEE; the Marco Geoestadístico Nacional. Catálogo Único de Claves de Áreas Geoestadísticas Estatales, Municipales y Localidades (INEGI, 2018).

Table 4. Percentage of sixth-grade students by school type and level of educational attainment achieved in the domains evaluated in the PLANEA-SEN tests (2018).

School type	I %	(se)	II %	(se)	III and IV %	(se)
Language and communication						
Public general	50.7	(0.6)	33.9	(0.5)	15.4	(0.3)
Indigenous[1]	79.0	(3.7)	17.0*	(2.9)	4.0**	(1.4)
Community	70.7*	(2.6)	24.4*	(2.5)	4.8**	(1.2)
Private	14.9	(0.8)	35.0	(0.9)	50.1	(1.1)
National	49.1*	(0.6)	32.9	(0.4)	17.9	(0.3)
Mathematics						
Public general	60.9	(0.6)	17.8	(0.4)	21.3	(0.4)
Indigenous[1]	77.5*	(3.1)	11.8*	(1.9)	10.7*	(1.7)
Community	76.6*	(2.4)	14.7	(1.9)	8.7*	(1.7)
Private	30.9*	(1.2)	22.3*	(0.9)	46.9*	(1.2)
National	59.1*	(0.5)	17.9	(0.3)	23.0*	(0.4)

[1] These estimates do not meet the participation rate criterion.
* Statistically different from public general schools in each grade, using the t-test.
** Estimate with a coefficient of variation greater than 20 percent.
se. Standard error. Data obtained from "Panorama Educativo de México. Indicadores del Sistema Educativo Nacional 2018" (INEE, 2019).

equations; nor do they recognize and express relationships of direct or inverse proportionality.

Secondary schools located in rural areas, which serve a greater proportion of children in conditions of social vulnerability than urban schools, have higher percentages of students with insufficient mastery of key learning objectives in the two subjects under discussion. In language and communication, six out of every 10 community secondary students (60.2 percent) and about half of those studying in a telesecondary school (48.8 percent) are at Level I of achievement (see Table 5).

Table 5. Percentage of third-grade secondary students by level of educational attainment attained in domains as assessed on Plan-ELSEN Tests by type of school (2017).

	I (Insufficient)		II		III and IV (Satisfactory and outstanding)	
	%	(se)	%	(se)	%	(se)
Language and communication						
General public	31.6	(0.9)	42.8	(0.5)	25.6	(0.8)
Technical public	32.2	(0.7)	41.8	(0.6)	25.9	(0.6)
Telesecondary	48.8*	(1.2)	36.6*	(0.8)	14.6*	(0.6)
Community	60.2*	(2.6)	31.3*	(2.2)	8.5*	(1.2)
Private	10.6*	(0.7)	32.2*	(0.7)	57.3*	(1.1)
National	33.8*	(0.6)	40.1*	(0.3)	26.1	(0.5)
mathematics						
General public	66.2	(0.9)	21.7	(0.5)	12.1	(0.6)
Technical public	66.8	(0.7)	21.2	(0.4)	12.0	(0.5)
Telesecondary	69.9*	(1.1)	19.6*	(0.7)	10.4*	(0.6)
Community	86.7*	(1.5)	10.9*	(1.3)	2.4**	(0.5)
Private	37.0*	(1.3)	29.1*	(0.6)	33.9*	(1.1)
National	64.5	(0.6)	21.7	(0.3)	13.7*	(0.3)

Note: * Statistically different from public general schools in each grade, using the t-test.

** Estimate with a coefficient of variation greater than 20 percent. se. Standard error

Data obtained from "Panorama Educativo de México. Indicadores del Sistema Educativo Nacional 2017", INEE (2018).

In math, the figures for insufficient achievement were 86.7 percent of community secondary students, 69.9 percent of telesecondary students, 66.8 percent of technical secondary students, 66.2 percent of general school students, and 37 percent of private school students (see Table 5 above).

Main educational challenges faced by children at the bottom of the pyramid

Children in conditions of social vulnerability have difficulty accessing quality education, as can be seen in the assessment of key learnings. In addition, the schools they attend generally have more deficiencies in infrastructure, educational materials, and equipment, as well as in educational and organizational processes. This section shows the extent to which vulnerable children are accessing and completing preschool, primary, and secondary education, and the barriers to learning that these children face.

Access to and progress in compulsory education: Analysis by age group

Table 6 below displays for different subpopulations of children (by age group): (i) the school attendance rate; (ii) the attendance rate at the educational level corresponding to the typical age; and (iii) the percentage of the population by age group that completes each educational level following an uninterrupted schooling path. These are estimates using data from ENIGH (INEGI, 2018).

All children in the age groups 3–5, 6–11, and 12–14 must attend preschool, primary, and secondary school, respectively. At the national level, only children aged 6–11 are very close to achieving universal school attendance (98.8 percent), whereas 93.5 percent of the 12–14 age group and only three-quarters (76 percent) of children aged 3–5 attend school. Children with social vulnerability attend school less than those in better conditions (see Table 6 below).

It is desirable that students enter school at a certain age and follow uninterrupted paths, as this is associated with a greater probability of completing compulsory education. In secondary education and following levels, there are significant proportions of children who study at older than typical ages (over-age students). This situation may be due to temporary dropout or grade repetition, which is usually associated with poor school performance. When this occurs, a vicious circle is created, since rarely does the school resolve the learning deficits of its students to ensure their full inclusion in the educational process. This means that over-age children are more likely to fail and drop out again.

The *attendance rate* indicator at the *education level that typically corresponds to age* roughly measures an uninterrupted school progression—that is, timely school attendance. Only 84.5 percent of 12–14-year-olds attend secondary school and almost 10 percent still attend primary school (see Table 6 below). Uninterrupted school progressions are less common among vulnerable children than among their non-vulnerable peers.

The social mandate that establishes that all children must complete the compulsory educational levels can be partially monitored with the percentage of students that complete a certain level following an uninterrupted path. Thus, if a child is in the first grade when he or she is six years old and continues to make uninterrupted progress in school—without failing or repeating grades or temporarily dropping out—then by the age of 12 this child should have completed primary education. This would be the case if the MES were effective in guaranteeing universal access to schooling for all children, and in reducing school dropout and grade repetition.

By 2018, 88.9 percent of children aged 12–14 had completed primary education, and 81.6 percent of those aged 15–17 had completed secondary education. There are no statistically significant differences by gender for children aged 12–14 with completed primary education, but in the age group 15–17, more girls (83.8 percent) than boys (79.3 percent) complete their secondary education in time (see Table 6 below). Given that late entry to school, dropout, and grade repetition are more frequent among children in vulnerable conditions, lower rates of completion in primary and secondary education are observed in these children (see Table 6).

Barriers to learning

Children and young people at the bottom of the pyramid have, for all the reasons described above, fewer opportunities to learn, which is the ultimate purpose of the right to education. In addition to the difficulties described in having access to and remaining in school long enough to achieve the necessary skills to meet the demands of society, these population groups face special challenges in language, teacher preparation, and limited infrastructure.

In the case of indigenous children, in addition to poverty, a fundamental challenge is the language of instruction. Indigenous students who attend school almost always receive instruction in

Table 6. School attendance rate, percentage of population with complete education levels, and school attendance rate at educational level typically corresponding to age by selected subpopulation (2018).

	School attendance rate by age group				Attendance rate at educational level typically corresponding to age			Percentage of children with complete primary or secondary education by age group	
	3–5	6–11	12–14	15–17	Secondary school 12–14	High school 15–17		Primary education 12–14	Secondary education 15–17
Total population	76.0	98.8	93.5	74.2	84.5	66.4		88.9	81.6
Sex									
Male	75.9	98.7	92.8	73.1	84.1	64.6		89.0	79.3
Female	76.2	98.8	94.2*	75.4*	85.0*	68.2		88.7*	83.8*
Type of community									
Rural	75.7	98.4	90.3	60.9	81.3	53.9		88.0	76.1
Semi-urban	75.7	98.9	92.7*	75.5*	83.1*	69.1*		87.6*	82.9*
Urban	76.3	98.9	95.2*	80.1*	86.4	71.5		89.6	83.7
Ethnic status									
Indigenous population	73.0	97.8	88.0	64.0	78.4	54.6		85.7	71.1

240 Learning, Marginalization, and Improving the Quality of Education

Non-indigenous population	76.4	98.9*	94.1*	75.5*	85.3*	67.8*	89.2*	82.8*
Disability status								
With disabilities	71.7	89.3	73.4	54.0	56.4	43.5	66.3	58.4
Without disabilities	76.1	99.0*	94.1*	74.8*	85.4*	67.1	89.5*	82.2*
Education level of head of household								
No education	64.6	94.0	84.3	50.5	72.6	40.7	81.2	63.0
Incomplete basic	71.5*	98.2*	89.1*	61.4*	79.9	53.3*	87.7*	74.6*
Complete basic	75.4*	99.4*	95.6*	77.4*	86.7*	69.9*	89.3*	85.6*
Complete high school	81.6*	99.6	98.2*	90.3*	89.6*	83.5*	91.0*	89.7*
Complete higher education	89.1*	99.8	99.4*	95.7*	91.8*	87.2*	92.1*	90.0
Income quintile								
I	71.8	97.7	88.9	63.9	79.5	54.5	86.5	73.9
II	73.7	98.9*	93.1*	71.7*	83.6*	63.8*	88.4*	79.7*
III	75.5	99.0	94.5	73.3	86.4*	66.5	89.9*	84.1*
IV	79.6*	99.4	96.2*	79.7*	88.3	71.7*	91.2*	84.1
V	85.9*	99.6	97.2	86.7*	87.2	80.0*	89.2	88.2*
Work status								
Extra-domestic work ≥ 20 h	n.d.	n.a.	37.9~	26.5~	33.5~	16.5~	80.0	56.2

8. Mexico: Education and Learning at the Bottom of the Pyramid   241

Mixed work ≥ 20 h	n.d.	100.0	59.9*	40.0*	49.6*~	30.4*	80.3	63.1*
Domestic work ≥ 20 h	n.d.	93.5*	71.7*	39.5	59.1*	29.4	79.0	61.5
No work or < 20 h	n.d.	99.1*	97.0*	90.6*	73.5*	63.6*	75.5	68.4*
Poverty status[2]								
Poverty	69.3**	98.0**	90.3**	66.6**	80.9**	58.0**	87.3**	76.7**
Extreme poverty	54.9**	94.7**	77.2**	44.9**	66.7**	32.7**	81.5**	52.6**
Moderate poverty	73.5**	98.8**	93.2**	70.9**	84.0**	63.0**	88.5**	81.4**
Not poor or vulnerable	100.0	100.0	99.6	95.2	90.8	88.8	90.8*	93.2*

Note: ~ Adjusted Coefficient of Variation greater than 10 percent. See technical note "Criterio de precisión" in Panorama Educativo de México 2017 (INEE, 2018, p. 171).

[1] See technical note "Subpoblaciones, nivel de escolaridad y población atendible" in Panorama Educativo de México 2017 (INEE, 2018, pp. 167–170).

[2] These categories are not entirely exclusive. Poverty comprises extreme poverty and moderate poverty.

* Statistically significant difference at a 95 percent confidence interval from the previous category.

** Statistically significant difference at a 95 percent confidence with respect to the "not poor or vulnerable" category.

n.d. Not available. n.a. Not applicable.

Calculations based on the Encuesta Nacional de Ingresos y Gastos de los Hogares 2018 (INEGI, 2019), for total population and the following subpopulations: sex, type of community, ethnic status, educational level of head of household; on Medición de la Pobreza en México 2018 (Coneval, 2019), for the income variables, income quintile, and poverty variables, and Encuesta Nacional de Ocupación y Empleo, 2nd trimester 2019 (INEGI, 2019) and Encuesta Nacional de Ocupación y Empleo, Módulo de Trabajo Infantil, 4th trimester 2017 (INEGI, 2017), for the work condition variable.

Spanish, although in some cases teachers who speak the same language, about half of them, use it to teach. Working materials, textbooks, and the school environment in general are all in Spanish. In these circumstances, children take much longer to learn to read and write (many succeed only at the age of 10), and their mastery of the content included in the curriculum is consequently much lower. This helps explain their low achievement on the learning tests described above.

In small and/or dispersed rural communities, where schools do not have one teacher per grade, there is a lack of teaching methodologies that take advantage of grade and age diversity. Teachers who have not been trained to deal with multigrade groups tend to divide time between grades, which places students at a disadvantage compared to schools with one teacher per grade (Schmelkes & Aguila, 2018).

Children and young people living in poverty attend schools that have suboptimal infrastructure, equipment, and resources for learning more frequently than their peers not in poverty. Teachers are less experienced, have less access to in-service training opportunities and, in general, their classroom practice is teacher-centered, based on rote learning, non-inclusive, and does not integrate learning with the students' contexts, making the school experience alien to them. This also partly explains why students at the bottom of the pyramid achieve lower scores on school tests. In schools in indigenous and rural areas, and in some cases in marginal urban areas, teacher absences tend to be more frequent, and less time is spent in school for instructional purposes (see Anzures Tapía, 2020, for preschool). When culturally and linguistically diverse populations are present in schools, such as in urban areas or migrant agricultural camps, discrimination often occurs, making the school environment more difficult and causing students to drop out.

These situations combine to prevent those at the bottom of the pyramid from learning: they have more difficulty accessing school; they have more difficulty remaining and progressing through the school system; and they face poorer material conditions, teachers with less training, pedagogical practices that constitute barriers to learning, and non-inclusive—sometimes even discriminatory and hostile—school environments. The result of this perverse synergy of hostile conditions for those who are most disadvantaged is early school abandonment, truncated or incomplete compulsory schooling, and, most distressingly, the absence of the necessary learning to live a dignified life. The education system, not designed with an equity perspective, fails to break the intergenerational transmission of poverty.

Education policies currently in place to serve the bottom of the pyramid[6]

In this section, we briefly describe the pro-equity programs promoted by the administration of President López Obrador and report on the budget assigned to them in the year 2020, on the understanding that the expenditure allocated to their implementation is a fundamental indicator of the priority given to them. It is highly probable that these programs have experienced important budget cuts due to the austerity measures implemented by the federal government in 2020, and further affected by the COVID-19 pandemic. When this chapter was written there was no information available on the size of these cuts.[7] Nevertheless, we consider it important to show the changes in educational expenditure that the present administration has carried out until now.

Federal spending on basic education is carried out through budgetary programs (BP) that can be divided into federalized spending programs (FSP) and federal programs (FP). Through the FSPs, resources are transferred to the federal entities for specific purposes, mainly to maintain the regular operation of school services (LCF, 2018, January 30). In general, this spending is inflexible. The FPs, on the other hand, are based on agreements between the federal and state governments, and their purpose is to finance actions to promote integral education. These programs are subject to change. For the purposes of this section, FPs are explicitly labeled to distinguish them from programs for the general student or teacher populations.[8] It is worth mentioning that, in the year 2020, about 89 percent of federal spending on basic education will go to

---

6 The authors wish to thank Raúl Guadalupe Antonio for his contribution to this section.
7 In September 2020, Congress received the federal proposal budget for 2021 with important planned reductions for some equity programs described here. The approval of the final budget will occur at the end of the year.
8 FPs that benefit the general population, without targeting any population group or type of service, also include programs with administrative activities, educational policy design, and production and distribution of educational materials. FPs with a specific target population target subpopulations of children in vulnerable conditions such as children in poverty, in highly marginalized localities, indigenous, with some disability, in a situation of violence, or with low results in learning tests.

federalized spending programs, and the rest to federal programs (see Table 7 below). This information comes from the Federal Expenditure Budget 2019 and 2020 (DOF, 2018; 2019h), which is the only available resource that reveals the structure of federal education spending. This chapter reviews the operating rules of such pro-equity programs (see Table 7).

In 2020, there were 11 ongoing federal programs that were designed to promote equity, six of which were new initiatives. The three most important initiatives continuing from previous administrations include:

- *Benito Juárez Basic Education Scholarship Program for Welfare*, which replaced the Prospera program launched in 1997.[9] This program seeks to promote attendance, permanence, and graduation from compulsory education for children and young students enrolled in basic education institutions, whose families: (i) are located in priority localities and/or with children under five years of age residing in those localities, or (ii) have an estimated monthly per-capita income below the Coneval Income Poverty Line (LPI)[10] (DOF, 2019a). In 2020, the planned budgetary allocation for this cash transfer program is $1,348.5 million (30,475.1[11] million pesos), an amount that is 50 percent higher, in real terms, than what Prospera spent in 2018, a share of 63.3 percent in the total planned spending for federal programs on basic education for vulnerable populations. It is expected that each beneficiary family will be granted a scholarship consisting of 800 pesos ($36.34) per month during 10 months of the year.

- *The Full-Time Schools Program*,[12] in effect since 2007, aims to establish full-time schools in basic education, with 6–8-hour-long days, to better promote the well-rounded education of their students. Eligible schools are single-shift public basic

---

9 This program is described in greater detail in Section 5 of this document.
10 In 2019, the average rural and urban LPIs monthly per capita were equal to $104.55 and $161.36, respectively. In Mexican pesos these figures were 2,011.27 and 3,104.30 pesos, respectively.
11 Nominal budget is translated into dollars at the exchange rate of 22.012 pesos to 1 US dollar. Rate of exchange is unstable now in Mexico. This rate of exchange corresponds to July 29, 2020 (Banxico, 2020).
12 This program is described in greater detail in the next section.

Table 7. Federal spending on basic education by budget program (millions of pesos) (spent in 2018; planned for 2019 and 2020).

Type of program	Target population	Nominal (% of total)							In 2018 prices[2]			Diff.
		2018	(%)	2019e	(%)	2020e	(%)	2018	2019e	2020e	2018–2020
Federalized spending program	General	418,933.4	91.1	428,241.0	88.1	443,135.3	89.2	418,933.4	413,216.6	413,128.8	−5,804.6
Federal program	General	4,896.3	1.1	4,768.5	1.0	5,385.8	1.1	4,896.3	4,601.2	5,021.1	124.8
	In vulnerability conditions	35,968.0	7.8	52,996.4	10.9	48,167.6	9.7	35,968.0	51,137.0	44,905.9	8,937.9
		40,864.4	8.9	57,764.9	11.9	53,553.3	10.8	40,864.4	55,738.3	49,927.0	9,062.7
Total in federalized spending programs and federal programs		459,797.7	100.0	486,005.9	100.0	496,688.6	100.0	459,797.7	468,954.9	463,055.8	3,258.1
	(Real percentage change compared to 2018)								2.0	0.7	

[1] The target population was determined based on the Rules of Operation or Guidelines of each budget program.

[2] Nominal values were deflated by the National Consumer Price Index (INPC). The monthly INPC was annualized and the 2018 average was taken as a reference. For 2020, we used the expected inflation according to the Encuesta sobre las Expectativas de los Especialistas en Economía del Sector Privado: Enero de 2020 (Banxico, 2020, February 4), which was 3.5%.

e Estimations, according to the approved budget in the Presupuesto de Egresos de la Federación for 2019 and 2020. Source: Calculations based on Cuenta de la Hacienda Pública Federal 2018 (SHCP, 2019); Presupuesto de Egresos de Federación 2019 and 2020 (SHCP, 2020); and Índice Nacional de Precios al Consumidor (INEGI, 2020).

education institutions that meet at least one of the following criteria: (a) they are indigenous or multigrade schools; (b) they offer primary or telesecondary education; (c) they serve a population in a situation of vulnerability or in contexts of social risk; or (d) their students have low levels of educational achievement or high dropout rates. In 2020, this program was allocated a budget of $231.7 million USD (5,100 million pesos), which amounts to 10.6 percent of the federal government's pro-equity spending, much lower than the 29.9 percent share it received in 2018.

- *The Early Childhood and Community Education Program* is aimed at subpopulations in localities with high and very high levels of marginalization and social backwardness that should be served by the CONAFE system, especially the indigenous population. In early childhood education, the target population comprises pregnant women, and children aged 0–3 and their mothers, fathers, and caregivers. In basic community education, the target population is children and youth aged 3–16. This program intends to ensure the completion of the basic education provided by CONAFE (DOF, 2019b). In 2020, the planned expenditure for this program is $204.6 million (4,503.1 million pesos), which is less than the budget allocated in previous years (in 2018, $210.6 million or 4,634.6 million pesos).

There are six pro-equity FPs in basic education created between 2019 and 2020 by the current federal administration. In 2020, the aggregate expenditure allocation of the six new programs is $349.65 million (7,696.4 million pesos). Key examples are:

- *This School Is Our School*, created in 2020, aims to improve the infrastructure and equipment conditions of public basic education facilities, giving priority to those located in areas with the greatest backwardness, preferably in localities with high or very high levels of marginalization and a high concentration of indigenous people (DOF, 2019c). This is the second most important program of the current federal government, as it receives 15.1 percent of federal spending for vulnerable populations, amounting to $330.7 million

(7,280.3 million pesos), equivalent to just under a quarter of what is allocated to the Benito Juárez Scholarship Program (23.9 percent). The amount defined for each school is given to the PTA to administer, and is a major innovation supporting previous school infrastructure programs.

- *The Program for the Development of Meaningful Learning in Basic Education* seeks to contribute to the improvement of the academic achievement of students in public basic education schools that concentrate the greatest number of students with the lowest academic achievement levels on the PLANEA standardized tests. It is designed to prioritize schools located in communities with high rates of extreme poverty and violence or a high concentration of indigenous population (DOF, 2019d). In 2020 it was allocated $7.4 million (163.9 million pesos), which represents less than one-third of a percentage point of federal pro-equity spending on basic education.

- *The Support for Diversity in Indigenous Education Program* aims to improve education in indigenous schools. It will give priority to schools in localities with high and very high levels of marginalization, those with lower levels of educational achievement according to PLANEA, and those with greater needs for educational materials (DOF, 2019e). However, in 2020 it will receive only $4.2 million (92.5 million pesos), one-fifth of a percentage point of federal pro-equity spending.

In closing, it can be seen that the expenditure planned by the new federal administration represents an important change in the public spending policy, but it is also clear that such spending is only a fraction of what is needed to support educational equity. The economic crisis due to the COVID-19 pandemic will likely lead to significant reductions in the pro-equity education expenditure.

Education programs that have proven effective, and their challenges

This section reports on the most important elements of three federally-driven programs that have sought to improve educational opportunities for children and youth at the bottom of the pyramid and have achieved good results. The three programs bear little similarity to each other in terms of their specific objectives, operational strategies, and timing. Fortunately, there is evidence on the achievements of each of these three programs, as described below.

Progresa-Oportunidades-Prospera, 1997–2019[13]

The Education, Health, and Nutrition Program (Progresa) was launched in August 1997, under President Zedillo's administration, with two objectives: 1) to improve the welfare of families by increasing their purchasing power, and 2) to develop the human capital of its members, mainly children and young people, in order to improve their future welfare and income. Underlying the design of Progresa was the conviction that investment in human capital (education, health, and food) was the best way to break the cycle of poverty (Rodríguez, 2019; Yaschine, 2019).

To address the education component, cash scholarships were provided to mothers for each child that attended school, from third grade of primary school to third grade of secondary school. The scholarship was conditional on school attendance and the amount was higher for girls and children in secondary school, in order to discourage the early entry of children into the workforce. The health component involved access to a preventive health package, health education, and the provision of food supplements for young children and pregnant or breastfeeding women, since malnutrition was proven to have long-term effects on school and work performance. The food component was addressed by providing cash transfers to families, subject to attendance to health consultations and educational sessions. These transfers represented one-third of the average monetary income of families living in extreme poverty (Yaschine, 2019).

The original beneficiaries were families living in rural areas where poverty was much more acute than in the urban environment. In 1997,

---

13 The main source of information for this section is the book published by the CONEVAL in 2019 to commemorate the 20 years of Progresa-Oportunidades-Prospera, especially the chapter written by Iliana Yaschine (2019) on the history of the program.

300,000 families living in extreme poverty were assisted. A few years later, coverage was extended to semi-urban and urban localities.

In 2002, educational scholarships were extended to high-school students in order to encourage secondary-school graduates to continue their studies. As of 2012, support was extended to children in rural areas in the first two grades of primary school to avoid lagging behind and encourage them to stay in school. Starting in 2017, students who were entering public universities were given scholarships and transportation aid.

The program remained a nodal part of the poverty reduction strategy for three additional administrations. During President Peña Nieto's administration (2012–2018), the name changed to Prospera, Social Inclusion Program. By the end of Zedillo's administration, the program was reaching 2.5 million predominantly rural households. In 2004 it reached 5 million rural, semi-urban, and urban families; in 2010 the figure rose to 6 million; and in 2017 to 6.6 million, amounting to a total of 27 million people distributed in 114 thousand localities. According to CONEVAL (Yaschine, 2019), this figure only covers 63 percent of the potential target population, since the number of people in poverty has been increasing during the last few decades.

An important contributor to the success of Progresa-Oportunidades-Prospera (POP) was its built-in robust evaluation system to describe its results and give feedback on its design and operation. All evaluation databases are public so that anyone can replicate the measurements or carry out their own analyses (Rodríguez, 2019). Thanks to this system, we know that POP did have significant positive impacts on the human capital of the beneficiary families. In spite of these results, the evidence does not show results in improving school-based learning of the beneficiaries, as measured by standardized tests (Yaschine, 2019).

Program for the Improvement of Educational Achievement, 2009–2012

The Program for the Improvement of Educational Achievement (PMLE) was created in 2009 to improve school achievement in the public primary and secondary schools with the lowest scores. The central strategy of the program consisted of developing training and personalized support networks based on tutoring relationships, taking advantage of the human resources available in the education system (SEP, 2010).

The PMLE focused mainly on the development of independent text-based learning through tutoring relationships. At the federal level—as well as in states, school zones, and schools—collegial work teams (nodes) were created to study the topics in which students performed the poorest in the ENLACE test.[14] The focus on this curriculum content was complemented by the establishment of mentoring relationships within and across the nodes, allowing for the modeling and practice of the type of instruction teachers were expected to develop in their classrooms (Rincón-Gallardo, 2016).

Between 2010 and 2012, 9,072 schools were supported with training networks and personalized accompaniment based on tutoring relationships (SEP, 2012). Although only some of these schools were visited regularly by an advisor, it is possible to say that their teachers were directly exposed to the practice of tutoring networks. In those same years, more than 200 exchanges were carried out between schools, regions, and states in order to show, practice, consolidate, and disseminate the methodology of tutorial relationships (Rincón-Gallardo, 2016).

An analysis of the results obtained in ENLACE in 11,500 secondary schools was carried out, including 4,101 schools that participated in the PMLE (UPEPE, 2012). The study assumed that progress in the adoption of the tutoring-relationship methodology in each school would be strongly associated with the number of advisory visits that their teachers received: the more visits, the higher the quality of the tutoring competence in the classrooms. The program consists of three phases. In Phase 1, participants have some knowledge of the tutoring relationship methodology, but their experience is limited and they have received no counseling visits; in Phase 2, teacher networks have been established and counseling visits to schools are carried out sporadically (a maximum of five visits); in Phase 3, networks of students as well as parents have been established and regular counseling visits to the school (six or more) have taken place. As shown in Figures 1 and 2, PMLE secondary schools, in any phase, show greater increases in the percentage of students in the good and excellent levels than in non-participating schools. In addition,

---

14   The ENLACE test was used from 2006 to 2013 and was replaced by PLANEA starting in 2015.

the progress of secondary schools whose teachers received five or more advisory visits is greater than the rest of the schools, some of which even show declines. Improvements are greater in mathematics than in Spanish.

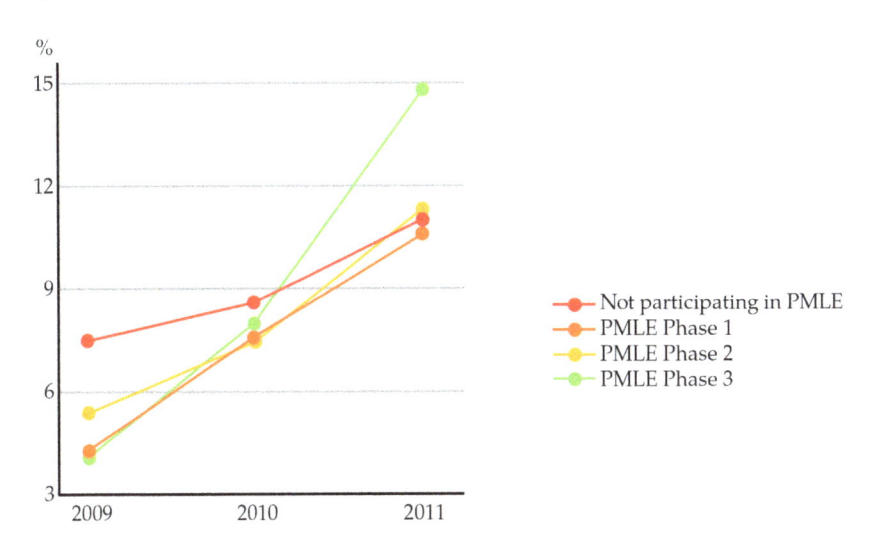

Fig. 1. Percentage of general secondary school students at "good" and "excellent" levels in mathematics, by degree of involvement in the PMLE. Source: Data obtained from UPEPE (2012).

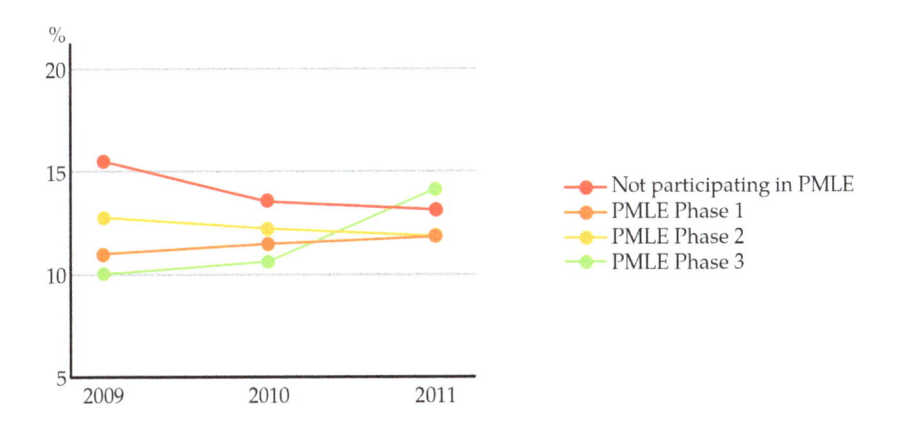

Fig. 2. Percentage of general secondary students at "good" and "excellent" levels in Spanish, by degree of involvement in the PMLE. Source: Data obtained from UPEPE (2012).

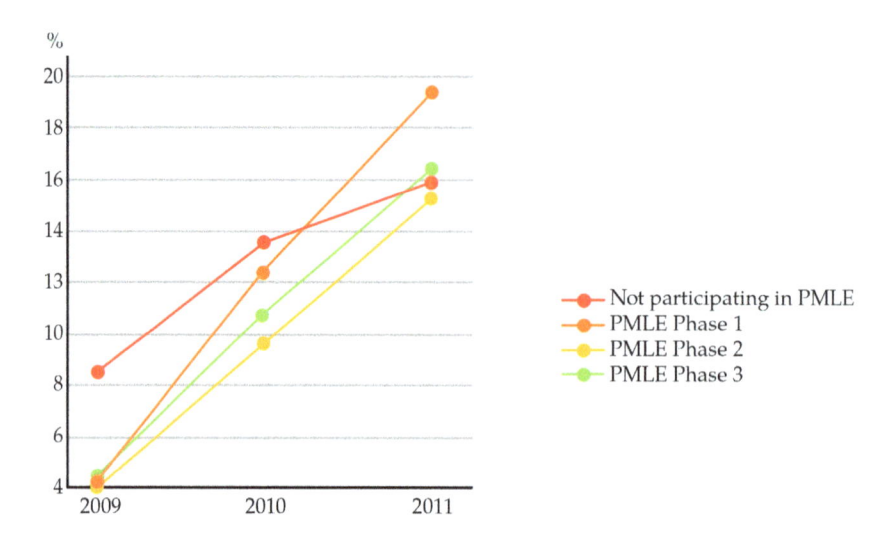

Fig. 3. Percentage of telesecondary students at "good" and "excellent" levels in mathematics, by degree of involvement in the PMLE. Source: Data obtained from UPEPE (2012).

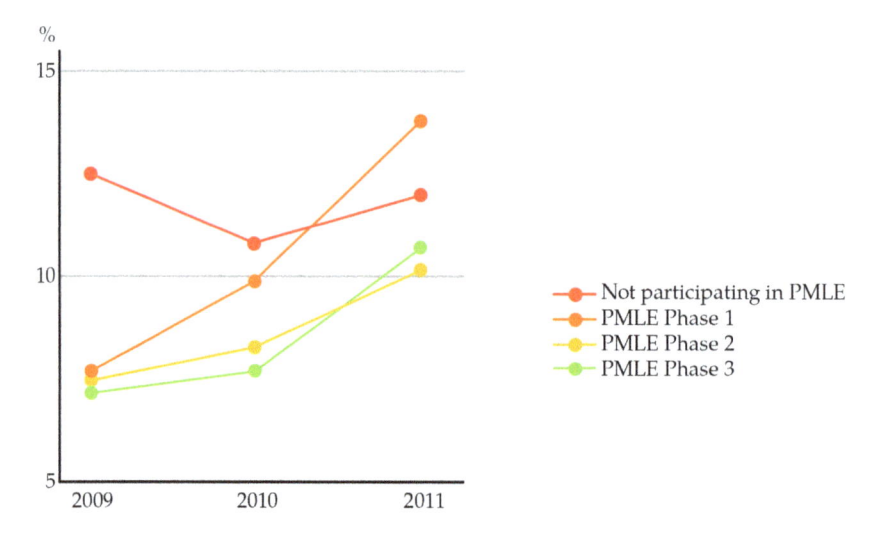

Fig. 4. Percentage of telesecondary students at "good" and "excellent" levels in Spanish, by degree of involvement in the PMLE. Source: Data obtained from UPEPE (2012).

In the case of telesecondary schools (Figures 3 and 4), PMLE schools also achieved greater increases than those that did not participate in the program. In both topic areas evaluated (mathematics and Spanish), it is the schools located in Phase 1—teachers who have been exposed to the practice through workshops, but have not received advisory visits to help them with implementation in their classrooms—that show the most progress, even more so than the schools that received more visits. One hypothesis for this result is that contact with a new methodology enhances motivation for teaching change and creates a motivational feedback loop.

The PMLE ended abruptly in December 2012 when a new federal administration took office.

Full-Time Schools Program, 2007 to date

The Full-Time Schools Program (PETC) is the only federal intervention targeting public basic education schools that has remained in place over the past three presidential six-year terms. It was launched in the 2007–2008 school year as a pilot initiative intended to improve learning opportunities for girls and boys by increasing the time they spend in school each day, on the assumption that this additional time would be devoted to strengthening the teaching of curricular content. Over the years, this mandate has been expanded to include other objectives beyond strengthening the curriculum, and additional actions have been taken to tackle malnutrition and improve social harmony (Luna & Velázquez, 2019).

For the year 2020, the general objective of the PETC is: "To establish, gradually, progressively, and in accordance with budgetary sufficiency, schools with a full schedule in basic education, with six-to-eight-hour-long days, to promote better use of available time, improve academic performance and encourage participation in activities related to the knowledge of civics, humanities, science and technology, the arts—especially music—physical education and environmental protection" (DOF, 2019j).

Like all schools in Mexico, full-time schools operate for 200 school days a year, but extend their hours from 4–4.5 to 6–8,[15] depending on whether they are primary or secondary schools and whether they offer

---

15 Mexican public-school days are four to four-and-a-half hours long in primary education and six hours long in secondary education.

food service or not. Full-Time Schools (FTS) can decide how to use the additional hours to work on their School Improvement Program, taking into consideration the seven Educational Lines of Work defined by SEP.[16]

In its early days, the PETC was aimed at public basic education schools that served populations in unfavorable conditions in urban contexts with poor educational results (Luna & Velázquez, 2019). As the program has expanded, its target population has been extended to cover rural populations; by 2020, the target population comprises single-shift public basic education schools that meet at least one of the following criteria: a) are indigenous or multigrade education schools; b) offer primary or telesecondary education; c) cater to populations in vulnerable situations or in contexts of social risk; and, d) have low levels of educational achievement or high dropout rates (DOF, 2019j).

During the administration of President Enrique Peña Nieto (2006–2012), the number of FTS increased considerably. As can be seen in Figure 5, in 2013, the number of schools incorporated into the program grew 129 percent to 15,349 schools and, in 2014, it grew a further 50 percent to a total of 23,182 schools. From 2015 to date, the number of schools has stabilized, as growth rates have not exceeded 2.5 percent since then. The figure reported for 2019 is 25,697 primary and secondary schools.

In the current school year (2019–2020), half of all FTS offer food service. This figure rises to 75 percent for indigenous primary schools, 62 percent for indigenous preschools, and 56 percent for telesecondary schools—the three types of schools that serve populations at the bottom of the pyramid (see Figure 5).

The results of the PETC, SEP (2017) include two independent investigations that show evidence of its impact. Both Andrade (2014) and Cabrera (2014) observed a positive effect on student performance in reading and math—as measured by the ENLACE test—and found cumulative effects. Another study, conducted by Padilla (2016), found that during the first year of implementation of PETC, the extension of the day does not affect Spanish and math scores, but during the second year, increases are observed in both subjects. Padilla also states that the effects

---

16 A description of the seven Lines of Work and their educational materials is available at: https://educacionbasica.sep.gob.mx/site/proetc#PP_PETC_Basica.

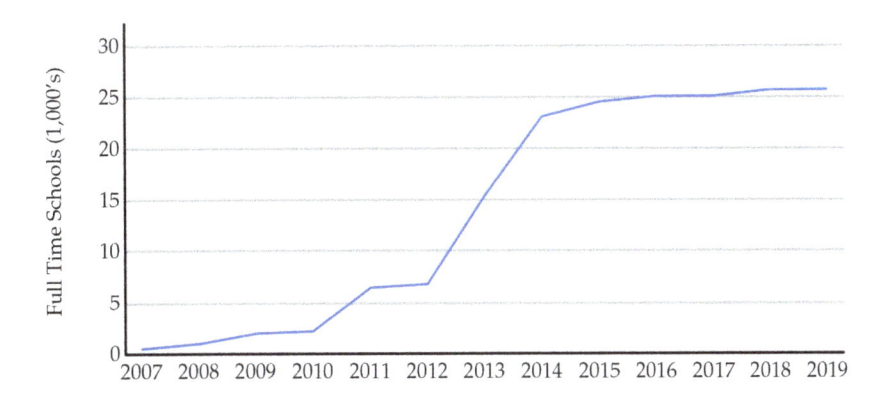

Fig. 5. Full-time schools, 2017–2019. Source: Prepared by the authors using varied sources.

are greater for students from schools located in highly marginalized areas and for those in the lower grades.

Sylveira and colleagues (2018) report that "participation in PETC reduces the proportion of students at the lowest level of performance on standardized tests by about 4.6% in Mathematics and 1.77% in Language. On the other hand, there is an increase in students at the highest performance level" (1.62 percent in mathematics and 0.63 percent in language). The results of the study revealed that the schools with the most marginalization participating in the PETC showed "greater reductions in the proportion of students at the lowest level of achievement in Mathematics and Language, and with severe educational lag" (p. 8).

From the results of these evaluations, it can be stated that the PETC has contributed to improving the school performance of students, especially the least advantaged among them. However, it cannot be concluded that the improvements are due to better use of time for teaching, as the program does not provide teacher training support. Among the hypotheses to explain the improvements in test outcomes is, of course, the feeding of children in poverty. However, it seems even more plausible that the gains are due to the increased time that children spend away from activities that do not promote learning (Cabrera, 2018).

Initiatives that address educational challenges at the bottom of the pyramid

There are several pilot projects at different scales that are aimed at improving learning among those at the bottom of the pyramid. Unfortunately, they have not been evaluated and there is not enough evidence that they actually improve learning. We have chosen to describe two of these initiatives because of their wide acceptance and their potential for impact.

Tutoring Networks

When the PMLE (discussed above) ended in December 2012, several of its promoters formed a civil society organization[17] that continues working to promote the adoption of this alternative methodology in primary schools, secondary schools, and high schools, both in Mexico and abroad.[18]

Tutoring Networks (TN) is based on two fundamental pedagogical purposes: 1) to generate collaboration and dialogue between those who want to learn and those who are able and willing to share what they have previously learned, and 2) to achieve in each student the commitment and capacity to learn autonomously, through the development of reading, writing, oral expression, and mathematical reasoning skills. Both purposes involve placing at the center of interactions between tutors and learners their confidence and ability to become aware of their own personal learning process while recognizing that of others.

Tutoring begins when the student chooses the topic of study from a variety of options offered by the tutor, over which the tutor has already acquired mastery. Once the learner has chosen the topic he or she is interested in learning about, the individual process of inquiry and study begins. The student works at his or her own pace, puts learning strategies into play, and decides what to do. The tutor keeps an eye on this process and offers support when the learner has a need, encouraging him or her to identify and overcome his or her difficulties. Errors are key to

---

17 Tutoring Networks, in Spanish, is Redes de Tutoría.
18 TN has been taken to rural and urban schools in Chile through the Education 2020 Foundation, as well as to schools in Thailand, Singapore, Indonesia, and Argentina.

the learning process; the learner has the opportunity to analyze the logical sequence followed to construct a statement and cannot continue until he/she understands how he/she reached an incorrect or a correct answer. The tutor must help the learner to identify the specific elements of success in the topic at hand (Lopez, 2016).

As the tutoring progresses, the learner records, in writing, the learning process. Writing helps organize ideas, express doubts, identify findings, and clarify how the learner has managed to understand the chosen topic—that is, to reconstruct the mental process by which the learner synthesized the known with the unknown in order to achieve an understanding of the new topic.

The written record of the learning process functions as evidence of achievement and as support for preparing the public demonstration, which must be made in front of the group (and sometimes also family members and the community) to share with others what has been studied and how it has been learned. This public "demonstration" is also evidence of learning; in addition, it allows the tutor to know if a learner is able to provide tutoring on the subject to another person. By demonstrating a topic, the learner becomes a tutor.

The possibility for each apprentice to become a tutor after learning a subject in-depth is a core part of TN. No one learns something as well as when teaching it (Cámara, 2014; Rincón-Gallardo, 2012). When tutoring occurs among peers, it contributes to the formation of a support network in which personalized attention does not depend on the teacher or the number of members in a group. Everyone learns from everyone else and, therefore, the roles of teacher and students are reconfigured by the creation of a community that is willing to learn and share (López, 2016; Rincón-Gallardo, 2016).

TN is a highly portable methodology and, once it is learned, few seem to wish to return to conventional practices; it only requires the will to learn and textual resources in various formats. It has been easily rooted in marginalized schools, where needs are greater, while institutional controls and resistance to disrupting conventional school culture are weaker. In these contexts, it has been possible to attempt to transform the core of instruction—the relationship between teachers and students—in large part because this change makes improvements in learning more visible (Rincón-Gallardo, 2014).

While no formal studies have assessed the impact of TNs so far, there are testimonies from students, teachers, supervisors, and graduates,[19] as well as some writings from leading education scholars that remark on their promising benefits for learning.[20] The results of the PEMLE, described above, give credibility to the potential of this approach for learners at the bottom of the pyramid.

Attendance, Permanence, and Learning model

The Attendance, Permanence, and Learning (Asistencia, Permanencia, Aprendizaje or APA) model was designed[21] to support state governments as they converged their education policy decisions around three fundamental objectives: student attendance, retention, and learning in compulsory education. The APA model was first implemented in the state of Puebla[22] during the 2011–2017 administration. The state education authorities sought to address problems of quality and equity through an accessible, high-impact model of education policy that could be easily communicated and understood by all stakeholders, so that they could integrate and work towards common goals (INEE, 2018c). The objectives proposed by the APA model are:

- Attendance. All girls and boys aged 3–17 should attend school.
- Permanence. All students should complete high school (Grade 12).
- Learning. Each student should acquire at least the basic knowledge established in the curricula.

These objectives would be achieved by promoting an education policy centered on four management strategies:

1. *Focalization.* Since the available resources (human, budgetary, material) are insufficient, all actions must be targeted so as

---

19 The testimonies can be read on the webpage redestutoria.com.
20 See El aprendizaje bajo la lupa published by UNICEF in 2015 and authored by Inés Aguerrondo y Denisse Vaillant.
21 Proyecto Educativo, S.C. was responsible for the design. According to its webpage (https://www.proyectoeducativo.org/), the APA model adapts the logic of a model used in the province of Ontario, Canada, which had similar objectives.
22 In 2018, Puebla had a population of 6.3 million people. That same year it ranked fifth (out of 32) in poverty with 58.9 percent of its population in poverty and 8.6 percent in extreme poverty, according to CONEVAL figures.

to achieve greater equity and reduce inequality gaps, which means giving priority to those most in need of support. Resources should target schools in a number small enough to guarantee a significant impact.

2. *Articulation.* Good coordination between state and federal programs, educational levels, and agencies within the education sector and outside of it is essential to ensuring the complementarity of the actions.

3. *Implementation.* Coordinated action by the education system requires communication that ensures that everyone involved agrees on the various efforts and its objectives, and understands their powers and responsibilities. A good part of the success of the model lies in the ease of understanding and sharing these objectives.

4. *Accompaniment.* The articulated implementation must be accompanied so that the actions developed and the perception of the different actors can be monitored in order to identify risks and opportunities at the right time.

In the case of Puebla, the model was applied to 500 schools—200 primary schools and 200 secondary schools selected for their low results in the ENLACE test—as well as 100 preschools whose graduates were mostly served by the targeted primary schools. Although academic performance was the only criterion used to choose these schools, the high correlation with socioeconomic level meant that the selected schools were located in the lowest income deciles. Participation was voluntary, so that schools that did not wish to be included were replaced.

Multiple actions were promoted to serve each of the four levels of compulsory education, seeking to involve all actors (students, teachers, principals, supervisors, and parents). Supervisors (950) were trained in leadership skills and the Puebla Supervisors' Academy was created. An APA report was generated for each at-risk student in each of the state's schools.[23]

---

23 To learn more about the actions implemented at each level, see the interview published in the Gaceta del INEE (2018) and the 5th Report of the Secretariat of Education in the State of Puebla.

The results of the implementation of the APA model in academic performance were very positive, as reflected in the national evaluations (Figure 6)[24] that shows the annual rank occupied by Puebla in standardized tests as compared to the other 31 states.[25]

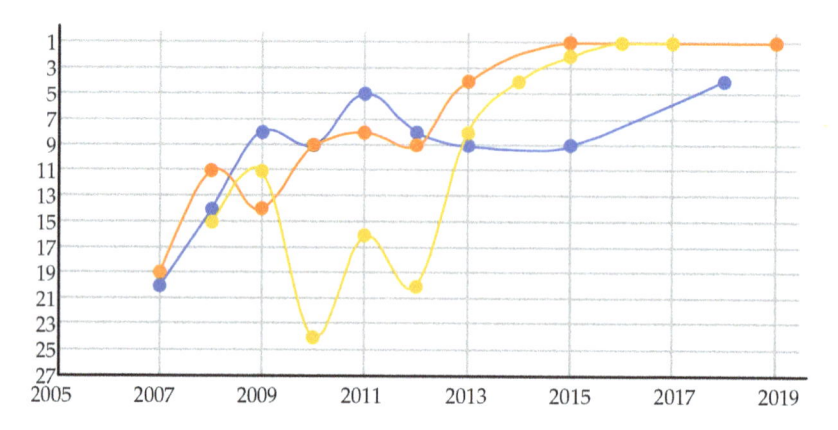

Fig. 6. Puebla's ranking relative to both rich and poor states. Source: Data from SEP, ENLACE 2006 to 2013, and PLANEA 2015.

Although all schools increased their achievement scores (de Hoyos, in press), Puebla's 200 targeted secondary schools, between 2013 and 2015, not only ceased to be in the last quartile of performance in language and mathematics, but in both subjects exceeded the national average recorded in the PLANEA test. In 2015, for the very first time, Puebla's secondary schools achieved first place nationally in mathematics and third place in language and communication. These results also reflect progress in equity. Puebla has managed to remain in first place nationwide in terms of academic achievement, despite being one of the five most marginalized states in Mexico.

To some extent, the scalability of the APA Model is demonstrated by the fact that it has been implemented in a state that has a compulsory education enrollment (K-12) that is twice as large as Finland's. Other

---

[24] The graph is taken from the presentation "Puebla. Innovation and improvement for students' attendance, graduation and learning", made by Bernardo Naranjo (member of Proyecto Educativo, S.C.) and presented to the Bill & Melinda Gates Foundation in December 2019.

[25] The ENLACE test was used from 2006 to 2013 and was replaced by PLANEA starting in 2015. The use of relative rank allows us to eliminate biases derived from comparability between both tests.

important attributes are its sustainability and its transferability to other locations. In Proyecto Educativo's opinion, the fact that Puebla has remained at the top of the national tests for five consecutive years seems to be due to the work of the supervisors and the creation of collegial bodies in which teachers participate. It is worth mentioning that other Mexican states—Sonora and Coahuila—have already replicated it with some local changes, demonstrating that the APA model can be adapted to other national regions and beyond.

Improving educational policies for the poor

Historically, education policy in Mexico has been successful in improving access to school, as well as permanence. Since the creation of the Secretariat of Education in 1921, Mexico has achieved almost universal primary education, it has expanded preschool to three years, it has made lower- and higher-secondary education compulsory, and it has diminished dropout rates at the primary- and lower-secondary levels.

Even so, the expansion of the Mexican Educational System has been constant but unequal, benefiting those in urban and more developed regions first, and leaving small rural and indigenous communities to the last. This trickle-down model is still in operation with the educational levels that are still expanding, as is the case with preschool and higher-secondary education. Thus, it is the students in these conditions that find it more difficult to attend school and complete their compulsory education. Being in school is a condition for school-based learning, and thus it is a matter of concern that 4.8 million children and adolescents aged 3 to 17 are not in school. So even though the Mexican Educational System has shown a steady expansion of educational opportunities, around 15 percent of school-aged children and adolescents are not even enrolled at the different levels of education. They are at the bottom of the learning pyramid.

But what is really alarming is the number of children and adolescents who are in school but are not learning. We have shown that between one- and two-thirds of students enrolled in the Mexican Educational System is achieving below Level 2 in the standardized tests based on the national curriculum. PISA (OECD, 2019) and LLECE (UNESCO,

2015) assessments show similar results. Those that have been situated at the bottom of the learning pyramid are children and adolescents living in small rural communities, indigenous students, children that work, those living in highly marginalized areas, internal migrants, and disabled students. There is a strong correlation between all of these characteristics and learning results in standardized tests. Those that are located at the bottom of the learning pyramid according to standardized tests represent at least 50 percent of children and adolescents in school. This amount is alarming and does not correspond to what one would expect of a middle-income country. Mexico has not been successful in achieving the learning what standardized tests measure. Neither has it been successful in improving these results (Backhoff et al., 2017).

It is important to analyze the causes of this reality. An external cause is, of course, poverty and its consequences, such as the need to work, malnutrition, migration, as well as the fact that those in poverty tend to have parents with less schooling who are less able to help in school-related activities. But there are also at least three very important factors that can improve educational policy for the poor in Mexico.

The first is the training of teachers. In Mexico, teacher training was a technical career (three years after lower secondary) until 1984, when it became a tertiary-level education, lasting four years after higher secondary. Nevertheless, little changed in the way teachers were taught, because those training future teachers were the same as before. It has taken a long time for teacher-training institutions to evolve towards improved quality teaching. Teacher training does not take place in universities, but in normal schools, of which there are 464 in Mexico. Most of these normal (teacher-training) schools are very small and have no capacity for carrying out research. Normal schools in general have very few experts in the disciplines as professors; they are mainly people who have been trained as teachers themselves and who reproduce the way they were taught. The result is low-quality teaching of graduates who, once in the classroom, receive inadequate in-service training and little pedagogically oriented supervision. In many classrooms, and particularly in those in the poorer regions, teachers teach by rote instruction and have no training in inclusive pedagogy. Forty-six percent of primary schools in Mexico are multigrade (one teacher teaching more than one grade, sometimes even the six grades in small communities), and teachers receive no training in multigrade methodology.

The second is the curriculum and the language of instruction. When the modern school system was installed at the beginning of the last century, schools were conceived as the route towards integration into the mainstream culture. At that time, about 25 percent of the population were indigenous language speakers, but indigenous children attended schools where they were taught in Spanish. As a consequence, indigenous children learned very little and took a long time to become literate. Though things have changed somewhat over the years—and, at least in theory, indigenous primary schools teach their students to be fully bilingual—the force of the original momentum explains why even teachers themselves believe that using Indigenous languages is a sign of backwardness. Curriculum in Mexico has been national and uniform since the inception of the present system, and for non-mainstream children and youth, what they learn in school remains foreign to their context and interests. Thus, lack of relevance of school-based education for a large percentage of the population is another important cause, to which we must add the small degree of parent and community participation in schools, which helps to explain the likelihood of low educational aspirations.

The third cause is the fact that equity in education, and particularly equity in learning, has never really been a priority in the Mexican Educational System. The priority a country gives to equity in education is reflected in the way resources—financial, physical, pedagogical, and human—are distributed among the different sectors of the population. In Mexico, those who are dispossessed receive the least and poorest resources or all types. Traditionally, resources have been distributed according to political motives more than to equity-related criteria.

Conclusions

The learning problem of more than half of the Mexican school-aged population that is described in this chapter is based on information that is available but still incomplete. Further, and more detailed, information is needed in order to be able to carry out an in-depth analysis of those children who are not in school or not learning in school. Standardized achievement tests are partial because they only consistently measure the school-based areas of language and mathematics.[26]

Policies and programs have been put into place to mitigate the effects of poverty on education, but they continue to privilege access and permanence in education, rather than learning. Some have shown an ability to mitigate inequality, and some have been evaluated as to their impact (the case of Prospera or Full-Time Schools). Civil society organizations have developed interesting initiatives for improving learning at the bottom of the pyramid, which have shown signs of being successful on a smaller scale and should be looked into more deeply.

The government that came into office in December of 2018 modified the Constitution in 2019, and established educational equity as a priority. It also defined education in Mexico—in addition to the historical definition of free and lay—as *inclusive* and *intercultural*. Unfortunately, the programs that have been put in place to date are still oriented towards improving access and permanence, not learning that is both inclusive and intercultural. Hopefully, we can expect future changes that can bring about learning equity among those at the bottom of the pyramid.

Appendix

Information and knowledge gaps

Information is necessary in order to be able to identify educational problems and to design adequate policies to face them. The information that we have used to identify vulnerable and marginalized populations with respect to education gives us a clear idea of both the size and the location of the problems. Educational research uses this information to further explore causes and possible solutions.

However, in spite of continuous efforts to improve the information available, in Mexico we still have serious information gaps that prevent us from achieving these ends.

---

26 Context questionnaires that accompany the tests allow for the testing of hypotheses on different learning behaviors of different populations and their possible causes. In the Appendix, we provide an additional analysis what information is lacking.

Information on teachers of compulsory education

Historically, information on teachers in the national education system has been very limited. It has not been in the interest of the National Union of Education Workers to make this information accessible to the public. In 2014, a Census of Students, Teachers, and Schools of Basic Education (CEMABE) was carried out for the first—and, to date, the only—time. It yielded school-by-school information on enrolled students, teachers assigned to them, and some information on their working conditions. From this census we know, in broad terms, that the number of basic education workers that year was 1,949,105. Of them, 88.1 percent worked in basic and special education schools, 2 percent in special-education-support work centers, and 9.9 percent in other work centers. The number of people working as classroom teachers was 978,118.

In 2015, the National Institute for Educational Evaluation (INEE) published in its annual report for 2015 (INEE, 2015) a systematization of the information available on the teaching staff in the educational system, including the information derived from the results of the first two entrance examinations for teachers. Among the findings, it is worth noting that teaching as a career is losing its attractiveness since during the two school years prior to the publication of this report, the demand for teacher training had declined and 27.4 percent of the available positions had remained vacant.

Regarding teacher training in the 484 teacher training colleges, information was available on the results of mid-training and final examinations up to 2013, in which almost half the students had insufficient achievement. The year 2014 was the first year in which examinations were applied to start teaching, and only 40.4 percent of prospective teachers reached the level of sufficient achievement. It should be noted, however, that in the following years this figure increased, indicating that teacher-training colleges were striving to achieve better learning outcomes among their students in order to achieve better results in teacher entrance examinations.

The payroll for teachers used to be handled by the states, but in 2017, the lack of reliable information and the states' debts to the social security system and the treasury led to the centralization of the payroll. For transparency reasons, this payroll is now in a public database, and it is possible to know how many active teachers there are, by state and level, as well as their income levels. With time, studies can be made of teacher mobility.

The available information about teachers, their training, background, and performance is therefore partial at best and not yet entirely reliable.

Information on groups requiring special attention

In addition to information on teachers, which is fundamental for improving the initial and in-service training of teachers and for guiding their placement in schools according to the specific needs of their populations, in Mexico, as in many other countries, we lack the necessary information to be able to serve special population groups that would require special attention. Some of the data is structurally unavailable. For instance, we do not know how many children of migrant farmworkers there are, and the data on how many of them are in school and their background and performance are unreliable. It is estimated that around 350,000 children and young people aged 5–17 are in this condition. It is also estimated that only 10 percent of them are in school (INEE, 2016).

We do not have any information about their learning. We also lack information on the number of indigenous students and speakers of an indigenous language enrolled in schools that are not indigenous. Even in indigenous schools, some students are not indigenous but are nevertheless counted as such. Indigenous schools only exist at the preschool and primary levels and only 53 percent of indigenous students attend these schools (INEE, 2017).

Information about people with disabilities is scarce and incomplete, and we know even less about their access to education, their permanence in school, and their learning achievement (INEE, 2017). This incomplete and unreliable information is a reality that we have carried with us since the creation of the SEP in 1921 and its absence has not been addressed.

There are also emerging situations. There is a complete lack of information about students displaced by violence, as well as about schools that shut down because it's too dangerous for teachers to travel to their localities. Faced with an emerging reality of significant migration on the northern border, due to the deportation of undocumented Mexican people from the United States, and on the southern border, due to the migration of Central Americans and others who manage to cross this border to transit through Mexico and reach the United States, we lack timely and reliable information and cannot assume that this population is fulfilling its human right to education.

Information on learning

Since 2000 we have information about the learning of children and young people in school in Mexico. The INEE, founded in 2002, was responsible for the administration of the PISA test as well as the Latin American LLECE test. Beginning in 2005, it administered the EXCALE test to a sample of students in different grades of primary and secondary school, and as of 2015 EXCALE was substituted by the PLANEA ELSEN test (based on a representative sample of schools in each of the 32 states) to students at all levels of compulsory education.

There have also been evaluation efforts by the Secretariat of Public Education with tests applied to all students (ENLACE) or schools (PLANEA ELCE) since 2005. These tests measure students' reading ability and their level of achievement in Mathematics in a consistent manner. The INEE attempted to also measure achievement in natural sciences and civic and ethical education. This information, however, was not able to be measured consistently, and the picture that emerges from its results is incomplete. Other areas of learning, including social-emotional skills, have not been successfully measured, and the situation of the national population in this regard is still unknown.

Information on inequalities in compulsory education

Information on the ways in which different sectors of the population are served and on the differential results of their education is fundamental to adequately serve the bottom of the pyramid. The INEE made a systematic effort to record the gaps in educational achievement among various populations, types of school, places of residence and even the condition of speaking an indigenous language. As developed in the first two sections of this chapter, we are able to observe the profoundly unequal reality of the national education system, to assess the difficulty of reducing the identified gaps, and to identify the population groups that face special difficulties in learning at school. Over the years, recommendations were generated for equity to become a public policy priority and for specific population groups to be served with equity. Unfortunately, we must say that equity in the quality of educational inputs and materials, pedagogical processes in schools and, consequently, learning outcomes, has not visibly become a priority of education policy to date. The modification of Article 3 of the Constitution makes equity a priority for the first time in history.

Information on early childhood education

We know from recent research in the learning sciences that the first three years of life are essential to the development and learning over the life span. Changes in Article 3 of the Constitution in 2019 make early childhood education (0–3) part of compulsory and free education in the country for the first time. However, the information available on these first three years of life and the efforts to serve these children is still precarious and unreliable, and it will be necessary to strengthen data collection efforts in this area if the aim is to substantially expand and strengthen the care for children in this age group.

Concerns about the future of information on education

On 15 May 2019, Article 3 of the Constitution was amended and the National Institute for the Evaluation of Education ceased to exist. In 2013 the INEE became the autonomous institution responsible for evaluating the national education system. It was replaced by the Commission for the Continuous Improvement of Education (MEJOREDU) which, since its foundation, has not carried out any evaluation at the national level.

The INEE conducted an evaluation of teaching and learning conditions based on a representative sample of all school types. In only four years it managed to evaluate all levels of compulsory education. This evaluation was very important, as it showed the degree of compliance with the state's obligation to provide the minimum conditions for each school to fulfil the right to education. With the disappearance of the INEE, this evaluation will no longer be carried out, so we will not have reliable data on the degree to which the infrastructure, equipment, teaching materials, and management and living conditions in schools are adequate, nor will we know if the gaps discovered in these evaluations between types of school are diminishing.

Over the course of 15 years, the National Education Panorama systematically reported on key indicators regarding the structure and size of the national education system, the agents and resources of this system, the access to and achievement within the education system at a national level, educational processes, and school management, and the results of education, both in terms of learning and economic and social performance. Although the System for the Continuous Improvement of Education is expected to generate indicators on the results of educational improvement, and although educational equity is a declared priority of the new administration, there is still little progress in this regard by the new National Commission for the Improvement of Education, nor has it announced what it plans to do in terms of generating indicators. However, what we do know is that they will no longer be generated independently of the Secretariat of Public Education.

At the time of writing, nothing is known about whether MEJOREDU will continue to administer the PLANEA ELSEN test of student learning on a representative sample of schools through statistically controlled administration. The Secretariat of Public Education will probably continue to administer the PLANEA ELCE test, but without the counterweight of the equivalent controlled test, it risks presenting—as the ENLACE test did in the past—unexplained results inflation. With this, the learning data we have so far collected based on our own curriculum will be lost or become unreliable.

References

Andrade, G. (2014). *Improving academic achievement through extended school-days: Evidence from Escuelas de Tiempo Completo in Mexico* (Thesis). Graduate School of Education, Stanford University.

Anzures Tapia, A. (2020). *The promise of language planning in indigenous early childhood education in Mexico* (Doctoral thesis). University of Pennsylvania, Philadelphia.

Backhoff, R., et al. (2017). *Cambios y tendencias del aprendizaje en México 2000–2015*. Mexico: INEE. https://www.inee.edu.mx/publicaciones/cambios-y-tendencias-del-aprendizaje-en-mexico-2000-2015/

Banxico. (2020, February 4). *Encuesta sobre las Expectativas de los Especialistas en Economía del Sector Privado: enero de 2020.* https://www.banxico.org.mx/publicaciones-y-prensa/encuestas-sobre-las-expectativas-de-los-especialis/%7B7C6AD83D-D7F8-9C8F-A1F9-4460DD0A78D3%7D.pdf

Cabrera, F. (2014). *Impact evaluation of the full-time schools program in Mexican primary education.* Department of Economics, University of Sussex.

Cabrera, F. (2018). *Escuelas de Tiempo Completo: claroscuro en Distancia por Tiempos.* Blog de Nexos. https://www.nexos.com.mx/?p=39515

Cámara, G. (2014). *El entramado conceptual de la relación tutora.* https://redesdetutoria.com/el-entramado-conceptual/

Cámara, G. (2020). *Pedagogía que aprende de su práctica.* Mexico.

Consejo Nacional de Población (CONAPO). (2019). *Población a mitad de año (tabla de datos).* https://datos.gob.mx/busca/dataset/proyecciones-de-la-poblacion-de-México-y-de-las-entidades-federativas-2016-2050

Consejo Nacional de Evaluación de la Política de Desarrollo Social (CONEVAL). (2019a) *Metodología para la medición multidimensional de la pobreza en México (tercera edición).* México City: CONEVAL. https://www.coneval.org.mx/InformesPublicaciones/InformesPublicaciones/Documents/Metodologia-medicion-multidimensional-3er-edicion.pdf

Consejo Nacional de Evaluación de la Política de Desarrollo Social (CONEVAL) (2019b). *Diez años de medición de la pobreza multidimensional en México: avances y desafíos en política social* (Medición de la pobreza serie 2008–2018, presentation). https://www.coneval.org.mx/Medicion/MP/Documents/Pobreza_18/Pobreza_2018_CONEVAL.pdf

CONEVAL and UNICEF (2018). *Pobreza infantil y adolescente en México 2008–2016.* https://www.coneval.org.mx/Medicion/Documents/UNICEF_CONEVAL_POBREZA_INFANTIL.pdf

CPEUM. (2019). *Constitución Política de los Estados Unidos Mexicanos.* http://www.diputados.gob.mx/LeyesBiblio/htm/1.htm

De Hoyos, R., & Naranjo, B. Uno de los sistemas educativos más exitosos en América Latina. El caso de Puebla en el contexto internacional. In Nexos, México (in press).

Diario Oficial de la Federación (DOF) (2002). *DECRETO por el que se aprueba el diverso por el que se adiciona el artículo 3º, en su párrafo primero, fracciones III, V y VI, y el artículo 31 en su fracción I, de la Constitución Política de los Estados Unidos Mexicanos.* México. http://www.dof.gob.mx/nota_detalle.php?codigo=718015&fecha=12/11/2002

Diario Oficial de la Federación (DOF). (2004). *Ley General de Desarrollo Social.* México. http://www.diputados.gob.mx/LeyesBiblio/ref/lgds/LGDS_orig_20ene04.pdf

Diario Oficial de la Federación (DOF). (2017). *ACUERDO número 29/12/17 por el que se emiten las Reglas de Operación del Programa Educación Inicial y Básica Comunitaria para el ejercicio fiscal 2018*. México. https://www.gob.mx/cms/uploads/attachment/file/399680/ROP_2018_E066.pdf

Diario Oficial de la Federación (DOF). (2018). *Presupuesto de Egresos de la Federación para el año fiscal 2019*. México. https://dof.gob.mx/nota_detalle.php?codigo=5547479&fecha=28/12/2018

Diario Oficial de la Federación (DOF). (2019a). *Decreto por el que se crea la Coordinación Nacional de Becas para el Bienestar Benito Juárez*. México. https://dof.gob.mx/nota_detalle.php?codigo=5561693&fecha=31/05/2019

Diario Oficial de la Federación (DOF). (2019b). *Acuerdo Número 06/02/2019 por el que se emiten las Reglas de Operación del Programa Educación Inicial y Básica Comunitaria para el ejercicio fiscal 2020*. México. https://www.gob.mx/cms/uploads/attachment/file/524299/2019_12_29_RO__CONAFE.pdf

Diario Oficial de la Federación (DOF). (2019c). *Acuerdo por el que se emiten los Lineamientos de Operación del Programa La Escuela es Nuestra*. México. https://dof.gob.mx/nota_detalle.php?codigo=5574403&fecha=03/10/2019

Diario Oficial de la Federación (DOF). (2019d). *Acuerdo número 24/12/19 por el que se emiten las Reglas de Operación del Programa Desarrollo de Aprendizajes significativos de Educación Básica para el ejercicio fiscal 2020*. México. http://dof.gob.mx/nota_detalle.php?codigo=5583046&fecha=29/12/2019

Diario Oficial de la Federación (DOF). (2019e). *Acuerdo número 26/12/19 por el que se emiten las Reglas de Operación del Programa Atención a la Diversidad de la Educación Indígena (PADEI) para el ejercicio fiscal 2020*. México. https://dof.gob.mx/nota_detalle.php?codigo=5583048&fecha=29/12/2019

Diario Oficial de la Federación (DOF). (2019f). *Acuerdo número 27/12/19 por el que se emiten las Reglas de Operación del Programa Atención Educativa de la Población Escolar Migrante (PAEPEM) para el ejercicio fiscal 2020*. México. https://dof.gob.mx/nota_detalle.php?codigo=5583049&fecha=29/12/2019

Diario Oficial de la Federación (DOF). (2019g). *Acuerdo número 25/12/19 por el que se emiten las Reglas de Operación del Programa Fortalecimiento de los Servicios de Educación Especial (PFSEE) para el ejercicio fiscal 2020*. México. https://www.dof.gob.mx/nota_detalle.php?codigo=5583047&fecha=29/12/2019

Diario Oficial de la Federación (DOF). (2019h). *Presupuesto de Egresos de la Federación para el ejercicio fiscal 2020*. México. https://www.dof.gob.mx/nota_detalle.php?codigo=5581629&fecha=11/12/2019

Diario Oficial de la Federación (DOF). (2019i). *Ley General de Educación*. México. http://www.diputados.gob.mx/LeyesBiblio/index.htm

Diario Oficial de la Federación (DOF). (2019j). *Acuerdo número 21/12/19 por el que se emiten las Reglas de Operación del Programa Escuelas de Tiempo Completo para el ejercicio fiscal 2020*. México. https://dof.gob.mx/nota_detalle.php?codigo=5583043&fecha=29/12/2019

Encuesta Nacional de Jornaleros (ENJO). (2009). *Módulo de consulta de resultados*. Estimaciones ENJO. http://www.cipet.gob.mx/jornaleros/

Galeana, C. R. (2016). *Identificación de subpoblaciones de niños que no asisten a la escuela y caracterización de los factores asociados a la problemática. Conformando un marco inicial para la construcción de indicadores*. Mexico: Instituto Nacional para la Evaluación de la Educación. https://www.inee.edu.mx/wp-content/uploads/2019/01/P3B105.pdf

Gobierno de Puebla. (2015). *5o Informe de Labores*. Puebla: Secretaría de Educación Pública.

Instituto Nacional de las Lenguas Indígenas (INALI). (2009). *Catálogo de las Lenguas Indígenas Nacionales: Variantes Lingüísticas de México con sus autodenominaciones y referencias geoestadísticas*. México: Instituto Nacional de las Lenguas Indígenas. https://site.inali.gob.mx/pdf/catalogo_lenguas_indigenas.pdf

Instituto Nacional para la Evaluación de la Educación (INEE). (2007). *La educación para poblaciones en contextos vulnerables* (Informe anual 2007). Mexico: Instituto Nacional para la Evaluación de la Educación. https://www.inee.edu.mx/publicaciones/la-educacion-para-poblaciones-en-contextos-vulnerables-informe-anual-2007/

Instituto Nacional para la Evaluación de la Educación (INEE). (2010). *El derecho a la educación en México* *Informe 2009). Mexico: Instituto Nacional para la Evaluación de la Educación. https://www.inee.edu.mx/publicaciones/el-derecho-a-la-educacion-en-mexico-informe-2009-2a-edicion/

Instituto Nacional para la Evaluación de la Educación (INEE). (2014a). *El derecho a una educación de calidad* (Informe 2014). Mexico: Instituto Nacional para la Evaluación de la Educación. https://www.inee.edu.mx/publicaciones/el-derecho-a-una-educacion-de-calidad-informe-2014-resumen-ejecutivo/

Instituto Nacional para la Evaluación de la Educación (INEE). (2014b). *Evaluación externa de los servicios educativos dirigidos a los niños de familias de jornaleros migrantes*. Mexico: Instituto Nacional para la Evaluación de la Educación/UNPE. https://www.inee.edu.mx/portalweb/suplemento12/evaluacion-servicios-educativos-jornaleros-agricolas-migrantes.pdf

Instituto Nacional para la Evaluación de la Educación (INEE). (2015). *Los Docentes en México* (Informe 2015). Mexico: Instituto Nacional para la Evaluación de la Educación. https://www.inee.edu.mx/publicaciones/los-docentes-en-mexico-informe-2015/

Instituto Nacional para la Evaluación de la Educación (INEE). (2016). *Directrices para mejorar la atención educativa de niñas, niños y adolescentes de familias de jornaleros agrícolas migrantes*. Mexico: Instituto Nacional para la Evaluación de la Educación. https://www.inee.edu.mx/publicaciones/directrices-para-mejorar-la-atencion-educativa-de-ninas-ninos-y-adolescentes-de-familias-de-jornaleros-agricolas-migrantes/

Instituto Nacional para la Evaluación de la Educación (INEE). (2017). *La educación obligatoria en México* (Informe 2017). Mexico: Instituto Nacional para la Evaluación de la Educación. https://www.inee.edu.mx/publicaciones/la-educacion-obligatoria-en-mexico-informe-2017/

Instituto Nacional para la Evaluación de la Educación (INEE). (2018a). *Panorama Educativo de México. Indicadores del Sistema Educativo Nacional 2017*. Mexico: Instituto Nacional para la Evaluación de la Educación. https://www.inee.edu.mx/publicaciones/panorama-educativo-de-mexico-indicadores-del-sistema-educativo-nacional-2017-educacion-basica-y-media-superior/

Instituto Nacional para la Evaluación de la Educación (INEE). (2018b). *La educación obligatoria en México* (Informe 2018). Mexico: Instituto Nacional para la Evaluación de la Educación. https://www.inee.edu.mx/publicaciones/la-educacion-obligatoria-en-mexico-informe-2018/

Instituto Nacional para la Evaluación de la Educación (INEE). (2018c). *Origen, recorrido y logros del Modelo Educativo Poblano Asistencia, Permanencia y Aprendizaje* (Entrevista a Patricia Vázquez, Gaceta INEE). https://www.inee.edu.mx/origen-recorrido-y-logros-del-modelo-educativo-poblano-asistencia-permanencia-y-aprendizaje/

Instituto Nacional para la Evaluación de la Educación (INEE). (2019a). *Panorama Educativo de México. Indicadores del Sistema Educativo Nacional 2018*. Mexico: Instituto Nacional para la Evaluación de la Educación. https://www.inee.edu.mx/publicaciones/panorama-educativo-de-mexico-2018-educacion-basica-y-media-superior/

Instituto Nacional para la Evaluación de la Educación (INEE). (2019b). *La educación obligatoria en México* (Informe 2019). Mexico: Instituto Nacional para la Evaluación de la Educación. https://www.inee.edu.mx/publicaciones/la-educacion-obligatoria-en-mexico-informe-2019/

INEE-UNICEF. (2015). *Panorama Educativo de la Población Indígena*. Mexico: Instituto Nacional para la Evaluación de la Educación and Fondo de Población de las Naciones Unidas (UNICEF). https://www.inee.edu.mx/publicaciones/panorama-educativo-de-la-poblacion-indigena-y-afrodescendiente-2017/

INEE-UNICEF. (2018). *Panorama Educativo de la Población Indígena y Afrodescendiente*. Mexico: Instituto Nacional para la Evaluación de la Educación y Fondo de Población de las Naciones Unidas (UNICEF). https://www.inee.edu.mx/publicaciones/panorama-educativo-de-la-poblacion-indigena-y-afrodescendiente-2017/

INEE-UNICEF. (2019). *Panorama Educativo Estatal de la Población Indígena: Entorno Nacional*. Mexico: Instituto Nacional para la Evaluación de la Educación y Fondo de Población de las Naciones Unidas (UNICEF). https://www.inee.edu.mx/wp-content/uploads/2019/08/P3B112.pdf

Instituto Nacional de Estadística y Geografía (INEGI). (2014). *Censo de Escuelas, Maestros y Alumnos de Educación Básica y Especial (CEMABE)*. Atlas

Educativo. Instituto Nacional de Estadística y Geografía. https://www.inegi.org.mx/sistemas/mapa/atlas/

Instituto Nacional de Estadística y Geografía (INEGI). (2018). *Encuesta Nacional de Ingresos y Gastos de los Hogares 2018.* Instituto Nacional de Estadística y Geografía. https://www.inegi.org.mx/programas/enigh/nc/2018/

Instituto Nacional de Estadística y Geografía (INEGI). (2020). *Índice Nacional de Precios al Consumidor* (Año base 2018). Instituto Nacional de Estadística y Geografía. https://www.inegi.org.mx/temas/inpc/#:~:text=El%20%C3%8Dndice%20Nacional%20de%20Precios%20al%20Consumidor%20(INPC)%2C%20es,consumen%20las%20familias%20en%20M%C3%A9xico

Instituto Nacional de Estadística y Geografía (INEGI). (2017). *Módulo de Trabajo Infantil*: (MTI) *2017. Principales resultados.* INEGI-México. https://www.inegi.org.mx/contenidos/programas/mti/2017/doc/mti2017_resultados.pdf

Ley de Coordinación Fiscal (LCF). (2018). *Diario Oficial de la Federación.* México. http://www.diputados.gob.mx/LeyesBiblio/pdf/31_300118.pdf

López, D. (2016). La relación tutora y la mejora del aprendizaje. *Revista RED,* 3(1). https://www.inee.edu.mx/wp-content/uploads/2019/01/Red03-1PDF.pdf

López, D., & Rincón-Gallardo, S. (2003) *La capacitación artesanal y la profesionalización de la labor docente en Posprimaria.* Conafe, Mexico.

Luna, D., & Velázquez, P. (2019). Evaluación del impacto del Programa de Escuelas de Tiempo Completo en medidas de logro académico de centros escolares en México, *Revista Latinoamericana de Estudios Educativos*—Nueva Época, XLIX(2), 87–120. https://rlee.ibero.mx/index.php/rlee/article/view/19

Naranjo, B. (2019). Puebla. *Innovation and improvement for students' attendance, graduation and learning* (Presentation to the Bill & Melinda Gates Foundation).

Organization for Economic Co-Operation and Development (OECD). (2019). *Pisa results 2018, Vol. 1: What students know and can do.* https://www.oecd-ilibrary.org/education/pisa-2018-results-volume-i_5f07c754-en

Padilla, M. (2016). *The short and long run effects of full-time schools on academic performance.* Texas A&M University. https://sites.google.com/site/mariaspadillaromo/research

Proyecto Educativo. (2020). *Política educativa y el modelo APA.* https://proyectoeducativo.org/Hacemos/modelo_apa

Rincón-Gallardo, S. (2012). *Redes de tutoría académica. Orientaciones para su gestión en las regiones y escuelas.* Dirección General de Desarrollo de la Gestión e Innovación Educativa, Subsecretaría de Educación Básica, Secretaría de Educación Pública, Mexico.

Rincón-Gallardo, S. (2013a). *Educational change as a social, political, and instructional movement: Learning and expanding a countercultural practice in Mexican public middle-schools* (Doctoral thesis). Harvard University.

Rincón-Gallardo, S. (2013b). La tutoría para el aprendizaje independiente como práctica y principio rector del cambio educativo en escuelas públicas mexicanas. *Didac, 61*, 58–64. http://revistas.ibero.mx/didac/articulo_detalle.php?id_volumen=14&id_articulo=171

Rincón-Gallardo, S. (2014). Innovación pedagógica en gran escala: ¿lujo o imperativo moral? *Didac, 65*, 11–18. http://revistas.ibero.mx/didac/articulo_detalle.php?id_volumen=19&id_articulo=227

Rincón-Gallardo, S. (2016) Large scale pedagogical transformation as widespread cultural change in Mexican public schools. *Journal of Educational Change, 17*, 411–436. https://doi.org/10.1007/s10833-016-9286-4

Rincón-Gallardo, S., & Fullan, M. (2016). Essential features of effective networks in education. *Journal of Professional Capital and Community, 1*(1), 5–22. https://doi.org/10.1108/JPCC-09-2015-0007

Rives, R. (2010). *Texto original de la Constitución de 1917 y de las reformas publicadas en el Diario Oficial de la Federación del 5 de febrero de 1917 al 1º. de junio de 2009 en LA REFORMA CONSTITUCIONAL EN MÉXICO*. UNAM-México. https://archivos.juridicas.unam.mx/www/bjv/libros/6/2802/2.pdf and https://archivos.juridicas.unam.mx/www/bjv/libros/6/2802/8.pdf

Rodríguez, E. (2019). Progresa y su contexto, veinte años después. In Hernández Licona, G., De la Garza, T., Zamudio, J., & Yaschine, I. (Eds.). (2019). *El Progresa-Oportunidades-Prospera, a 20 años de su creación*. Mexico City: CONEVAL. https://www.coneval.org.mx/Evaluacion/IEPSM/Documents/Libro_POP_20.pdf

Rojas, T. J. (2017). Migración rural jornalera en México: la circularidad de la pobreza. *Revista de Ciencias Sociales de la Universidad Iberoamericana, XII*(23), 1–35. https://www.redalyc.org/articulo.oa?id=211053027001

Schmelkes, S., & Aguila, G. (Eds.) (2019). *La educación multigrado en México*. INEE-México. https://www.inee.edu.mx/publicaciones/la-educacion-multigrado-en-mexico/

Secretaria de Educación Pública (SEP). (2010). *Documento Base del Programa Emergente para Mejorar el Logro Educativo*. Mexico: Secretaría de Educación Pública.

Secretaria de Educación Pública (SEP). (2012). *Memoria documental de la Estrategia Integral para Mejorar el Logro Educativo*. Mexico: Subsecretaría de Educación Básica.

Secretaria de Educación Pública (SEP). (2017) *Evaluación de Consistencia y Resultados. Escuelas de Tiempo Completo. Resultados 2017*. Mexico: Instancia Evaluadora: N.I.K. BETA S.C.

SHCP. (2019). *Cuenta de la Hacienda Pública Federal 2018*. México. https://www.cuentapublica.hacienda.gob.mx/es/CP/2018

Silveyra, M., Yañez, M., & Bedoya, J. (2018). *¿Qué impacto tiene el Programa Escuelas de Tiempo Completo en los estudiantes de educación básica?* (Evaluación del programa en México 2007–2016). Washington, DC: World Bank.

United Nations Educational, Scientific and Cultural Organization (UNESCO). (2015). *Informe de resultados TERCE*. Ofina de Santiago. https://unesdoc.unesco.org/ark:/48223/pf0000243532

United Nations Population Fund (UNFPA). (2019). *SWOP Data 2019*. https://www.unfpa.org/sites/default/files/SWOP-Data-2019.xlsx

Unidad de Planeación y Evaluación de Políticas (UPEPE). (2012). *Documento de trabajo: Análisis del impacto del Programa para la Mejora del Logro Educativo (PEMLE) en las escuelas secundarias*. Mexico: Unidad de Planeación y Evaluación de Políticas, Secretaría de Educación Pública.

Yaschine, I. (2019). Progresa-Oportunidades-Prospera, veinte años de historia. In Hernández Licona, G., De la Garza, T., Zamudio, J., & Yaschine, I. (Eds.). (2019). *El Progresa-Oportunidades-Prospera, a 20 años de su creación*. Mexico City: CONEVAL. https://www.coneval.org.mx/Evaluacion/IEPSM/Documents/Libro_POP_20.pdf

9. India: Learning in the Margin

Reflections on Indian Policies and Programs for Education of the Disadvantaged

Rangachar Govinda

Introduction

India has witnessed enormous expansion of school infrastructure and near-universal enrollment of children in schools in recent decades. But it is common knowledge that improvement in quality has not kept pace with this expansion. What if all children get to attend school, but the majority fail to acquire even the basic skills of literacy and numeracy after several years of schooling?

While ASER (2015) and other achievement surveys have repeatedly pointed to persistent levels of learning deficit, it is well-recognized that learning enhancement for children from marginalized groups requires comprehensive strategies. This raises several questions: how has India been responding to this challenge? What policies and strategies have been adopted to provide quality education to children of communities afflicted by chronic poverty and social marginalization? What are the critical issues that confront Indian policymakers in creating an equitable system of school education? In the context of learning at the bottom of the pyramid, this chapter attempts to address these critical questions related to India's policies and strategies for educating the large mass of children living in the margin.

© 2022 Rangachar Govinda, CC BY-NC 4.0   https://doi.org/10.11647/OBP.0256.09

Retrospect on policies and strategies

India began its efforts to provide universal elementary education more than seven decades ago. The initial goal was to reach universal access within 10 years, but that did not happen, and the goal has remained elusive. Recognizing the complex nature of regional and social inequalities in education historically inherited from the colonial period, special clauses were incorporated in the Indian Constitution. Emphasizing a "right to equality", the Constitution explicitly specified: "The State shall not discriminate against any citizen on grounds only of religion, race, caste, sex, place of birth or any of them" (The Constitution of India, 1950). The Constitution also empowered the state to practice positive discrimination to ensure advancement of special category groups, including women, scheduled castes consisting of people belonging to (former) untouchable castes who had been patently discriminated against, and scheduled tribes consisting of aboriginal ethnic groups, largely isolated from mainstream society. There is no doubt that substantial progress has been made in the education status of these groups. Yet statistics for recent years point out that they continue to occupy the bottom of the hierarchy in educational progress. In fact, reviews have revealed persistent educational backwardness among religious minorities (particularly Muslims) and also among several other caste groups broadly classified as "other backward classes".

Over the years, both central and state governments have been launching a number of measures to offset the handicaps faced by various disadvantaged sections of society. We will not list out various schemes and projects launched over the years, which are still in operation with variable levels of success and failures. We would rather present an overall picture that will give an indication of the kinds of efforts being made. Broadly, these measures could be discussed under three categories, namely: (1) area-specific strategies; (2) target-specific strategies; and (3) programs of early childhood care and learning enhancement.

Area-specific strategies

The Indian scenario is too complex and varied to be effectively captured through aggregate national figures. On the one hand, there is Kerala, where practically every child attends elementary school, with an adequate number of teachers and classrooms. At the other end of the spectrum, there is Bihar, where only one out of two children are in school, invariably with subminimal infrastructure. By the beginning of 2000, it was estimated that three-quarters of out-of-school children lived in six states of the country—namely Andhra Pradesh,[1] Bihar, Madhya Pradesh, Rajasthan, Uttar Pradesh, and West Bengal (Govinda, 2008). Even within these states, the situation varies widely across different districts, castes, religious minorities, and ethnic groups.

Under an area-specific approach, programs and projects are designed based on the empirical observation that some geographical units, which are characterized by chronic educational backwardness, are inhabited by socially marginalized groups. One of the earliest projects to emerge with this perspective was the Integrated Tribal Development Program, which was specially designed to send developmental resources to ethnic minority groups or scheduled tribes inhabiting specific geographical pockets. It is debatable if this approach, which has been in operation for several decades, has really helped improve education in these areas. There is no systematic assessment to conclude if it has really worked. An empirical study taking place over 18 years in a cluster of villages in a tribal area revealed overwhelming interest among parents to get their children educated, marking a significant change from the attitude of parents in early 1990s. However, this was barely matched by the response from the state; no private providers seem to be interested within the locality, unlike other parts of the same state. Except for improved physical infrastructure in the schools, barely any improvement in the teaching learning facilities and conditions could be observed (Govinda, 2009).

In recent years, area-specific strategies have been adopted with an expanded framework. For instance, Sarva Shiksha Abhiyan (SSA) has identified more than 350 districts and blocks as special focus areas for targeted interventions, based on a composite set of education development indicators. These geographic units receive special consideration in matters of allocation of funds and school infrastructure. Based on this consideration, SSA has identified 61 districts with a high SC (scheduled caste) population, 106 districts with a high ST

---

1   Andhra Pradesh is now divided into two states but the overall situation remains unchanged.

(scheduled tribe) population, and 88 districts with a high Muslim population. Further, over 3000 blocks (subdistricts) with low female literacy levels and high gender gaps—called Educationally Backward Blocks (EBB)—have also been identified as part of the focus on girls' education (Government of India, 2017).

Relatively small habitations located in difficult-to-access pockets make the provision of schools fully equipped with physical and academic infrastructure really challenging. The problem is partially being tackled by establishing residential schools in central locations within the hard-to-reach tribal pockets. Special residential facilities are also being set up in low-female literacy blocks to improve the participation of girls.

Target-specific strategies

While area-specific initiatives can address the problem of marginalization to some extent, children from vulnerable groups have to be reached more directly if their educational conditions are to improve. With this in mind, several incentive schemes and direct support measures have been initiated. These include monetary support in the form of cash and scholarships to the students or their families, as well as non-monetary support specifically focusing on scheduled castes and differently-abled children. Further, a number of measures also focus on girls across social affiliations, with increased focus on girls from marginalized groups. Considering that many of the children from marginalized groups are first-generation learners, special attention in the form of additional coaching classes is also given to students in higher levels of education who are from educationally-backward families. Because incentives such as scholarship schemes have been in operation for several decades, some of them are no longer viewed as special measures. Rather, they are part of the regular process of financial allocations at the state government level.

It should of course be acknowledged that, notwithstanding constitutional measures and directives, transforming social practices is a slow process and there has, indeed, been progress on this front. Yet, empirical observations point to the continuance of subtle forms of discrimination in schools and classrooms that clearly impact children's learning. While special measures focusing on vulnerable groups and less developed pockets seem reasonable, they potentially lead to a hierarchy of schools corresponding to the marginalized status of the children, particularly affecting the educational progress of girls (Ramachandran, 2004). Addressing such unintended consequences of special-focus programs poses a difficult challenge.

Programs of early childhood care

There is increasing empirical evidence to suggest that, by the time children reach school-age, it might already be difficult to stop certain types of exclusions. In particular, it is clearly established that nutrition and cognitive stimulation early in life are critical for long-term skill development (Galiani & Manacorda, 2007; Shonkoff & Phllips, 2000; Shore, 1997; Sternberg, 1985). Indeed, there is a widespread conviction among educators that the benefits of pre-primary education are carried over to primary school. In particular, teachers identify a lack of academic skills as one of the most common obstacles children face when they enter school. Also, they perceive preschool education as facilitating the socialization and self-control necessary to make the most of classroom learning (Rimm-Kaufman, Pianta, & Cox, 2000; Currie, 2001). It is within this context that India operates a massive program under the banner of Integrated Child Development Scheme (ICDS) to provide developmental support to children ages 0–6, coupled with prenatal and post-natal care facilities for mothers. One of the six components of the program is to provide preschool education to children attending the ICDS center. The government is committed to expanding the program to ensure full coverage throughout the country, even though a lack of qualified preschool teachers and trained caregivers poses a major challenge to meeting this goal.

Another country-wide program in operation is the National Program of Nutritional Support to Primary Education, popularly referred to as the Mid-Day Meal (MDM) program. Evidence suggests that undernutrition, both protein-energy malnutrition and micronutrient deficiencies, directly affect many aspects of children's development (Ijarotimi, 2013). In particular, it retards their physical and cognitive growth, and increases susceptibility to infection and disease. Unfortunately, India's record in this regard is quite unsatisfactory. Around 35 percent of children in India have been identified as malnourished (UNICEF, 2019). This is an issue of direct relevance to the achievement of EFA/SDG goals, as there is disturbing evidence of *worsening* gender gaps in child malnutrition (although gender gaps in educational outcomes have decreased), particularly in rural areas of northern and eastern states where nutritional status has been improving substantially more for boys than girls (Tarozzi & Mahajan, 2005).

The MDM program recognizes the vulnerability of children without adequate nutritional input at home. Provision of nutritious food under the program, which is currently operating throughout the country and covers children in Grades 1 through 8, is now increasingly viewed from a "food security" and rights perspective, and not just as an incentive to attract and retain children in schools.

Programs with special focus on learning enhancement

The problem of poor learning levels is not a new finding of recent years. The National Policy on Education (NPE), issued in 1986, flagged this as a serious issue (MHRD, 1986). It declared that the universalization of elementary education was incomplete without universal achievement, and called for elementary education programs to look beyond reaching quantitative targets of enrollment and completion. In order to refocus classroom teaching on learning outcomes, in the early 1990s the government of India published a document delineating "Minimum Levels of Learning" to be mastered by the end of each grade, from 1 to 5. But the implementation of the corresponding program was disbanded within a few years without any systematic assessment. However, the launch of Sarva Shiksha Abhiyan in 2002 brought back the focus on learning outcomes, prompting the state governments to embark on major programs for enhancing learning levels in elementary schools. Further, the ASER Report on learning outcomes in 2006 attracted public attention to the poor state of learning among school children, and highlighted the need for devoting greater attention to the issue.

Interestingly, a number of programs have been initiated during the last two decades by various state governments with the goal of enhancing learning levels. Even though the goal has been to improve learning among the children, the approach and emphasis varies from state to state. We will present a synoptic view of three programs which are illustrative of different approaches with respect to their design and instrumentality.

Activity-Based Learning of Tamil Nadu

The main thrust of the Activity-Based Learning (ABL) program[2] is to recast classroom pedagogy to be more child-centered. The approach involves the provision of engaging and challenging learning materials in a carefully graded and planned sequence. It attempts to create an individualized tract for each child by enabling differentiated learning through the use of the "learning ladder", consisting of a sequence of steps that must be completed as a child proceeds through the curriculum. Learning is also self-directed by the child as they learn to recognize their position on the ladder and choose the appropriate "self-learning card" that corresponds to the step they have reached. The program has been, over the years, the subject of a number of evaluation studies, which have identified five key features of the model:

(a) *classroom organization* as multigrade with small groups on different mats carrying out independent learning activities with support from teachers and students following the "learning ladder";

(b) *curriculum structure* broken down into small learning units or milestones;

(c) *teaching and learning* through a series of activities and opportunities for independent and peer learning;

(d) *role of the teacher* as a facilitator rather than learning being solely teacher-driven, and

(e) *assessment*, which is non-threatening and built into the activities the child completes, moving onto the next milestone only after they achieve a certain "mastery of skills".

The ABL approach was an adaptation of the Rishi Valley Institute for Educational Resources' model of child-friendly education, practiced in its satellite schools. The model was tried out in a small number of schools in Karnataka under the banner "*nali kali*" as part of the District Primary Education Program (DPEP) in 1995. The success of the experiment led to subsequent expansion within Karnataka. In Tamil Nadu, the ABL program also began as a small experimental project in 13 schools of the Chennai Municipal Corporation in 2002–2003. Based on the positive

---

[2] See for more details: UNICEF (2012); Akila (2009); NCERT (2011); Singhal et al. (2017).

experience, the program was extended to the whole of the Corporation area, and within five years the Tamil Nadu government decided to adopt the approach throughout the state, covering all government and government-aided primary schools.

Evaluation studies of the ABL have tended to focus on the implementation of child-centered pedagogy; it is difficult to determine if the program made a significant impact on learning levels of the children. ABL is also one of the most replicated learning-improvement programs in India. The positive promise it held for ensuring a child-friendly education gained the attention of educational administrators across the country. Over the years, with encouragement from UNICEF, which was the original sponsor of *nali kali* in Karnataka as well as ABL in Chennai, adaptations of the ABL approach have been implemented in as many as 13 states.

Gunotsav of Gujarat

The *Gunotsav* (Celebrating Quality) program design assumes that assessment and feedback in a competitive framework spurs quality improvement in schools and enhances learning outcomes of students. The program was launched on a state-wide basis in 2009 as a Gujarat government initiative. The entire state-government machinery was mobilized to evaluate and grade the quality of teachers and schools. The main purpose of the annual exercise is to monitor school conditions and make sure that all children studying in primary schools (Std 2 to 8) achieve improvements in basic reading, writing, and numerical skills. The exercise is expected to build an environment of accountability. Some view the program as a mass-scale diagnostic assessment and remediation exercise.[3]

---

3 The program implementation consists of three sequential phases, repeated every year. Phase 1 consists of self-evaluation by all schools (around 34,000) and all students (more than 5,000,000) by head teachers and teachers. Phase 2 involves external evaluation by more than 3000 political representatives and government officials, who spend full days in randomly selected schools (three schools in three days). The assessment parameters are based on learning outcomes (with 60% weight), co-scholastic activities (20%), infrastructure, including human resources (10%), and community participation (10%). Based on the evaluation, schools are given a grade ranging from A+ to D. Phase 3 consists of remedial action for improving school conditions and bridging the gaps identified in learning outcomes.

Over the years, government reports indicate that, as a consequence of *Gunotsav* implementation, many schools have improved their grades, and practically none or very few can be found at the bottom of the ladder, with a D grade (Government of Gujarat). As a follow-up measure, a learning-based child tracking system was launched in 2013, in which the learning levels of each individual child were monitored along with teachers' profiles, competencies, and training needs. A database of 54 lakh (5.4 million) students was generated through a web-based application by assigning unique identification to each government primary school student. Self-assessment by the school was carried out using OMR sheets pre-printed with student names and unique IDs.

As the program has been consistently implemented in more or less the same format, cumulative progress in school quality and learning outcomes should be clearly discernible. Considering that the program covers the full cycle of elementary education, it should also be possible to identify and earmark critical stages in which progress in learning get disrupted, and thereby help launch corrective measures. Government reports indicate that many schools have moved to higher levels in the grading system, and that several agencies have been involved in implementation. However, there are no comprehensive studies available in the public domain which explore the progress made with respect to each of the eight objectives of the program. What is somewhat surprising is that its impact on improving learning outcomes does not get reflected in reports of ASER and NAS by NCERT for various years following the program.

Mentor Teacher program of Delhi

The program of "Mentor Teacher" (MT) was launched in recent years by the Delhi government[4] and is still taking shape. It is based on the assumption that teachers make the biggest impact on education quality and learning outcomes. It aims to leverage the creative expertise of around 200 experienced teachers to enhance the pedagogic and academic capacities of the rest of Delhi's 45,000 teachers. Each mentor

---

For a broader discussion of the theme of accountability, see: Ish, Singh, & Vaghela (2015) and Sankar (2013).

4   Government of NCT of Delhi (2019).

teacher has five to six schools assigned to them, which they visit at least once a week, to observe classroom practices and guide the teachers. They also create supplementary learning materials for children, in consultation with other teachers. Mentor teachers also act as critical pivots in implementing various other government programs which focus on improving school quality. Even though teachers, both the mentor teachers and others, are held accountable for learning outcomes of children, the program is carefully designed not to pose any threat to incumbent teachers. This is in contrast to the several other initiatives in the country where teachers seem to have felt intimidated by the grading of their performance.

Delhi has around 5700 schools, of which around 2400 are directly managed by the Delhi government. The remaining schools are managed by a number of private and semi-private organizations. The "Mentor Teacher" program is confined to the schools under direct government management. Thus, the MT initiative has a relatively small reach compared to state-wide programs of other states such as *Gunotsav* or ABL. Yet it is perhaps the largest experiment in quality improvement through peer learning and school-based on-site support through participatory process. This, unlike other state-wide programs, offers the opportunity to create interventions tailored to the unique requirements of each school and provide teachers with more personalized support. The program was extended to cover all state government schools based on positive feedback to an initial pilot. It is perhaps too early to judge if the initiative could be sustained and whether it can really bring about permanent improvement in school quality and learning outcomes.

Reflections

The core concern that has led to these innovative efforts is common—to improve the learning levels of children in school. But the approaches and underlying assumptions have been quite different. While the ABL program is anchored in the principle of pedagogic transformation leading to improvement in learning, Gunotsav considers assessment and remediation as the route to enhancing learning outcomes. The Delhi government initiative of "mentor teachers" seems to place its faith in supporting and empowering teachers through professional development for improving learning outcomes.

The increasing number and variety of programs for improving learning outcomes signify the recognition by the state of the magnitude and intensity of the problem, as well as the urgency of action. Many of the projects for learning improvement have been in operation for more than 10–15 years; some of them, such as the ABL in Tamil Nadu and *nali kali* in Karnataka, began nearly two decades ago. The basic principles on which the programs are designed cannot be questioned for their technical soundness. Yet, when India participated in PISA in 2010, the results were dismal, with India appearing at the bottom of the league.

Why have such large-scale interventions, implemented for a decade or more, made such little impact on the ground? Possibly because government projects are generally treated as refutation-proof. If the project works, the political leadership and the government bureaucracy is credited with the success; if it fails, implementation inefficiency is thought to account for it. Consequently, numerous evaluation studies—most of which are sponsored by the government or by development agencies with tacit consent by the government—opt to keep their critical observations muted. There are not many independent evaluation studies. Sponsored evaluation projects often fail to reveal the full story, as broad program evaluation exercises do not go deep enough to investigate school functioning and classroom dynamics. It is urgent that we engage in open debate and critical reflection on these initiatives, as well as the broader policy context. The following are a few reflective observations on some of the critical themes on the array of projects being pursued and the policy framework within which they operate.

On scaling up and standardization vs. local initiative and innovation

The large-scale projects for quality improvement in most states began as small-scale local innovations. The program design and learning materials were invariably the products of collective thinking and cooperative work by the direct stakeholders involved in implementation—teachers and local administrators. This was indeed the case in the *nali kali* project in Karnataka or ABL in Tamil Nadu. Even though a common design was arrived at, flexibility, improvization, and adaptation by the teachers in each school were the watch words. This was the precise element that disappeared when the government decided to upscale the project for state-wide implementation. Flexibility gave way to standardization and participatory action was replaced by adherence to pedagogic prescriptions from authorities. Enthusiasm among the teachers, which was high to begin with, waned over time. Robbed of such vital elements, the program has continued without much impact on quality of learning.

Similar stories have unfolded in most states in their efforts to improve quality of education. It may sound logical to argue that standardization is inevitable while going to scale. But such an argument is self-defeating. The answer likely lies in promoting multiple local-level innovations instead of hoisting a single state-wide model as the panacea for all the ills of the system. Can the government bureaucracy initiate and sustain such flexible initiatives? While this is a pertinent question, we have to recognize that there is no dearth of public-minded non-government entities engaged in education. It is time that school education is viewed as a genuinely public good, with synergic contribution from government and non-government sectors.

On large-scale testing

Most of the state governments also have embraced the practice of conducting mass-scale tests of student learning through specially created institutional arrangements. There is no doubt that these initiatives have raised general awareness among the public and presented useful benchmarks for planners and administrators regarding the health of the education system; they also present helpful pointers to curriculum framers and textbook writers. In fact, ample reference to these tests and their findings can be found in all contemporary policy-related documents at national and state levels. However, it is difficult to assess how effectively these findings have been used for redrawing policies that improve learning outcomes among the marginalized; one could possibly construe the emergence of state-level learning-focused projects as a demonstration of such consciousness. It is pertinent, however, to reflect on the way state governments attempt to utilize the findings of such achievement surveys.

Identifying learning gaps and bridging them through corrective action is specified as a core objective of the testing programs in most of the states. Diagnostic testing followed by remedial action is a time-honored practice used by all teachers. But that has been in the context of classroom teaching and school-based testing, where the focus is on specific problems faced by the learners. It is not an exercise for fixing the learning deficit or raising the average learning score of a district or a state. Could we use external testing (not school-based) for diagnosis and mass-scale remedial action in a generic fashion? This could be the subject of academic discourse and exploration. But it suffices to state that continued low scores on national achievement tests indicate that such measures have not worked in the Indian context.

Could the findings of such large-scale testing initiatives be used for holding an individual school or teacher accountable? This, again, has been an objective that the state governments have sought to achieve, though without much success. Even though state government reports claimed that almost all schools have moved up the ladder due to such efforts, NAS and ASER results do not show any significant progress in learning outcomes. In fact, the method of using test results as accountability measures for teachers was strongly resented by the teachers themselves, forcing the state to give up the practice of grading teachers based on *Gunotsav*. It should be recognized that poor scores in tests are only symptomatic of underlying malaise in the system, not all of which can be attributed to schools and teachers. Test results may not always help in identifying and rectifying the cause of the malaise. For that to happen, such testing exercises should be accompanied by carefully-designed analytical studies that are context-specific.

In any endeavor to improve school quality and learning outcomes, teachers have to be part of the solution framework, whereas using test results for fixing teacher accountability tends to treat them as adversaries. Viewed from this angle, the "Mentor Teacher" program of Delhi stands out as a unique example, even though it is too early to predict its future course when implemented on a large scale and over a longer period of time. If there has to be a "one-point agenda" for improving learning levels in Indian schools, it should be to significantly enhance investment in the professional development of teachers. This also points to the need for reflecting on broader policies and practices that help or hinder extending quality education to the children of the poor and marginalized.

Conclusion

Creating a comprehensive school system commonly accessible to all does not imply casting all schools in a single standard mold. No two schools are identical or even similar in terms of resources and outcomes, and some inequality among schools is inevitable. But it becomes problematic when the variation is based on social and economic considerations. This, indeed, is the situation that the Indian school system is slipping into. If the trend is not reversed, it would not take long for it to evolve into a highly discriminatory and exclusionary system, placing children from different backgrounds into designated slots in the name of schooling. Schools in the public realm are not only places of common provision, but also settings for civic education. Ideally, at least, they are places where children of all classes can mix and learn the habits of democratic citizenship (Sandel, 1998).

This is not in the least to suggest that such discriminatory policies and practices are being consciously pursued. In fact, Indian policy has always advocated for embedding concern for quality within a framework of equity and social justice. This, indeed, is the intent of incorporating education as a fundamental human right in the Indian Constitution. But translation of that intent into reality has proved elusive, particularly jeopardizing the prospect of quality education for the disadvantaged children living in the margin of the society. The goal is difficult but achievable, with appropriate restructuring of the system in order to create more robust and wider learning pathways that are inclusive and common for all.

References

Akila, R. (2009) *A Trigger for Change in Primary Education: An Evaluation of ABL in Tamil Nadu*. Evaluation report commissioned by Government of Tamil Nadu.

ASER. (2015). *Trends over time 2006–2014 (A supplement to ASER 2014)*. New Delhi: Pratham Education Foundation.

Currie, J. (2001). Early childhood education programs. *Journal of Economic Perspectives, 15*, 213–238.

Galiani, S., & Manacorda, M. (2007). *Giving children a better start: Preschool attendance and school-age profiles* (World Bank Policy Research Working Paper, No. 4240). Washington, DC: World Bank.

Government of Gujarat. (n.d.). *Good practices and new initiatives for education in Gujarat*. Government of Gujarat, Education Department, Gandhinagar.

Government of India. (2012). *12th five year plan*. New Delhi.

Government of India. (2017). *Annual report of the Ministry of Human Resource Development 2016–17*.

Government of NCT of Delhi (2019). *2015 and Beyond: Delhi Education Revolution*. http://www.edudel.nic.in/welcome_folder/delhi_education_revolution.pdf

Govinda, R. (2008). Literacy and elementary education: Regional imbalances and social inequities. In P. V. Prakash, & K. Biswal, *Perspectives on education and development: Revisiting education commission and after* (pp. 157–201). NUEPA and Shipra Publication.

Govinda, R. (2009). *Are schools improving: Revisit to 35 schools in three rural clusters*. CREATE Project. New Delhi: NUEPA.

Ijarotimi, O. S. (2013). Determinants of childhood malnutrition and consequences in developing countries. *Current Nutrition Reports, 2*, 129–133.

Ish, V. Singh, S. & Vaghela, P. D. (2015). Strategy to improve learning outcomes in primary schools, *The Administrator: Journal of LBSNAA, 56*(1), 42-63. https://www.lbsnaa.gov.in/upload/academy_souvenir/5cd016c90c9725513d9e5-3310-477d-a74c-41fdc0a80121.pdf

MHRD. (1986). *National policy on education: Programme for action*. Ministry of Human Resource Development, Government of India, Department of Education, New Delhi.

NCERT (2011). *Programme Evaluation Report: Activity Based Learning Tamil Nadu*, SSA Technical Cooperation Fund.

Ramachandran, V. (2004). Hierarchies of access. In V. Ramachandran (Ed.), *Gender and social equity in primary education*. Sage Publications India Pvt Ltd.

Rimm-Kaufman, S., Pianta, R., & Cox, M. (2000). Teachers' judgments of problems in the transition of kindergarten. *Early Childhood Research Quarterly, 15*, 147–166.

Sandel, M. J. (1998). *What money can't buy: The moral limits of markets* (Lecture notes). The Tanner Lectures on Human Values Delivered at Brasenose College, Oxford. https://tannerlectures/utah.edu/_documents/a-to-z/s/sandel00.pdf

Sankar, V. (2013). Large-scale diagnostic assessments: the Gujarat experience. *Learning Curve*, (20), 81-84. https://edu.in/SitePages/pdf/Publications/Learning-Curve/LCIssue20-Eng.pdf

Shonkoff, J. P., & Phllips, D. A. (2000). *From beurons to neighborhoods: The science of early childhood development*. Washington, DC: National Academy Press.

Shore, R. (1997). *Re-thinking the brain: New insights into early development.* New York: Families and Work Institute.

Singal, N., Pedder, D., Malathy, D., Shanmugam, M., Manickavasagam, S., & Govindarasan, M. (2017). Insights from within activity based learning (ABL) classrooms in Tamil Nadu, India: Teachers perspectives and practices. *International Journal of Educational Development.* http://dx.doi.org/10.1016/j.ijedudev.2017.08.001

Sternberg, R. (1985). *Beyond IQ: A triarchic theory of human intelligence.* Cambridge University Press.

Tarozzi, A., & Mahajan, A. (2005). *Child nutrition in India in the nineties: A story of increased gender inequality?* (SIEPR Discussion Paper, No. 04–29).

The Constitution of India. (1950). *Article 15(1).*

UNICEF. (2019). *The state of the world's children 2019. Children, food and nutrition: Growing well in a changing world.* New York: UNICEF.

10. India

Learning Challenges for the Marginalized

Udaya Narayana Singh, Rajarshi Singh, and Padmakali Banerjee

Introduction

There are numerous sources of inequality in India–linguistic, economic, sociocultural, class, and caste. In this chapter, we examine the heterogeneities and inequalities that characterize India and impact learning at bottom of its pyramid (BOP), focusing primarily on linguistic diversity and mother-tongue instruction.

India's people speak many languages, including 3592 numerically weak mother-tongues used by 705 tribes or ethnic groups, and 1284 castes scattered across the country's mostly rural landscape. Across 36 states and union territories of India there are 739 districts[1] and 5,572 sub-districts.[2] There are 7,935 urban areas[3] (4,041 statutory and 3,894 census towns) housing 31 percent of Indians (which is much lower by world standards) and 649,481 villages[4] often located in remote

---

1 "*Districts | Government of India Web Directory*". www.goidirectory.gov.in. Census 2011 shows 640 and Census 2001 has the figure 593 for districts. There are 687 unique names and others are similar or identical names.
2 https://en.wikipedia.org/wiki/List_of_tehsils_in_India.
3 http://mohua.gov.in/pdf/5c80e2225a124Handbook%20of%20Urban%20Statistics%202019.pdf. According to the World Urbanization Prospects, 2018, 55.29 percent of the world population lived in urban areas in 2018 as compared to 34.03 percent in India in 2018.
4 As per the census in 2011, out of which 593,615 are inhabited; IMIS database pegs it at 608,662, SBM-G at 605,805.

subdistricts[5] that support 68 percent of the population. According to the census in 2011, the number of urban agglomerations (with populations of over 100,000) stood at 474. Managing teaching and learning across this vast space poses many challenges and opportunities.

The biggest challenge comes from multilingual or pluricultural learning situations. Nearly 96 percent of India's mother-tongues are spoken by only 4 percent of the population. Plans for early grade education, textbook production, teacher-training programs, and so on, often do not take into account these linguistic minorities, despite constitutional provisions that require schools to impart education in everyone's mother-tongue. As a result, there are many smaller groups who must learn to read in "other"-tongues, and therefore fail almost invariably. Periodic national assessments of children's learning conducted by the Annual Status of Education Report (ASER), which tests children both in school and out of school, and the National Achievement Survey consistently highlight the sub-par academic capacities of these children, especially in foundational reading and numeracy in the state language.

Such diverse classrooms can be found not only in state-run schools of different types, but also in private schools, except that in most privately managed institutions, a monolingual regime is imposed from the top. There is often a vast linguistic distance between the "ideal" or the "standard" language the school systems expect all students to master vs. the dialectal or mother-tongue background of many students. The students coming to a city school from the districts are as challenged in this respect, as are the urban students coming from a certain class background. In many instances, the students from divergent backgrounds are able to "comprehend" academic language, but find it difficult to acquire fluency of speech or the standard pronunciation.

These challenges only increase as children become young adults who only possess an elementary level of reading and writing because of these previous challenges. Their advantage, unlike many adult

---

5   The subdistricts are known by different names – sometimes called Tehsils or Talukas, or Mandals (Andhra Pradesh and Telengana), Circles, C.D. Block (Bihar, Tripura, Meghalaya, West Bengal and Jharkhand), R.D. Block (Mizoram), Commune Panchayats (Pondicherry), and Subdivisions (Lakshadweep and Arunachal Pradesh), and even Police Stations (Odisha).

learners, is that they are less afraid of making mistakes. Assuming that none of them have speech disabilities or difficulties in pronunciation because of their base language influence, their teachers need to work on what could be done to improve their processes of learning, or how sociocultural and sociolinguistic barriers could be overcome to infuse confidence in them. However, getting the right kind (and quantity) of teachers or instructors is another major challenge. A trained and patient teacher can go a long way towards helping a struggling child or young adult overcome linguistic barriers, but many teachers are not sufficiently sensitive to this issue.

Another challenge is that, in the Indian Constitution, each of the 36 states (and Union Territories) has the right to come up with its own education policy vis-à-vis use of mother-tongues in elementary schools. Even as the "Right to Education" (RTE) was accepted as a legal instrument, there were numerous cases filed in different high courts about the policies of different state governments with respect to mother-tongue education. In the post-independence period, the States Reorganization Commission (SRC) of India reviewed this question based on linguistic principles. Thus, language diversity increased as more and more states were carved out of the existing huge provinces.

Managing a diversity of languages and cultures is perhaps the biggest challenge for education in India. Howarth and Andreouli's (2016) book *Nobody Wants to Be an Outsider* is valid today: they question how we can manage diversity so that it becomes a source of mutual enrichment rather than conflict, especially when "societies cannot manage cultural diversity due to assumed incompatibility" (Chryssochoou, 2014). The nature of globalized communities encourages dialogue and interactions across different sets of people. As societies diversify, psychological analysis shows that our identities become populated with "multiple selves" to respond to these complexities. Given this scenario, it is interesting to see if these heterogeneities also affect the bottom of our societies today. One may be a resident of Delhi living in the not-so-affluent colonies and settlement areas, but may also use one's identity as a Bihari where it may work, or may show allegiance to Bhojpuri speech community that would cut across several states, and make one a member of a larger network.

Heterogeneity at the "bottom of the pyramid"

The Indian population can be divided in myriad ways—by language, culture, socioeconomic conditions, religion, and gender, amongst others. The sheer number of tribes, castes, ethnic communities, speech groups, and mother-tongues active in a pluricultural India is immense. Language roles and their differences in power add to the complexities at the bottom of the pyramid. Some are immensely successful in the market, such as Hindi, Marathi, or Malayalam, while others are left behind. The languages on the margin (Singh et al., 2017) are viewed in much the same way economists view "the forgotten man at the bottom of economic pyramid" (Roosevelt, 1932). Of course, in this metaphoric "pyramid" what is on top is considered a dominant force or a commanding voice while the bottom remains powerless. Those at the "bottom of the pyramid" may feel alienated for different reasons, but a lack of opportunities and economic deprivation are the common factors for all of them. The learning issues of the children of these marginalized families need to be understood in the context of this heterogeneity.

At the bottom of the hierarchy in India is a set of heterogenous, under-developed, scantily published, and unprofitable (in terms of the market) speech communities, ethnic groups with thinning numbers, and scheduled castes that are both socioeconomically and culturally excluded. If we set aside the problems of methodology and accuracy with how one counts "languages", the sheer number of mother-tongues in India is intimidating: Sir George Abraham Grierson's *Linguistic Survey of India* (1903–1923) documented 179 languages and 544 dialects, while early census reports (1921) showed 188 languages. Post-independence, the 1961 census reports mentioned a total of 1,652 "mother-tongues" which kept on increasing until we reached the census in 2011.[6] Other sources, such as *People of India*—the Anthropological Survey of India,[7] identified 75 "major languages" out of a total of 325 languages used

---

6   The unclarity with respect to the concept of "mother-tongue" arose because the Indian Census authorities had passed on different instructions to the ground-level enumerators. The emphasis in the censuses in 1881 and 1891 was on counting mother-tongues "ordinarily spoken in the household". In 1901, enumerators were instructed to record names of languages "ordinarily used". This was extended to mother-tongues "ordinarily used in his own home" in 1911 and 1921. In 1931, and 1951, it was stipulated as the language first spoken "from the cradle".

7   Singh (1993).

in Indian households, and the *Ethnologue*[8] reported 398 languages, including 387 living and 11 extinct languages. Despite a lack of consensus on the language count, it is clear that the linguistic landscape is diverse. Using Greenberg's (1956) *Linguistic Diversity Index* (LDI), which measures the probability of two people selected from the population at random speaking different mother-tongues—ranging from 0 (everyone has the same mother-tongue) to 1 (no two people have the same mother tongue)—India ranks 9th out of 209 countries with an index of 0.930 (UNESCO, 2009). A visualization of India's linguistic diversity based on LDI is shown in Figure 1 below (Singh, 2018):

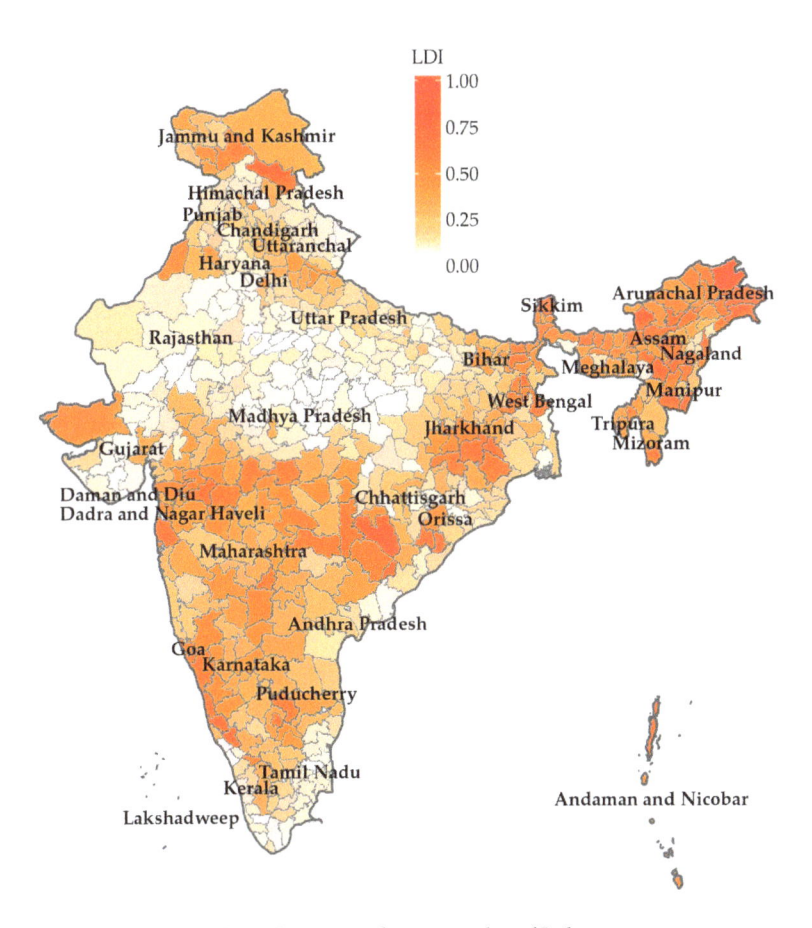

Fig. 1. Linguistic diversity index of India.

---

8   http://www.ethnologue.com/show_country.asp?name=India.

In India, language families roughly coincide with broad geographic division of the subcontinent, although their growth pattern shows the differences as Figure 2 below does:

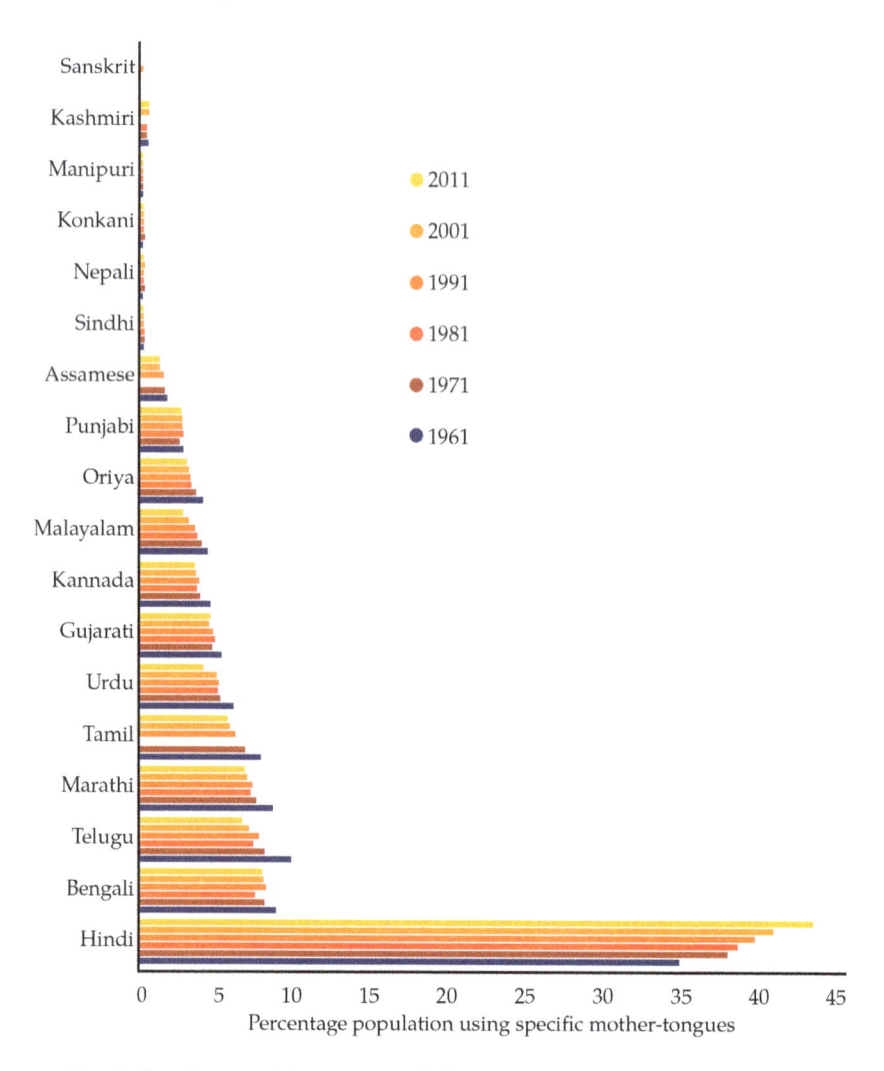

Fig. 2. Distribution of languages in India—comparative strength. Source: the authors.

The number of "castes" (usually referred to as "scheduled castes", or SCs) and tribes in the country is more numerous than the language count; the government of India's *Scheduled Castes Order 1936*[9] (Gazette of India on June 6, 1936) lists 16.23 percent of people categorized into 428 castes. This has now grown upwards to 1284 castes under Article 341 of the Constitution (cf. Table 1.2.8 in Handbook).

Article 366 (25) defines "scheduled tribes" as "such tribes or tribal communities or parts of or groups within such tribes or tribal communities as are deemed under Article 342 to be Scheduled Tribes for the purposes of this constitution". One could, of course, question their identification methods, but after the census in 1931 identified them based on indications of primitive traits, distinctive culture, geographical isolation, shyness of contact with the community at large, and backwardness, this was reiterated in the Reports of First Backward Classes Commission (1955), the Advisory Committee (Kalelkar), on Revision of SC/ST lists (Lokur Committee, 1965), the Joint Committee of Parliament on the Scheduled Castes and Scheduled Tribes Orders (Amendment) Bill (1967), and the Chanda Committee (1969). The 30 Indian states that have reported these tribes show that they constitute 8.6 percent of our total population, over 100 million people, and 705 distinct tribes. The IWGIA (International Work Groups for Indigenous Affairs), a Copenhagen-based human rights group, claims that: "In India, there are 705 ethnic groups officially recognized as 'Scheduled Tribes,' although there are several ethnic groups that are also considered Scheduled Tribes, but are not officially recognized".[10]

There is diversity in religious practices as well. Although 79.8 percent of people in India are, broadly speaking, followers of Hinduism, India also houses more than 172 million Muslims, comprising 14.2 percent of the population—making it one of the world's largest Muslim populations. The population also includes the following smaller religious minorities: Christian (2.3 percent), Sikh (1.7 percent), Buddhist (0.7 percent), Jains (0.4 percent), and other (0.9 percent).

McKinsey's 2007 report shows that roughly five out of every six Indians have an annual income of less that INR 200,000. Thus, 997 million people, (or 80 percent of the population) are at the bottom of the economic pyramid. For those in the urban areas, one may have to

---

9   http://www.socialjustice.nic.in/writereaddata/UploadFile/GOI-SC-ORDER-1936.pdf.
10 https://www.iwgia.org/en/india.

say that the qualifying income bracket is about INR 300,000, and those in the rural area earning below INR 160,000 could be included.

Amongst this diversity, implementing inclusive socioeconomic growth and prosperity becomes a great challenge. The current predominant emphasis on curriculum, syllabus, and enrollment has propagated an environment that is not learner-centric. Instead of promoting child-friendly and child-centric educational opportunities, the current system is more administration friendly. The Indian government's mantra of *Sabka Saath, Sabka Vikas* ("development for all") which is the cornerstone of its National Education Policy (2019) is generally oblivious to children's varying needs and non-uniform learning trajectories.

Weakness of "mother-tongues" and Education for All

Given this background, the core tenets of Education for All—namely the right to attend school and learn one's mother-tongue—become practically meaningless pronouncements. As the UNESCO 2013 report rightly observed, for inclusive education to become a reality, the world education scene needs to undergo a systemic change. Quoting a World Bank Report of 2016, Roche (2016, p. 131–132) observes that "not only is lack of education generally recognized as a cause of poverty, it has come to be recognized as one of three core dimensions alongside living standard and health". Despite strong economic growth in countries with high per-capita GDP, poverty continues to persist, which has encouraged many observers to doubt the meaning of "development".

In implementing many of the ideal programs and curricula, the problems are twofold: there are quite diverse school populations, containing children and guardians from varied backgrounds; rural-urban immigration and displacement could also increase variation. As Ghiso (2013, p. 23) observes, "educators themselves are cultural beings... their backgrounds may be useful in promoting multicultural learning and global sensitivity in early childhood classrooms". Experiments with children as collaborators (Kirmani, 2007) have yielded success, although in small-scale environments.

Teachers who are aware of the local context are therefore necessary. Recruitment of teachers across India's government schools is currently not sufficiently decentralized to meet this demand. Additionally, there is a great need to construct school environments that encourage culturally responsible learning and help children retain and evolve their own identities, so as to create a pluralistic school education space, and develop close home-school partnerships for successful school-based learning outcomes. It is well-known that the public schools in India are constrained by budget.

Ejele (2016, p. 141) comments that Western development ideals often promote the belief that multilingual and multicultural societies are "prone to the 'inevitable clash of cultures and civilizations'". These non-harmonious sentiments are echoed by Huntington's (1993) *Clash of Civilizations* thesis as well. However, according to Annamalai (1995, p. 216), the Indian experience shows the opposite: "Europe promoted monolingualism as part of nation formation... This contrasts, for instance, with the situation in India, where contact with the English language, via colonisation, did not result in language loss, but triggered renaissance in the major Indian languages...". There are also alternative positions, such as that of Appadurai (1996), who would say that the margins are where languages and cultures interact and allow greater understandings to develop, giving rise to spaces for creativity.

Nevertheless, in the real world, there aren't many incentives for supporting non-market-friendly heterogeneity. This coexistence of a large number of marginalized people governed by majority communities is a source of constant tension and political negotiation. While the language of education may not be a practical means of promoting marginalized cultural dimensions, including the knowledge system of marginalized communities would only enrich the education of India's children.

Empowering marginalized learners

"Marginality" refers to an uncontrolled and involuntary position that a group finds itself in with respect to sociopolitical, cultural, economic, ecological, and biophysical systems. Such groups are unable to or are not permitted to access the resources available to all other groups, or to assets and public services. Thus, the marginal groups are restrained in using their freedom of choice, which in turn affects their capabilities, and delays their development, causing them to remain on the margin within the confines of poverty. The Centre for Development Research[11] tells us that although global poverty has decreased substantially, the ultra-poor are now concentrated in South Asia and sub-Saharan Africa. Even though India has seen rapid economic growth, poverty still affects a large proportion of the population. In this matter, the lingua-ethnic minority groups have suffered the most. Using evidence from the Sustainable Development Goals Index released by Niti Aayog and the UN, Khan (2020) showcases worrying trends that "India is losing its footing in key areas such as poverty alleviation, ending hunger, economic growth, and preserving life on land. It's a setback for the country's efforts to rapidly raise standards of living".

For any planned "sociocultural development", the thrust must be on empowerment of the marginalized. Once empowered, those at the bottom of the ladder have the freedom of choice and social action. Tagore, one of India's premier educationists, had a deep dissatisfaction for the hodgepodge that emerged in the name of modern education in India, which led him to conceive of a practical form of "de-schooling" reflected in the practices at Viswa-Bharati. He tried to build a true human community with no marginalization.[12] Tagore was not alone in this goal Freire's Critical Pedagogy approach promoted emancipation of students and learning (Freire 2000; 2007; Freire & Faundez, 1989). Critical Pedagogy aimed at guiding students to become responsible members of a society where the voices and opinions of the marginalized are also heard. "Through these opportunities, students can comprehend their position in society and they can take positive steps to amend their society and ultimately eliminate problems, inequities, and oppressions in their future life" (Mahmoudi, Khoshnood, & Babaei, 2014, p. 86). In fact, the Critical Pedagogy approach aims at encouraging learners not only to interpret the situation and understand the problems, but also to develop the much-needed critical consciousness that is so crucial to changing the world. Those at the BOP then would be encouraged to intervene in the affairs of their society and culture to make a difference. Once this leadership or ownership is accepted by those at the bottom, one may see many changes in mitigating the problems.

---

11 https://www.zef.de/fileadmin/webfiles/downloads/projects/margip/downloads/Poster-marginality-tropentag.pdf.
12 As quoted in http://research.news.yorku.ca/2011/02/25/professor-ananya-mukherjee-reed-rabindranath-tagores-teachings-particularly-relevant/.

Mitigation of challenges: Recommendations

Language and education planners in India must come up with plans and strategies to manage and celebrate diversities in schools, rather than only depending on legal mandates to teach several languages in schools. How education can liberate India from the seemingly inevitable problems of poverty, unemployment, environmental degradation, violence, and so forth, was a concern of the visionaries of India's past—Gandhi, Tagore, Sri Aurobindo, and Jiddu Krishnamurti, among others. In their writings and their experiments, each one of them tried to envision a better reality for India, one unmarred by the greed and destruction associated with the Western model of development, facilitated by the Western style of schooling. They believed that India could only grow and regenerate itself by seeking out those tried and tested beliefs, values, languages, cultures, knowledge, and wisdom upon which it had developed and lived for a long time.

Policies that systemically promote marketable skills and employability of learners within a socially inclusive framework can act as catalytic force to fulfil the priorities of NEP 2019 and SDG4. We present here a tentative model that can ensure universal quality education based on "bottom of the pyramid" framework:

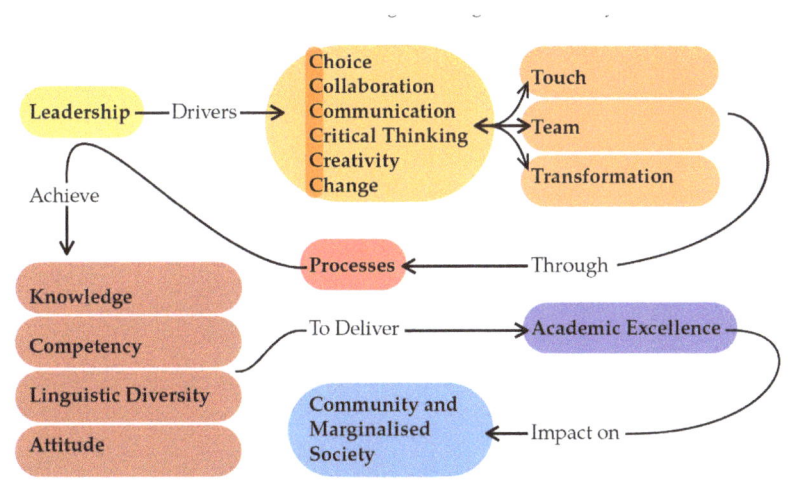

Fig. 3. A model of learning in diverse linguistic contexts of India. Source: based on the work of P. Banerjee (co-author).

The model integrates the six Cs (choice, collaboration, communication, critical thinking, creativity, and change management) along with academic excellence and leadership traits. The model promotes the use of mother-tongue communication to improve the targeting of socially underprivileged and marginalized populations and bring them into the "educational mainstream". Harmonizing the educational expectations and standards across the different states and central boards of education would surely help in educational mainstreaming.

The foremost component of the 6C model is "choice". In the model, the learning pathway is chosen by the student, or by the parents on their behalf, depending upon their ability, aptitude, and interest. Teachers design and develop the curriculum based on the directions of an academic leader or mentor who influences the choice to move in a particular direction when there are diverse course options.

An important component of the 6C model is "collaboration". The primary focus is on mutual efforts and activities worldwide, keeping in mind processes that create academic excellence in ideal schools. Technology could be an accelerator for this kind of education, given the variety and accessibility of options. This entire process is planned and handled by teachers to help learners become more communicative. The term "change" refers to the fact that change is unavoidable as the learners' progress. Repetitive teaching of expressions and "vocables" (that are in the process of becoming "vocabulary" for these learners), often introduced through rhymes, poems, and role-playing at the elementary level, can be one method.

The six Cs of the model are strengthened by touch, team, and transformation, where touch refers to the teacher's investment, team refers to the group effort required for knowledge creation, and transformation to the changing paradigms of teaching and learning and the role of a teacher (Banerjee et. al., 2019).

In conjunction with the above-stated approach, there is also a need to institutionalize inclusive education by involving communities, social workers, other students, and volunteers. Here, inclusive education "involves the right to education for all students... and revolve[s] around fellowship, participation, democratization, benefit, equal access, quality, equity and justice" (Haug, 2017, p. 206). Even though there is some degree of uncertainty about defining "inclusive education" across countries, there is no doubt about the necessity of securing quality education for every learner.

To begin tackling the challenge of educational disparity, one could harness a well-devised technology-driven solution, which could promote the inclusion of marginalized populations in accordance with the Digital India Campaign, Fourth Industrial Revolution as propounded by 10th BRICS Annual Summit Joint Statement, SDG4 and 8.

Lastly, to make any universal education framework successful, there is an urgent need to foster a vibrant and holistic educational environment as envisaged by NEP 2019 and SDG4, especially in primary and secondary schools, by instituting smart classrooms, libraries, laboratories, auditoriums, and playgrounds, among other things. Explaining to students the purpose of education—and that their attempts to succeed will only reflect positively in their own lives—is important. In addition to creating a climate of positivity and safety where risk-taking is encouraged, such tactics would create an open and authentic conversation where trust and respect are fostered, making learning "relevant" to the students. Loveless (2020) shows that these strategies could have a number of results and manifestations such as:

1. Establishment of a good feeling and development of positive self-image;
2. Positive wellness-related actions such as nutrition, exercise, and sleep;
3. Actions leading to problem-solving, decision-making, and thinking skills;
4. Inculcating empathetic and respectful feelings towards others;
5. Positive actions in both time management and managing emotions;
6. Positive actions such as admitting mistakes and taking responsibilities for actions; and
7. Help in goal-setting, leading to personal growth and improvement.

Concluding remarks

We have examined the nature of heterogeneities and inequalities in India that are based on linguistic, economic, sociocultural, class, and caste-based factors. Given this diversity, planning for early grade education or preparing teachers and textbooks are huge challenges, no matter what constitutional provisions are made. Variations across regions and communities have emerged (even after ASER and the National Achievement Surveys) which, coupled with economic, political, and psychological barriers, have led to deprived marginalized communities.

We have identified several challenges and have argued that academic, socioeconomic, and psychological support systems that account for India's heterogenous populace can enhance behavioral and learning competencies, leading to resilience and lifelong learning of children. However, since so many people in India are often juggling multiple identities, what we need is an efficient and responsible system of diversity management. It will be important for our teacher education managers to keep in mind how intercultural tensions could be turned into interethnic bonds.

References

Annamalai, E. (1995). Multilingualism for all: An Indian perspective. In T. Skutnabb-Kangas (Ed.). *Multilingualism for all: European studies on multilingualism* (pp. 215–219). Lisse, the Netherlands: Swets & Zeitlinger.

Appadurai, A. (1996). *Modernity at large: Cultural dimensions of globalization (Public Worlds Series). Minneapolis, Minnesota:* University of Minnesota Press.

Banerjee, P., Ludwikowaska, K., Adhikari, B., & Bandyopadhyay, R. (2020). 6C model of leadership excellence in higher education. In *Academic Leadership Framework for Sustainable Environment: Capacity Building in Higher Education* (pp. 11–27). Warsaw: Diffin, SA.

Chryssochoou, X. (2014). Identity processes in culturally diverse societies: How cultural diversity is reflected in the self. In R. Jaspal & G.M. Breakwell (Eds.), *Identity process theory: Identity, social action and social change* (pp. 135–154). Cambridge: Cambridge University Press.

Ejele, P. E. (2016). The challenges of linguistic and cultural diversities as the common heritage of humanity: The Nigerian experience. In O. Ndimele (Ed.), *Convergence: English and Nigerian languages: A festschrift for Munzali A. Jibril* (pp. 141–158). M & J Grand Orbit Communications.

Freire, P. (2000). *Pedagogy of the oppressed* (M. Bergman Ramos, Trans.). New York: Continuum (Original work published 1996).

Freire, P. (2007). *Critical education in the new information.* Oxford: Rowman & Littlefield Publishers, Inc.

Freire, P., & Faundez, A., (1989). *Learning to question.* New York: Continuum.

Ghiso, M. P. (2013). Every language is special: Promoting dual language learning in multicultural primary schools. *YC Young Children, 68*(1), 22–26.

Greenberg, J. H. (1956). *The measurement of linguistic diversity. Language, 32*(1), 109–115.

Haug, P. (2017). Understanding inclusive education: Ideals and reality. *Scandinavian Journal of Disability Research, 19*(3), 206–217.

Howarth, C., & Andreouli, E. (2016). "Nobody wants to be an outsider": From diversity management to diversity engagement. *Political Psychology, 37*(3), 327–340.

Huntington, S. P. (1993). The clash of civilizations? *Foreign Affairs*, 72, 22–49.

Khan, M. (2020). *Cloud over India's growth story: Poverty and inequality rose in most states in 2019.* ET Prime. https://prime.economictimes.indiatimes.com/news/74232740/economy-and-policy/cloud-over-indias-growth-story-poverty-and-inequality-rose-in-most-states-in-2019

Kirmani, M. H. (2007). Empowering culturally and linguistically diverse children and families. *YC Young Children, 62*(6), 94–98.

Loveless, B. (2020). Strategies for building a productive and positive learning environment. educationcorner.com

Roche, S. (2016). Introduction: Education for all: Exploring the principle and process of inclusive education. *International Review of Education, 62*(2), 131–137.

Singh, K. S. (Ed.). (1993). *Tribal ethnography, customary law, and change.* New Delhi: Concept Publishing Company.

Singh, R. (2018) Choosing the right path: People, development and languages (Plenary talk given at the National Seminar-Cum-Workshop on Revitalization of Heritage Languages and Culture with Special Reference to the NER). Amity University Haryana, Gurugram & Sahitya Akademi, New Delhi.

Singh, U. N. (2009) Status of lesser-known languages of India. In A. Saxena & L. Borin (Eds.) *Lesser-known languages in South Asia: Status and policies, case studies and applications of information technology.* Mouton de Gruyter.

Singh, U. N. (2010). Erosion of cultural and linguistic bases in South Asia (Keynote address, 21st ECMSAS). Universität Bonn; Institut für Orient und sienwissenschaften Abteilung für Indologie, Germany.

Singh, U. N. (2014). Education and what it does to us. *Visva-Bharati Quarterly*. Santiniketan: Visva-Bharati.

UNESCO. (2009). *Policy guidelines on inclusion in education* (ED.2009/WS/31). Paris: UNESCO.

UNESCO. (2013). *Inclusive education* (Education sector technical notes). Paris: UNESCO.

11. India

The Role of Civil Society Organizations and Scalable Technology Solutions for Marginalized Communities

Rajarshi Singh, Annapoorni Chandrashekar, and Nishant Baghel

Introduction

In this chapter, we look at innovations led by civil society organizations (CSOs) that have improved learning outcomes of children at the bottom of the pyramid (BOP) in India. In doing so we hope to explore questions regarding (i) the role of CSOs in developing innovative and effective solutions; (ii) the value of indigenous knowledge and innovations; and (iii) methodologies of creating positive impact by taking innovations to scale, especially by leveraging technology for education. We also realize that there are several other questions that we may not be ready to ask and answer on this issue; for instance, could we build a staircase to ascend to the top and flatten out the pyramid in due course (Prahalad & Hart, 2002)? Can private players, including non-government organizations (NGOs), serve a public cause in poor societies by treating the BOP not as a constituency but as a group who deserves to be shown how to climb up (Prahalad, 2009)?

Civil society space in India

South Asia has had a rich history of non-state actor involvement in elementary education. While educational institutions were attached to temples, mosques, and monasteries in medieval India, and residential colleges of learning in advanced subjects were set up quite early in its history, the picture changed dramatically after 1854, when the British introduced the first formal Colonial Education Policy. This policy allowed some non-state actors and private schools to develop institutions in the region (Day Ashley et al., 2014). While public schooling initiatives were focused on increasing access, improving quality, reducing inequalities, and reducing costs (Patrinos, Barrera-Osorio, & Guáqueta, 2009), some public private partnerships were attempting to standardize what was being taught and optimize government-backed support.

Jhingran (2015) outlines the evolution of public education in India, and argues that, during the post-independence period, CSOs—and particularly NGOs—increased their participation and collaboration with the central and state governments through the DPEP and SSA programs in education. He observes that large NGOs such as the Pratham Education Foundation (since 1994) and Azim Premji Foundation (since 2001) have developed close collaborations with the state and central governments. In addition, more such organizations of different sizes and capabilities have joined in helping out with education. The notable among them include Make A Difference (or "MAD", from 2006), Teach for India (since 2009), The Akshaya Patra Foundation (since 2000), Akanksha Foundation (since 1991), Child Rights & You (since 1979), Bhumi (since 2006), Deepalaya (since 1979), and Bachpan Bachao Andolan (working since 1980, and supported by KSFC). Together they are able to impact government policy and programs around curriculum, pedagogy, textbooks, and teacher training. Finally, Jhingran observes that "some of them have actually started to set up state teams housed in the SCERTs or state offices. Many of them now have leverage because they are also providing man- or woman-power to the state SSA societies".

The CSOs are not only partners to public institutions, they also help hold those institutions to account (WEF, 2013). They serve as advocates for positive change, supply subject matter experts, support capacity building, incubate innovations and solutions, represent marginalized communities, encourage citizen participation, promote fundamental rights and values, and set standards that shape the market and activities. The stakeholders of any generalized education system must provide support that is social, economic, and environmental (Salvioni

& Cassano, 2015). Civil society partnerships provide support and resources (both financial and non-financial) to the education system, in addition to integrating policy with grassroot needs and accountability.

Civil society, in addition to government and private business, is a key change lever for the growth and improvement of education, especially for those at the bottom of the pyramid and those at the primary level. Bjorn Lomborg's work (2014) at the Copenhagen Consensus Center has shown that investing in early learning has phenomenal benefits. Investing in the education of children under five years of age not only increases the likelihood of healthier life, but also reduces future costs of special and remedial education, as well as achievement gaps and overall social costs. Research suggests that "every dollar invested in high-quality early childhood education produces a 7 to 10 percent per annum return on investment" (Heckman et al., 2010).

Driven by this zeal, the government of India spent INR 23,500 crores (FY 2017–2018) on Sarva Shiksha Abhiyan (Accountability Initiative, 2018) to provide free and compulsory education for all children between the ages of 6 and 14 under the Right to Education Act. Mired by multiple inefficiencies and leakages, this investment has not resulted in equivalent benefits. Pritchett and Aiyar (2014) show the difference between the accounting cost and economic cost of publicly funded education, implying that "the excess cost of achieving the existing private learning levels at public sector costs is Rs. 232,000 crores (2.78% of GDP, or nearly US$50 billion)". In other words, public education is expensive in addition to being inefficient.

If economists were to calculate the Herfindahl-Hirschman Index[1] for schooling in India, they would find a trend showing decreasing government monopoly in education after 2000. Furthermore, while the government is the largest funder of education, the private and civil society sectors are the leading innovators and providers of novel solutions. The ability of CSOs and NGOs to provide low-cost innovations has encouraged the government to view CSOs as partners, rather than competitors. With few exceptions, NGOs typically are more community-oriented, and therefore have a better understanding of local-speak and local sociocultural landscapes—what some call an indigenous

---

1 As developed by Orris C. Herfindahl and the economist Albert O. Hirschman; see https://en.wikipedia.org/wiki/Herfindahl–Hirschman_Index.

approach. The NGOs' ground-level connections also serve as crucial marketing channels that enable effective scaling of innovations with greater community buy-in.

Indigenous knowledge and sustainable development

Indigenous or traditional knowledge refers to the "long-standing information, wisdom, traditions and practices of certain indigenous peoples or local communities" (Kothari, 2007). Typically, sectors related to agriculture, forestry, fisheries, and traditional housing make extensive use of indigenous knowledge that is passed down from generation to generation (Posey, 1999). More recently, the adoption of traditional practices has enhanced the sustainability of many production chains across secondary and tertiary sectors such as textiles, pharmaceuticals, and medicine.

Ellen and Harris (1996) characterize indigenous knowledge as having 10 salient features (see Fig. 1.). Much of this knowledge was devalued and even ridiculed by nineteenth-century social scientists, who often held an antipathy towards indigenous knowledge systems (Warren, 1989). As a result, traditional and indigenous knowledge, which is considered the social capital of the poor, was grossly overlooked by the colonial education system (Senanayake, 2006). Furthermore, cross-cultural studies have shown that transmission and maintenance of indigenous knowledge depends on economic, social, cultural, and ecological factors. Conservation of this knowledge can only be achieved by local preservation and growth strategies (Paniagua-Zambrana et al., 2016). Thus, the question before us is, how do we blend local and global knowledge and technologies to offer the best practices of both worlds to children at the bottom of the pyramid? (see Figure 1)

The indigene and learning technology

Comparative analyses have demonstrated that globalization, global competition, and a need for 21st-century skills have resulted in the homogenization of some aspects of child development and education curricula across nations (Sparapani et al., 2014). Learning through play, problem-solving, learning by doing, and experiential pedagogies are

Fig. 1. Characteristics of indigenous knowledge. Source: the authors.

some examples of common, yet experimental, approaches being used throughout the world. Research shows that large gains in children's learning outcomes can be achieved when instruction is aligned with learners' learning levels (Banerjee et al., 2016). Gamified teaching-learning aids and learning through play are adaptive techniques that organically align with a capability-based teaching methodology.

Pratham Education Foundation (Pratham), one of India's largest education NGOs, observed substantial gains in foundational mathematics outcomes of 10,000 slum children who participated in a longitudinal randomized experiment, where they played mathematics computer games targeting math learning (Banerji & Chavan, 2016). Similarly, the Bridges to the Future Initiative, a technology-based intervention, implemented in primary schools in West Godavari and secondary schools in Ranga Reddy districts "had a modest (marginally significant) impact on the reading skills of both young children and youth/young adults who had no prior experience with computers" (Wagner, Daswani, & Karnati, 2010); later work in South Africa, using a similar approach, had much more robust learning outcomes (see Castillo et al., this volume). Evidence from remedial reading and math interventions has also shown that children are able to sustainably learn foundational skills if the lessons are mapped to their capacity.

The positive impact of educational games on the development of children is well-known. Yet existing or even innovative solutions that are "ported" from the Global North often fail to assist children in rural and developing contexts in their learning journeys. Kam et al. (2009) analyzed 28 traditional games across villages in India that children engage with on a regular basis and compared them to the characteristic features of digital games to understand the difference in uptake. Contextually constructed games create "virtual environments with rich backgrounds where players participate actively", where these games continuously "challenge players to develop new skills". As argued by Fine (2012), our world is constructed of "tiny publics" that allow us to share affiliations with others. These small groups are spaces where social actors operate within the bounds of society—a phenomenon that is observed in games involving groups. Shared "social experiences" ultimately develop shared contexts for growth and social communication (Kam et al., 2009).

Arvind Gupta, a renowned scientist and inventor, has demonstrated how science and math can be taught in low-income environments by using locally sourced materials. This is where children are encouraged to use their own imagination and problem-solving capacities to find solutions to puzzles, which often leads to higher learning gains. He states that the best way for children to learn is by doing (Krithika, 2019). Although the tradition of learning from indigenous technologies is on the decline, from a design perspective they "show remarkable examples of the creative and thoughtful use of materials" (Khanna, 2018). The key strengths of indigenous technologies that can be leveraged to improve learning outcomes are: (1) dynamism; (2) simplicity of materials; (3) affiliation with cultural ethos; and (4) alignment with scientific principles and technology. In the remaining sections we showcase instances of learning technologies developed and propagated by NGOs that have substantially moved the needle in the Indian context. In each example the problem, solution, and benefits are presented. We are aware that technology alone will not solve all the problems with education (Toyama, 2015), but that it is a crucial lever in maximizing improvement (Garton, 2017).

PraDigi Open Learning: An example of a scalable indigenous tech-based solution

The story of low foundational learning levels is not new (see Crouch & Slade, this volume). In India, it goes back to 2005, when Pratham Education Foundation, now one of India's largest educational NGOs, launched the Annual Status of Education Report (ASER). Volunteers were trained and marshalled to collect evidence about children's reading and numeracy skills across India's rural districts. What was discovered was critical for educational planning, though distressing. This Indian innovation found acceptance in other countries that faced similar challenges. Citizen-Led Assessments (CLAs), which are characterized by their robust design yet simple-to-use tools and processes, were taken up by eight organizations that eventually came to be known as the People's Action for Learning (PAL) Network. Today, the PAL Network has 15 members who have cumulatively assessed more than 7.5 million children by engaging about 690,000 volunteers over the past 15 years

PAL Network conducted the International Common Assessment of Numeracy (ICAN, 2020) between October 2019 and February 2020, where it assessed the foundational math competencies of more than 26,000 children from approximately 15,000 households in 779 rural communities (villages) across 13 countries. A cluster of 60 villages was selected from one subnational region (district) per country.

As a cross-national assessment, ICAN has the potential to provide a Global-South-based platform for comparative and benchmarking purposes. In addition to its policy-level impacts at the international and sub/national levels, ICAN also has the necessary characteristics to significantly influence regional educational responses towards foundational learning. As pointed out by Schwantner and Walker (2020), ICAN promises to: (1) provide a single source citizen-led assessment that can be adapted to various local contexts and languages; (2) broaden our understanding of numeracy and increase the scope of early grade assessments through a collaborative effort; and (3) provide insights about foundational learning necessary for monitoring educational outcomes of children at all levels. With the support of the Global Partnership for Education's Knowledge and Innovation Exchange (KIX) grant, PAL Network and its partners are in the process of a common-scale adaptation of the ICAN tool that assesses children's pre-numeracy and early numeracy skills. Evidence from assessments inform in-class practices and intervention designs to improve children's foundational learning. In what follows, we will discuss an innovative, digitally-supported intervention by Pratham that not only uses data on children's learning outcomes, but also their daily interaction with the digital system to enhance engagement and uptake.

Building on its work across rural India, Pratham's PraDigi Open Learning program is a community-based, digitally enabled open-learning intervention that spans multiple cognitive and non-cognitive skills (Singh, Sharma, & Verma, 2017). The program has been evolving since its inception, experimenting with content, delivery mechanisms, learning structures, and other programmatic aspects. PraDigi Open Learning's iterative design has created an open learning space for children and youth to prepare for school, work, and life. The program has achieved this through three pillars:

- Social structure—systems and structures to encourage the community to actively participate in children's learning.

- Digital infrastructure—mobile devices and technology placed in the hands of children, used for guided learning and fun activities.

- Learning content—a wide array of contextualized content created in the form of videos and games.

PraDigi Open Learning is a non-formal (out-of-school) learning experiment that dynamically tries to improve how children learn in rural India. It draws on the belief that children are naturally curious and interested in learning. In the absence of traditional teaching, the program's hybrid model of blending the three support pillars (social, digital, and content) has enabled responsive learning experiments. The programs help children build their skills and learn, even outside a school setting. In the absence of a prescribed curriculum (a conscious choice), children are encouraged to choose what they want to learn, set their learning goals, and participate in group activities where they manage their own learning, including assessments to measure their progress on topics. Youth volunteers who support the groups in the learning activities are called coaches.

PraDigi Open Learning has undergone multiple stages of evolution. Beginning as a proof of concept called "m-learning program" in early 2015, the program was scaled up from 50 villages in the Pisangan block of Rajasthan to 400 villages across Uttar Pradesh, Rajasthan, and Maharashtra in 2015. About 26,000 children between Grades 5 to 8 were enrolled. However, the number of children who benefited from the program was higher, as quite often friends and siblings of participants also participated. PraDigi Open Learning utilized the close-knit *"mohulla"* structure of villages to involve and encourage the participation of children's guardians, and every child in the village was welcome to be part of the groups that were engaging with Pratham's digital content. The program leveraged the natural group-based activities of children, as well as the potential of digital content and devices.

After a controlled trial in 2017 to study the PraDigi Open Learning model in Rajasthan's Dausa district, the program expanded and evolved further, with a renewed focus on self-organized learning and delivery of project-based learning content. Children were encouraged to select courses themselves, set their own targets, and manage their own learning experiences within the program. A majority of the experiences continued to be rooted in group-based learning activities, but personal practice was also built in through mock assessments and a final assessment managed by the program facilitators. The content for the open learning initiative is broadly clustered in three domains: preparation for school, preparation for work, and preparation for life.

The PraDigi approach seeks to blend technology with indigenous social support systems, and had a unique impact on children's learning habits. In the period of 2017–2019, the digital learning tools reached more that 300,000 learners through 22,000 tablets and organized more than 19,800 learning groups. With minimal intervention, learners engaged with the app for 12–14 days a month on average for 55–60 minutes per day. A total of 70+ million minutes were clocked on the app over an 18-month period. A controlled learning experiment with 139 treatment villages and 99 control group villages with no intervention found that children with access to the PraDigi Open Learning showed the maximum improvements in science, English, and Hindi assessments. Participants in the program outperformed children in the control group by 12 percentage points in school curricular subjects (World Economic Forum, 2020).

The curiosity of children, communities, and staff has enabled multiple innovations. One such experiment was Pratham's Code Club Pilot.[2] This experiment was launched in 2019, across 40 villages in Aurangabad (Maharashtra) and Sitapur (Uttar Pradesh), with 50 coaches mentored 244 code clubs, reaching 1109 learners. Children in these low-resourced communities were given the opportunity to learn and utilize computer programing to execute a live project. Approximately 40 percent of the groups that started their project managed to complete it, with the support of their peers and coaches.

Conclusion

The PraDigi Open Learning program is a unique program that blends technology, children's curiosity, and traditional social structures to engage communities in children's learning. In this program, children manage their own learning outside a school environment and were found to have outperformed their counterparts who only engaged with the traditional school-based learning model. Its architect, Madhav Chavan, summed up this child-friendly learning and education by stating that education needs to "move away from the age-grade system.... Instead we need an age-stage system that allows children to meet learning goals in both the social and academic sphere when they are ready, transitioning to each stage at their own pace".

Educational technology is not a magic wand that can solve all the ills ailing education, especially inequity and non-inclusion. However, technology can be leveraged to improve access to education and buttress delivery of quality learning modules. Furthermore, recent evaluations of tech-based products such as instructional aids, individual-use products, and personalized adaptive products have reported that it is important for solutions to be tailored to children's capability levels and deliver

---

2   Pratham Education Foundation's internal document, "Code Club Pilot".

child-friendly content in vernacular languages (Sampson et al., 2019). One hopes that, with continued partnerships between public, private, and non-profit agencies, technology can be prudently used to improve learning in India.

References

Accountability Initiative. (2018). *Budget briefs: Sarva Shiksha Abhiyan (SSA) GoI, 2017–18*. Centre for Policy Research.

ASER. (2016). *Annual status of education report*. Pratham Education Foundation.

Ashley, L. D., Mcloughlin, C., Aslam, M., Engel, J., Wales, J., Rawal, S., & Rose, P. (2014). *The role and impact of private schools in developing countries: A rigorous review of the evidence* (Unpublished Final Report). Education Rigorous Literature Review, UK Department for International Development.

Banerjee, A., Banerji, R., Berry, J., Duflo, E., Kannan, H., Mukherji, S., & Michael, W. (2016). *Mainstreaming an effective intervention: Evidence from randomised evaluations of 'Teaching at the Right Level' in India* (NBER Working Papers, No. 22746).

Banerji, R., & Duflo, E. (2015). *Let's remake the classroom*. The Indian Express.

Banerji, R., & Chavan, M. (2016). Improving literacy and math instruction at scale in India's primary schools: The case of Pratham's Read India program. *Journal of Educational Change, 17*(4), 453–475.

Chavan, M. (2013). Who needs classrooms? In C. Chandler & A. Zainulbhai (Eds.), *Reimaging India: Unlocking the potential of Asia's next superpower* (pp. 221–226). New York: Simon and Schuster.

Ellen, R., & Harris, H. (1996). Concepts of indigenous technical knowledge in scientific and developmental studies literature: A critical assessment. In R. Ellen, P. Parkes, & A. Bicker (Eds.), *Indigenous environmental knowledge and its transformations: Critical anthropological perspectives* (pp. 1–34). Routledge.

Fine, G. A. (2012). *Tiny publics: A theory of group action and culture*. Russell Sage Foundation.

Garton, S. (2017). The case for investing more in people. *Harvard Business Review*, September. https://static1.squarespace.com/static/5a6c0b97f43b554 3ff1f502e/t/5a80b8cb8165f5c700abb46a/1518385356105/The+Case+for+In vesting+More+in+People.pdf

Heckman, J. J., Moon, S. H., Pinto, R., Savelyev, P. A., & Yavitz, A. (2010). The rate of return to the HighScope Perry Preschool Program. *Journal of Public Economics, 94*(1–2), 114–128.

ICAN. (2020). *International common assessment of numeracy report.* Nairobi: People's Action for Learning (PAL) Network.

Jamil, B. R. (2020). *Introducing ICAN (International Common Assessment of Numeracy) as a global learning metric.* PAL Network. https://palnetwork.org/introducing-ican-international-common-assessment-of-numeracy-as-a-global-learning-metric/

Jhingran, D. (2015). *Systemic change in education and the role of Civil Society Organizations.* The Educationist. http://www.theeducationist.info/systemic-change-in-education-and-the-role-of-civil-society/

Kam, M., Mathur, A., Kumar, A., & Canny, J. (2009). Designing digital games for rural children: A study of traditional village games in India. In *Proceedings of the 27th International Conference on Human Factors in Computing Systems.* Boston, MA, USA.

Khanna, S. (2018). *Indian toys and toy makers.* Arvind Gupta Toys. http://www.arvindguptatoys.com/arvindgupta/sudarshan.pdf

Kothari, A. (2007). *Traditional knowledge and sustainable development.* Canada: International Institute for Sustainable Development (IISD).

Krithika, R. (2019). *Let children learn by doing.* The Hindu. https://www.thehindu.com/education/schools/a-conversation-with-renowned-scientist-and-educator-arvind-gupta/article28098701.ece

Lomborg, B. (2014). *Fixing the world, bang-for-the-buck edition (Ep. 181): Full transcript of Freakonomics Radio.* Freakonomics. https://freakonomics.com/podcast/fixing-the-world-bang-for-the-buck-edition-a-new-freakonomics-radio-podcast/

Paniagua-Zambrana, N., Camara-Leret, R., Bussmann, R. W., & Macía, M. J. (2016). Understanding transmission of traditional knowledge across northwestern South America: A cross-cultural study in palms (Arecaceae). *Botanical Journal of the Linnean Society, 182*(2), 480–504.

Patrinos, H. A., Barrera-Osorio, F., & Guáqueta, J. (2009). *The role and impact of public-private partnerships in education.* Washington, DC: World Bank.

Posey, D. A. (1999). *Cultural and spiritual values of biodiversity.* https://www.unep.org/resources/publication/cultural-and-spiritual-values-biodiversity

Prahalad, C. K. (2009). *The fortune at the bottom of the pyramid: Eradicating poverty through profits* (Revised and updated 5th anniversary edition). FT Press.

Prahalad, C., & Hart, S. (2002). The fortune at the bottom of the pyramid. *Business Strategy Review, 2,* 1–14.

Pritchett, L., & Aiyar, Y. (2014). *Value subtraction in public sector production: Accounting versus economic cost of primary schooling in India* (Working Paper No. 391). Center for Global Development.

Rose, P. (2020). *More than the sum of its parts: Internationally-comparable citizen-led assessments to ensure no child is left behind.* UK FIET. https://www.ukfiet.org/2020/more-than-the-sum-of-its-parts-internationally-comparable-citizen-led-assessments-to-ensure-no-child-is-left-behind/

Salvioni, D. M., & Cassano, R. (2015). Improvement of management performance in the school system. *Proceedings of the 3rd Virtual Multidisciplinary Conference,* (pp. 108–112).

Sampson, R., Johnson, D., Somanchi, A., Barton, H., Joshi, R., Seth, M., & Shotland, M. (2019). *The EdTech Lab Series: Insights from rapid evaluations of EdTech products.* IDinsight and Central Square Foundation.

Schwantner, U., & Walker, M. (2020). *Supporting quality education through citizen-led assessment.* ACER. https://www.acer.org/in/discover/article/supporting-quality-education-through-citizen-led-assessment

Senanayake, S. G. (2006). Indigenous knowledge as a key to sustainable development. *Journal of Agricultural Sciences–Sri Lanka,* 2(1).

Singh, R., Sharma, N., & Verma, K. (2017). Learning and evolving in hybrid learning: A PAR perspective. In *Participatory action research and educational development* (pp. 161–183). Cham: Palgrave Macmillan.

Sparapani, E. F., Perez, D. C., Gould, J., Hillman, S., & Clark, L. (2014). A global curriculum? Understanding teaching and learning in the United States, Taiwan, India, and Mexico. *SAGE Open,* 4(2), 1–15.

Toyama, K. (2015). *Why technology alone won't fix schools.* The Atlantic.

Wagner, D., Daswani, C., & Karnati, R. (2010). Technology and mother-tongue literacy in Southern India: Impact studies among young children and out-of-school youth. *Information Technology and International Development,* 6(4), 23–43.

Warren, D. M. (1989). Linking scientific and indigenous agriculture systems. In J. L. (Eds.), *The transformation of international agricultural research and development* (pp. 153–170). Boulder: Lynne Rienner.

World Bank. (2018). *World Development Report 2018: Learning to realize education's promise.* Washington, DC: World Bank.

World Economic Forum. (2020). *Schools of the future: Defining new models of education for the fourth industrial revolution.* World Economic Forum.

12. Ivory Coast

Children at the Bottom of the Pyramid and Government Policies

*François Joseph Azoh
and Zamblé Théodore Goin Bi*

Introduction

The main goal of the initiative "learning at the bottom of the pyramid" (Wagner et al., 2018) is to broaden the debate on educational inequality and improve the quality of learning among poor and marginalized populations in low-income countries. The initiative aims to draw more attention to learning inequalities in these countries, identify the populations who face the most barriers to education and learning, examine the socioeconomic conditions of vulnerable populations, and propose suggestions for policies and further research.

This contribution focuses on the specific case of Ivory Coast, and aims to:

- identify the populations at the bottom of the pyramid;
- describe the current state of schooling; and
- present government education policies that curb inequalities in access to quality education.

Who are the children at the bottom of the pyramid in Ivory Coast?

Children from economically disadvantaged families

Ivory Coast's economy has improved in recent years. As a matter of fact, the growth rate went from 4.4 percent in 2011 to 7.4 percent in 2019. However, according to the Human Development Index (HDI), Ivory Coast was among the countries with the lowest overall HDI values, ranking 165th out of 189. And, despite solid economic growth, poverty is still significant. In 2016, nearly 46 percent of Ivorians lived on less than $1.30 per day and were in a multidimensional poverty situation. Rural areas had a higher concentration of poor people (56.8 percent), and children from poor families were mostly out of school or failing to achieve expected learning benchmarks (UNDP, 2019).

The State Report on the National Education System (RESEN, by its French acronym, 2016) shows that financial problems are the primary reason cited by families for not enrolling children in school. Moreover, many children from poor families who attend school repeat grades, thus increasing the risk of dropping out before completing the cycle. This suggests that being poor and living in a rural area increases the probability of both not attending school and dropping out.

Girls

The net primary-school intake and enrollment rates show that girls have less access to school than boys. In terms of access to primary school, intake rates for girls went from 67.80 percent to 71.90 percent between 2013 and 2019, which indicates that around one-third of school-aged girls still do not have access to primary school.

Completion rates for primary and lower-secondary school show progress over the period 20132019. However, 20 percent of girls do not complete their primary school education and almost half of girls do not complete their lower-secondary-school education.

In Ivory Coast, pregnancy during the school years is another barrier to girls' education. Over the past five years, an average of 311 pregnancies have been recorded in primary school compared to 4,190 in secondary

Table 1. Girl's completion rates in primary and lower-secondary school in Ivory Coast from 2013 to 2019.

School year	Primary school	Lower-secondary school
2013–2014	54.20%	29.0%
2014–2015	58.80%	30.5%
2015–2016	64.70%	35.4%
2016–2017	71.60%	42.7%
2017–2018	75.00%	49.2%
2018–2019	79.80%	52.8%

Source: Ministry of National Education, Technical Education and Vocational Training (2014; 2015; 2016; 2017; 2018; 2019).

school (Ministry of National Education, Technical Education and Vocational Training, 2016). In 2016, the Ministry of National Education, Technical Education and Vocational Training reported that students who become pregnant during their school years usually come from a disadvantaged social background. Very often, these girls come from rural areas and their arrival in the cities to undertake secondary studies becomes a daily struggle to ensure the minimum subsistence (food, body care products, etc.). To support themselves, girls are sometimes forced to carry out transactions of a sexual nature, ending in pregnancies during the school years and associated with a high risk of dropout.

Data collection of pregnancy cases during the school years appears in the statistical yearbooks of the Ministry since 2014. This information has not yet been analyzed in depth to know more about these girls' dropout from and reintegration into the system.

Children living with a disability

In Ivory Coast, 65 percent of people with disabilities are illiterate and 71 percent of them live in rural areas (Ministry of National Education, Technical Education and Vocational Training, 2017). Of children aged 3 to 18, about 48,200 are diagnosed with a disability, representing 11 percent of school-aged children from pre-primary to high school. Children with disabilities are mostly out of school. Of these children, 44 percent have never attended school, and this rate is higher in rural areas, where it reaches 60 percent. Among children with disabilities, the primary school dropout rate is 95 percent.

Economically disadvantaged parents often believe that sending children with disabilities to school is a waste of time and money (Azoh & Goin Bi, 2019). Parents doubt the learning abilities of their children and the system's ability to integrate them into the socioeconomic fabric. From the start, any financial commitment is seen as a waste.

The structures required for these children to achieve their full potential are not in place. Public schools were not designed to accommodate children with disabilities and do not have adequate human and material resources.

Children without a birth certificate

Birth registration in Ivory Coast is not systematic. The registration rate in 2018 was 72 percent compared to 74.8 percent in 2014. The rate of timely registration regressed from 2014 to 2018, i.e., it went down from 70 percent to 55.4 percent throughout the country. One-third of children do not have a birth certificate, and as a result will face difficulties in enrolling in primary school.

Table 2. Overall birth registration rate.

Year	Registrations (%)	Timely registration of births
2014	74.8	70
2015	72.8	60.5
2016	74.8	59
2017	70.8	54
2018	72.2	55.4

Source: Ministry of the Interior and Security, 2019, p. 27–28.

Other children outside the school system

Sika and Kacou (2018) observed that in 2015, school exclusion in Côte d'Ivoire affected more girls (3,289,400) than boys (2,771,800) and that children in rural areas (3,845,800) are more affected than those in urban areas (2,215,400).

Regarding 12–15-year-olds—i.e., the age group corresponding to Secondary 1—there were about 797,100 total, of which rural areas accounted for 533,000 (66.9 percent). The same study showed that 706,000 children with schooling had not yet entered secondary school and risked never reaching that level.

According to the same authors, children with no schooling generally live in large households with an average size of seven people. The parents or guardians of these Children Outside the School System (COSS) are mostly employed in agriculture (38.5 percent), service activities (28.9 percent) and trade (7.9 percent).

The *Rapport d'Etat sur le Système de l'Education* report (RESEN; 2016) comes to similar conclusions, analyzing data from the DHS-MICS 2012 survey. COSS are most often girls living in rural areas with poor parents. In the first quintile, representing the poorest 20 percent of the population, the prevalence rate of children who are not in school is 43.9 percent. The majority (28.8 percent) of children who are not in school belong to this category of the population.

Table 3. Characteristics of COSS aged between 6 and 11 years old in 2012.

	Prevalence rate of COSS	Distribution of COSS
Gender		
Girls	34.1%	53.9%
Boys	28.4%	46.1%
Area of residence		
Rural	36.6%	72.3%
Urban	22.5%	27.7%
Income quintiles		
Q1 (Poor)	43.9%	28.8%
Q2	31.2%	22.6%
Q3	36.7%	24.0%
Q4	27.7%	17.6%
Q5 (Rich)	13.1%	7.1%

Source: RESEN (IMF, 2016).

Schooling in Ivory Coast

School statistics for Ivory Coast indicate that many children either do not enter school (Figure 1) or else drop out very early (Figure 2). The net intake rates to CP1 are between 70 percent and 74 percent for the periods between 20142015 and 2019–2020, showing that about a quarter of applicants fail to enroll. However, the net enrollment rate has increased over the past five years from 78.9 percent to 91.5 percent. Despite everything, nine percent of children still do not receive achieve age-appropriate schooling or progress through the school system (UNICEF, 2014).

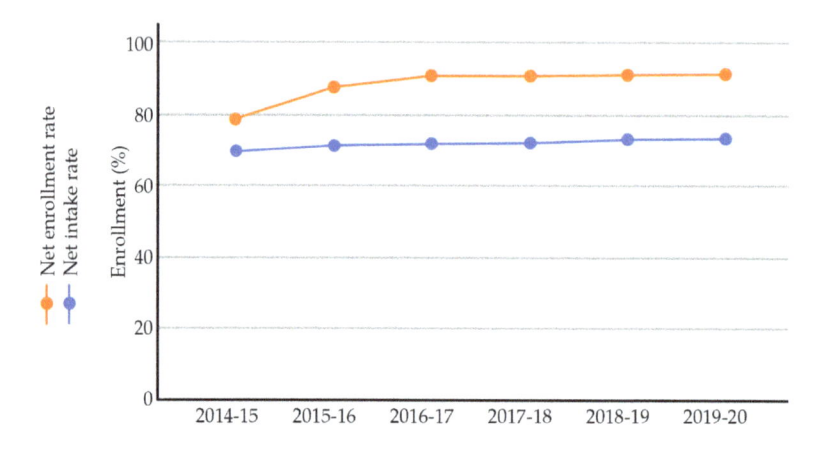

Fig. 1. Net intake and enrollment rates in Ivory Coast from 2014/15 to 2019/20. Source: Ministry of National Education, Technical Education and Vocational Training (2014, 2015, 2016, 2017, 2018, 2019, 2020).

Primary school dropouts have been around 5 percent during the last five years and repeaters represented 10 percent (see Figure 2).

Children denied access to CP1

The Statistical Analysis Report 2018–2019 revealed that between 2015 and 2019, the proportion of children who were denied enrollment in primary school varied between 9.8 percent and 7.4 percent. One of the causes was the lack of national coverage of the school infrastructure, which decreased from 43.5 percent to 31.5 percent during the same period.

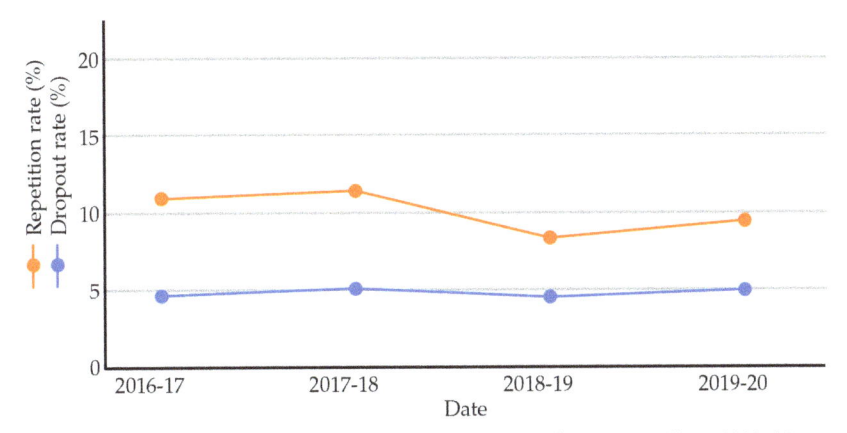

Fig. 2. Repetition and dropout rates in Ivory Coast from 2016/17 to 2019/20. Source: Ministry of National Education, Technical Education and Vocational Training (2014; 2015; 2016; 2017; 2018; 2019; 2020).

Table 4. Children denied enrollment in CP1 in Ivory Coast from 2015–2019.

		2015/16	2016/17	2017/18	2018/19
Number of children who applied to CP1		793,848	764,488	759,362	783,638
Number of children not admitted to CP1		77,915	72,695	54,630	58,241
Proportion of not-admitted children		9.8%	9.5%	7.2%	7.4%
Number of children not admitted to CP1 by reason	Number of children not admitted because of insufficient accommodation capacity	33,865	27,027	19,666	18,325
	Number of children not admitted because of their young age	40,634	42,372	32,776	37,587
	Over-aged children	3,416	3,296	2,188	2,329
Proportion of children not admitted to CP1 by reason	Accommodation capacity	43.5%	37.2%	36.0%	31.5%
	Under-aged children	52.2%	58.3%	60.0%	64.5%
	Over-aged children	4.4%	4.5%	4.0%	4.0%

Source: Ministry of National Education, Statistical Analysis Report 2018–2019, p. 22.

Alternative educational offers for children at the bottom of the pyramid

Low-cost private schools

Goin Bi and Koutou (2019) showed that low-cost private schools often did not meet the necessary conditions to operate. Most of them operated without authorization—i.e., illegally—and ran dilapidated and unhealthy infrastructures. In these schools, teachers started the job without any pedagogical training or experience and worked with insufficient and poor-quality didactic and pedagogical materials. Parents' interest in such schools was directly related to their limited financial resources.

Islamic schools

During the 2019–2020 school year, Ivory Coast had 2,536 Islamic schools with 8,573 classrooms attended by 512,811 students, out of which 161,052 were girls (31.4 percent).

These schools were strongly established in the north and northeast of Ivory Coast, which were areas of under-enrollment in government schools. There were 112 schools and 7,807 students, out of which 5,464 (70 percent) were boys and 2,343 girls (Guiré, 2010, cited by Silué and Ndjore, 2016). Silué and Ndjore (2016) described the difficult educational conditions in Islamic schools, where didactic material and infrastructure was very limited. Learning takes place on the ground—i.e., on mats or animal skins. Students used ink, a pen, a small board or *walaga*, the Koran, and related books. The majority of these schools did not provide the skills and content level expected in the national curriculum. Furthermore, teachers in these schools received lower remuneration than teachers in formal schools (Kanvaly, 2009). Children enrolled in Islamic schools came from socially and economically disadvantaged families. Interpeace (2019) reported that children went to Islamic schools for two main reasons: financial and geographical constraints, as they are usually tuition-free (though require additional expenses during the school year), and the fact that they are sometimes the only viable schooling option in remote rural areas.

Community schools

Community schools have emerged recently as a form of resilience in rural areas without school infrastructure (public and private). For the 2018–2019 academic year, 888 community schools were inventoried; they had 2,287 classrooms and 69,301 enrolled students, including 31,488 girls (45 percent). Community schools represent two percent of all educational offerings, but five percent of primary-school enrollment.

However, the quality of the education provided in these schools is typically poor because of a lack of qualified teachers, pedagogical supervision, and resources. In fact, teachers are often out-of-school high-school students who have no pedagogical training and who teach in an approximate manner, which rarely meets the standards of public education. Ouattara and Aya (2016) found that teachers are "volunteers"[1] who serve the community. Their remuneration is not fixed and is based on the number of students enrolled and other arrangements with the community, such as in-kind donations (food).

Institutional framework of educational policy

The educational policy in Ivory Coast is based on the Constitution, which states that "school attendance is compulsory for children of both sexes, under the conditions determined by law", and two specific acts: Law No. 95696 of September 7, 1995 and Law No. 2015635 of September 17, 2015.

The 1995 law

Law No. 95696 of September 7, 1995, outlines the fundamental principles governing the public service of education in Ivory Coast, as follows:

- Enable each citizen to acquire knowledge, develop her/his personality, raise her/his level of education, integrate into social, cultural, and professional life and exercise citizenship;

---

[1] This is the name chosen by the Ministry of National Education for this category of teachers.

- Promote the neutral, free, and equal nature of the public service of education, where neutrality is defined in relation to any political, philosophical, or religious current of thought;
- Ensure free education in public institutions, with the exception of enrollment fees, social benefits, and the cost of textbooks and other school supplies;
- Enable the acquisition of knowledge, soft skills, and a critical mind, as well as the development of sensitivity and curiosity.

Article 2 of this law reaffirms the right to education and equal treatment of all citizens (regardless of their race, sex, political, philosophical, or religious convictions, or their social, cultural, or geographical origin), particularly in public education. It also emphasizes the need for increased participation of all stakeholders, especially the community, in the management of institutions.

The 2015 law

To curb inequalities among children in school, the State of Ivory Coast initiated a series of additional educational measures. In 2015, the policy of compulsory schooling came into force through Law No. 2015–635. Article 2.2 states that "the State is obliged to keep children between the ages of six and sixteen in the school system, including those with special needs, and to set up a mechanism to integrate or reintegrate children between the ages of nine and sixteen who are outside the system; in particular by means of crossover classes for the nine-to-thirteen age group, as well as vocational training for the fourteen-to-sixteen age group".

According to this policy, all children are required to be enrolled in school and complete 10 years of education—i.e., have a minimum education level equivalent to third grade, regardless of their identity or ability. During this period, all children should acquire a common base of knowledge, skills, and culture. Additionally, this base must enable children to pursue further studies, build a personal and professional future, and prepare them for civic life. This policy is inclusive of all children, regardless of their vulnerable situation. The 20162025 Education and Training Sector Plan emphasizes this mandate by defining the following objectives: access, equity, respect for the right to education, and inclusive education.

Government responses to children at the bottom of the pyramid

Integration of Islamic and community schools

In Ivory Coast, UNICEF has made a major contribution to the process of integration of Islamic schools. Silué and Ndjoré (2016) note that, starting in 2004, UNICEF, supported by local NGOs, invested in a program to equip Islamic faith-based schools and train teachers. The formal integration, as of 2012, of Islamic and community schools into the formal education system helps to offer children at the bottom of the pyramid opportunities similar to those of other children. The recognition of these schools by the state assures that they meet the key standards, including having training programs for teachers, pedagogical supervision, and status as civil servants.

In 2018, the state established the National Commission for the Support of Islamic Educational Institutions (CNAESI, by its French acronym), which is in charge of the integration of Islamic structures into the formal education system following a two-level compliance analysis (see Table 5).

In 2019–2020, there were 385 integrated Islamic schools with 98,291 enrolled students, compared to 54,298 students in non-integrated Islamic schools, out of a total of 373,300 students in all Islamic education structures, which means that the rate of integration of students into the formal system was 26.3 percent (see Figure 3).

The state recognizes community schools that meet integration standards by charting them on the school map. The Statistical Analysis Report 2018–2019 shows that, from 2014/15 to 2018/19, the number of community schools, classrooms, and students declined. As a matter of fact, the number of community schools decreased from 1,084 to 888 (an 18 percent regression), classrooms from 2,592 to 2,287 (a 12 percent regression) and students from 81,539 to 69,301 (a 15 percent regression). This downward trend could be explained by the fact that some community schools that meet school mapping standards are being converted into traditional public elementary schools.

Table 5. Levels of the compliance analysis for Islamic faith-based schools.

First level	Second level
Analysis of the minimum criteria	In-depth analysis of official standards
Assesses whether the school...	This level has three stages:
has clean facilities. has buildings made of permanent or semi-permanent materials. has administrative staff. has permanent teaching staff. has tables and benches. has a wall board per classroom. teaches the basic disciplines. uses French as the language of instruction.	A more exhaustive analysis of the components in terms of infrastructure, equipment, human resources, and pedagogy. Ranking of the different categories (infrastructure, equipment, human resources, and pedagogy) along the scale (very satisfactory, satisfactory, or not satisfactory). The summary of the rankings, leading to the classification of schools.
Result 1	Result 2
First classification in two groups: Category C school (non-compliant). School eligible for an in-depth analysis (Level 2).	Second classification in two groups: Category A school = integrated. Category B school = standby.

Source: Ministry of National Education, 2012, p. 8.

Number of integrated Islamic schools

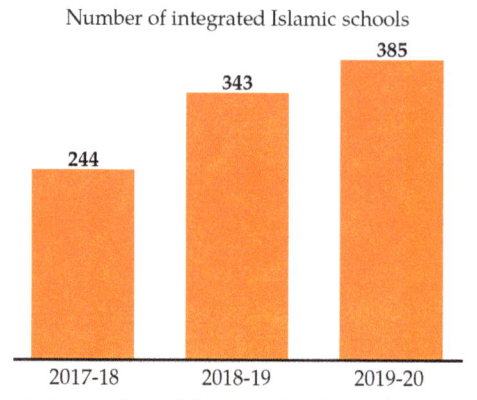

- 2017-18: 244
- 2018-19: 343
- 2019-20: 385

Fig. 3. Evolution of the number of Islamic schools integrated in Ivory Coast's public system from 2017 to 2020. Source: Ministry of National Education, Technical Education and Vocational Training (2018; 2019; 2020).

School canteens

To help keep vulnerable children in school, the state of Ivory Coast committed in 1989 to the implementation of a school canteen development program with the support of the World Food Program (WFP). A targeting policy has been implemented to define priority areas for intervention. Selection criteria are based on the level of food insecurity, the prevalence of chronic malnutrition, the poverty rate, the enrollment rate, and the primary education completion rate.

The WFP, which supported the supply of food and equipment to school canteens from 1989 to 1999, withdrew to make way for the "Integrated Program for the Continued Existence of School Canteens" (PIP/CS, by its French acronym) which was initiated by the government in 1998. In 2000, with the support of the WFP and UNDP, the government launched the pilot phase of the PIP/CS project, but the program was suspended as a result of the sociopolitical crisis of 2002–2010.

The percentage of schools without a canteen has increased every year, moving from 55 percent in 2017 to 69 percent in 2020. Additionally, due to limited supply, school canteens only provide meals on 18 of the 128 days of the school year. This state policy is clearly insufficient, and does not currently do enough to impact or improve the academic performance of learners from disadvantaged families.

Distribution of school kits

In 2000, Ivory Coast opted for free public primary schooling. Two major actions support this choice: free CP1 enrollment, and the distribution of school kits and textbooks. School kits consist of notebooks, pens, plastic notebook covers, pencils, and textbooks. They are assembled according to the level of study. The state allocates an average of 3 billion CFA francs for school kits, an amount that represents less than 1 percent of spending on education (UNICEF, 2014). The coverage rate has been over 80 percent except for the 2018–2019 school year.

Table 6. Number of school kits distributed to primary school students from 2016 to 2020.

School year	Total students	Number of kits delivered	Coverage ratio
2016–2017	3,169,641	2,731,423	86%
2017–2018	3,255,797	3,159,004	97%
2018–2019	3,308,667	2,257,796	68.2%
2019–2020	3,336,678	3,256,248	98%

Source: Ministry of National Education, Technical Education and Vocational Training (2017; 2018; 2019; 2020).

Reform of lower-secondary school

Prior to the implementation of the lower-secondary-school reform, the transition from primary to lower-secondary school was the cause of many grade repetitions and dropouts. The CM2 class with the sixth-grade competitive examination was a major obstacle to learners' progress. The abolition of the sixth-grade competitive examination (2012) has made this transition easier in recent years. Since 2012, a grade of 10 out of 20 is required for admission to the sixth grade (85 points out of 170, or an average of 10). Before 2012–2013, the transition rate from primary to lower-secondary school was around 50 percent. With the new provision, this rate reached 75 percent in 2019–2020. For girls, the gross intake ratio to lower-secondary school has increased over the past five years, from 55.30 percent in 20152016 to 74.30 percent in 2019–2020.

To accommodate the large influx of students entering lower-secondary school, the state started to build "outreach schools", which are public secondary schools with two classrooms per level of study. Outreach schools are built in rural areas to keep learners in their usual living environment and, in particular, to reduce the number of pregnancies during schooling.

The catchment area of outreach schools covers two to three elementary schools (i.e., two to three villages), with a total of at least 90 students in the CM2 class. To reduce gender disparities, outreach schools target primarily the most disadvantaged districts, with a focus on rural areas. The construction of outreach schools began in 2012 with two schools and, in 2019, there were already 152 open throughout the country, with an almost equal distribution between urban and rural areas. Statistical data on student numbers and characteristics are not available.

Table 7. Evolution of the number of open outreach schools from 2012 to 2019.

Year	Rural area	Urban area	Number of open outreach schools
2012	1	1	2
2013	1	0	1
2014	2	3	5
2015	23	20	43
2016	17	23	40
2017	5	10	15
2018	17	14	31
2019	9	6	15
Total	75	77	152
%	49%	51%	100%
2019–2020	3,336,678	3,256,248	98%

Source: Ministry of National Education, Technical Education and Vocational Training (2017; 2018; 2019).

At the national level, outreach schools represent 6.5 percent of the lower-secondary educational offering and serve 2.11 percent of the students. Girls represent 43 percent of the enrollment compared to 44 percent nationally. In the 20182019 school year, outreach schools enrolled 36,729 students, including 14,995 girls who represented 41 percent of the enrollment. In 2019–2020, there were 52,866 students enrolled, which means a 44 percent increase in enrollment within one school year. The proportion of girls was 41 percent in 20182019, but it reached 43 percent in 2019–2020. Trends are similar in rural areas.

Integration of children with disabilities

In accordance with the law of 2015, the government started to develop inclusive education by enrolling children with disabilities in regular schools; this policy is consistent with the right to education recognized for every individual in Ivory Coast. The integration of children with disabilities into regular public schools increased between 2016 and 2020. The number of children who were integrated went up from 9,569 in 2016 to 13,716 in 2020, a 43 percent growth. This development highlights the willingness of the state to make inclusive schooling a reality for all children.

Inclusive education currently targets motor (reduced mobility) and sensory (deaf, blind, mute) disabilities, and the school system has succeeded in integrating 12 percent of children with disabilities between the ages of 0 and 15. Mentally handicapped children have not been integrated into this system yet because for these severe disabilities, regular schools have neither the human resources capable of ensuring their care, nor the equipment and infrastructure to accommodate them.

Number of children with disabilities in public schools

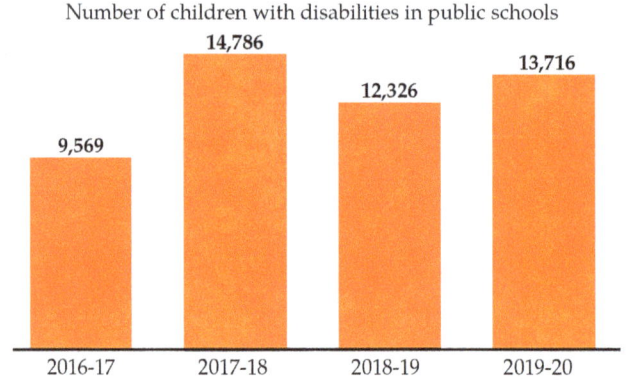

2016-17	2017-18	2018-19	2019-20
9,569	14,786	12,326	13,716

Fig. 4. Evolution of the integration of children with disabilities in public schools from 2016 to 2020. Source: Ministry of National Education, Technical Education and Vocational Training (2016; 2017; 2018; 2019; 2020).

Authorization to enroll without a birth certificate

Adopted in 2012, a national measure to allow children to enroll without a birth certificate has enabled many children to enter school. Over the past five years, more than a million children per year were able to access school who previously could not. Children who benefit from this initiative come largely from disadvantaged rural backgrounds.

Number of children enrolled without a birth certificate

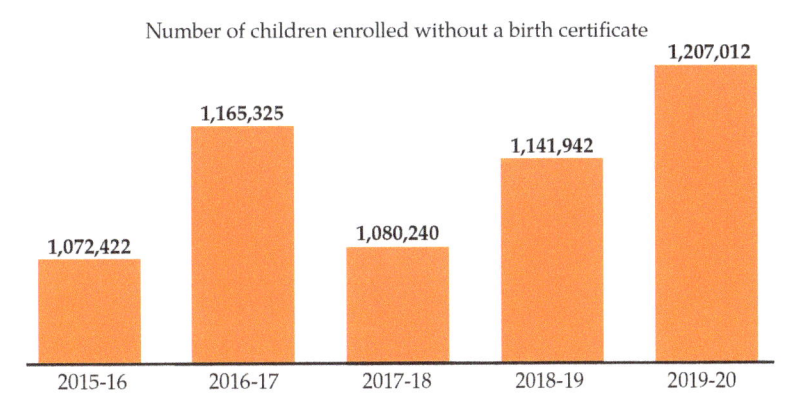

Year	Number
2015-16	1,072,422
2016-17	1,165,325
2017-18	1,080,240
2018-19	1,141,942
2019-20	1,207,012

Fig. 5. Number of children allowed to enroll without a birth certificate from 2015 to 2020. Source: Ministry of National Education, Technical Education and Vocational Training (2016; 2017; 2018; 2019; 2020).

Retention and reintegration of pregnant girls

In 2010, the Ministry of National Education adopted an administrative provision allowing the retention in school of pregnant girls who want to continue their education as well as the reintegration of those who interrupted their schooling. To date, there are no statistical data on pregnant girls who postpone their schooling.

Conclusion

Children at the bottom of the learning pyramid in Ivory Coast struggle to access quality schooling. This group of children includes motor and sensory handicapped disabled children, as well as those who are considered "socially handicapped" by virtue of family poverty, rural context, and gender discrimination. The literature shows that based on the length of the time spent in the school system, boys in Ivory Coast consume 20 percent more resources than girls, urban children consume almost twice as many resources as rural children, and children in the richest quintile consume 3.7 times more resources than children in the poorest quintile.

As reviewed above, multiple important state educational policies have been implemented to reach out to and support children at the bottom of the pyramid. These policies have improved children's access to education and honored their right to education. At present, the data indicate that these policies need to be significantly reinforced in order to reduce the large gaps that remain between children at the bottom of the pyramid and those at higher levels. Only through ensuring quality education for all will every child be able to make independent choices for her or his future.

References

Azoh, F. J., & Goin Bi, Z. T. (Eds.). (2019). *Tous les enfants ont le droit d'aller à l'école* (Film documentary). http://www.aire.ci

Goin Bi, Z. T., & Koutou, N. C. (2019). De la privation à la marchandisation de l'éducation en Côte d'Ivoire, *Revue Internationale d'Éducation Sèvres, 82,* 85–92.

Gouvernement de Côte d'Ivoire. (2016). *Rapport d'État du système éducatif national de la Côte d'Ivoire: Pour une politique éducative plus inclusive et plus efficace.*

IMF (International Monetary Fund) (2016). Economic Development Plan (2016–20). Country Report No. 16. Washington, DC: IMF. https://www.imf.org/external/pubs/ft/scr/2016/cr16388.pdf

Interpeace. (2019). *Enfants talibés et écoles coraniques en Côte d'Ivoire: Enjeux et perspectives.* www.interpeace.org

Kanvaly, K. (2009). *Pourquoi peu d'agrément et la marginalisation des écoles islamiques.* Unpublished.

Ministère de l'Éducation Nationale. (2012). *Processus d'intégration des écoles confessionnelles islamiques dans le système d'enseignement officiel en Côte d'Ivoire* (Évaluation de la conformité de 43 écoles confessionnelles islamiques aux normes officielles d'enseignement, rapport final, Abidjan, p. 144).

Ministère de l'Éducation Nationale. (2016). *Statistiques Scolaires de poche 2015–2016.*

Ministère de l'Éducation Nationale et de l'Enseignement Technique et de la Formation Professionnelle. (2016). *Les grossesses en milieu scolaire en Côte d'Ivoire* (rapport final).

Ministère de l'Éducation Nationale et de l'Enseignement Technique et de la Formation Professionnelle. (2020). *Annuaire statistique de l'enseignement primaire 2019–2020.*

Ministère de l'Éducation Nationale et de l'Enseignement Technique et de la Formation Professionnelle. (2019). *Statistiques scolaires de poche 2018–2019.*

Ministère de l'Éducation Nationale et de l'Enseignement Technique et de la Formation professionnelle. (2018). *Statistiques Scolaires de poche 2017–2018*.

Ministère de l'Éducation Nationale et de l'Enseignement Technique et de la Formation professionnelle. (2017). *Statistiques Scolaires de poche 2016–2017*.

Ministère de l'Éducation Nationale et de l'Enseignement Technique et de la Formation professionnelle, (2019), *Rapport d'Analyse Statistique 2018–2019*.

Ministère de l'Éducation Nationale et de l'Enseignement Technique et de la Formation professionnelle. (2018). *Rapport d'Analyse Statistique 2017 – 2018*

Ministère de l'Éducation Nationale et de l'Enseignement Technique et de la Formation professionnelle. (2017). *Rapport d'Analyse Statistique 2016–2017*.

Ministère de l'Éducation Nationale et de l'Enseignement Technique et de la Formation professionnelle. (2016). *Rapport d'Analyse Statistique 2015–2016*.

Ministère de l'Éducation Nationale et de l'Enseignement Technique et de la Formation professionnelle. (2017). *Étude nationale sur les enfants et adolescents de 3 – 18 ans en situation de handicap hors du système scolaire en Côte d'Ivoire: l'éducation inclusive, solution à l'insertion des enfants handicapés* (Rapport d'Étude).

Ouattara K. I., & Aya, A. (2016). Réalité et défis des écoles communautaires de Côte d'Ivoire. In J. F. Azoh & Z. T. Goin Bi (Eds.), *Nouveaux défis de l'éducation en Côte d'Ivoire: Mutation et Résiliences* (pp. 91–120). Éditions Eburnie.

PNUD. (2020). *Rapport sur le développement humain 2019: Les inégalités de développement humain au XXIe siècle* (Note d'information à l'intention des pays concernant le Rapport sur le développement humain 2019). Côte d'Ivoire.

Sika, G. L., & Kacou, A. E. (2018). La Scolarisation des enfants en dehors du système scolaire en Côte d'Ivoire. *European Scientific Journal, 14*(31), 1–14. https://doi.org/10.19044/esj.2018.v14n31pl

Silué, O., & Ndjoré, Y. A. B. (2016). Intégration des écoles confessionnelles islamiques dans le système éducatif officiel. In J. F. & Z. T. Goin Bi (Eds.), *Nouveaux défis de l'éducation en Côte d'Ivoire: Mutation et Résiliences* (pp. 35–90). Éditions Eburnie.

UNICEF. (2014). *Pour une société plus équitable dans un pays émergent: La situation de l'enfant en Côte d'Ivoire*.

Wagner, D. A., Wolf, S., & Boruch, R. F. (Eds.) (2018). *Learning at the bottom of the pyramid: Science, measurement, and policy in low-income countries*. Paris: UNESCO-IIEP.

13. Ivory Coast

Promoting Learning Outcomes at the Bottom of the Pyramid

Kaja Jasińska and Sosthène Guei

Introduction

Millions of children in low- and middle-income countries (LMICs) do not realize their learning potential, and this has profound consequences: in sub-Saharan Africa, 30 percent of youths aged 15–24 and 41 percent of adults aged 15+ are illiterate, creating severe economic and social disadvantage within local communities and globally (UNESCO Institute for Statistics, 2019).

In Ivory Coast specifically, literacy rates remain poor, particularly for children growing up in impoverished rural communities where access to quality education remains a challenge. Although the number of out-of-school children in Ivory Coast has declined from 1,463,648 in 2009 to 241,575 in 2018, and primary school enrollment increased from 55.8 percent in 2009 to 90.3 percent in 2018, the literacy rate has remained largely unchanged (UNESCO Institute for Statistics, 2019). The literacy rate among the Ivorian population aged 15 and older was 48.7 percent in 2000 and 47.2 percent in 2018, and similarly, the literacy rate among the population aged 15–24 was 60.7 percent in 2000 and 58.4 percent in 2018 (UNESCO Institute for Statistics, 2019).

Literacy rates are lowest in rural areas of the country, where only 14 percent of sixth-grade students attain sufficient competency in both math and language (World Bank, 2014). Rural children in particular fail to realize their academic potential due to two key factors. First, children lack access to quality educational opportunities and developmentally appropriate curricula, for many reasons. For instance, because rural schools are a greater distance from the central government, often requiring travel over poor-quality roads, teachers receive fewer visits from pedagogical advisors and have less opportunity for professional development. In turn, the implementation of policies that target learners at the bottom of the pyramid (BOP) suffer. Second, economic insecurity and exposure to adversity (including child labor and hazardous work) undermine learning. Many rural children are managing the dual demands of school and working on family farms.

Ivory Coast is the largest producer of cocoa in the world. In rural cocoa-producing communities, poverty is rampant and has reached levels as high as 61.2 percent (Fonds monétaire international, 2009), with many households surviving on $1–2 a day (Institut National de la Statistique du Ivory Coast, 2015). The pressure to produce cocoa often means it is a family affair—it is estimated that 1.3 million school-aged children (out of a population of 3.7 million) are working in cocoa production (Tulane University, 2015), largely concentrated in rural areas. Children's agricultural responsibilities may interfere with their education, and they may, for example, be forced to drop out of school temporarily during harvest season. In other cases, work may result in fatigue or other negative health impacts, or just leave little time for homework and other school-related tasks.

However, child cocoa farming in Ivory Coast is a multifaceted issue. Contributing to family farming is one of the ways that parents teach their children how to farm cocoa. Child cocoa workers also contribute to the household income which, in turn, often funds their ability to go to school. Moreover, the perceived low quality and irrelevance of the education available to them pushes many children into work, rather than continuing to attend school (e.g., Canagarajah & Nielsen, 2001; Coulombe, 1998; Coulombe & Canagarajah, 1997).

To meaningfully meet the learning goals of all of Ivory Coast's children, policies need to direct attention to the unique needs of these BOP learners, their parents, teachers, and communities. Practically, this means measuring learning as well as learning inequities (e.g., Learning Gini Index; see Crouch and Slade, this volume) specifically at the

BOP, and requires research aimed at understanding education quality, teacher training and professional support, family systems to support learning, and the unique considerations for learning as a member of an ethnolinguistic minority, among other things, at the BOP.

A number of innovative, research-based programs are currently underway in Ivory Coast, which seek to improve education quality, and in turn, support children's optimal learning outcomes, specifically focusing on the BOP. Broadly, these programs incorporate three strategies: (1) changing classroom structure to better meet children's learning needs; (2) effectively leveraging educational technologies to provide access to quality education for more children; and (3) systematically addressing a major underlying cause of poor school participation and learning outcomes: poverty. Each of these programs showcases a public-private partnership between the Ivorian government and industry, not-for-profit entities, and/or international organizations, with scientific research embedded within program design.

Changing classroom structure to meet learning needs of children at the bottom of the pyramid

In Ivory Coast, children enroll in Grade 1 at six years old, and continue for six grades in the primary-school cycle. There are key underlying assumptions in this structure—namely, that children enroll in Grade 1 at the mandated age of six, that they remain continuously enrolled, and that they master the curriculum at each level to successfully advance to the next grade each year. However, in Ivory Coast, as is the case in many LMICs, many children enroll at different ages. Often, enrollment in Grade 1 happens as young as four years old, or as late as age 10, and is predominantly driven not by official policy on the age of school enrollment, but rather on the availability of family resources to support schooling. Furthermore, because births in rural regions are not always officially recorded, many children do not have a birth certificate, or their birth date is approximate. As a result, a child's true age at school enrollment is not always known.

When children do enroll on time, they may still experience significant gaps in their schooling. They may not remain in attendance for the full duration of the academic year, or stay continuously enrolled each year.

Poor attendance also contributes to grade repetition, which is common in Ivory Coast, and adds to the variability in ages and skills in each grade. Experiencing educational gaps is explicitly tied to experiencing poverty; limited family resources may prevent a child from attending school regularly, and/or enrolling continuously each year. Although public primary schooling is free in Ivory Coast, families still face financial hurdles to sending their children to school. For example, parents may struggle to buy adequate school supplies and uniforms. Parents may also depend on their children for income, either directly or indirectly.

Taken together, variability in age at enrollment, lack of consistent attendance, and high grade-repetition rates negatively impact learning, and these negative factors are more commonly experienced by children at the BOP. Many children finish primary school without acquiring functional literacy and numeracy skills. Practically, this means that many children advance in grades without effectively mastering grade-appropriate skills, which has a cumulative effect over a child's primary schooling—children continue to fall further behind. This also has a larger, systemic impact on primary education, as classrooms become increasingly composed of more children with very different skill levels. The variability in both age and skill levels creates a challenge for teachers, who are unable to simultaneously teach at all the levels required by students in their classrooms, and ensure learning for all. Classrooms that incorporate pedagogical approaches to target a child's actual level are better suited for BOP learners as compared to teaching a curriculum that is too advanced for children. In Ivory Coast, programs adapted to the learning needs of children at the BOP include the "bridging program" and "Teaching at the Right Level" (TARL). These programs are implemented by the National Ministry of Education in partnership with national and international NGOs.

Bridging program: Classrooms for out-of-school children

The policy of free and compulsory education for all children aged 6–16 is enshrined in two main laws, passed respectively in 1995 and 2015. It is still a challenge to achieve in Ivory Coast. In 2013, the number of out-of-school children was estimated at 1,136,993 with a predominance in rural areas (UNESCO Institute for Statistics, 2019). To curb that situation, the Ivorian government highlighted the need to provide an alternative education offering in its 2016–2025 Education/Training Sectoral Plan, namely bridging classes targeted at this segment of school-aged children.

Bridging classes are remedial emergency lessons based on a speed-learning approach, targeting out-of-school children aged 9–14. Children are taught for eight months with an accelerated curriculum that covers the first two grades of primary school. The approach allows children to catch-up and be reintegrated, following their assessment, into the formal schooling system.

Bridging classes use child-centered and active learning approaches to improve children's learning outcomes. In Ivory Coast, Save the Children's globally validated evidence-based *Literacy and Numeracy Boost* approaches are implemented by local NGOs and approved by the Ministry of Education as part of the bridging classes curriculum. The approach has been contextualized to include instruction in local languages in addition to the official language of instruction (French), and map onto the local curriculum. The approach mobilizes teachers, parents, and the community's engagement to support children inside and outside the school. *Literacy Boost* aims at improving children's reading skills across five core competencies including letter identification, phonological awareness, vocabulary, fluency and accuracy, and comprehension. *Numeracy Boost* targets three core competencies including numbers and operations, geometry, and measurement.

A pilot bridging project implemented by Save the Children in 2015 in cocoa-growing communities in Ivory Coast has shown significant effects on children's reading skills across all five core reading competencies compared to a control group. At the end of the project, 70 percent of the girls from the intervention group who scored lower in reading at baseline were able to recognize 10 words (out of 20 words), compared to only 30 percent of girls from the comparison group in a peri-urban environment.

Teaching at the Right Level: Classrooms that target children's skills

Teaching at the Right Level (TARL) is a pedagogical approach developed by the Indian NGO, Pratham (Banerjee et al., 2007; Banerjee et al.,

2016; Banerji & Chavan, 2016; Akyeampong, Chapter 3 this Volume). The TARL program is a learner-centered approach that supports the acquisition of literacy and numeracy skills in children who have been left behind. By teaching classes as a whole, one assumes that all children have similar skills and can therefore similarly engage with the curriculum. In reality, classrooms in Ivory Coast, and in many LMICs, contain children with very different skill levels and only a few children who have sufficiently mastered the prerequisite skills from earlier grades to learn the course content. The TARL program changes how teaching is done in the classroom. Children are grouped according to their level, and lesson plans are tailored to their needs. The TARL approach starts with a basic assessment of children's learning levels, and then groups for instruction are formed based on a child's level, rather than their grade. Teachers use interactive techniques to teach to the level of each group, rather than lecture-style teaching. As children progress, they can quickly move to more advanced groups that match their skills. Teachers receive professional training and ongoing mentoring throughout the academic year to support the implementation of the TARL program.

In 2017, the Ivorian National Ministry of Education joined Abdul Latif Jameel Poverty Action Lab (J-PAL), Pratham, and Transforming Education in Cocoa Communities (TRECC) to launch TARL in Ivory Coast. The Ivorian model of TARL (Le Programme d'Enseignement Cible; PEC) aimed to (1) test the efficacy of TARL in an Ivorian context, specifically focusing on this first-time French language implementation of TARL, and (2) develop a government-led TARL program, by amassing an understanding of the government's capacity for TARL implementation, using primarily government structures and agents. In the 2018–2019 academic year, a pilot program was launched in 50 schools. In this pilot program, TARL was implemented in the classroom for 90 minutes each day for the duration of the school year. Pilot-program results showed positive impacts. Children's reading and math skills improved significantly and teachers who adopted the TARL assessment methods and teaching tools found them simple and easy to use (Pratham, 2020). However, challenges remain. Teachers appreciated the support of the mentor, an integral part of TARL, but a need for further improvements in the mentorship process was identified. The TARL program has since been expanded for the 2019–2020 academic year, with an additional

150 schools participating in the program. A formal framework for the implementation of TARL at the national level has been created in 2020 (Arrêté N°0067; Ministry of National Education, 2020).

Educational technology to support learning at the bottom of the pyramid

Educational technologies (EdTech) can be leveraged to provide educational access to more children and to maximize learning impact, particularly for vulnerable children in remote rural regions who may not be attending school regularly. Several meta-analyses of educational intervention in sub-Saharan West Africa have found that investments in instructional technologies had the largest impact on children's learning outcomes in comparison to other investments, including nutritional and health interventions, reducing class sizes, or cash transfers conditional on school attendance (Conn, 2017; McEwan, 2015; Castillo et al. Chapter 4, this Volume). EdTech tools can complement traditional educational models by offering supplementary at-home lessons, resources for teachers, and/or targeted messaging to parents and caregivers. To provide effective support, successful EdTech solutions must be easy to use, engaging, inexpensive, and crucially, leverage technology that is readily available in the target community.

In Ivory Coast, over 50 percent of the population still does not use mobile internet, which can create barriers to access for internet-based remote learning services, such as educational content delivered over smartphones, tablets, or laptops (GSMA, 2017). Many families in rural communities, in particular, lack sufficient internet access to effectively make use of some educational technologies. However, simple mobile phones offer key advantages: mobile phone penetration in Ivory Coast is widespread at 122 percent, and parents (and often children) are already familiar with using simple mobile phones (GSMA, 2017). While many rural families are less likely to own a smartphone or have a mobile internet subscription, teachers, on the other hand, tend to have greater access to smart technologies. Teachers may be more likely to own a smartphone, and therefore, interventions that use mobile internet may be more appropriate. The success of an EdTech program depends on the target recipient (e.g., the child, parent, or teacher), and their unique access to technology.

We review three EdTech interventions currently implemented in Ivory Coast: Allô Alphabet, Eduq+, and TARL+DIA. Each intervention targets children, parents, and teachers, respectively, and differentially incorporates simple and smart technologies.

Allô Alphabet: Simple mobile technology for literacy

The Allô Alphabet intervention is a child- and parent-facing simple mobile phone literacy program. Allô Alphabet is designed to be accessed at home and complements primary-school children's in-school curriculum. It delivers a French-language literacy program to children using simple mobile feature-phones and existing, widely available 1G and 2G networks that extend to remote, rural regions. This literacy intervention supports children's awareness of the sound structure of the French language and mapping between letters and sounds; these language skills are essential to emergent literacy (e.g., Jasińska & Petitto, 2018). Because many families in rural Ivory Coast are low-literate, Allô Alphabet is designed and implemented as an interactive voice response (IVR) system on simple phones. This follows many others (e.g., Patel et al., 2010; Thies, 2014) in using IVR for low-literate users.

The Allô Alphabet curriculum includes tasks that ask children to identify and manipulate phonemes—the smallest unit of spoken language—and link print to syllable sounds by audio message and SMS. For example: 1) Type the letter that makes the /s/ sound. 2) Do the words coin and pain rhyme? If they do, type 1. If they do not, type 2. The system provides instructions, questions, and feedback via voice messages recorded by an Ivorian researcher, with answers inputted via touchtone. The users call in to a specified number, which immediately ends the call and calls the user back to avoid fees for the users. Parents access a parent module where they can monitor their child's progress through the curriculum.

Since simple mobile phones have high penetration rates in Ivory Coast, most families already have the required technology to access the Allô Alphabet platform. Because parents are already users of the technology, they can also help guide children and troubleshoot any potential issues.

Importantly, using existing technologies can address cultural barriers to tech adoption. For example, distributing a high-value item such as a tablet to a child for use at home has challenges. Parents are unlikely to permit their child to play with an expensive item; indeed, a tablet could be among the most valuable possessions of a household, and it can be culturally inappropriate to permit a low-rank member of the household (child) to use an expensive item; such items may be reserved for only senior members of the household (parent).

A randomized control trial is underway with 1,200 fifth-grade children in the Adzope region of Ivory Coast (Chatterjee et al., 2020; Madaio et al., 2019; Madaio, Tanoh, Seri, Jasińska, & Ogan, 2019; Madaio et al., 2020) for the academic year 2020–2021. This trial is a partnership between the Ivorian National Ministry of Education, an African EdTech industry partner, and a team of Ivorian and international researchers. Allô Alphabet is a valuable model of government-industry-research partnerships that collaboratively design evidence-based solutions, implement and deliver the program, evaluate its impact, and create the structures to support transition to scale.

Eduq+: Using technology to engage parents in children's education

The Eduq+ program is a mobile-phone platform that targets parental engagement and teacher support in education, which is a known predictor of children's academic achievement (Castro et al., 2015). The Eduq+ technology platform engages parents in children's education through behavioral nudges and provides pedagogical support and tips for teachers. Eduq+ sends text and audio messages to mobile phones with suggestions of simple activities that aid children's social-emotional development and learning, but which do not require curricular knowledge of math or literacy (Lichand & Wolf, 2020). For parents, these nudges are designed specifically to increase their engagement in their child's education, including suggesting that they show up in school to monitor teachers. Parents received nudges twice a week for the duration of a school year. Nudges start with a motivating fact, followed by a suggested activity, an interactive message (soliciting feedback), and a growth message.

Using technology to engage parents in their children's education has been shown to be effective for increasing both children's school attendance and grades in Brazil (Bettinger et al., 2020). In Ivory Coast, a randomized control trial of the Eduq+ intervention was conducted in the academic year 2018–2019. 20,000 children and their parents across 100 schools participated in the intervention study; 50 percent of participants received the intervention, and 50 percent of participants served as a control group. The study found that nudges to parents significantly decreased student drop-outs by 2.47 percentage points, a large effect given a base level of 4.7 percent. In schools where parents received nudges, 24 percent of teachers reported that a parent showed up at the school at least once a week, in comparison to 14 percent in the control schools (Lichand & Wolf, 2020). The Ivorian National Ministry of Education is currently exploring a national expansion of the Eduq+ program.

TARL+DIA: Using technology to optimize an already-effective program

EdTech can also be used to enhance existing programs, such as Teaching at the Right Level (TARL), discussed above. There is robust evidence to suggest that teaching to groups of children according to their skill levels has a positive impact on children's learning outcomes, both from RCTs conducted in India, where TARL was first implemented (Banerjee et al., 2007; Banerji & Chavan, 2016), and in sub-Saharan Africa (Duflo, Dupas, & Kremer, 2011; Innovations for Poverty Action, 2018), including Ivory Coast (Pratham, 2020). However, implementation challenges remain. The success of TARL is mediated by the availability of pedagogical advisors who can provide ongoing mentorship and professional support for teachers. Given the remoteness of many rural schools, one key barrier to increasing educational quality even for effective programs is teachers' lack of opportunities for professional development and continuous mentorship and support (Komba & Nkumbi, 2008; Pryor et al., 2012). Current approaches to professional development in Ivory Coast use an in-person teacher-training model, but in-person models are limited in their ability to provide frequent, ongoing support. In rural locations, a visit from a pedagogical advisor requires travel across long distances and poor road conditions to reach schools. In fact, in Ivory Coast, most schools receive teacher professional support visits from the regional education directive only about two times per year (Jasińska et al., 2017).

Adaptive technology that allows for two-way communication between a teacher and a pedagogical advisor can help to provide ongoing support and development opportunities for teachers in rural communities. A meta-analysis found that adaptive technology-based augmentations to traditional classroom approaches are among the most effective ways to improve educational quality in sub-Saharan Africa (Conn, 2017), above other interventions such as decreasing class size or increasing teacher pay. The current implementation of the TARL program in Ivory Coast has highlighted the need for improvements to teacher mentorship and support. Teachers participating in the TARL program receive in-person training at the beginning of the school year and are typically more motivated to incorporate TARL in their classrooms immediately after their training. Over time, implementation fidelity of the TARL intervention decreases. Teachers in remote rural schools may struggle with aspects of implementation and encounter new challenges they may not feel prepared to meet, leading to gradually reduced and/or poor program implementation. A technology-enhanced implementation of TARL can address these outstanding challenges.

The widespread usage of social media messaging applications (i.e., WhatsApp, Facebook messenger) in LMICs opens up new possibilities for communication between a teacher and a pedagogical advisor. Expert content (i.e., from a master trainer or a pedagogical advisor) shared over messaging applications can reach teachers in remote locations. Moreover, teachers who have access to an expert advisor can receive ongoing support that complements their in-person training. Currently, in Ivory Coast, a pilot program is underway that explores how a human-chatbot hybrid system, DIA (Cannanure, Brown, & Ogan, 2020), implemented over a social media messaging application, can augment the existing TARL program. DIA is powered by artificial intelligence and can learn topic-specific knowledge (such as TARL) from user interactions. However, DIA is a human-chatbot hybrid system, which means that a human, such as a pedagogical advisor or another teacher, can offer support when the AI has no answers. A pilot deployment of

DIA with 38 teachers in Ivory Coast found that the system can support dialogue, understand teachers' smartphone usage, and collect data through conversation interactions (Cannanure et al., 2020; 2022). Teachers were responsive to using DIA, showing regular engagement with the platform despite having irregular connectivity. The pilot study suggests that an AI-powered human-chatbot system may effectively complement, and enhance, an existing educational quality program. An RCT of the DIA-enhanced TARL program is scheduled for the 2020–2023 academic years.

Addressing causes of poor learning outcomes: Poverty

Poverty and poor-quality schooling act in tandem to prevent Ivorian children at the BOP from realizing their learning potential. Interventions that address the quality of education—by changing classroom structures to meet BOP children's learning needs and leverage EdTech to support learning—have been shown to be effective in Ivory Coast. Yet, without robust strategies to reduce poverty—the single most important issue at the heart of the learning crisis facing children at the BOP—other intervention approaches will have limited impact. Reducing poverty by directly providing cash transfers to families can eliminate or reduce some of the barriers to enrollment and attendance.

Cash transfers (CTs) are one of the most extensively implemented and evidence-based approaches to poverty reduction. CTs offer families small amounts of regular money to ease economic hardship and potentially increase the chance that their child will attend school rather than work on a family plantation, or offset the income generated by the child. There is growing evidence that families use cash transfers to enhance household nutrition and economic wellbeing (e.g., Haushofer & Shapiro, 2016; McIntosh, 2018). Conditional cash transfers were actually developed to address child labor and school enrollment, and growing evidence suggests that unconditional cash transfers may have similar effects. Unconditional cash transfers have the added benefit of being relatively easy to implement administratively. One study in Ecuador found that CTs lead families to keep children in school and postpone child entry into the labor market (Edmonds & Schady, 2012). A second study in Nepal found that a CT conditional on education increased school enrollment and decreased child labor (Edmonds & Shrestha, 2014).

Currently, the Ministry of Solidarity, Social Cohesion and the Fight Against Poverty in Ivory Coast, in partnership with the World Bank, is conducting an unconditional cash transfer program to 127,000 families under the UGP *Filets Sociaux Productifs* initiative (Ministère de la Solidarité, 2019). Households who represent the bottom economic quintile are beneficiaries of the program. Households receive 36,000 XOF (approximately $65) every three months for a period of three years. The first phase of the program was launched in 2017. Phase 2 of the program, launched in 2020, benefits an additional 75,000 households (55,000 rural, 20,000 urban) in 1,500 villages spanning 21 regions (Ministère de la Solidarité, 2020). A smaller-scale cash transfer program supported by the NGO 100WEEKS (100weeks.org) is also underway. Beneficiaries of the 100WEEKS program receive a weekly unconditional cash transfer (approximately $10) for 100 weeks alongside participating in a peer-group coaching program that provides training in financial literacy, entrepreneurship, and life skills on a weekly basis (van der Linden, 2018). Cash transfer programs in Ivory Coast vary with respect to the amount, frequency, and duration of transfers, and whether they are implemented by the government, international organizations, NGOs, the private sector, or through partnerships between multiple stakeholder entities. These programs can reduce some of the key financial barriers to learning for children at the BOP.

When cash transfer programs are implemented alongside education interventions, such as the programs discussed above, the potential benefit for children at the BOP is greater. If programs that improve the quality of education are implemented, but school attendance is low, children will not benefit from such interventions. Similarly, if programs that reduce barriers to school attendance are implemented (i.e., poverty reduction strategies), but the quality of education that children receive at school is low, children's learning will not improve. Integrated interventions that simultaneously address the leading causes of poor learning outcomes among Ivory Coast's most vulnerable children—poverty and education quality—are more likely to have positive impacts.

Conclusion

This chapter describes several evidence-based interventions in Ivory Coast that aim to improve learning for children at the BOP. These programs focus on changing classroom structures to meet the learning needs of children at the BOP (e.g., bridging classes for out-of-school children, Teaching at the Right Level) and leveraging EdTech to provide low-cost access to education (e.g., Allô Alphabet mobile phone literacy intervention), improve parent and teacher engagement (e.g., Eduq+ behavioral nudges), and enhance existing, effective programs (TARL+DIA human-chatbot hybrid professional support for teachers). The impacts of such programs may be further enhanced if implemented in combination with a poverty reduction strategy, such as providing cash transfers to poor families.

To substantially address the learning challenges faced by children at the BOP, we need to better understand children's learning in these contexts. This requires rigorous child development and educational research specific to the Ivorian context. The programs reviewed are evidence-based, and many incorporate research that is focused on understanding learning in Ivory Coast specifically. Ultimately, these research insights can inform the design of policy and programming in order to have maximal impact on children's learning outcomes.

References

Banerjee, A. V., Cole, S., Duflo, E., & Linden, L. (2007). Remedying education: Evidence from two randomized experiments in India. *The Quarterly Journal of Economics, 122*(3), 1235–1264. https://doi.org/10.1162/qjec.122.3.1235

Banerjee, A., Banerji, R., Berry, J., Duflo, E., Kannan, H., Mukherji, S., & Walton, M. (2016). Mainstreaming an effective intervention: Evidence from randomized evaluations of "Teaching at the Right Level" in India. *National Bureau of Economic Research*.

Banerji, R., & Chavan, M. (2016). Improving literacy and math instruction at scale in India's primary schools: The case of Pratham's Read India program.

Journal of Educational Change, 17(4), 453–475. https://doi.org/10.1007/s10833-016-9285-5

Bettinger, E., Cunha, N., Lichand, G., & Madeira, R. (2020). Are the effects of informational interventions driven by salience? *SSRN Electronic Journal.* https://doi.org/10.2139/ssrn.3633821

Canagarajah, S., & Nielsen, H. (2001). Child labor in Africa: A comparative study. *Annals of The American Academy of Political and Social Science, 575,* 71–91. https://doi.org/10.1177/0002716201575001005

Cannanure, V. K., Brown, T. X., & Ogan, A. (2020). *DIA: A human AI hybrid conversational assistant for developing contexts* (Paper presented at the Proceedings of the 2020 International Conference on Information and Communication Technologies and Development). Guayaquil, Ecuador. https://doi.org/10.1145/3392561.3397577

Cannanure, V.K., Avila-Uribe, E., Adji, Y.T., Wolf, S., Jasińska, K., Brown, T. X. & Ogan. A. (accepted). "We dream of climbing the ladder, of getting there, we have to do our job better:" Designing for Teacher Aspirations in Rural Côte d'Ivoire. *ACM SIGCAS Conference on Computing and Sustainable Societies* (COMPASS '22).

Castro, M., Expósito-Casas, E., López-Martín, E., Lizasoain, L., Navarro-Asencio, E., & Gaviria, J. L. (2015). Parental involvement on student academic achievement: A meta-analysis. *Educational Research Review, 14,* 33–46. https://doi.org/10.1016/j.edurev.2015.01.002

Chatterjee, R., Madaio, M., & Ogan, A. (2020). *Predicting gaps in usage in a phone-based literacy intervention system* (pp. 92–105). Springer International Publishing.

Conn, K. M. (2017). Identifying effective education interventions in sub-Saharan Africa: A meta-analysis of impact evaluations. *Review of Educational Research, 87*(5), 863–898. https://doi.org/10.3102/0034654317712025

Coulombe, H. (1998). *Child labor and education in Côte d'Ivoire* (Background paper). Washington, DC: World Bank.

Coulombe, H., & Canagarajah, S. (1997). *Child labor and schooling in Ghana* (Policy Research Paper, No. 1844). Washington, DC: World Bank.

Duflo, E., Dupas, P., & Kremer, M. (2011). Peer effects, teacher incentives, and the impact of tracking: Evidence from a randomized evaluation in Kenya. *American Economic Review, 101*(5), 1739–1774. https://doi.org/10.1257/aer.101.5.1739

Edmonds, E. V., & Schady, N. (2012). Poverty alleviation and child labor. *American Economic Journal: Economic Policy, 4*(4), 100–124. https://doi.org/10.1257/pol.4.4.100

Edmonds, E. V., & Shrestha, M. (2014). You get what you pay for: Schooling incentives and child labor. *Journal of Development Economics, 111*, 196–211. https://doi.org/10.1016/j.jdeveco.2014.09.005

Fonds monétaire international. (2009). *Stratégie de Relance du Développement et de Réduction de la Pauvreté*. Côte d'Ivoire.

GSMA. (2017). *Country overview: Côte d'Ivoire*. London, UK: GSMA.

Haushofer, J., & Shapiro, J. (2016). The short-term impact of unconditional cash transfers to the poor: Experimental evidence from Kenya. *The Quarterly Journal of Economics, 131*(4), 1973–2042. https://doi.org/10.1093/qje/qjw025

Innovations for Poverty Action. (2018). *Evaluating the teacher community assistant initiative*. https://www.poverty-action.org/study/evaluating-teacher-community-assistant-initiative-ghana

Institut National de la Statistique du Côte d'Ivoire. (2015). Enquete sur le niveau de vie des menages en Côte d'Ivoire (ENV 2015). In Institut National de la Statistique Ministère d'état (Ed.), *Ministère du plan et du développement*: Direction Générale du Plan et de la Lutte contre la Pauvreté.

Jasińska, K. K., Hager, C., Amon, A., Guei, S., Kakou, C., Koffi, S., & Seri, A. (2017). *Literacy development in rural cocoa communities in Côte d'Ivoire: Child development research and local scientific capacity building initiatives* (Paper presented at the Society for Research in Child Development). Austin, TX.

Jasińska, K. K., & Petitto, L. A. (2018). Age of bilingual exposure is related to the contribution of phonological and semantic knowledge to successful reading development. *Child Dev, 89*(1), 310–331. https://doi.org/10.1111/cdev.12745

Komba, W. L., & Nkumbi, E. (2008). Teacher professional development in Tanzania: Perceptions and practices. *Journal of International Cooperation in Education, 11*(3), 67–83.

Lichand, G., & Wolf, S. (2020). *Arm-wrestling in the classroom: The non-monotonic effects of monitoring teachers* (Working Paper, No. 357). University of Zurich, Department of Economics.

Madaio, M. A., Kamath, V., Yarzebinski, E., Zasacky, S., Tanoh, F., Hannon-Cropp, J., & Ogan, A. (2019). *"You give a little of yourself": Family support for children's use of an IVR literacy system* (Paper presented at the Proceedings of the 2nd ACM SIGCAS Conference on Computing and Sustainable Societies). Accra, Ghana. https://doi.org/10.1145/3314344.3332504

Madaio, M. A., Tanoh, F., Seri, A. B., Jasińska, K., & Ogan, A. (2019). *"Everyone brings their grain of salt": Designing for low-literate parental engagement with a mobile literacy technology in Côte d'Ivoire/Ivory Coast* (Paper presented at the Proceedings of the 2019 CHI Conference on Human Factors in Computing Systems). Glasgow, Scotland. https://doi.org/10.1145/3290605.3300695

Madaio, M. A., Yarzebinski, E., Kamath, V., Zinszer, B. D., Hannon-Cropp, J., Tanoh, F., & Ogan, A. (2020). *Collective support and independent learning with *a voice-based literacy technology in rural communities* (Paper presented at the Proceedings of the 2020 CHI Conference on Human Factors in Computing Systems). Honolulu, HI. https://doi.org/10.1145/3313831.3376276

McEwan, P. J. (2015). Improving learning in primary schools of developing countries. *Review of Educational Research, 85*(3), 353–394. https://doi.org/10.3102/0034654314553127

McIntosh, C., & Zeitlin, A. (2018). *Benchmarking a child nutrition program against cash: Experimental evidence from Rwanda*. https://www.poverty-action.org/sites/default/files/publications/Benchmarking.pdf

Ministère de la Solidarité, de la Cohésion Sociale, et de la Lutte contre la Pauvreté. (2020). *127 000 ménages bénéficiaires du Programme Filets Sociaux Productifs ont perçu leurs deux (02) premières allocations trimestrielles au titre de l'année 2020*. https://filetsociaux-ci.org/127-000-menages-beneficiaires-du-programme-filets-sociaux-productifs-ont-percu-leurs-deux-02-premieres-allocations-trimestrielles-au-titre-de-lannee-2020/

Ministère de la Solidarité, de la Cohésion Sociale, et de la Lutte Contre la Pauvreté. (2019). *Extension du Projet Filets Sociaux productifs: Les nouveaux villages bénéficiaires sont connus*. http://filetsociaux-ci.org/extension-du-projet-filets-sociaux-productifs-les-nouveaux-villages-beneficiaires-sont-connus/

Patel, N., Chittamuru, D., Jain, A., Dave, P., & Parikh, T. S. (2010). *Avaaj otalo: A field study of an interactive voice forum for small farmers in rural india* (Paper presented at the Proceedings of the SIGCHI Conference on Human Factors in Computing Systems).

Pratham. (2020). *Teaching at the Right Level (TaRL)*. Programme d'Enseignement Ciblé (PEC).

Pryor, J., Akyeampong, K., Westbrook, J., & Lussier, K. (2012). Rethinking teacher preparation and professional development in Africa: An analysis of the curriculum of teacher education in the teaching of early reading and mathematics. *Curriculum Journal, 23*(4), 409–502.

Thies, I. M. (2014). User interface design for low-literate and novice users: Past, present and future. *Foundations and Trends in Human-Computer Interaction, 8*(1), 1–72.

Tulane University. (2015). *2013/14 survey research on child labor in West African cocoa growing areas*. School of Public Health and Tropical Medicine.

UNESCO Institute for Statistics. (2019). *Côte d'Ivoire*. http://uis.unesco.org/en/country/ci

van der Linden, M. (2018). *Measuring impact and developing the 100WEEKS model*. https://100weeks.nl/uploads/100WEEKS-ImpactReport-group-1.pdf

World Bank. (2014). *The programme for the analysis of education systems*. Washington, DC: World Bank.

14. Kenya

Education, Learning, and Policy-Framing for Children at the Bottom of the Pyramid

Sara Ruto, Ann Gachoya, and Virginia Ngindiru

Introduction

The year 2020 will likely be remembered for its global disruption of the education system. At the peak of the health pandemic caused by COVID-19, schools were closed in more than 190 countries, with 90 percent of the world's student population asked to remain at home (UNESCO, 2020a). Though schools closed, learning continued for children in wealthy nations and from high socioeconomic households across countries. Remote learning options, coupled with innovative e-learning solutions, sprung up or were expanded to facilitate learning, but its inequitable spread exacerbated the situation where the "haves have it, and have nots do not". Already, many countries in the Global South face a learning crisis in which six of every 10 children are not learning (World Bank, 2020; UNESCO, 2017).

The theme of learning equity is topical in Kenya, and it is increasingly shaping educational decisions. For instance, with respect to returning to school after the COVID-19 school closure, the Ministry of Education declared that it would be informed by the character of the disease, and the current learning situation, which showed that 24.6 percent of school age children unfortunately remained outside of the e-learning fixes (KNBS, 2020). The Ministry hence decided to favour the learning circumstances of children excluded from the current e-fixes and declared that formal curriculum coverage would continue from where it stopped after the March 2020 disruption. It is a decision that hinges on the UN Sustainable Development Goals (SDG) principle to prioritize those furthest behind.

In some ways, the effort to embrace the more vulnerable in society is not surprising. Analysis of key policy documents in independent Kenya affirm a consistent promotion of social justice, equity, and fairness. Indeed, the concepts of access, equity, quality, and relevance of education frame almost all educational-policy visioning, resulting in structural adjustments that have reshaped governance and funding streams and expanded the social safety nets. Many examples of repositioning services to reach rural and marginalized populations stand as illustrations. The Ministry of Education continues to receive one of the highest allotments of recurrent expenditure. In 2019, spending on education accounted for 5.4 percent of the Gross Development Product (Economic Survey, 2020, p. 243). An ambitious curriculum reform process is underway that seeks to provide every child with an education that enables them to thrive and reach their highest potential. It seems however, that many of these efforts have not become deeply entrenched or successful enough to ensure a more egalitarian Kenyan society. The special rapporteur (UNESCO, 2020b) observation of a "global lack of preparedness" to meet the education needs of the vulnerable and marginalized in society confirms that many countries, including Kenya, have to do more to ensure an inclusive and equitable education for each child.

Inequality in education is visible on many fronts, school types being one of them. The number of private schools has grown steadily since the introduction of Free Primary Education (FPE) and Free Day Secondary Schools (FDSE). Private primary schools, for instance, increased by 16 percent between 2012 and 2016, compared to a 12 percent growth in public primary schools during the same period (MoEST, 2016). This happened as parents sought for quality learning (usually measured through performance means in national end-of-cycle examinations). While exploring the dynamics of low-fee private schools in Kenya, Edwards et al. (2017) note that, though policies designed to regulate the operations of these schools exist, they do not operate as effectively as envisioned. The tensions and trade-offs have compromised on quality and equity. For learners facing socioeconomic disadvantages,

Alternative Providers of Basic Education and Training (APBET) have catered for them. While APBET institutions enhance access, they do not guarantee quality education.

Analysis framework

The inequitable distribution of learning opportunities has historical, sociocultural, and economic underpinnings. To date, administrative zones in Kenya's arid north continue to register poorer learning outcomes. Children with special needs and disabilities have yet to be fully served, and ethnic minorities still lag behind. The chances of not being in school for a girl with a disability—born in an arid district with an illiterate mother—are high. Using learning assessment data from ASER and Uwezo, Rose et al. (2016) estimate that such a child, even if in school, would experience a 20 percent deficit in learning outcomes. An equally important lens of inequality is the comparative wealth of a nation. Montoya (2018) is among those who point to the widening rift between countries, with most African countries retaining the bottom quintile. Such is the picture of exclusion, and indeed, the child considered to be at the bottom of the pyramid. A good understanding of exclusion demands unearthing these layers of vulnerability.[1]

This chapter will primarily draw on a desk review of policy documents and related critiques. It will adopt a "4A" analytic framework, in which the four As include: availability, accessibility, acceptability, and adaptability (UNESCO, 2020b; Tomasevski, 2001). These authors suggest that:

A) Availability addresses whether or not services exist, and whether they are sufficient in terms of quantity and type (such as schools, teachers);

B) Accessibility includes physical accessibility (such as distance to school, safety) and financial accessibility (free schooling, school types);

---

[1] Vulnerable groups include ethnic minorities, older persons, persons with disability, child- and woman-headed households, and vulnerable children (including those in arid districts, or facing cultural negative practices, like early marriage).

C) Acceptability includes respect to the culture of all, including minority communities; and

D) Adaptability suggests that all barriers have been removed to allow for full participation in education.

The questions to be posed, as informed by this 4A framework, would include: are inputs such as schools, teachers, materials, funding, and IT facilities available? Are these learning inputs and opportunities accessible to all learners regardless of gender, socioeconomic background, geographic location, or disability status? Are the education provisions deemed to have relevance and quality? Have issues related to the language of instruction been addressed? Finally, have adaptations been made to ensure that children with disabilities or in disadvantaged geographies can thrive within the system? Existing evidence will be used to examine the extent to which education systems have sought to be equitable in their provision, with a focus on basic education.

In order to assess the current policy-framing to see if the country will meet the SDG goals for education by 2030, the analysis will further be informed by the six policy issues identified by UNESCO (2019) meant to accelerate progress. These urge a shift away from the "availability" and "accessibility" domains identified above to focus on lifelong learning, relevance, and cooperation by going:

A) Beyond averages, towards equality and inclusion;

B) Beyond access, towards quality and learning;

C) Beyond basics, towards content fit for sustainable development;

D) Beyond schooling, towards lifelong education;

E) Beyond education, towards cross-sector collaboration, and

F) Beyond countries, towards regional and global collaboration.

These six policy issues, coupled with the 4As, provide a solid framework with which to analyze Kenya's progress towards meeting its educational goals.

Policy-framing

Policy recommendations in Kenya have been crafted through a series of commissions on education and task forces, and thereafter formally adopted as official government policy through sessional papers. In this section, we shall attempt to see to what extent learning equity has permeated through policy articulation. Children at the bottom of the learning pyramid can be identified though their special circumstances, hence the review shall highlight sub-sector policies that seek to hasten education for excluded children, such as children with special needs, and children in Kenya's arid and semi-arid lands (ASAL).

Historical perspectives on education policy: 1960–1990s

Early educational policy direction was offered through the Kenya Education Report of 1964, popularly known as the Ominde commission. This commission was constituted against a backdrop of disproportionate educational opportunities across the races and regions, and tasked to envision a system of education for the newly independent state that would foster nationhood, identity, and unity. Critical of the colonial education system that was inaccessible to many, the Ominde report recommended that at least primary education ought to be free. This report sought to give preferential treatment to regions lagging behind, and recommended higher grant allocations, boarding schools, and mobile schools as strategies to expand access to schooling in the ASAL regions of Tana River, Garissa, Wajir, Mandera, Isiolo, Marsabit, Narok, Kajiado, Turkana, Samburu, and West Pokot.

Sessional Paper No. 10 of 1965 on African Socialism and its application to planning in Kenya formally adopted the Ominde report to guide educational development in Kenya. Wary of the colonial legacy of unequal development, it asserted that: "Every effort will be made to ensure that equal opportunities are provided for people in less developed parts of the country" (GoK, 1965, p. 56). It announced that Universal Primary Education (UPE) would start in 1965 and be achieved by 1971. While the UPE goal remained elusive for several decades, the Ominde report fermented the "access quest" that has generally been abided to by subsequent political manifestos and governments. For instance, in 1971, a presidential decree abolished tuition fees in the ASAL districts—thus, in part, implementing the recommendations suggested by the Ominde Commission and affirmed through Sessional Paper No. 10. In December 1973, another presidential decree outlawed fee payment for all children in Grades 1–4. The presidential decree of 1978 abolished school fees in all classes in primary school. It would take the Free Primary Education call of 2003 to assure free access to primary education for all grades, though even then, as the analysis will show, specific pockets of children remained excluded. Secondary schooling received special attention in the Report of the National Educational Objectives and Policies of 1976 (or Gachathi Report; GoK, 1976) which recommended government support for the self-help *Harambee* schools that had mushroomed to offer secondary education. These early policies showed an intent to expand access to basic education, with some differential treatment being attempted for children in remote and rural areas. However, early policies were rather silent about other adaptations needed to make learning accessible to all children, including those with special needs.

Sessional Paper No. 10 of 1965 embarked on a policy shift towards inclusion. It was grounded "African Socialism", a term that some scholars deem a misnomer, while others like Ochola (2016) see it as the foundation of the concept of equity, as it stresses that policy should be directed with impartiality, fairness, and justice for socioeconomic development to spread divergently across communities. Munene and Ruto (2015, p. 139) observe that the 1965 policy directive sought to "combat educational inequalities through the provision of universal primary education". The Ominde report viewed education as an equalizer, stating that "education must promote social equality". Similarly, the Gachathi Report observed that "the fundamental purpose of national development is to effect social improvement of lives of the people as a whole".

A slight departure is seen in the social-justice framing of the Kamunge report of 1988 that was subsequently adopted into policy through Sessional Paper No. 6 of 1988 on education and training for the next decade and beyond. Introduced under the aegis of the World Bank's Structural Adjustment Programs for African States, this policy sought to rationalize budgets and decrease public expenditure. This resulted in a cost-sharing policy that strained educational access, leading to pronounced exclusion of vulnerable groups including the urban poor, rural communities, and ASAL peoples. Many have faulted this policy with a failure to acknowledge the community resourcing that had always existed, and gave impetus to the first wave of secondary-school expansion. Kenya, therefore, joined the rest of the world in Jomtien for the 1990 World Conference on Education for All (EFA) against a backdrop of strained access, despite always having the policy intent to achieve universal education for all children. Economic growth had reduced from an average of 6.6 percent in the 1970s to 4.2 percent in the 1980s to an average of 2.1 percent in 1990s (Nthia & Njeru, 2005). It was an era in which low-income households and the educational system suffered, exemplified by a high rate of dropouts, low transitions to secondary school and beyond, poor learning outcomes, and growing populations of schooled yet unemployed youths/citizens.

It is also during this period that presidential directives initiating special programs to boost secondary-education participation for vulnerable groups were started. The secondary-school education bursary fund of 1993/4 was established through a presidential announcement to cushion children from disadvantaged communities from the high cost of secondary education. The fund received allocation from the Ministry of Education, and was coordinated by the constituency bursary committee. Affirmative action was practiced, as a specific amount was reserved for children from ASAL. There were often allegations of favoritism in allocation, and a generally poor identification system diminished its reach to needy children. In a bid to consolidate the fund with other bursary and scholarship schemes, its management was handed over to the Constituency Development Fund (CDF) in 2013/14. The CDF Act (2015, p. 1963) stipulates that up to 35 percent of total allocated funds per financial year may be used to support education, bursaries, and assessments. In general, many constituencies prefer the practice of giving secondary-school merit scholarships, based on the performance rather than need of learners.

Recent education policy developments: The year 2000 onwards

Kenya is signatory to, and has drawn impetus from, a series of international declarations, such as:

A) The 2000 Dakar Education for All declaration, that committed to "ensuring that by 2015 all children, with special emphasis on girls, children in difficult circumstances and from ethnic minorities have access to and complete free and compulsory primary education of good quality";

B) The 2015 Sustainable Development Goal (SDG) 4 that commits to "ensure inclusive and equitable quality education and promote lifelong learning opportunities for all". The SDG centers on a moral impetus that "no goal will be considered met, unless met for all" which reaffirms the equity threshold that the state needs to aim for.

The spirit articulated in these declarations is evident in public policy in Kenya. There have been several economic, social, and government reforms meant to invigorate economic growth and improve social services. Given the stagnant growth witnessed during the previous decades, policy-based strategies to reduce poverty were introduced, including the Economic Recovery Strategy (ERS) 2003–2007, which harmonized previous economic plans and strategies in a bid to accelerate economic growth. This plan focused on economic recovery by developing sound macroeconomic policies; enhancing efficient public service delivery; reducing inequalities in access to productive resources, basic goods, and services; and designing policies that reduced the cost of doing business. The ERS proposed several targeted programs such as the social action fund, the ASAL program, the vulnerability program, and the slum upgrading and low-cost housing program (Nthia & Njeru, 2005). These would later shape the three pillars of the Vision 2030. The anecdotal view is that the low-income households were hard hit, perhaps implying that the policies were not "pro-poor".

In education, planning was contained in Sessional Paper No. 1 of 2005 on education, training, and research (GoK, 2005), which ushered in the Sector-Wide Approach to Planning (SWAP); this was instrumental in shaping the Kenya Education-Sector Support Program (KESSP) 2005–2010/11. KESSP is credited for two key movements that greatly influenced access to education. Its pooled funding approach allowed the Free Primary School scheme to be sustained. It is also during this period, in 2008, that Free Day Secondary schooling was introduced.

In addition, a series of sub-sector issue-focused policies that targeted excluded groups were developed, as illustrated below. Some of these policies have since been revised:

A) 2007 Gender in Education Policy (Revised in 2015 to Education and Training Sector Gender Policy);

B) 2009 Special Needs Education Policy (Revised in 2018 to Sector Policy for Learners and Trainees with Disability);

C) 2009 Policy Framework for Nomadic Education in Kenya (Revised 2015);

D) 2009 Safety Standards Manual for Schools in Kenya: Schools as Safe Zones;

E) 2009 National School Health Policy (MoE, 2009) (Revised in 2018 to Kenya National Health Policy);

F) 2009 Alternative Provision of Basic Education and Training.

Sessional Paper No. 10 of 2012 on Kenya Vision 2030 offers the long-term development blueprint created under the backdrop of the Economic Recovery Strategy. It has three pillars: economic, social, and political. The social pillar seeks to create just, cohesive, and social development in a clean and secure environment. Vision 2030 is very forward-thinking and, indeed, a perfect fit in terms of phrasing with the SDGs. It retains the call for special investment in ASAL, as well as other communities with high rates of poverty. It is cognizant that effort is needed to reach the unemployed youth, women, and vulnerable groups. All in all, Vision 2030 strategies to achieve equity have prioritized access, an emphasis that is retained in other sector-wide planning documents, such as the "Big Four Agenda" (Kenya Yearbook, 2019) that views access to education as a critical enabler to achieve the priority goals of food security, healthcare, manufacturing, and housing. The National Education Sector Strategic Plan 2018–2022 in based on access, equity, quality, and relevance of education as a means of achieving social development.

One of the more consistent Kenyan educational policy priorities has been to increase basic education for 8-to-12-year-olds, and this necessitated the implementation of several nationwide interventions that help needy populations participate in secondary schooling. Some examples are provided below:

A) The presidential secondary-school bursary scheme started in the 2013/14 financial year. Administered by the Children's Department, this fund seeks to enhance secondary-school enrollment, attendance, and completion for orphaned and vulnerable children.

B) The primary and secondary school examination fees waiver commenced in 2017 for all candidates. Some have observed that this waiver could have been targeted to reach those in need, allowing those who could afford to pay for the already subsidized fees to continue to do so.

C) The sanitary towels program for schools was initiated in 2011 by the Ministry of Education. Since 2018, this program provides free sanitary towels to girls from disadvantaged backgrounds and is run by the State Department for Gender Affairs.

D) The Elimu Scholarship was supported by the World-Bank-funded Secondary Education Quality Improvement Project (SEQIP). One component of the project provides scholarships for secondary education to students from needy families, and 9000 students benefited in 2019/20. The scholarship fund is managed by Equity Foundation, which runs the Wings to Fly scholarship program. Indeed, in the last decade, public-private partnerships offering scholarships and bursaries to expand participation in secondary education have grown. Some of the sought-out scholarship schemes by corporate firms targeting needy children include Equity Wings to Fly, Kenya Commercial Bank, Safaricom Foundation, and Kenya Tea Development Authority. There is a gradual and steady emergence of corporate social responsibility to boost public education participation.

E) Since 2016, the Ministry of Labour and Social Protection has led a multi-agency effort known as "Inua Jamii"(Empower the Community) that operates a common operational platform offering cash transfers to orphaned and vulnerable children, older people, and people with severe disabilities. It also runs the hunger safety net program (only in the Turkana, Marsabit,

Mandera, and Wajir counties). This effort is part of the governments' national safety-net program aimed at uplifting the lives of "poor and vulnerable citizens", where deserving individuals/households receive KES 2000.

F) The school meals program, initiated in 2009, provides meals to children from needy counties at school, to both enhance attendance and achievement, and also stimulate local agricultural production through the purchase of food from small farmers and local suppliers.

G) The National Council for Nomadic Education in Kenya (NACONEK) was established—a semi-autonomous agency —to steer efforts towards the attainment of education for all in nomadic communities.

The Basic Education Act provides for the establishment of private schools, in which Clause 5.1 states that any person requiring basic education may attend a private school. This sector has grown exponentially over the years, under a progressive regulatory framework by the government. The most rapid growth was witnessed between 1999 and 2006, when the number of private primary schools increased from 569 to 1,839, a growth attributed to the declaration of FPE in 2003. Enrollment in private secondary schools increased by 19 percent between 2015 and 2016. This increase is consistent with improved transition rates. The private sector continues to play a critical role in strengthening access to education in Kenya, even though it is seen as a cause of the widening gap between the rich and the poor.

A major education reform is currently underway that is progressively phasing out the 8–4–4 system, to be replaced by competency-based education and training. The impetus for the reforms is contained in the Odhiambo report (2012), *The Realignment of the Education Sector to Vision 2030 and the Constitution of Kenya*, whose recommendations were adopted into policy in Sessional Paper No. 2 of 2015 on reforming education and training for Kenya. To ground the visioning of the reforms, the Basic Education Curriculum Framework (MoE, 2016) was developed. The National Curriculum Policy (2018) and the Sessional Paper No. 1 of 2019 on reforming education and training for sustainable development in Kenya articulate the policy standpoints.

The mission of the Competency-Based Curriculum (CBC) is to "nurture the potential of every child", and is grounded on seven guiding principles: opportunity, excellence, inclusion, diversity, differentiated curriculum and learning, parental empowerment, and engagement and community-service learning. These guiding principles need to be cushioned by issue-specific policies and accompanying plans to allow grounded visioning, planning, and monitoring. For example, while the CBC Framework is guided by the principle of promoting multiple languages, and even gives prominence to sign language, it is very likely that progress in language and education will be muted, as it draws its policy direction from the language policy in education policy last revised in 1976. A better approach would be to revise the language policy and develop costed strategies whose implementation can be monitored.

Discussion

Access to education is a basic human right, enshrined in the bill of rights of the Constitution of Kenya (2010). Article 2(6) of the Constitution of Kenya further states that: "Any treaty or convention ratified by Kenya shall form part of the law of Kenya". Kenya is a signatory to several regional and international conventions and declarations such as The African Charter on the Human and Peoples Rights, The African Charter on the Rights and Welfare of the Child, and The Convention on the Rights of the Child. These all express the right of each child to free and compulsory education. The national intent to offer equal opportunity to all as a right, and not a privilege, is domesticated and expressed in the following articles of the Constitution of Kenya 2010:

- 43 (1): Every person has the right to (f) education;
- 53 (1) Every child has a right to (b) free and compulsory basic education;
- 54 (1): A person with disability is entitled (b) to access educational institutions and facilities... that are integrated into society;
- 56: The state shall put in place affirmative action programmes designed to ensure that minorities and marginalised groups (b) are provided special opportunities in education.

The imperatives communicated in the Constitution have been domesticated in the Education Act of 2013. The Education Act states that educational provision shall be guided by:

- the right of every child to free and compulsory basic education;
- equitable access for the youth to basic education and equal access to education or institutions;
- protection of every child against discrimination;
- advancement and protection of every child… to be instructed in a language of his or her choice where this is reasonably practicable;
- provision of adequate equipment, infrastructure, and resources that meet the needs of every child in basic education.

To compel the right to education, Section 30 of the Act provides a fine of KES 100,000 for anyone who does not take their child to school, and KES 5 million for anyone found culpable of child labor.

These legal instruments mainly stress access, and the associated inputs needed to actualize this access. The evidence at hand, when viewed in terms of averages, confirms satisfactory progress. Current government statistics as contained in the Economic Survey (KNBS, 2020, pp. 241–251) indicate that:

A) There are a total of 89,331 learning institutions in basic education in Kenya, comprised of 46,530 pre-primary schools; 32,344 primary schools; 10,463 secondary school, and 2,191 technical and vocational education training centers. Pre-primary and TVET institutions registered a 10 percent increase from the previous year, while primary and secondary schools registered a lower number due to more stringent compliance measures being implemented.

B) Primary-school enrollment between 2015 and 2019 consistently stood at slightly over 10 million, with near gender parity (5.1 million boys and 4.96 million girls), while secondary-school enrollment increased from 2.9 million in 2018 to 3.3 million learners in 2019, with gender parity having been achieved.

C) Primary-school completion rates have witnessed a marginal increase from 82.7 percent in 2015 to 85.4 percent in 2019.

D) Transition rates to secondary schooling have increased from 81.9 percent in 2015 to 85.5 percent in 2019. The 2020 drive for 100 percent transition had resulted in a rate of over 95 percent, but this progress was interrupted by the COVID-19 pandemic.

E) The Teachers Service Commission manages a teaching force of 218,760 teachers in public primary schools, of whom slightly more are female (114,076), and 105,234 teachers in secondary school (43,124 being female). All these teachers are trained. There is an estimated 30 percent teacher shortage, and any recruitment drive attracts hundreds of thousands of applications from qualified teachers.

Three critiques can be levelled against the current data on educational progress in key government documents. First, key statistical documents tend to provide national data that is often not disaggregated by lower administrative zones, or by regions and populations of policy interest to allow proper monitoring of policy issues. For instance, while the review affirms that policies have always intended to address the educational disadvantage in ASAL areas, data-reporting in national documents such as the Economic Survey—or integrated reports by the government such as the Kenya Yearbook (2019)—do not offer ASAL-specific data. Similarly, while policy documents have improved in their recognition that vulnerable communities must be reached, data capture fails to consistently report education participation against disability and socioeconomic status. UNESCO (2019) urges the necessity of going "beyond averages" to allow for a true assessment of whether each learner is truly being included. Such reporting would automatically lead to focus on the 15 percent of children who do not complete primary schooling and give clarity to the nature and type of interventions they need. Data is an important way to measure commitment.

Second, while the culture of annual reporting on all sectors, including education, in the Economic Surveys is appreciated, the data capture and monitoring has tended to focus on numbers closely related to "availability" and "access". It is now time to move "beyond access". The next frontier of reporting should therefore include learning-outcome data from assessments, not just summative examinations. It should focus on adaptations that have been made to address the learning needs of children with disabilities, who at the moment are covered under blanket access numbers. Overall, reporting will need to address the more qualitative indicators related to learning.

Finally, the Ministry of Education should regularly capture and report on data based on a broader set of indicators. The last comprehensive data released by MoE is irregularly published. After the Basic Education Statistical Booklet of 2014, another set was released in 2016, and the latest in 2020. A more regular rhythm will enable its users to plan accordingly and articulating an open data policy and operationalizing an online data platform would help. These statistical booklets include data on learners with special needs and undertake cohort analysis, informing on internal efficiency of the system. Unfortunately, the MoE data are limited to access numbers. The National Assessment Centre for Monitoring Learning Achievement based at the Kenya National Examination Council can play a bigger role in undertaking and consolidating studies on learning outcomes, which currently show that learning outcomes remain low (PAL Network, 2020; Uwezo, 2014). There is a need to invest in research on policy issues that would result in more equitable learning opportunities. For example, analyses by Alcott and Rose (2016) show that private schooling does not narrow learning inequalities. These data support the resolve to expand public education for underserved populations, like the urban poor or children with special needs. Likewise, the PAL Network (2019) analysis of age by grade rates—which shows that children who are in incorrect grades for their age are likely to be learning less, and that their mothers also have educational needs—should inform policy actions.

It is agreed that good policy formulation needs to be accompanied with good data and strategies. Kinyanjui (2020; this volume) observes the current policy limitation to lie in the:

- lack of comprehensive data sets;
- lack of broad indicators that are continuously reported against;
- lack of baseline data prior to development of policies, which makes it difficult to determine the effectiveness of the policy; and

- lack of clear methodologies and criteria to determine which policy contributes to which change in the sector.

Conclusion

The education policy vision in Kenya has been one of promise, underscored by the belief that education will lead to a more equal society and better opportunities for all. Government policy initiatives have made commendable progress in fermenting this vision. Learning inputs are available, the number of learning institutions continues to increase to meet demand, and there is an oversupply of trained teachers. All of the ingredients needed for a functional education system are available. The issue that has arisen, however, is one of inequitable opportunity. This is where attention is needed as efforts move toward building a resilient system that works for all children, including those most marginalized.

The next frontier is to make education more acceptable and adaptable, as these considerations are at the heart of educational quality. Operationalizing the language policy, for example, will go a long way in bridging the gap between home and school for marginalized communities. Institutionalizing periodic assessments and enforcing a culture of data use for classroom decision-making will help these disadvantaged learners as well. Teachers must also be empowered to adjust the curriculum pace to match the level of their learners, which will ultimately result in improved learning for all.

Public participation has found its way into national decision-making, since the inauguration of the Kenyan constitution in 2010. There has been constant engagement with communities, so that, as much as possible, their diverse array of cultures and aspirations are catered to in the curriculum. However, the role of communities in augmenting certain aspects of the formal curriculum remains unclear. COVID-19 has led to notable incidences of parents and communities stepping up with alternative ways to ensure continued learning for their children. We must not lose the momentum when schools fully reopen. This has been a period to augment parental engagement as envisioned in the Competency-Based Curriculum, and lessons learnt should shape community involvement in improving learning going forward.

In an effort to improve on service delivery, specifically for those at the bottom of the Kenyan pyramid, there has been a recent proliferation of multi-sectoral programs uniting different government ministries. In the last decade, these programs have expanded, with new variations springing up during the COVID-19 period, in which vulnerable youths were identified and offered services and funds. There is still an unfinished agenda that continues to propel the education reforms currently being witnessed. A more outcome-driven approach to policy-making, with correct mechanisms to monitor progress, may support growth in education, especially for Kenya's most vulnerable populations.

In summary, two key observations emerge from this policy review. First, policy-making processes have generally matured in Kenya. There is a consistent focus on expanding access, and huge strides have been made in that regard. Another positive trend in the last decade has been the multi-sectoral approach to planning and execution. However, policies now must move from being input-driven to being outcome-based. They must shift from reporting only on access numbers to including data on learning outcomes. Finally, they must follow through on promoting and implementing sub-sector-specific policies, which allow further focus on needed areas and marginalized populations. The seven CBC principles would benefit from clear and specific policies, supported with a culture of data capture to monitor implementation.

References

Kenya National Bureau of Statistics. (2020a). *Survey on socio-economic impact of COVID-19 on households report*. https://www.knbs.or.ke/?wpdmpro=survey-report-on-socio-economic-impact-of-covid-19-on-households

Kenya National Bureau of Statistics. (2020b). *Economic survey 2020*. https://www.knbs.or.ke/?wpdmpro=economic-survey-2020

Kenya Yearbook. (2019). *The big four agenda: Road to prosperity*. Nairobi: Kenya Yearbook Editorial Board.

Ministry of Education. (2014). *Basic education statistical booklet*. https://kicd.ac.ke/wp-content/uploads/2017/10/2014-Basic-Education-Statistical-Booklet.pdf

Ministry of Education. (2015). *Policy framework for nomadic education in Kenya*. https://education.go.ke/index.php/downloads/file/631-policy-framework-for-nomadiceducation-in-kenya

Ministry of Education. (2016). *Basic education statistical booklet.* https://www.education.go.ke/images/REPORTS/Basic-Education-Statistical-Booklet---2016.pdf

Ministry of Education. (2018). *Sector policy for learners and trainees with disability.* https://education.go.ke/index.php/downloads/file/510-sector-policy-for-learners-and-trainees-with-disabilities

Ministry of Education & Ministry of Public Health. (2009). *National school health policy.* https://www.prb.org/wp-content/uploads/2018/05/National-School-Health-Policy-2009.-without-cover..-Kenya.pdf

Montoya, S. (2018). What is the bottom of the pyramid in the case of low-income countries? In D. Wagner, S. Wolf, & R. Brouch (Eds.), *Learning at the bottom of the pyramid: Science measurement and policy in low-income countries.* UNESCO IIEP. https://unesdoc.unesco.org/ark:/48223/pf0000265581

Munene, I., & Ruto, S. (2015). Pastoralist education in Kenya. Continuity in exclusion in arid and semi-arid Lands (ASAL). *Journal of Third World Studies, 32*(1). https://nau.pure.elsevier.com/en/publications/pastoralist-education-in-kenya-continuity-in-exclusion-in-arid-an

Nthia, N., & Njeru, P. (2005). *Policy-based approaches to poverty reduction in Kenya: Strategies and civil society engagement.* Nairobi: UNDP. https://profiles.uonbi.ac.ke/enjeru/publications/policy-based-approaches-poverty-reduction-kenya-strategies-and-civil-society-eng

Ochola, S. (2016). *Assessment of Sessional Paper No. 10 1965 in the context of equity and development in Kenya.* https://www.internationalbudget.org/wp-content/uploads/ibpkenya-equity-week-2016-sessional-paper-10-critique-shem-ochola-9-19.pdf

PAL Network. (2020). *ICAN (International Common Assessment of Numeracy).* https://palnetwork.org/wp-content/uploads/2020/07/2020_PAL-Network_ICAN-Report_EN.pdf

Republic of Kenya. (2019). *Sessional Paper No. 1 of 2019 on a policy framework for reforming education and training for sustainable development in Kenya.* Nairobi: Government Printers. https://www.education.go.ke/index.php/downloads/file/643-sessional-paper-no-1-of-2019

Republic of Kenya. (2013). *Basic Education Act No. 14 of 2013.* https://www.education.go.ke/index.php/downloads/file/96-basic-education-act-no-14-of-2013

Republic of Kenya. (2012). *Sessional Paper No. 10 of 2012 on Kenya Vision 2030.* http://www.foresightfordevelopment.org/sobipro/54/1263-sessional-paper-no-10-of-2012-on-kenya-vision-2030

Republic of Kenya. (2010). *The Constitution of Kenya.* https://www.constituteproject.org/constitution/Kenya_2010.pdf

Republic of Kenya. (2005). *Sessional Paper No. 1 of 2005 on a policy framework for education, training and research.* http://www.knqa.go.ke/wp-content/uploads/2018/10/sessional-paper-sept.-2005-final.pdf

Republic of Kenya. (1965). *African Socialism and its application to development: Sessional Paper No. 10.* Nairobi: Government Printers.

Republic of Kenya. (1976). *Report of the National Committee on education objectives and policies: Gachathi Report.* Nairobi: Government Printers.

Rose, P., Sabates, R., Alcott, B., & Ilie, S. (2016). *Overcoming inequalities within countries to achieve global convergence in learning* (Background paper for The International Commission on Financing Global Education Opportunity Report). https://www.repository.cam.ac.uk/bitstream/handle/1810/262418/Overcoming-Inequalities-within-Countries%20%282%29.pdf?sequence=1&isAllowed=y

Ruto, S., Ongwenyi, Z., & Mugo, J. (2009). *Educational marginalisation in Northern Kenya.* https://unesdoc.unesco.org/ark:/48223/pf0000186617?posInSet=1&queryId=29fcab0c-f01f-4a95-8e6f-73c01f0af65f

Tomasevski, K. (2001). *Human rights obligations: Making education available, accessible, acceptable, and adaptable.* https://www.right-to-education.org/sites/right-to-education.org/files/resource-attachments/Tomasevski_Primer%203.pdf

UNESCO. (2017). *More than one-half of children and adolescents are not learning world wide* (UIS Fact Sheet No. 46., UIS/FS/2017/ED/46). http://uis.unesco.org/sites/default/files/documents/fs46-more-than-half-children-not-learning-en-2017.pdf

UNESCO. (2019). *Beyond commitments: How countries implement SDG 4.* Paris: UNESCO. https://unesdoc.unesco.org/ark:/48223/pf0000369008/PDF/369008eng.pdf.multi

UNESCO. (2020a). *Re-opening schools: When, where and how?* https://en.unesco.org/news/reopening-schools-when-where-and-how

UNESCO. (2020b). *Right to education: Impact on the COVID-19 crisis on the right to education: Concerns, challenges and opportunities* (Special rapporteur). https://www.right-to-education.org/sites/right-to-education.org/files/resource-attachments/UNSR_Education_Report%20on%20Covid19_HRC_2020.pdf

Uwezo. (2014). *Are our children learning?* https://www.twaweza.org/uploads/files/Uwezo_EA_Report-EN-FINAL.pdf

World Bank. (2020). *The COVID-19 pandemic: Shocks to education and policy responses.* https://openknowledge.worldbank.org/handle/10986/33696

15. Kenya

Free Primary and Day Secondary Education Policies and Their Contributions to Learning at the Bottom of the Pyramid

Emmanuel Manyasa
and Mercy G. Karogo

Introduction

The 2000 United Nations (UN) Millennium Declaration highlighted universal primary education as one of eight global goals, which led to unprecedented enrollment of children in primary school. In response to these Millennium Development Goals (MDGs), Kenya implemented Free Primary Education (FPE) in 2003, with significant support from multilateral development partners. Both the UN and the Kenyan government sought to address the challenge of intergenerational transmission of illiteracy, marginalization, and poverty.

FPE implementation significantly increased access to primary school. The Gross Enrollment Rate (GER) in primary school rose from 88.2 percent in 2002 to 103.21 percent in 2016. Among those who enrolled was the late Kimani Maruge, who holds the Guinness World record for being the "oldest person to begin primary school" at age 84. Buoyed by this success, the government implemented Free Day Secondary Education (FDSE) in 2008. As a result, GER in secondary school rose from 41.9 percent in 2009 to 58.2 percent in 2014. More recently, the government implemented the 100 percent transition policy, pushing up the primary to secondary transition rate from 76.1 percent in 2014 to 83.3 percent in 2018 (Republic of Kenya, 2019).

© 2022 Manyasa and Karogo, CC BY-NC 4.0   https://doi.org/10.11647/OBP.0256.15

MDG2 (primary-school access) was largely achieved, but there is no evidence that the core mission for universalizing basic education and learning was. Indeed, Uwezo learning assessments have consistently reported low learning outcomes among children aged 6–16 years in the country. In 2015, up to eight percent of children exiting primary school had not acquired the basic literacy and numeracy competencies expected of a Grade 2 child. Without learning, universal schooling will not disrupt the intergenerational transmission of illiteracy, marginalization, and poverty. Indeed, it might contribute to the polarization of society by widening the learning gaps and the attendant social dysfunction (Manyasa, 2015). Yet the learning crisis is not just a Kenyan phenomenon. It is a global problem (Bashir et al., 2018), a fact that informed the formulation of the Sustainable Development Goal (SDG) 4 as part of the broad 2030 Global Development Agenda. SDG4 acknowledges the fact that schooling is not the same as learning.

In this chapter, we explore whether the FPE policy is contributing to quality learning for all. We use the Kenya Certificate of Secondary Education (KCSE) examination results for 2017–2019 to demonstrate that universal schooling at the basic level, implemented without a deliberate mechanism to ensure equitable learning opportunities, may still marginalize those at the bottom of the pyramid. We draw on a rich family of sorting models to analyze and interpret secondary school data to achieve the following objectives:

1. Establish the relationship between the type of primary school attended and the category of public secondary school attended by learners;

2. Establish the relationship between the category of secondary school attended and the performance of learners in the national examinations at the secondary-school level; and

3. Determine the equity implications of FPE as currently implemented in Kenya for the children at the bottom of the learning pyramid.

We demonstrate that children at the bottom of the pyramid constitute a significant proportion of all children, and yet despite being in school, their learning levels remain low. According to Uwezo (2016), a Grade 3 pupil in a private school in Kenya was twice as likely to successfully complete a Grade 2 task as a pupil in the same grade in a public school. We highlight the steady decline in budgetary allocation to the Ministry of Education (MOE) as a percentage of total government spending from 21.3 percent in the financial year 2013/14 to 8.8 percent in the year 2020/21 (Republic of Kenya, 2019; 2020). Additionally we argue that implementation of FPE and FDSE in an environment of diminishing budgetary support may deepen the learning poverty of those at the bottom of the pyramid.

Theoretical framework

Manyasa (2015) underscores the impact of the FPE policy on sorting children, based on household poverty, into public and private primary schools. This view differs from Kremer (1997), who studied the effect of sorting in marriage and neighborhoods and assessed parental and neighborhood effects on steady-state inequality, as proxied by the standard deviation in educational attainment. By measuring educational attainment in years of schooling, Kremer (1997) found that "changes in sorting will have only a small impact on steady-state inequality of characteristics that are only moderately heritable, such as education and income". He concluded that inequality is insensitive to sorting and, further, that sorting has been declining.

According to his model, sorting would have a greater effect on the distribution of the quality of schooling if it was based on the individual rather than parental characteristics. It is further argued that: "Since sorting increases the intergenerational correlation of education, inequality among dynasties will be more sensitive to sorting than inequality among individuals" (Kremer, 1997, p. 128). Thus, he concludes that sorting is an insignificant factor that has received undue attention in inequality discourse.

This view is not shared by Fernandez and Rogerson (2001). In a model that includes the ability to borrow against a child's future income, they argue that sorting affects inequality except in circumstances where it does not affect the families' credit constraint. Their model also includes the price of skill, which is not included in Kremer (1997). They postulate that the price of skill is determined by three factors: "the existence of a nonlinear relationship between parental years of education and those of their children; a negative correlation between fertility and parental education; and wage rates that are sensitive to changes in the skill" (Fernandez & Rogerson, 2001, p. 1330).

Fernandez and Rogerson argue that, when parents are unable to borrow against their children's future income, they are constrained financially in investing in their children's education. This makes parental income an important factor in children's access to "quality education". It is this constraint that the Kenyan FPE and FDSE policies may have sought to remove, but the current quality gaps between public and private primary schools, as well as sub-county and higher-ranked secondary schools, indicate that the policies may in fact have tightened the constraint. This may be the case due to the worsening quality of education in the schools where children of the poor go, yet according to Psacharopoulos (1984), quality of education, however it is measured, has an impact on children's learning and later, earnings.

Methodology

This study utilized secondary data consisting of the KCSE examination results for the candidates whose scores were in the top and bottom 25 percent across three years: 2017, 2018, and 2019. Both descriptive and inferential statistics were obtained and are presented in the next section. For inferential analysis, we fitted a Poisson regression model to assess the relationship between KCSE performance against a student's gender, age, KCPE score (marks), secondary-school type (national, county, extra-county, sub-county, and special), primary-school category (rural-public, urban-public, and private), KCPE exam year, and a binary variable to show whether the student repeated grades. To fit the KCSE grades in a Poisson count model, the grades were assigned corresponding values equivalent to their assessment strength, where grades A, A-, B+ ... D, D-, and E were assigned numerical values 12, 11, 10 ... 3, 2, 1, respectively. By fitting a Poisson regression model, we assumed that the response variable (KCSE grade) assumes a count variable where the lowest grade, E, is assigned lowest count (1) and the highest grade, A, is assigned highest count (12).

Letting $y_1, y_2 ... y_n$ be the KCSE grades from n students, we assumed that these sample random observations can be treated as a realization of independent Poisson random variables and fitted a Poisson model shown by Equation (1).

$$Y_i \sim P(\mu_i) \quad \quad (1)$$

where μ_i is the mean and variance of a Poisson distribution. The mean vector μ_i depends on the explanatory variables X_i. A simple Poisson regression model can be expressed in the form given by Equation (2).

$$\log(\mu_i) = X_i\beta \quad \quad (2)$$

where β is a vector of coefficients and X is a matrix consisting of data from the explanatory variables. By mimicking the ordinary regression equation, the Poisson Equation (2) can be expressed as Equation (3).

$$\mu_i = \exp\{X_i\beta\} \quad \quad (3)$$

Thus, the fitted Poisson model is used to assess the effect of different learning and demographic characteristics on the probability of the student scoring one grade higher.

Empirical findings

We analyze the performance of 901,128 secondary-school leavers who sat KCSE examinations in the years 2017–2019, and were either in the top or bottom 25 percent of the performance table. We depart from the assumption that the KCSE results follow a normal distribution. This then means that the bottom 25 percent forms the bottom of the pyramid, while the top 25 percent is the top of the pyramid, with the remaining 50 percent forming the middle of the pyramid. Therefore, the learners whose KCSE scores put them in the bottom 25 percent are the main focus of this analysis, but the top 25 percent are useful to contextualize the discussion of the findings. Table 1 shows the analyzed school-leavers' distribution among three types of primary schools, with the majority attending rural-public schools (65.8 percent), followed by private schools at 20.3 percent, and urban-public schools at 13.9 percent. The distribution is stable across the three years under consideration (see Table 1).

Table 2 shows consistent over-representation of the school leavers who attended rural-public primary schools in the bottom quarter of KCSE examination performance, and over-representation of those who attended private primary schools in the top quarter. Across the three years, secondary-school leavers who attended rural-public primary

Table 1. Distribution of school leavers by type of primary school attended and KCSE examination year.

Primary school type	2017 No.	2017 %	2018 No.	2018 %	2019 No.	2019 %	Total No.	Total %
Private	54,147	20.6	62,801	20.1	66,088	20.3	183,036	20.3
Public (U)	37,393	14.2	43,298	13.8	44,592	13.7	125,283	13.9
Public (R)	171,775	65.2	206,544	66.1	214,490	66.0	592,809	65.8
Total	263,315	100.0	312,643	100.0	325,170	100.0	901,128	100.0

schools account for over 75 percent of the bottom achievers in KCSE examinations, which is higher than their overall percentage in the population of approximately 66 percent. Those who attended private primary schools account for approximately 11 percent of the bottom achievers, against their overall percentage in the population of 20.3 percent. Those who attended urban-public primary schools account for a proportionate percent of both bottom and top achievers to their overall percentage in the population under study. It is important to note here that most urban-public primary schools are expensive, and many of them are located in affluent parts of cities, thus attracting children from households that differ significantly from those of their rural counterparts.

Table 2. KCSE mean score distribution between top and bottom performance quarters by type of primary school attended.

KCSE level	2017 Priv.	2017 Pub (R)	2017 Pub (U)	2017 Total	2018 Priv.	2018 P(R)	2018 Pub (U)	2018 Total	2019 Priv.	2019 Pub (R)	2019 Pub (U)	2019 Total
Bottom	11.0	76.0	13.0	100	11.4	75.4	13.1	100	11.4	75.5	13.1	100
Top	30.5	54.0	15.5	100	28.9	56.6	14.6	100	29.2	56.5	14.3	100
Total	20.6	65.2	14.2	100	20.1	66.1	13.8	100	20.3	66.0	13.7	100

Table 3 and Figure 1 show the distribution of the study population by Kenya Certificate of Primary Education (KCPE) examination marks and type of primary school attended. Table 3 shows that, while private primary schools were attended by 20.3 percent of the school leavers in this study, they account for 72.7 percent of those who scored over 400 in KCPE examinations, and only 8.9 percent of those who scored less than 200. This contrasts sharply with school leavers who attended rural-public schools, who account for 65.8 percent of the population under study, but account for only 16.4 percent of those who scored over 400, and 75.8 percent of those who scored less than 200.

Table 3. Distribution of study population by KCPE examination marks and type of primary school attended.[1]

School categories	>400	350–399	250–299	200–249	<200	Total
Private	72.7	47.4	12.7	9.4	8.9	20.3
Rural-public	16.4	37.8	74.3	78.2	75.8	65.8
Urban-public	10.9	14.9	13.0	12.5	15.3	13.9
Total	100	100	100	100	100	100

Figure 1, on the other hand, shows that among the school leavers in this study, 10.5 percent of those who attended private primary schools scored over 400 marks on the KCPE examinations, compared to only 0.7 percent of their compatriots who attended rural-public schools. The figure also shows that 60 percent of those who attended private primary schools scored 350 and above, compared to 12.4 percent of those who attended rural-public primary schools, and attained similar marks. Importantly, however, the figure shows that while 24.4 percent of the private-schoolers scored below 250 marks (which is the pass mark), 60.7 percent of rural-public-schoolers failed to reach this pass mark, with 23.3 percent of them scoring below 200 marks.

The marks scored in primary school have implications for the secondary-school mean grade, as indicated in Table 4 and Figure 2. From Table 4, the color green shows the school leavers who qualified for university, orange indicates those that were within the top 25 percent but did not qualify for university, and red indicates those in the bottom quarter in the KCSE examinations performance for the respective KCPE examination score brackets. The table shows that, on aggregate, 23.4 percent and 63.7 percent of the study population qualified to join university and fell in

---

[1] Note that the table does not include children whose KCPE marks were in the range of 300–349. This is because none of them fell in either the bottom or top quarters in their KCSE performance. The table also does not have any candidates who scored mean grade D and D+ because the candidates with those grades fell in the middle 50 percent in their KCSE performance.

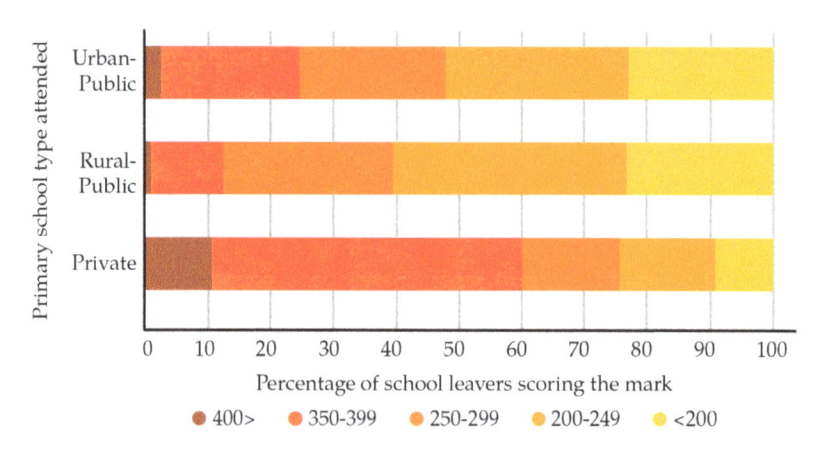

388   *Learning, Marginalization, and Improving the Quality of Education*

Fig. 1. Distribution of study population by KCPE examination scores and type of primary school attended.

the bottom quarter of KCSE examinations performance, respectively. However, 95.1 percent of those who scored at least 400 marks on the KCPE examination qualified to join university, compared to 0.1 percent of those who scored below 200 marks. Conversely, 99.6 percent of those who scored less than 200 marks in KCPE examinations fell in the bottom quarter in KCSE examination performance, compared to 0.1 percent who scored at least 400 marks.

Table 4. KCSE mean grade distribution by marks scored in KCPE examinations.

KCSE mean grade	KCPE examination score					
	>400	350–399	250–299	200–249	<200	Total
A	4.2	0.2	0.0	0.0	0.0	0.2
A-	25.1	4.3	0.0	0.0	0.0	1.6
B+	26.7	12.1	0.3	0.0	0.0	3.3
B	19.7	18.6	2.0	0.1	0.0	4.9
B-	12.1	21.0	5.5	0.4	0.0	6.1
C+	7.3	20.5	10.9	0.9	0.1	7.3
Sub-Total	95.1	76.7	18.7	1.4	0.1	23.4
C	3.7	16.5	17.3	1.6	0.1	8.2
C-	1.1	6.3	12.2	1.2	0.2	4.7
Sub-Total	4.8	22.8	29.5	2.8	0.3	12.9

KCSE mean grade	KCPE examination score					
	>400	350–399	250–299	200–249	<200	Total
D-	0.1	0.5	49.0	85.2	59.3	51.3
E	0.0	0.0	2.9	10.7	40.3	12.4
Sub-Total	0.1	0.5	51.9	95.9	99.6	63.7
Total	100	100	100	100	100	100

Table 5 shows the distribution of KCSE examination mean grades by category of secondary school attended by the population under study. The green shows the school leavers who fell in the top 25 percent, and red indicates those in the bottom quarter in KCSE examination performance for the respective secondary-school category attended. Among those who attended national secondary schools, 97.1 percent fell in the top performance quarter, while 2.9 percent fell in the bottom performance quarter. For those who attended sub-county schools, the lowest-rated public-secondary-school category, 27.2 percent fell in the top quarter while 72.8 percent fell in the bottom quarter.

Table 5. Distribution of KCSE mean grade by category of secondary school attended.

KCSE mean grade	National	Extra-county	County	Sub-county
A	1.3	0.1	0	0.0
A-	9.9	2.1	0.2	0.1
B+	15.8	6.9	1.4	0.6
B	18.2	12.9	4.6	1.9
B-	17.1	17.8	9.2	4.1
C+	15.8	22.1	14.5	6.5
C	13.6	23.7	19.8	8.4
C-	5.4	10.3	13.8	5.6
Sub-Total	97.1	95.9	63.5	27.2
D-	2.2	3.8	32.8	60.5
E	0.7	0.3	3.7	12.3
Sub-Total	2.9	4.1	36.5	72.8
Total	100	100	100	100

Figure 2 shows that 14.9 percent of the population under study who attended private primary schools also attended national secondary schools, while 20.1 percent of private primary-schoolers attended sub-county secondary schools. This contrasts sharply with rural-public primary-schoolers, among whom only 4.3 percent attended national secondary schools and 63 percent attended sub-county secondary schools. We underscore the fact that sub-county secondary schools educate most of the children who come from public primary schools, while most of those who come from private primary schools end up either in the national or extra-county secondary schools. Although allocation of spaces in the secondary schools is purely meritocratic, it ignores the differential learning opportunities that children in public and private primary schools are exposed to. This underlies the observed fact that most children from poor households wind up in sub-county secondary schools, which are generally low-performing. This is a significant equity issue of concern in light of the performance gap between these two sets of secondary schools, as indicated in Table 5.

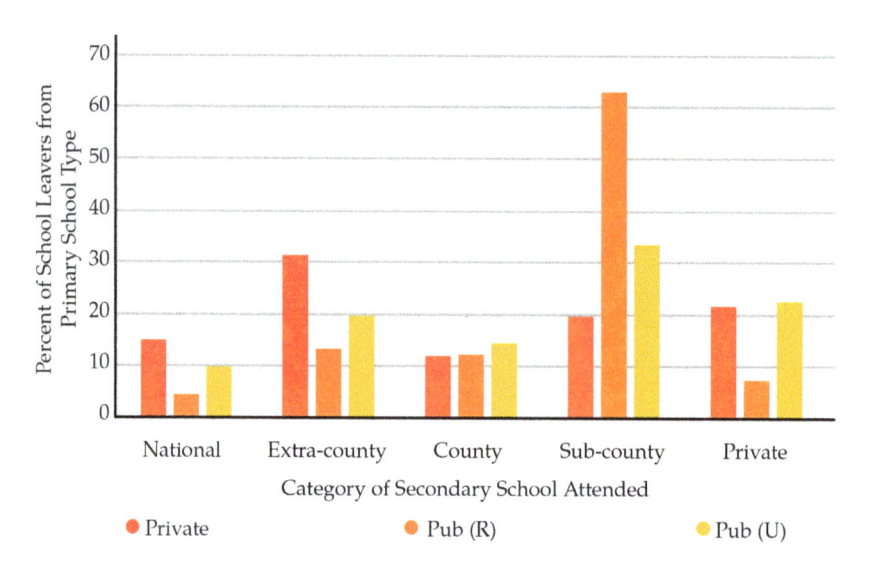

Fig. 2. Distribution of school leavers by type of primary and category of secondary schools attended.

Table 6 shows that 41.9 percent, 39.2 percent, and 18.9 percent of the school leavers who attended national secondary schools had attended private, rural-public, and urban-public primary schools, respectively. In contrast, 8.1 percent, 82.6 percent, and 9.3 percent of those who attended sub-county secondary schools had attended private, rural-public, and urban-public primary schools, respectively.

Table 6. Distribution of the study population by type of primary and category of secondary schools attended.

Secondary-school category	Primary school attended			Total
	Private	Pub (R)	Pub (U)	
National	41.9	39.2	18.9	100
Extra-county	36.0	48.6	15.4	100
County	19.4	64.5	16.1	100
Sub-county	8.1	82.6	9.3	100
Private	35.6	39.1	25.3	100

We also analyze two other important policy issues from the data: grade repetition and age of learners, to assess their impact on school leavers' KCSE examination results. An estimated 11.6 percent, 11.1 percent, and 14.5 percent of those who attended private, urban-public, and rural-public primary schools respectively repeated at least one grade during their secondary education. The difference in repetition rate was insignificant across the primary school types attended. However, from the regression results in Table 7, being a repeater increases the chances of achieving one grade higher by 37 percent, and the difference is statistically significant. This finding contradicts the basis of the government's non-repetition policy that prohibits learners from repeating grades.

The school leavers in this study ranged from 15 years to over 25 years old. The age range violates the MOE age guidelines, which expect learners to join primary school at the age of 6 and complete Form 4 at the age of 18. 15-year-olds are proportionately represented in the bottom quarter, 16- and 17-year-olds are under-represented in the bottom quarter, while the rest are over-represented. The extent of over-representation increases with age, with 24-year-olds being over-represented by up to five times and the 25-and-older group being over-represented by more than five times in the bottom quarter. This finding is corroborated by the regression results in Table 7. From the results, one more year on the age of the learner decreases the chances of achieving one grade higher by seven percent, other factors held constant. This finding is statistically significant.

Table 7. Regression model results based on Poisson Regression Model (probability of getting higher grade).

Factor		Incidence rate	p-value	95% Conf. interval	
Gender of the student (ref: female)					
	Male	1.04	0.000	1.03	1.04
KCSE category (ref: county)					
	Extra-county	1.02	0.000	1.02	1.03
	National	1.04	0.000	1.03	1.04
	Private	0.91	0.000	0.91	0.92
	Sub-county	0.95	0.000	0.95	0.96
Primary-school category (ref: rural-public)					
	Private	1.09	0.000	1.08	1.09
	Urban-public	1.08	0.000	1.08	1.09
KCSE grade category (Ref: >400)					
	350–399	0.83	0.000	0.82	0.83
	250–299	0.48	0.000	0.47	0.48
	200–249	0.26	0.000	0.26	0.27
	<200	0.21	0.000	0.21	0.21
Age of the student		0.93	0.000	0.93	0.93
Repeating a grade (Ref: no)					
	Yes	1.37	0.000	1.36	1.37

These findings also show a statistically significant gender gap in performance among the study population. Boys have a 4 percent probability of scoring a grade higher than girls. Similarly, with rural-public primary schools as the base category for the primary school attended, attending a private and an urban-public primary school increases one's chances of scoring a grade higher by nine percent and eight percent, respectively. With county schools as the base category for secondary school attended, attending an extra-county school and a national school increases one's chances of scoring a grade higher by two percent and four percent respectively. Conversely, attending a sub-county or a private secondary school increases one's chances of scoring a grade lower by five percent and nine percent respectively. These findings are statistically significant

With the cohort that scored more than 400 on the KCPE examinations as the base group, scoring between 350 and 399 increases one's chances of scoring a grade lower by 17 percent; scoring between 250 and 299 increases one's chances of scoring a grade lower by 52 percent; scoring between 200 and 249 increases one's chances of scoring a grade lower by 74 percent; and scoring less than 200 increases one's chances of scoring a grade lower by 79 percent. These findings are also statistically significant.

Conclusion

We define children at the bottom of the learning pyramid as those who would not attend school without the government's free education policies. While Kenyan government policies have facilitated children's access to school, the findings of this study tell a simple story about learning for these children: there is little learning happening in their early years of schooling, and this problematic start to education exacerbates the initial disadvantages into a burden which they will carry with them for their entire school journey. The children who would otherwise have been out of school due to their inability to pay school fees are in school thanks to the free education policy of the government. But parents of these children are only able to send them to public primary schools or the poorly equipped and staffed low-cost private schools (which unfortunately we could not separate from other private schools due to data limitations). They learn much less compared to their counterparts in private schools, perform comparatively dismally in KCPE examinations, and get placed in the lowest-ranked secondary schools, which are also often poorly equipped and staffed.

Two factors direct children at the bottom of the pyramid into these sub-county secondary schools: low KCPE examination marks that limit their choice of secondary school, and their inability to pay fees. This leaves them with the option of FDSE, accessible through day/sub-county secondary schools. Once in these ill-equipped and often inadequately staffed schools, and given the weak academic foundation bequeathed by their primary schools, these disadvantaged children learn less than they should and find it hard to excel in KCSE examinations. As Fernandez and Rogerson (2001, p. 1312) argue: "This would then affect both the amount of human capital obtained from high school attendance and the probability that the child attends college". Indeed, our findings illustrate how low the probability of qualifying for university is, having attended a rural-public primary school.

Failure to qualify for university education, which is highly subsidized by the state, augments the initial disadvantage by tightening the households' borrowing constraints. These findings illustrate the fact that, under the FPE and FDSE policies as currently implemented, "...schooling is open to all children in the society but acquisition of vital skills remains a preserve of those from privileged households, who can afford private school fees" (Manyasa, 2015). The implication of this is failure to achieve SDG4 despite increasing enrollments, but more importantly it is the imminent failure to realize the core mission of education as envisaged at Kenya's founding, and further elucidated in the country's Vision 2030.

Given the pivotal role of formal education in social mobility (Becker, 1964; Psacharopoulos, 1984; Romer, 1990; Fernandez & Rogerson, 2001; Desjardins & Schuller, 2006; Martin & Pimhidzai, 2013; McKnight, 2015), we argue that this state of affairs is unsustainable. Indeed, it is inconsistent with the Global 2030 Development Agenda, which is built on a vision of shared prosperity.

In light of these outcomes, we suggest three possible solutions to ensure that well-intentioned government interventions deliver equitable learning opportunities for all children in Kenya, especially those afflicted most by learning poverty: first, there is a need for a comprehensive review of FPE and FDSE policies as currently implemented. This is to identify systemic and conceptual gaps in their design that may have been overridden by their political popularity, but which may be undermining their efficacy. Second, there is a need to redesign the programs implemented under these policies with a clear focus on equity. The programs currently lay more emphasis on promoting access, which we have demonstrated in this paper to be an incomplete solution to the problems underpinning learning poverty and increasing inequity. Third, we suggest a review of the education financing model implemented by the government. This will help to refocus government investments to ensure efficient and optimal utilization of the scarce public resources invested in the sector for those most in need.

References

Bashir, S., Lockheed, M. E., Ninan, E., & Tan, J. (2018). *Facing forward: Schooling for learning in Africa*. Washington, DC: World Bank.

Becker, G. S. (1964). *Human capital: A theoretical and empirical analysis, with special reference to education*. New York: NBER.

Desjardins, R., & Schuller, T. (2006). Understanding the social outcomes of learning. In OECD (Ed.), *Measuring the social effects of education on health and civic engagement: Proceedings of the Copenhagen symposium* (pp. 11–18). Paris: OECD.

Fernández, R., &. Rogerson, R. (2001). Sorting and long-run inequality. *The Quarterly Journal of Economics, 116*(4), 1305–1341.

Kremer, M. (1997). How much does sorting increase inequality? *The Quarterly Journal of Economics, 112*(1), 115–139.

Manyasa, E. (2015). Schooling without learning: The long-term implications of free primary education for income and welfare inequalities in Kenya. In N. Aworti & H. Musahara (Eds.), *Implementation of millennium development goals: progresses and challenges in some African countries*. Addis Ababa: Ossrea.

Martin, G. H., & Pimhidzai, O. (2013). *Education and health services in Kenya: Data for results and accountability*. New York: World Bank.

McKnight, A. (2015). *Downward mobility, opportunity hoarding and the 'glass floor'*. Centre for Analysis of Social Exclusion (CASE), London School of Economics.

Psacharopoulos, G. (1984). The contribution of education to economic growth: International comparisons. In J. W. Kendrick (Ed.), *International comparisons of productivity and causes of the slowdown* (pp. 335–355). American Enterprise, Ballinger.

Republic of Kenya. (2019). *Medium term expenditure framework 2020/21–2022/23* (2019 Education Sector Report). Nairobi: Government Printers.

Republic of Kenya. (2020). *2020/2021 Estimates of recurrent expenditure of the Government of Kenya for the year ending 30th June, 2021* (Vol. I, Votes R1011 – R1162). Nairobi: Government Printers.

Romer, P. (1990). Endogenous technological change. *Journal of Political Economy, 98*, 71–102.

Uwezo. (2016). *Are our children learning?* Uwezo Kenya Sixth Learning Assessment Report. Nairobi, Twaweza East Africa.

16. Kenya

Disability and Learning at the Bottom of the Pyramid

John K. Mugo, Diana Makau, and David K. Njengere

Introduction

Globally, estimates of the number of children ages 0–14 with disabilities range between 93 million and 150 million (WHO, 2011). At least in policy, those with disabilities have been entitled to basic human rights since the Universal Declaration of Human Rights in 1948. The rights specific to people with disabilities were better defined and confirmed by the Convention on the Rights of Persons with Disabilities (UN, 2006) — key among them the right of all children with disabilities to schooling within general education systems. However, more than half a century later, the world is far from delivering on this promise. For instance, a recent analysis of available datasets from developing countries established that, in seven out of the eight countries included, more than 85 percent of primary school age children with disabilities had never attended school (Mizunoya, Mitra, & Yamasaki, 2016).

In Kenya, the education of children with disabilities has been a focus since the birth of the nation in 1963. Immediately after independence, the Ominde Commission (Kenya, 1964) recommended a focus on education for learners with special needs, and this same year, the government appointed the Ngala Commission to advise on matters of special needs education. As a result, enrollment over the past six decades has increased ten-fold. In the financial year 2017/2018, the Ministry of Education disbursed capitation grants to 108,221 learners with disabilities, who were enrolled in 290 special primary institutions and 2,057 special units/integrated programs (MoE, 2018).

Despite this focus, there is emerging evidence that students with disabilities continue to lag behind their peers without disabilities, and that disability continues to exacerbate the learning crisis (World Bank, 2019). Among the factors attributed to this is the lack of curriculum adaptation, and the exclusion of disability measurement in assessment.

This chapter seeks to unmask the multidirectional learning exclusions at the bottom of the pyramid, linked to disability categories, gender, and age. The analysis further examines the effectiveness of the examination accommodations instituted by the Kenyan National Examinations Council, among them time extensions. The conclusions and policy recommendations of this analysis are summed up into three key messages:

1. The effect of age and disability type on performance is high. Early screening and assessment, and other age-of-entry support, might benefit learning at the bottom of the pyramid;

2. Despite the accommodations in place, end-of-cycle examinations continue to marginalize learners with disabilities. Adapting accommodations to the type and severity of disability may be among the policy considerations to make;

3. Disability is a key driver of learning at the "bottom". Topics such as language deprivation and early cognitive development of deaf children might constitute the most urgent and key strategic choices for addressing learning at the bottom of the pyramid.

Objectives and key questions

This analysis adapts an *exclusion in exclusion* lens to understand learning outcomes in children with disabilities, focusing on three key questions:

4. How do learning outcomes compare across learners with and without disabilities?

5. Exclusion in exclusion—how do learning outcomes compare across different disability categories, and within the same disability category across age and gender?

6. Which examination accommodations exist, and how adequate and effective are these in facilitating better outcomes for learners with disabilities?

Methodology

While factors such as disability, socioeconomic class, age, gender, and rural residence each affect learning independently, the combined effect becomes even more instructive. Indeed, many of these are not mutually exclusive in the way they affect education. Many studies on disability and education have just focused on disability categories, and have hardly scratched below the surface to unearth the interactions between disability and gender, or disability and age in the driving of learning outcomes.

This analysis adapts an *exclusion in exclusion* lens to analyze official examination data from the Kenya National Examinations Council (KNEC)[1], looking at both the end-of-primary and end-of-secondary summative assessments, covering the period 2016 to 2019. Even though high-stakes examinations may not be an accurate measure of learning outcomes, the lack of recent and large-scale formative assessment data leaves few options. The analysis therefore adopts a narrow definition, by using examination results as a proxy for learning for children with disabilities. The Kenya examination data for the period only captures four disability categories, which were catered to with examination modifications—physical disability, low vision, blindness, and deafness—even though other disability categories are also known to exist.

---

1 Data in the tables in this chapter are drawn from the KNEC, https://www.knec-portal.ac.ke.

Design, data, and analysis

The Kenya Certificate of Primary Education (KCPE) is a summative norm-referenced examination given at the end of Grade 8, or the last year of primary education. This examination test contains mostly multiple-choice items in five academic subjects—mathematics, English, Kiswahili, science, and social studies, as per the national curriculum. The Kenya Certificate of Secondary Education (KCSE) is a summative, criterion-referenced examination that marks the end of secondary education at Grade 12. This is a high-stakes examination that contains theoretical, project, and practical components in a wide range of academic subjects. Both the examinations are administered by the Kenya National Examinations Council (KNEC).

Quantitative data

This study utilizes KCPE and KCSE examination data for four cohorts (2016–2019). Different analyses are conducted to answer the research questions, including both descriptive (means and percentages) and inferential (regression) analyses. The main independent variables considered include age, gender, and disability classification. The dependent variable is the examination results across the four years.

Qualitative data

Over the last decade, several examination reforms have been passed for disability accommodation. Many of these accommodations are also described in the various policies governing education. This study analyzes these policies to understand the examination accommodations in each disability area, and is complemented by interview data on the key challenges constraining learning across the disability areas. The findings from these qualitative data are used to interpret examination results.

Sample

The study analyzes the results of all learners with and without disabilities who sat for the KCPE and KCSE in the four cycles—2016, 2017, 2018, and 2019. The study excludes learners with intellectual or cognitive disabilities, and includes only those with perceptive or physical disabilities in the four categories mentioned above. Combined, there were a total of 14,620 students in the four disability categories who sat for the two examinations over the four years, constituting less than 0.5 percent of all examination candidates. Around 60 percent of them (8,856) sat for KCPE, while 40 percent (5,764) sat for KCSE. In terms of disabilities, 813 of these were blind (6 percent), 3,602 had low vision (25 percent), 4,773 were deaf (33 percent) while 5,432 had physical disabilities (37 percent).

Findings

In 2019, a total of 2,398 learners with visual, hearing, or physical disabilities sat for the KCPE examination, accounting for 0.002 of the over one million candidates for that year. Though this number was lower than in 2018 (2,469), the completion figures have been on a general upward trend. At the primary-school level, the gender ratio has averaged at 55 percent of boys and 45 percent of girls, with notable variations across the disability categories. The findings in this paper include a total of 8,856 KCPE candidates over the four-year period (2016–2019), 4,863 male and 3,993 female. Among these are 404 blind children, 2,974 deaf children, 2,135 with low vision, and 3,343 with physical disabilities.

At the secondary-school level, a total of 1,672 candidates with the four disabilities sat for the KCSE examination in 2019 (0.002 of all candidates), up from 1,499 in 2018, which also shows a distinct upward trend. Contrary to the primary level, there are more female than male candidates at the secondary level, with an average gender ratio of 42 percent male and 58 percent female. The findings presented in this paper involve a total of 5,764 KCSE candidates over the four-year period, 2,426 male and 3,338 female. Among these are 409 blind and 1,799 deaf candidates, as well as 1,467 with low vision and 2,089 with physical disabilities.

Disability accommodation and documented modifications

Recognizing the barriers to learning with disabilities, governmental policy in Kenya recommends the provision of differentiated curricula, intervention programs, and curriculum support materials to suit these learners' diverse needs, while strengthening the adaptation of assessment for learners and trainees with disabilities at all levels. In line with this, the Kenya National Examinations Council Act (Kenya, 2012) includes three key adaptations in the examination rules.

The KCPE examination Rule 12 provides for braille and large-print papers, provision of an alternative paper to English (Kenyan Sign Language—KSL) for learners with hearing impairments, and time extensions when appropriate. The KCSE examination Rule 19 provides for these three accommodations also, and goes further to add a fourth one—adapted question papers for candidates with hearing impairments. Further, prior assessment of learners with other diverse special needs is also undertaken before administration of both examinations to determine the specialized/individualized accommodations needed for each unique case.

While welcoming these adaptations, the report by the National Gender and Equalization Commission (NGEC) noted that only English and science subjects had been adapted for learners with hearing impairments by the year 2016 (NGEC, 2016). The report observed that even the extra time allowed (30 minutes) was not adequate to accommodate the slower pace of learning for children with disabilities.

Achievement for students with and without disabilities

The first question raised by this study was the difference between students with and without disabilities in learning attainment at the end of the primary and secondary school cycles. The primary examination (KCPE) performance is evaluated out of 100 for each of the five tested subjects, adding up to a total of 500. Scoring is different for the secondary-school examination (KCSE). Learners are graded using scores of the seven best performed subjects out of eight subjects taken. All the subjects are ranked on a scale, and an average is calculated across all the subjects. The results are presented in Tables 1 and 2 below:

Table 1. Overall means for learners with and without disabilities for primary-school examinations (KCPE).

Year	National means	Mean for learners with disabilities	Difference (%)	p-values (.05) in mean difference
2019	249.1	200.7	19.4	0.038
2018	248.45	191.97	22.7	0.354
2017	248.32	196.23	21.0	0.496
2016	251.13	215.15	14.3	0.048
Average	249.25	201.01	19.4	

Table 2. Overall means for learners with and without disabilities for secondary-school examinations (KCSE).

Year	National means	Mean for learners with disabilities	Difference (%)	p-values (.05) in mean difference
2019	4.26	3.1	27.2	0.084
2018	3.9	3.1	20.5	0.071
2017	3.68	3.06	16.8	0.088
2016	3.99	3.2	19.8	0.125
Average	3.96	3.12	21.3	

Overall, learners with disabilities scored an average of about 20 percentage points below their counterparts without disabilities for both primary and secondary levels. At the primary level, the difference was widest in 2018 (23 percentage points), while at secondary level, the difference was widest in 2019 (27 percentage points). However, statistical significance has only been established in three of the eight result areas. Lack of significance may be driven by the low numbers of students with disabilities compared to the total number of students, which was below 0.4 percent at both levels.

Achievement across the four disability categories

The analysis raised a second question: what are the learning attainment differences across the four categories of disability? To answer this, further analysis was undertaken to establish the differences in means at both KCPE and KCSE examinations. The results are provided in Tables 3 and 4 below.

Table 3. Examination means for the four disability categories at primary-school level (KCPE).

Year	2019	2018	2017	2016	Average means	Difference from average mean (%)
Low vision	227.21	229.51	227.85	261.39	236.5	14.5
Blind	209.35	215.37	198.86	230.44	213.5	3.3
Physical disability	211.66	192.81	203.97	227.94	209.1	1.2
Deaf	165.71	159.88	164.33	178.61	167.1	-19.1
Average	203.48	199.39	198.75	224.6	206.6	

Table 4. Examination means for the four disability categories at secondary-school level (KCSE).

Year	2019	2018	2017	2016	Average means	Difference from mean (%)
Blind	3.92	4.24	3.66	4.39	4.05	22.4
Low vision	3.94	3.56	3.47	3.87	3.71	12.1
Physical disability	3.32	3.24	3.31	3.45	3.33	0.6
Deaf	2.00	2.25	2.27	2.12	2.16	-34.7
Total	3.3	3.32	3.18	3.46	3.31	

These analyses reveal remarkable differences in learning attainment across the disability categories. The striking finding is that "deaf" is the only category that lies below the mean for learners with disability, and far below the mean. Overall, being deaf contributes to a drop in attainment of up to 19 percentage points at the primary level and nearly 35 percentage points at the secondary level. Candidates with physical disabilities lie just around the mean in both levels, while those with visual impairments lie a little above the disability mean. Dispersal from the mean is starker at secondary than primary level, extending to nearly 35 percentage points below the mean (deaf) and 22 percentage points above the mean (blind). Interestingly, the blind perform better on average than the learners with low vision at the secondary level, while the reverse is true for the primary level.

Achievement of different genders within the disability categories

The third question is whether gender impacts learning attainment across the four disability categories. KCPE and KCSE results were analyzed to establish the difference in the performance of male and female candidates overall, and in the performance of each gender within each disability category. Findings are presented in Tables 5 and 6 for the two levels.

Table 5. Means for various categories of disability by gender for primary examinations (KCPE).

Year	Gender	Blind	Deaf	Low vision	Physical disability	Average
2019	M	206.25	164.88	234.72	210.08	203.98
	F	214	166.63	218.53	213.78	203.24
2018	M	219.68	160.16	233.74	192.06	201.41
	F	209.48	159.56	224.03	193.8	196.72
2017	M	207.28	165.18	230.77	205.83	202.27
	F	188.98	163.48	224.16	201.24	194.47
2016	M	229.36	180.72	267.65	227.39	226.28
	F	231.49	176.07	253.43	228.56	222.39
Overall mean		213.3	167.1	235.9	209.1	206.3
Mean for male		215.6	167.7	241.7	208.8	208.5
Mean for female		211.0	166.4	230.0	209.3	204.2
Gender difference (male)		4.7	1.3	11.7	-0.5	4.3

Table 6. Means for various categories of disability by gender for secondary examinations.

Year	Gender	Blind	Deaf	Low vision	Physical disability	Average
2019	M	3.0	2.0	3.7	3.1	3.0
	F	4.4	2.0	4.1	3.5	3.5
2018	M	3.9	2.3	3.5	3.3	3.3
	F	4.5	2.2	3.6	3.2	3.4
2017	M	3.2	2.1	3.2	3.1	2.9
	F	3.9	2.4	3.7	3.4	3.4
2016	M	4.5	2.1	3.6	3.4	3.4
	F	4.3	2.2	4.1	3.5	3.5
Overall mean		4.0	2.2	3.7	3.3	3.3
Mean for male		3.7	2.1	3.5	3.2	3.1
Mean for female		4.3	2.2	3.9	3.4	3.4
Gender difference (male)		-0.6	-0.1	-0.4	-0.2	-0.3

The results establish differences in gender, though not as wide, among a class gender ratio of 55:45 (more male). These attainment differences are, however, inconsistent both across the school levels and disability categories. At the primary level, male candidates outperform their female peers by an average of 4.3 points across the four years. Within disability categories, male candidates who were blind, deaf, and with low vision outperformed their female counterparts, but female candidates with physical disabilities outperformed their male counterparts. The most consistent category across gender differences (in favor of males) is candidates with low vision, where male candidates performed better than female candidates by nearly 12 marks on average, and across all the years. This is the only category in which the differences reached statistical significance.

At the secondary level, by contrast, female candidates perform better than their male counterparts, consistent across both the four disability categories and across all four years. While the average difference is 0.3 points (or 2.5 percent in every paper), the difference is widest among the blind candidates (0.6 points or 5 percent in every paper), and narrowest among the deaf candidates (just 0.1 points, less than 1 percent per paper). The difference was widest in the years 2017 and 2019, with 0.5 points difference in each case, as compared to the 0.1 points difference in the two other years (2016 and 2018).

Though some differences are clearly visible, in only three instances were the differences statistically significant: among blind candidates in the KCPE of 2016, and among the deaf candidates in the KCPE of 2017 and KCSE of 2019.

Achievement and the age of learners with disability

The fourth question posed by the analysis was on the effect of age on learning for students with disabilities. To answer this, KCPE and KCSE candidates were grouped into three categories—right age, over-age, and under-age, and analysis of their learning achievement was conducted for the four-year period. We begin with a short overview of the distribution of the candidates and their ages.

Trends in age

In 2019, 76 percent of the candidates with disability who sat for KCPE were over-age (16 years old or above), while 24 percent were of the right age (13–15 years old). The under-age candidates (12 and below) constituted less than 1 percent of the population. Though the proportion of over-age candidates reduced over the four years (from 80 percent in 2016), the challenge persists. The analysis also reveals disturbing variation in the proportions of over-age candidates across the disability categories, ranging from 88 percent for blind candidates, 87 percent for the deaf, 75 percent among those with physical disabilities, and 67 percent among the candidates with low vision. Figure 1 summarizes these results (see Figure 1).

At the secondary-school level, the proportion of candidates of the right age (17–20 years old) was higher than that of over-age candidates (21+ years old), across all four years. There were no under-age candidates (16 and under) recorded. Notably, the definition of the "right age" for the secondary level for students with disabilities has a somewhat generous bracket (17–20) compared to that of students without disabilities

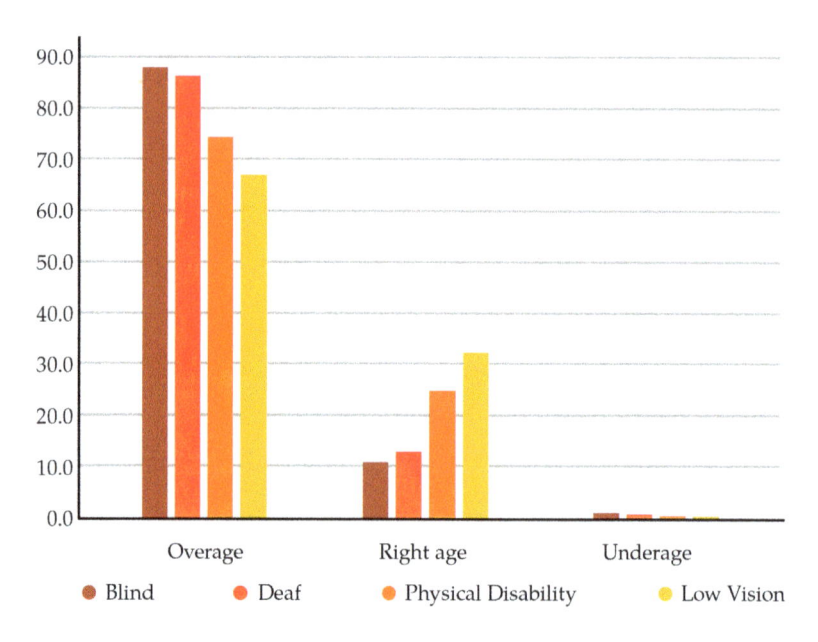

Fig. 1. Proportions of over-age, right-age, and under-age learners (KCPE 2016–2019).

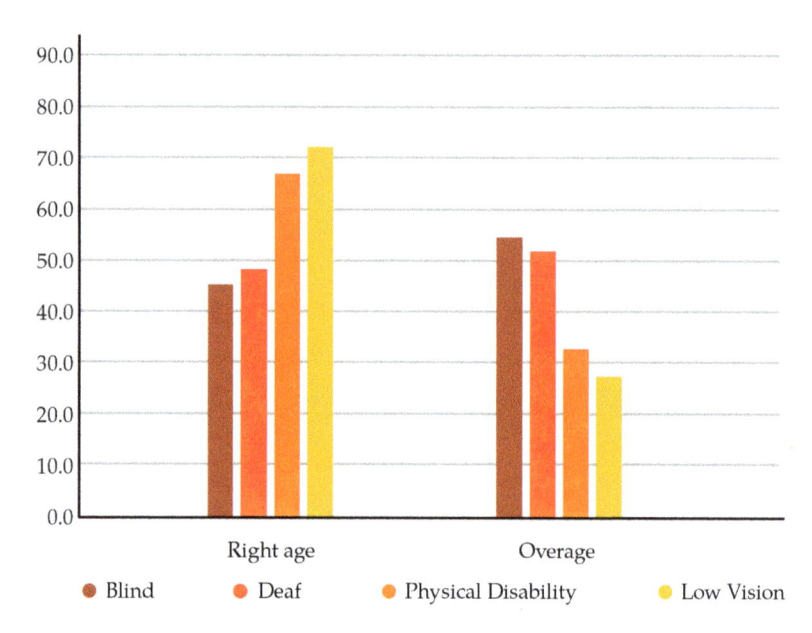

Fig. 2. Proportions of over-age, right-age, and under-age learners (KCSE 2016–2019).

(14–17), pegged at three years above. The same applies to the definitions of over-age—19 years and above for students without disabilities and 21 years and above for students with disabilities.

Comparison of age and disability across the years reveals a story consistent with that of primary school. The highest proportions of over-age candidates are found among blind (55 percent) and deaf (52 percent) candidates, while this is significantly lower among learners with physical disabilities (33 percent) and those with low vision (27 percent) (see Figure 2).

Learning achievement among right-age, over-age, and under-age students

This analysis confirms that age is a good determinant for the examination performance of students with disabilities at both the primary- and secondary-school levels. Results are presented in Tables 7 and 8.

Table 7. Performance scores of right-age, over-age, and under-age candidates (2016–2019) at primary level (KCPE).

Age	Total candidates	%	Mean
16+	6879	77.7	198.4
13–15	1972	22.2	229.7
12 and below	5	0.1	244.5

Table 8. Performance scores of right-age and over-age candidates (2016–2019) at secondary level (KCSE).

Age	Total candidates	%	Mean
21+	2232	38.7	2.81
17–20	3491	60.6	3.65
16 and below	41	0.7	3.16

At the primary level, candidates who are under-age (12 years old and below) outperform their right-age and over-age peers by 14.6 and 46.1 points respectively. The widest gaps in learning attainment between right-age and over-age candidates was among those with physical disabilities (11 percent on every subject) and low vision (10 percent), with narrower gaps among the blind candidates (3 percent). The effect of age was lowest among the deaf students, accounting for an average of only 1 percent on every subject between right-age and over-age candidates.

At the secondary level, the candidates of the right age (17–20 years old) performed better than their over-age peers (21 years old and above) by 0.84 mean points, or an average of 7 percent on every subject, and by 0.49 mean points for their under-age counterparts (16 years old and below). Consistent with the primary level, the effect of age on achievement was lowest among deaf candidates, where on average, right-age candidates outperformed their over-age peers by only 1 percent on every subject. The gap in performance in every subject (average) was widest among the candidates with visual impairments (10 percent blind and 9 percent low vision), followed by those with physical disabilities at 7 percent.

An analysis revealed isolated statistical significance among the KCPE examination results of 2018 and 2016 for the deaf students, and only in 2017 for the blind students. All other results were not significant. However, the results of the secondary-school candidates revealed significance for the deaf candidates, but not for the other disability categories (save for KCSE 2017 for the low-vision category).

Combining all

A multi-level regression analysis was undertaken to establish if there was any cross-variable relationship across the learners' disability, age, and gender for both primary and secondary exit examinations. The results are presented in Tables 9 and 10.

Table 9. Regression analysis of performance for learners with disabilities in primary (KCPE) examinations.

Variable	Coef.	Std. err.	T	P:t	[95% conf. interval]	
Age group (13–15)						
12 and below	13.6255	23.11	0.125	0.046	-66.24	38.46
16 and above	-31.396	23.11	0.332	0.145	-94.51	1.456

Variable	Coef.	Std. err.	T	P.t	[95% conf. interval]	
ii) Gender (male)						
Female	-4.28	4.73	-0.91	0.37	-13.99	5.42
iii) Disability type (LV)						
Blind	-22.57	6.69	-3.37	0	-36.29	-8.85
Deaf	-68.79	6.69	-10.29	0	-82.51	-55.07
Physical	-26.79	6.69	-4.01	0	-40.51	-13.07
Constant	236.04	4.79	43.62	0	224.5	251.2

The regression analysis further affirms that, at primary level, under-age learners (12 and below) are likely to perform better than right-age learners (aged 13–15) by 13.3 points. This was found to be significant at a p-value of 0.046. Though boys were likely to perform better than girls in KCPE examinations by 4.28 points, the result had no statistical significance.

Table 10. Regression analysis of performance for candidates with disabilities in secondary examinations (KCSE).

Variable	Coef.	Std. err.	T	P.t	[95% conf. interval]	
i) Age group (17–20)						
16 and below	-0.46	0.31	-1.23	0.056	-0.89	0.36
21 and above	0.12	0.32	1.2	0.146	0.061	0.097
ii) Gender (male)						
Female	-0.31	0.11	-2.87	0.01	-0.53	-0.09
iii) Disability type (LV)						
Blind	0.29	0.15	1.9	0.07	-0.02	0.6
Deaf	-1.54	0.15	-10.16	0	-1.85	-1.23
Physical	-0.38	0.15	-2.53	0.02	-0.69	-0.07
Constant	3.85	0.12	32.11	0	3.6	4.09

The candidates of the right age (17–20) are likely to score 0.46 more points than those 16 years old and below in KCSE examinations; however, this finding was not significant.

Discussion

Examination modifications and accommodations

Research on modifications and accommodations for students with disabilities has largely been based on students in the US. For example, a study by Zurcher and Bryant (2001) established that, when American college students with learning disabilities were provided with examination accommodations, their scores as a group were similar to those of examinees without learning disabilities taking the test under standard administration conditions, confirming that modifications are useful in equalizing examination opportunities. Further, Zuriff (2010) found that only students with learning disabilities benefit from extra examination time. He also questioned the validity of test scores under time extension, because students with non-learning disabilities already faced such other limitations. Similarly, Mandinach et al. (2005) determined that, while some extra time improves SAT examination performance for both students with and without disabilities, too much time may be detrimental.

In the present study in Kenya, students with disabilities performed well below their counterparts without disabilities, even though a time extension was provided. Though examination accommodations are useful to support students with disabilities generally, they may be insufficient for Kenyan students, for reasons we do not fully understand.

Disability, age, and learning

There seems to be scientific consensus in the evidence that learners of the right age perform better than over-age learners. Our results also indicate that the majority (76 percent) of candidates are over-age. A closer look at this points to either delayed school entry and/or delayed functional assessment and identification of the disabilities that yield to grade repetition. While little documentation is available on disability and grade repetition, Moyi (2017) found that many obstacles stand in the way for learners with disabilities in Kenya, and that most learners face delays in enrollment, grade progression, and course completion. Confirming this, one key informant argued that Kenya's educational opportunities for learners with disabilities are still relegated to special, segregated schools, most of which are boarding schools. Parents are often uncomfortable sending their little children to far-away institutions, and often delay enrollment until ages 8–10.

While inclusive education may be the solution to this problem in Kenya, it could realistically take time before this could be achieved, given the conditions, capacities, and low learning outcomes in the regular schools. However, regular neighborhood schools might be able to accommodate children with disabilities in early grades, so that later on, children would transition to the special schools. At this time, they would be old enough to move away from home. To complete this curve, the special schools would also need to invent accelerated learning opportunities for such learners, so that they attain maximal age-grade-learning levels within a reasonable timeframe.

Disability type and learning

The study showed major achievement variations across the various disability types. Uniquely, students who were deaf performed much more poorly than their counterparts who were blind, or had low vision or physical disabilities. Close examination of this finding leads to a language-barrier discussion. One expert interviewed in our study argued that deaf students have equal learning potential to their hearing peers, but what makes a difference is language deprivation. Deaf learners in Kenya acquire language late, and when they do, they are proficient in Kenyan Sign Language, while subjects are typically examined in English.

Language deprivation among deaf children is a widely confirmed phenomenon (Mayberry & Squires, 2006; Olusanya & Newton, 2007), and occurs mainly in deaf children born to hearing parents (Cheng et al., 2019). While learning interventions should compensate for language deprivation, two other possibilities may also be feasible. The first is addressing early language acquisition through creating language-rich home environments, and the second is adapting the examinations into appropriate languages and formats. Recorded, signed responses over written responses might be one such adaptation.

Conclusion

Our study has confirmed that students with disabilities face myriad exclusions in the high-stakes examinations in Kenya. While no significant gender differences were found, the effect of age and disability type on performance is high, pointing to the need for targeted interventions. There is also the need to re-examine the accommodations that the Kenya National Examinations Council has put in place for examinations, to ensure that they are better adapted to disability types and severity, and go beyond the simple time extension. It is important to note, however, that more focus is being given to learners with special needs and disabilities in the ongoing education reforms in Kenya, including the incoming Competency-Based Curriculum and Assessment (CBC and CBA). Clearly, we need greater investment and support for the specific needs of students with disabilities in Kenya, as a key part of improving learning at the bottom of the pyramid.

References

Cheng, Q., Roth, A., Halgren, E., & Mayberry, R. I. (2019). Effects of early language deprivation on brain connectivity: Language pathways in deaf native and late first-language learners of American Sign Language. *Frontiers in Human Neuroscience, 13*. https://doi.org/10.3389/fnhum.2019.00320

Kenya. (2003). *Persons with Disabilities Act, No. 14, 2003*. Nairobi: Government Printers.

Kenya. (1964). *Kenya Education Commission report*. Nairobi: Government Printers.

Klingner, J. K., Vaughn, S., Schumm, J. S., Cohen, P., & Forgan, J. W. (1998). Inclusion or pull-out: Which do students prefer? *Journal of Learning Disabilities, 31*(2).

Mayberry, R. I., & Squires, B. (2006). Sign language acquisition. In K. Brown (Ed.), *Encyclopedia of language and linguistics* (pp. 291–296). Amsterdam: Elsevier.

Mandinach, E. B., Bridgeman, B., Cahalan-Laitusis, C., & Trapani, C. (2005). *The impact of extended time on SAT® test performance* (Report to College Board, New York, Research Report No. 2005–8). http://www.ets.org/Media/Research/pdf/RR-05-20.pdf

Ministry of Education. (2018). *Sector policy for learners and trainees with disabilities*. Nairobi: Kenya.

Mizunoya, S., Mitra, S., & Yamasaki, I. (2016). Towards inclusive education: The impact of disability on school attendance in developing countries. *SSRN Electronic Journal.* https://doi.org/10.2139/ssrn.2782430

Montoya, S. (2018). What is the bottom of the pyramid in the case of low-income countries? In D. A. Wagner et al. (Eds.), *Learning at the bottom of the pyramid: Science, measurement, and policy in low-income countries* (pp. 31–56). Paris: UNESCO-IIEP.

Moyi, P. (2017). School participation for children with disabilities in Kenya. *Research in Comparative and International Education, 12*(4).

National Gender and Equality Commission (NGEC). (2016). *Access to basic education by children with disability in Kenya* (Commission's Report).

Olusanya, B., & Newton, V. (2007). Global burden of childhood hearing impairment and disease control priorities for developing countries. *The Lancet, 369*, 1314–1317.

Pitionak, M. J., & Royer, J. M. (2001). Testing accommodations for students with disabilities: A review of psychometric, legal, and social policy issues. *Review of Educational Research, 71*(1).

UN. (2006). *Convention on the Rights of Persons with Disabilities (CRPD).*

WHO. (2011). *World Report on Disability.*

World Bank. (2019). *Every learner matters: Unpacking the learning crisis for children with disabilities.* https://www.leonardcheshire.org/sites/default/files/2019-10/Every-Learner-Matters.pdf#page=56&zoom=auto,87,434

Zurcher, R., & Brant, D. P. (2001). The validity and comparability of entrance examination scores after accommodations are made for students with LD. *Journal of Learning Disabilities, 34*(5). http://citeseerx.ist.psu.edu/viewdoc/download?doi=10.1.1.819.4498&rep=rep1&type=pdf

Zuriff, G. E. (2010). Extra examination time for students with learning disabilities: An examination of the maximum potential thesis. *Applied Measurement in Education, 13*(1), 99–117. https://doi.org/10.1207/s15324818ame1301_5

17. Kenya

Education in Marginalized Communities

Joyce Kinyanjui

Introduction

The Kenyan Constitution (Articles 53, 54, 55, 56, 57, and 59) states that all children have a right to free and compulsory basic education, including children with disabilities. Despite these constitutional provisions, education marginalization in Kenya persists. UNESCO (2010) defines education marginalization as a form of acute and persistent disadvantage rooted in underlying social inequalities. In order to know where education marginalization is most likely to occur, one needs to first identify marginalized communities in Kenya.

Under Article 260, the Constitution states that a "marginalized community" is: (a) A community that, because of its relatively small population or for any other reason, has been unable to fully participate in the integrated social and economic life of Kenya as a whole; (b) A traditional community that, out of a need or desire to preserve its unique culture and identity from assimilation, has remained outside the integrated social and economic life of Kenya as a whole; (c) An indigenous community that has retained and maintained a traditional lifestyle and livelihood based on a hunter or gatherer economy; or (d) Pastoral persons and communities, whether they are—(i) Nomadic; or (ii) A settled community that, because of its relative geographic isolation, has experienced only marginal participation in the integrated social and economic life of Kenya as a whole.

The entirety of Northern Kenya—including upper parts of the eastern region (Moyale, Marsabit, Isiolo), northern and southern parts of the Rift Valley region (Turkana, West Pokot, Samburu, Kajiado, Narok, Transmara), and the northern part of the coastal region (Tana-River)—is occupied by nomadic pastoralists. Fishing nomads are found in parts of Homabay County (around Lake Victoria) and northern parts of the Rift Valley region (around Lake Turkana and Lake Baringo). Hunters and gatherers are mostly found in northern parts of the coastal region (Lamu district) and parts of the Rift Valley region (Marakwet, Baringo, and Narok districts) (MoEST, 2014). The government recognizes the fact that the educational needs of nomadic communities are generally complex and underserved. It is therefore not surprising that 11 counties—West Pokot, Turkana, Garissa, Isiolo, Kwale, Narok, Marsabit, Mandera, Tana River, Samburu, and Wajir—account for 733,765 (57 percent) of 1,292,675 out-of-school children in the country.

This chapter analyzes the social, cultural, political, and economic factors driving educational marginalization in the above 11 counties in Kenya. The paper also proposes how the government can ensure the right to quality basic education for children from marginalized communities. Gross Enrollment Rate (GER) will mainly be used to capture the percentage of pupils accessing education. Various recommendations are made in the conclusion that derive from the present findings.

Methodology

The main purpose of this chapter is to identify children and communities who are experiencing education marginalization in Kenya. The researcher used secondary data that were collected through a desk-review of government documents and policies, particularly the Ministry of Education and other line ministries both at national and subnational levels, the National Gender and Equality Commission, and the National Council for Nomadic Education in Kenya. In addition to official government documents, official international documents—especially from UNICEF and UNESCO—were reviewed.

To generate a comprehensive review on education marginalization in Kenya, the researcher utilized a systematic approach with two key steps, namely:

1. Identification of potential documents for review. These were identified through discussions with colleagues and online

searches using Google Scholar. Snowballing of bibliographies as a way to search for relevant literature was successfully applied to identify additional documents. Government data from the Kenya National Bureau of Statistics and the Ministries of Education and Health were used extensively.

2. Examination of relevance and credibility of the data and documents. This was done by verifying data through multiple sources and the materials referenced.

Once documents were selected, quantitative data were collated, summarized, aggregated, and organized into tables. Qualitative data were synthesized and formed part of the report. Additional grey literature, especially from newspapers and local studies by UNICEF, was also reviewed. One disadvantage of using this methodology is the fact that, in many cases, government data are a couple of years behind, and therefore somewhat outdated.

Education marginalization in Kenya

Access

Since Kenya introduced free primary schooling in 2003, and free secondary education in 2008, the education sector continues to expand at all levels. With regards to primary education, the introduction of Free Primary Education (FPE) in 2003 enabled 1.3 million poor children to benefit from primary education for the first time through the abolishment of fees and levies for tuition (MoEST, 2014; see also Manyasa & Karogo, this volume). The Gross Enrollment Rate in primary education jumped from 86.8 percent in 2002 to 104 percent in 2018, while the GER for secondary schools increased from 35.7 percent in 2008 to 70.3 percent in 2018. The net enrollment rates are the highest ever—77.2 percent for Early Childhood Development and Care (ECDE), 92.4 percent for primary schools, and 53.2 percent for secondary schools. The Pupil Completion Rate (PCR) was 84.2 percent in 2017, and there was a Primary-to-Secondary Transition Rate (PSTR) of 83.3 percent (KNBS, 2019). Despite this expansion, education marginalization continues.

In order to understand education marginalization, one needs to analyze education data. In 2014, a total of 1,292,675 (580,921 boys and

711,754 girls) children aged 6–13 years were not enrolled, either because they never attended school or dropped out (MoEST, 2014). This number was the ninth highest of any country in the world (UNESCO, 2015). The following 11 out of 47 counties accounted for almost 57 percent of all out-of-school children in the country: West Pokot, Turkana, Garissa, Isiolo, Kwale, Narok, Marsabit, Mandera, Tana River, Samburu, and Wajir (MoEST, 2014). Education access and retention have since increased in these 11 counties, but they remain at the bottom of the pyramid with regards to education attainment.

The 2019 national census established that there are 17,834,572 school-aged children in Kenya (KNBS, 2019). In 2018, more than 850,000 children aged between 6 and 17 years were out of school, with Mandera accounting for 15 percent (12,000) of all children out of school. Turkana accounts for 10 percent, Garissa 8.9 percent, and Wajir 6.7 percent, indicating that these counties are truly at the bottom of the pyramid (Mghenyi, 2018). The most comprehensive and accurate data on education in Kenya is found in the Basic Education Statistical Booklet of 2014 (MoEST, 2014)[1].

The national Early Childhood Development and Education (ECDE) centers' Gross Enrollment Rate (GER) stood at 73.6 percent in 2014. Compared to the national averages, only Garissa (69.4 percent), Marsabit (51.5 percent), Wajir (25.6 percent), and Mandera (20.70 percent) have GER lower than the national average of 73.6 percent (MoEST, 2014). The reason for high ECDE GERs is that, in most centers, children attending ECDE receive free meals.

At the primary level, the numbers begin to decrease. Figure 1, below, presents the Primary Enrollment Rates per county. Only West Pokot (109.4 percent) and Kwale (107.5 percent) had a higher primary GER than the national average of 103.5 percent (MoEST, 2014). The bottom six counties with regards to primary enrollment were Turkana (77.40 percent), Tana River (77.20 percent), Samburu (73.70 percent), Garissa (71.40 percent), Wajir (35.20 percent), and lastly Mandera (29.20 percent).

The secondary GER decreases further when one compares it to the national average. Figure 2 below shows the Secondary Enrollment Rate for counties in Kenya.

---

[1] This paper has referred extensively to the BESB 2014 booklet, as the information contained in it is regarded as official government data.

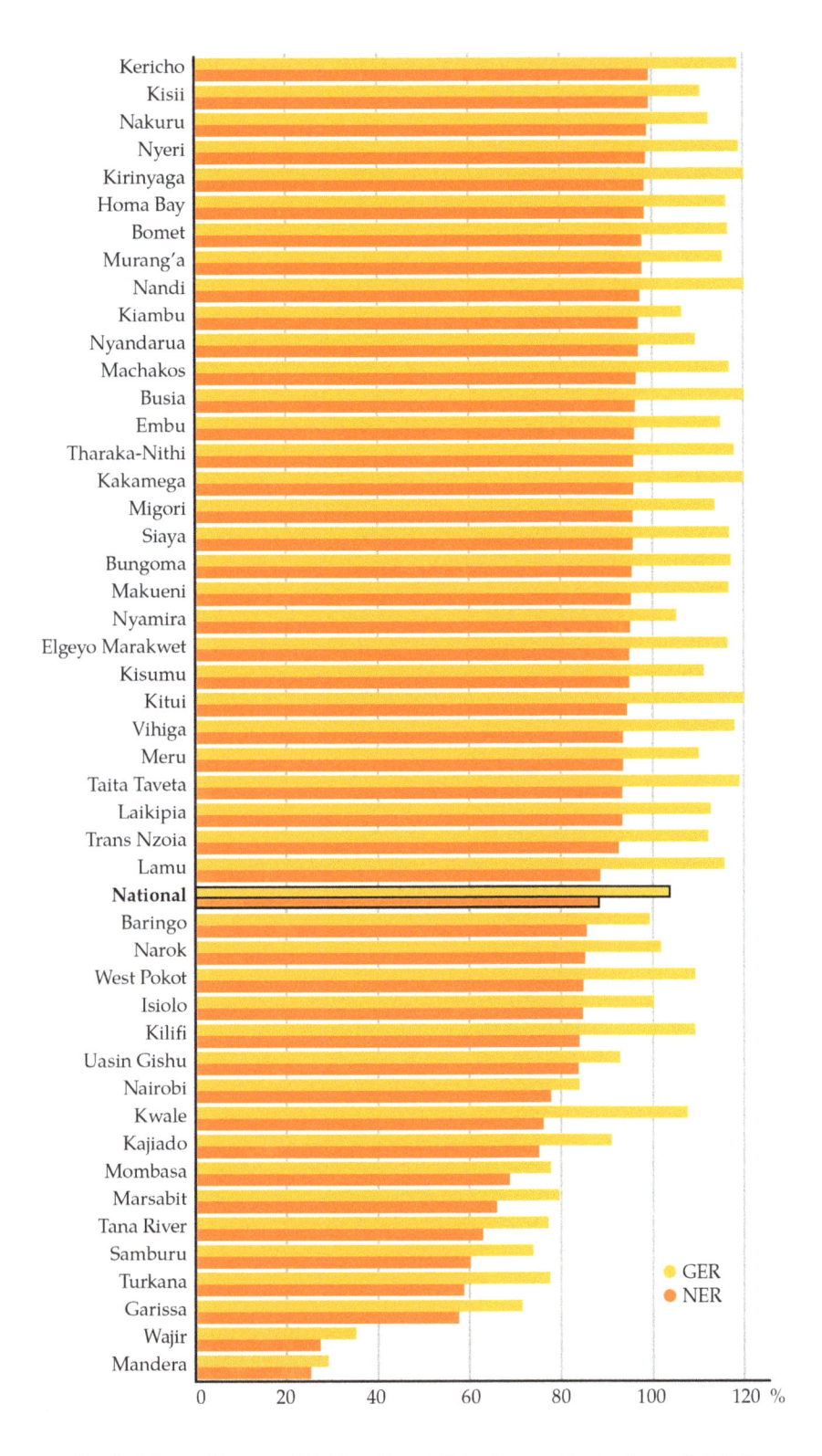

Fig. 1. Primary Gross and Net Enrollment Rates for counties in Kenya (MoEST, 2014). Source: the author.

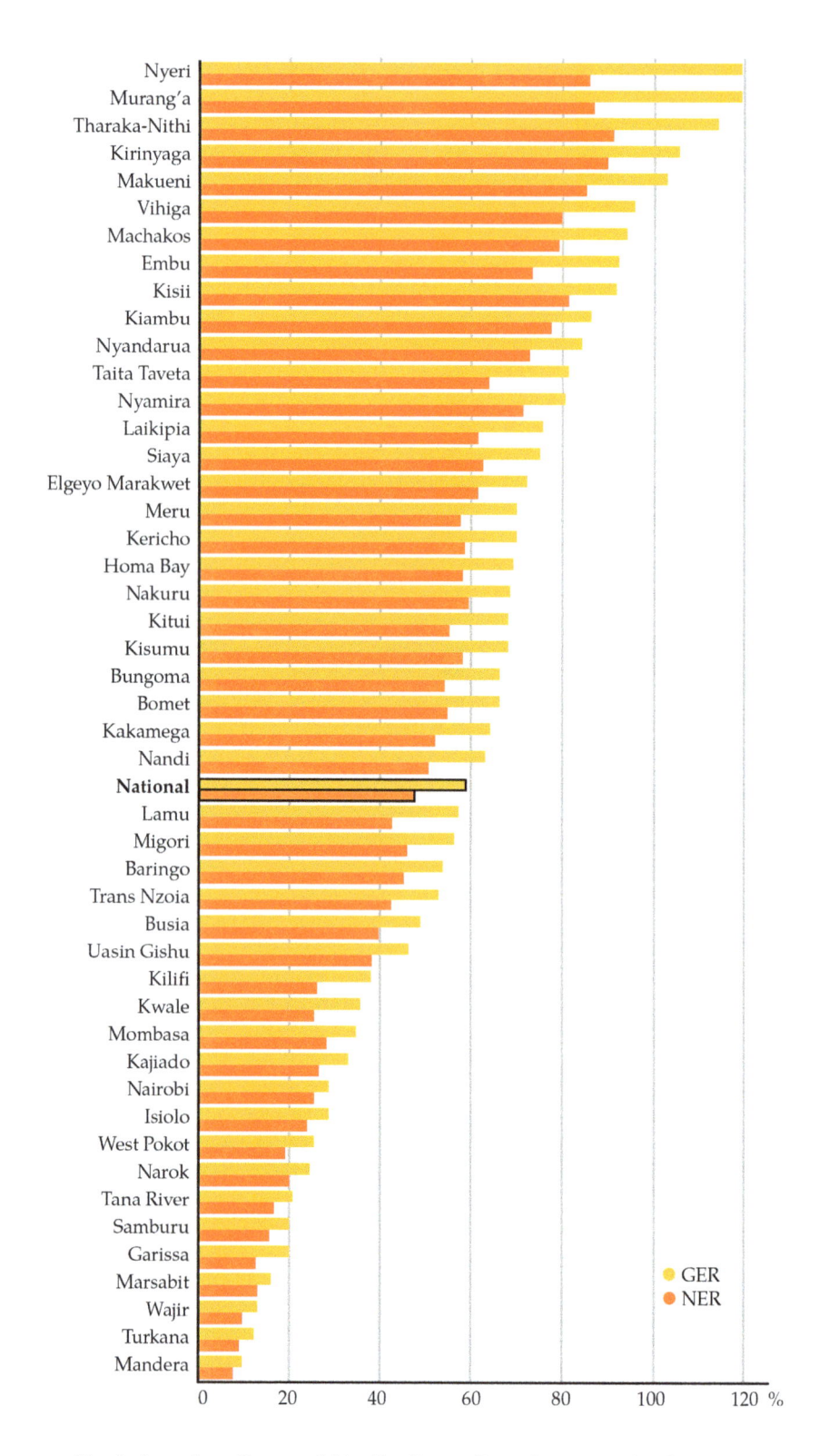

Fig. 2. Secondary Gross and Net Enrollment Rates for marginalized counties (MoEST, 2014). Source: the author.

At the secondary level, 10 out of the 11 counties under study had the worst secondary GER in the country. Mandera had the lowest secondary Gross Enrollment Rate of 9.40 percent, followed by Turkana at 12.10 percent. The national GER was 58.7 percent. Secondary enrollment in these counties is low when one compares the rates to those of counties like Nyeri with a GER of 132 percent, Muranga with a GER of 128 percent, and Tharaka Nithi with a GER of 114 percent.

Retention

Enrollment, however, does not tell the whole story. Equally important is retention. This is true for marginalized counties whose ECDE GER was higher than the national average of 73.6 percent. Such counties include West Pokot (98.9 percent), Turkana (97.6 percent), Isiolo (107.7 percent), Kwale (83.7 percent), and Samburu (113.0 percent), where the Gross Enrollment Rate at ECDE level was higher than the national average of 73.6 percent. West Pokot had a primary GER of 100.4 percent, which was higher than the national average of 103.5 percent. However, several counties had high access rates, but low retention levels. In 2014, the national retention rate was 88.2 percent. Turkana had the lowest retention rate at primary level (31.4 percent), followed by Garissa at 40.2 percent, and Narok at 61.4 percent. Out of the 11 marginalized counties, Kwale had the highest retention rate at 77.2 percent (MoEST, 2014).

With regards to primary education, the Mandera, Wajir, Marsabit, Samburu, and Tana River counties, in that order, have the worst education indicators with regards to access and retention. Mandera has a primary access rate of 39.3 percent and a retention rate of 13.6 percent, making it the most marginalized county with regards to education (MoEST, 2014).

Factors contributing to education marginalization

Marginalization in education is linked to factors such as poverty, politics, gender, ethnicity, disability, location, refugee status, and so on. This section looks at how some of these barriers are contributing to education marginalization in the 11 counties identified in the previous section.

Poverty

There is a high correlation between poverty and education marginalization. 36.1 percent of all Kenyans live below the poverty line (KNBS, 2018). All the counties that experience high rates of education marginalization have higher poverty rates than the national averages except for Narok,[2] which has a poverty rate of 22.6 percent. The following (Figure 3) presents the poverty levels and GER of marginalized counties in Kenya.

Turkana County has the highest poverty incidence in Kenya, with 79.4 percent of the residents living below the poverty line. The Mandera and Samburu counties are second and third at 77.6 percent and 75.8 percent respectively.

With regards to extreme poverty,[3] 8.6 percent—or 3.9 million people—lived in conditions of abject poverty and were unable to afford the minimum required food-consumption basket (KNBS, 2018). The incidence of extreme poverty at the county level ranges from a low of 0.2 percent in Nyeri to a high of 52.7 percent in Turkana. Likewise, the Samburu (42.2 percent), Mandera (38.9 percent), Busia (26.8 percent), West Pokot (26.3 percent), and Marsabit (23.8 percent) counties recorded a higher extreme poverty incidence. More than one-third (37.5 percent) of the total population living in conditions of extreme poverty reside in these six counties. Turkana County recorded the highest incidence of 66.1 percent (KNBS, 2018).

Poverty contributes to education marginalization in many ways. Children from poor homes in these 11 counties are unlikely to be enrolled in school due to the costs associated with schooling. Education at primary and secondary levels is free in Kenya, but there are still associated costs, such as school uniforms. Perhaps the greatest cost parents incur are levies in the form of examination fees, contributions to the salaries of teachers employed by Boards of Management, and building and other

---

2   Narok County is host to the Massai Mara, the eighth wonder of the world. This has led to increased direct and indirect employment, enhanced standard of living, more investments, infrastructural development, and new business linkages and opportunities. However, for the indigenous Masaai living in rural Narok, these benefits are not always in reach, hence contributing to education marginalization.
3   Households and individuals whose monthly adult equivalent total food and non-food consumption expenditure per person is less than KES 1,954 in rural and peri-urban areas, and less than KES 2,551 in core-urban areas (KNBS, 2018).

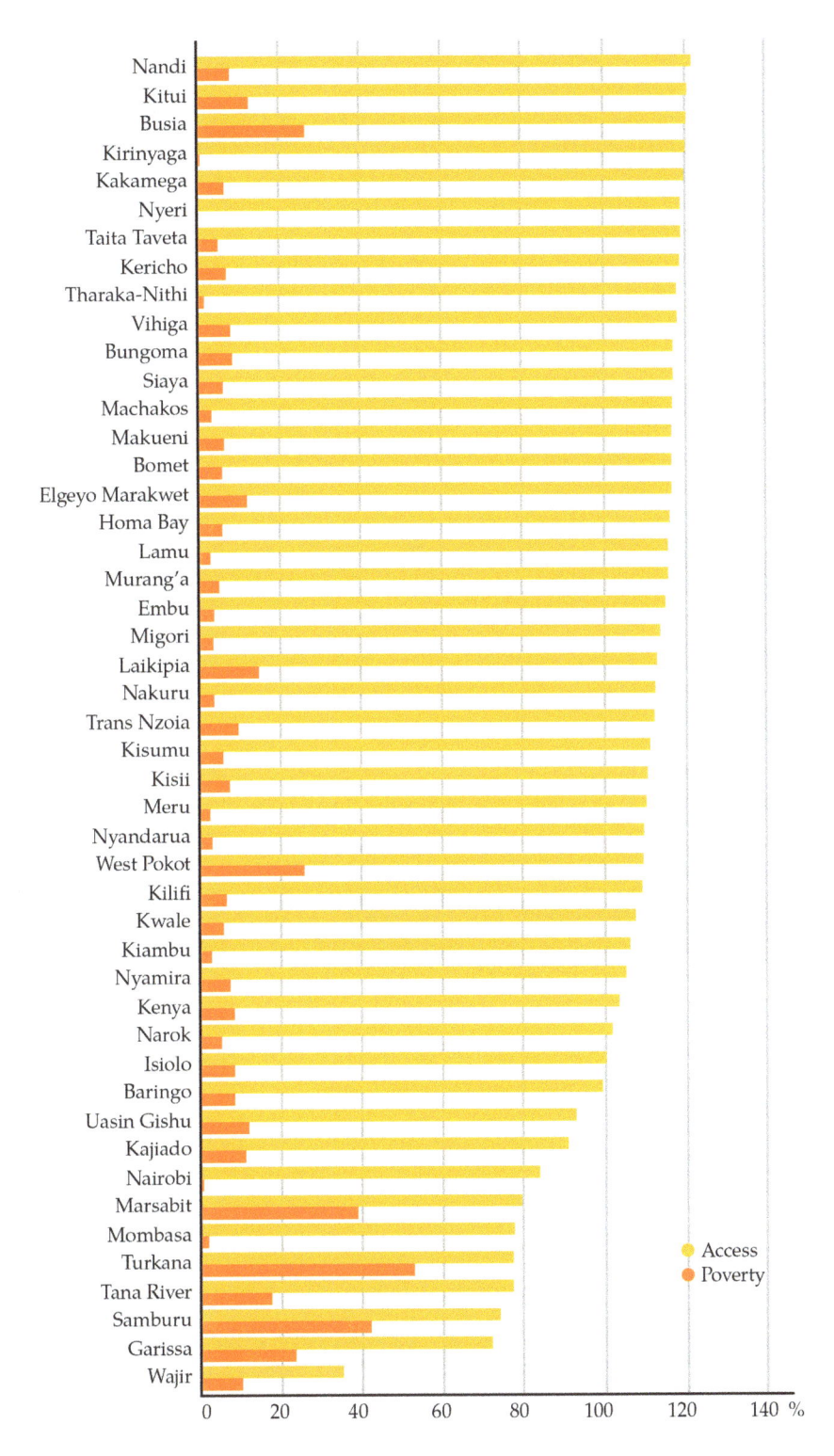

Fig. 3. GER and poverty levels in education marginalized counties (KNBS, 2015; 2018).

levies that are agreed upon by schools. In addition, the majority of communities living in the 11 counties practice pastoralism. Pastoralism is labor-intensive and children are sometimes withdrawn from school to take care of the family animals. In some cases, the families migrate to very remote areas in search of water and pasture where there are no schools.

Sociocultural barriers

Education marginalization cannot be entirely attributed to poverty. Complex sociocultural challenges affect education opportunities, especially for girls. These challenges include: negative cultural practices like female genital mutilation (FGM); early and forced marriages; tasks associated with family care and housework; and early pregnancies. In addition, the socializing processes are designed and rigorously applied to instil a feeling of superiority in boys, while girls are groomed to accept subjugation and inferiority with apathy (KNBS, 2015). Girls grow up with feelings of being inferior and suffer from low self-esteem. These two outcomes contribute to girls dropping out of school. Parents also prefer to send their sons to school over their daughters. Subsequently, boys are more likely to complete primary education than girls.

In counties experiencing education marginalization, the number of boys completing primary-level education is more than that of girls. Figure 4 shows the primary-level completion rate in the marginalized counties.

In order to calculate the Gender Parity Index, absolute numbers were used. In Garissa, the Gender Parity Index (GPI) is 2.02, in Mandera, 2.0, while in Wajir it is 1.94, all in favor of boys. The national GPI primary completion rate is about 0.99.

Gender, teen pregnancy, and early marriages

In 2020, the government of Kenya launched a national campaign against teenage pregnancies, through the National Council for Population and Development (NCPD, 2020). The campaign is focused on galvanizing communities to end teen pregnancies through awareness and advocacy, citing their negative impact on socioeconomic growth.

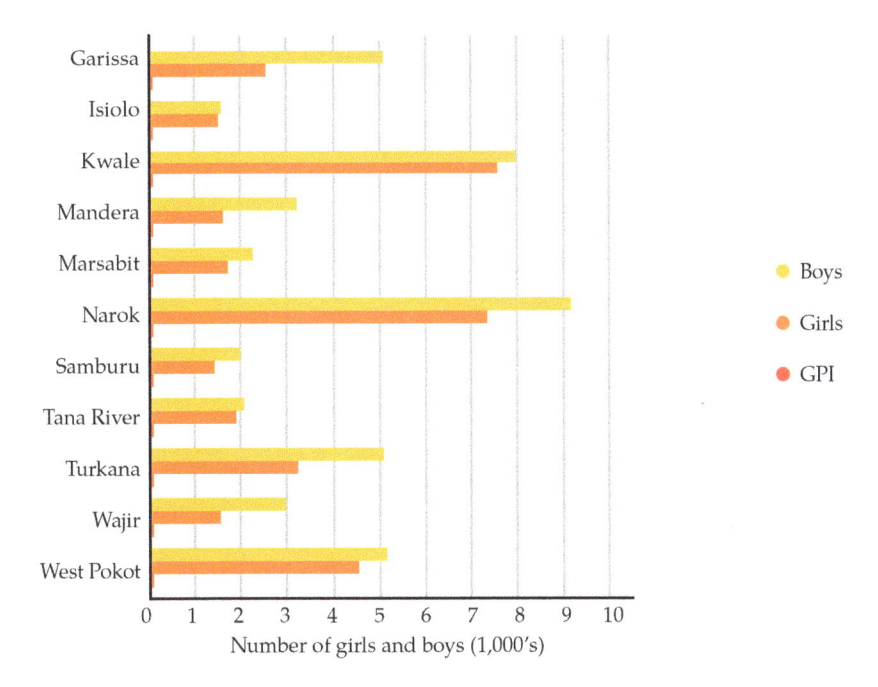

Fig. 4. Primary-level completion rate by gender.

Data from the Kenya Demographic and Health Survey (2014) show that one in every five girls between 15–19 years is either pregnant or already a mother. As a result, over 13,000 teenage girls drop out of school annually because of pregnancy (KNBS, 2015). As of 2019, based on the latest statistics from the Global Childhood Report (Save the Children, 2019), Kenya has a teen-pregnancy rate of 82 births per 1000.

Recent media reports show that 449 girls are failing to sit for their final examinations, while others complete examinations in maternity wards. This is a detriment to these girls' educations, health, and opportunities. The case of Narok County is especially profound, with 40 percent of teenagers being pregnant, compared to Garissa, Wajir, and Lamu at 10 percent (Mghenyi, 2018).

The 11 counties are all characterized by high fertility rates. Wajir and Garissa are the two counties with the highest Total Fertility Rates[4] in Kenya, at 7.8 and 7.2 respectively, against a national average of 3.9. Their GERs are 35.2 percent and 109.2 percent. Kirinyaga has the lowest

---

4   Fertility rate is defined in this paper as the average number of children born to women during their reproductive years.

Total Fertility Rate, at 2.3, and subsequently has the highest GER of 120.2 percent. High fertility rates contribute to increased poverty, as this strains the budgets of poor families. Other effects of high fertility rates include high infant mortality, malnourished children, and lack of education for children, especially girls, which in turn leads to intergenerational transmission of poverty.

Fertility rates decrease as women's education and wealth increase. Table 1 below shows that the total fertility rate decreases from 6.5 among women with no education to 4.8 among women with some education, and further to 3.0 among women with a secondary or higher education. Fertility is also closely associated with wealth, with women in the lowest quintile (6.4) having more children than those in the highest quintile (2.8) (KNBS, 2015). Wajir, Mandera, and Garissa are located in the northeastern part of the country. This region has the highest total fertility rate, at 6.4.

Table 1. Correlation between poverty and total fertility rate.

Background characteristic	Total fertility rate
Urban	3.1
Rural	4.5
Region	
Coast	4.3
Northeastern	6.4
Eastern	3.4
Central	2.8
Rift Valley	4.5
Western	4.7
Nyanza	4.3
Nairobi	2.7
Education	
No education	6.5
Primary incomplete	4.8
Primary complete	4.2
Secondary+	3
Wealth quintile	
Lowest	6.4

Background characteristic	Total fertility rate
Second	4.7
Middle	3.8
Fourth	3.1
Highest	2.8
Total	3.9

In Narok, 33 percent of women aged 15–19 years have had a live birth, while 7.4 percent are expecting their first child. West Pokot (22.8 percent), Tana River (20.4 percent), Samburu (19.7 percent), Isiolo (18 percent), and Turkana (17.6 percent) have higher percentages of girls aged 15–19 having a live birth, compared to the national average of 14.7 percent.

Sociocultural issues, such as female genital mutilation and early marriage, contribute to education marginalization. The government established the Anti-Female-Genital-Mutilation Board, a semi-autonomous government agency in December 2013, following the enactment of the Prohibition of Female Genital Mutilation Act 2011. It is within the Ministry of Public Service, Youth, and Gender Affairs. The fight against FGM has gained momentum recently, with the president promising to end the practice by 2022. Although the timeline may be unrealistic, religious and community leaders are joining the crusade against it.

HIV and AIDs

Kenya is one of the four HIV "high burden" countries in Africa—about 1.5 million people were living with a HIV infection at the end of 2015. Women in Kenya are more vulnerable to HIV infections than Kenyan men, with the national HIV prevalence at 7.0 percent for women and 4.7 percent for men, as per the 2015 HIV Estimate report (Kenya Ministry of Health, 2017). Young people aged 15–24 years constituted 51 percent of all new adult HIV infections in 2016 (Kenya Ministry of Health, 2016).

With regards to children below 14 years old living with HIV and AIDs, Turkana was ranked 21 out of 47 counties, with almost 2,000 children with HIV and AIDs. Narok was number 23, Kwale number

26, and Kilifi number 12 (KNBS, 2015). It is worth noting that the HIV and AIDs pandemic is affecting the entire country, and not just the 11 marginalized counties that are the focus of this chapter. The epidemic has also negatively affected the country's economy by lowering per-capita output by 4.1 percent. Kenya has an estimated 71,034 new HIV infections among adults and about 6,613 new infections among children annually.

Location, agriculture, and education of nomads

The Arid and Semi-Arid Lands (ASALs) of Kenya make up 89 percent of the country, encompassing 29 counties and a population of about 16 million people. The ASAL regions are characterized by low and irregular rainfall of less than 500mm per year, high temperatures of over 35° Celsius, and a sparse population whose main economic activity is pastoralism. The 11 counties under study are all located within the ASALs. For decades, these areas were marginalized and seen as unproductive due to persistent drought and famine. Investment in infrastructure was minimal as a result. Insecurity occasioned by cattle rustling and violent incidents due to terrorist attacks by Al-Shabaab have often led to humanitarian situations. Except for Marsabit and Isiolo, the other nine counties located in the northeastern part of Kenya borders with Somalia, Ethiopia, South Sudan, and Northern Uganda, which for many years have also suffered from insecurity.

Kenya is currently experiencing the worst locust invasion in 70 years. Currently, there are 17 counties invaded by locusts. So far, approximately 70,000 hectares of land have already been infested (FAO, 2020). Of the 11 counties under study, Mandera, Wajir, Marsabit, Garissa, Isiolo, Samburu, Turkana, Narok, and West Pokot have had such invasions. Only Tana River and Kwale have not had invasions, but it is predicted that by June 2020, 75 percent of the country will be covered by locusts. In conjunction with the fragile economy and the outbreak of COVID-19, this will lead to major loss of livelihoods. It is expected that many more children may not access education due to increased poverty.

Providing quality education to nomadic communities will enhance their socioeconomic growth. With this in mind, the government has established the National Council for Nomadic Education in Kenya

(NACONEK) whose mandate is to steer and coordinate efforts towards quality education for all in nomadic communities. Among the issues the Council is addressing are poor school infrastructure, shortage of teachers, low-quality education, and low access to primary and secondary education.

The mobility of nomadic communities, the hardships associated with the ASALs, and the few teachers with a nomadic background make recruitment, deployment, and retention of teachers difficult. Since the current teacher management policies, including delocalization,[5] have not adequately addressed staffing problems, there is a need to review the whole spectrum of teacher training, recruitment, and deployment.

Refugee education crisis

As of March 2020, there were 494,585 refugees and asylum seekers in Kenya, 51 percent male and 49 percent female. Of these, 53.6 percent are children aged 0–17 years, 43.7 percent are aged between 18–59, and only 2.7 percent are aged beyond 60. The refugee-hosting communities of Kakuma, Kalobeyei, and Dadaab are located in some of the most marginalized and food insecure counties in Kenya. Out of the total refugees and asylum seekers, 84 percent of the refugees and asylum seekers live in rural camps, while 16 percent live in urban areas, mainly Nairobi.

Among the refugee population in Kenya, over half are children of school age (4–18 years) (UNHCR, 2020). The majority of refugee children are enrolled in pre-primary, primary, secondary, and tertiary institutions located in Dadaab and Kakuma refugee camps and the Kalobeyei settlement established in 2016. Despite significant gains in enrollment at all levels, almost half of school-age children and refugees are still out of school. The gap in enrollment widens with progression through the levels. Only 30 percent of eligible refugees have access to secondary education. In Kenya, 16% have access to technical and vocational education and training, and only 1% of qualified learners acquire places to study in public and private universities across Kenya and abroad each year (UNHCR, 2020).

---

5   The delocalization policy was introduced by the Teachers Service Commission (TSC) to make teachers work outside their home counties.

According to UNICEF (2018), reasons for low education attainment among refugees include extreme poverty, overcrowded classrooms, inadequate numbers of schools, long distances to schools, poor-quality education, drug abuse, lack of role models—especially for girls—and lack of interest in education due to feelings of hopelessness, occasioned by the fact that there are very few opportunities for meaningful employment.

The refugee scenario is very similar to that of other marginalized communities, as they have large numbers of out-of-school children. However, in Kakuma, refugee children have better education levels than the children from Turkana host communities, when one considers mean years of schooling.[6] Congolese refugees have 8.2 mean years of schooling, South Sudanese refugees have 6.6 years, and Somalis have 5.7 years, compared to 2.7 years for the Turkana. In Garissa, Somali refugees have lower education levels, with an average of 8 years of schooling, compared to Kenyan Somalis with an average of 10.1 years of schooling. Kenyan Somalis have better education levels than Somali refugees because they are able to travel to Nairobi where there are more education opportunities (Betts, Omata, & Sterck, 2018).

The education sector in Dadaab refugee camps consists of preschools, primary schools, secondary schools, adult literacy centers, special education schools, accelerated learning centers, vocational training providers, and scholarships for tertiary education. One of the important tertiary education projects is the Borderless Higher Education for Refugees (BHER) project, a multi-partner initiative that delivers university education to refugee and local community populations in Dadaab, Kenya. The project is run by a consortium of four universities (York University, University of British Columbia, Kenyatta University, and Moi University) and is implemented by Windle International Kenya. The BHER project aims to enhance the life chances of vulnerable refugee and local communities, and build educational and teaching capacity *in situ*. Its ultimate goal is to afford refugees a greater likelihood of successful and productive repatriation to their home country when possible, and raise the quality of education in host/home countries so

---

6   Mean years of schooling: this is the number of completed years of formal education at primary level or higher, not counting years spent repeating individual grades.

as to build more peaceful, equitable, and socially inclusive societies (UNICEF, 2019).

Perhaps the greatest challenge is the inadequate number of learning institutions. For example, within the Dadaab refugee camp, there are only 22 ECDE Centers, 34 primary schools, 12 secondary schools, and 9 education institutions offering Alternative Basic Education (ABE). With regards to Technical Vocational Education and Training (TVETs), there are 15 registered TVETs in Garissa County, 13 of which are private and two of which are public (UNICEF, 2019). At the Turkana refugee camp, there are 21 primary schools, with 12 schools having an Accelerated Learning Programme (ALP), and five secondary schools and three education institutions offering ABE. At the Kalobeyei settlement, there are five primary schools, two secondary schools and one education institution offering ABE. With regards to TVETs, there are 11 TVET institutions, four of which are private and seven of which are public.

The Kenyan Constitution (2010) and the Basic Education Act (2013) stipulate that access to education is the right of every child in Kenya, including non-citizens. In October 2017, Kenya recognized the need for greater responsibility-sharing to protect and assist refugees and support host states by adopting the Comprehensive National Education Sector Plan 2019: Refugee Response Framework (CRRF)[7], and in December 2017, signing the Djibouti Declaration.[8] Education, training, and skill development for all refugees and host communities is an important component of the CRRF approach, which places emphasis on the inclusion of displaced populations in national systems. When refugees gain access to education and labor markets, they can build their skills and become self-reliant, contributing to local economies. The Djibouti Declaration also commits IGAD member states and development

---

7 On September 19th 2016, the United Nations General Assembly adopted a set of commitments to improve the manner in which we respond to large movements of refugees and migrants. These commitments, endorsed by 193 member states, are known as the New York Declaration on Refugees and Migrants. The New York Declaration calls upon UNHCR to develop and initiate the application of the Comprehensive Refugee Response Framework (CRRF). The objectives are to: ease pressure on host countries; enhance refugee self-reliance; expand access to third-country solutions, and support conditions in countries of origin for safe and dignified return.

8 Details about the Djibouti declaration can be found at: https://igad.int/attachments/article/1725/Djibouti%20Declaration%20on%20Refugee%20Education.pdf.

partners to take collective responsibility to ensure that every refugee, returnee, and member of host communities has access to quality education in a safe learning environment, without discrimination.

In November 2017, President Uhuru Kenyatta rejected a bill that gave refugees living in camps the right to work and use land for business and farming. Without freedom of movement, refugees will remain unable to access education, especially tertiary education, economic opportunities, or employment.

COVID-19 pandemic

The first case of COVID-19 in Kenya was confirmed on March 13th 2020. One of the first measures taken was the presidential directive to shut down all learning institutions from March 15th 2020, which affected all schools, colleges, and universities, or about 17.5 million learners.

The government introduced online learning for students in ECDE, primary, and secondary schools. However, very few learners are accessing these digital materials. A recent study by Usawa Agenda (2020) and Uwezo (2020) established that, on average, only 22 out of 100 children are accessing digital learning. The higher the grade the learner is in, the higher the probability of their accessing digital learning. The majority of learners not accessing digital learning are from marginalized counties. The implication is that they will continue lagging behind in terms of learning outcomes. Figure 5 presents findings on the status of digital learning during COVID-19 school closures. Although closure of schools has affected most learners, those from marginalized communities have experienced greater education marginalization (see Figure 5).

Conclusion

Education is at the center of Kenya's future human and economic development (Kenya Ministry of Education, 2016). It is therefore critical that all children have access to education and quality learning. Where this is not happening, there is the risk of a continued cycle of poverty. The ideals of the country as envisioned in Vision 2030, of having Kenya become a newly industrialized country, may not happen. We have seen that there are many interconnected and continuing causes of

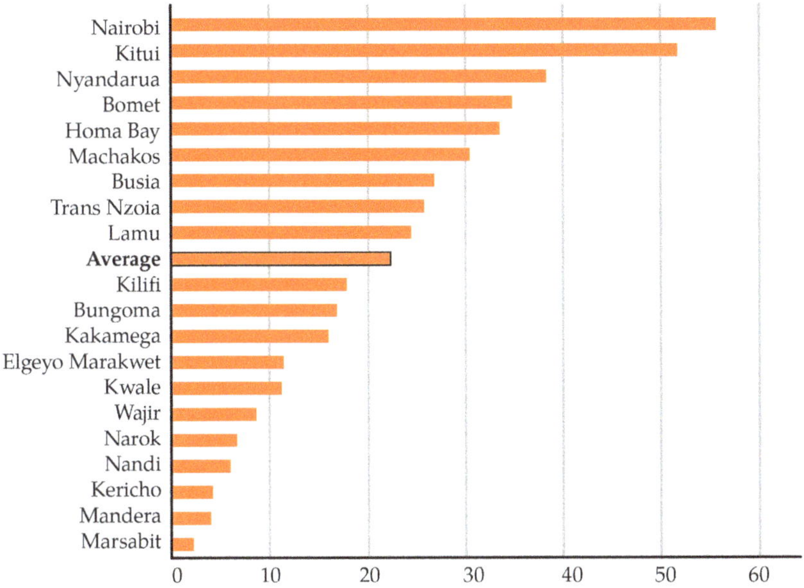
Nairobi
Kitui
Nyandarua
Bomet
Homa Bay
Machakos
Busia
Trans Nzoia
Lamu
Average
Kilifi
Bungoma
Kakamega
Elgeyo Marakwet
Kwale
Wajir
Narok
Nandi
Kericho
Mandera
Marsabit
0
10
20
30
40
50
60

Fig. 5. Access to digital learning materials during the COVID-19 pandemic. Source: Uwezo (2020).

marginalization in Kenya, such as geographical location, gender, health, and the current pandemic. And while these factors affect all children in Kenya, we have seen that there is increased impact on the 11 marginalized counties in this review. As such, it is possible—and, indeed, crucial—to find ways of improving the lives of those at the bottom of the pyramid, including the following recommendations.

Recommendations

1. **Ensure implementation of Vision 2030,** especially components that deal with increased investments in ASAL regions for increased economic growth.
2. **Strengthen institutions like NGEC,** which support gender equality in Kenya.
3. **Strengthen NACONEK** to manage and administer quality education that is sensitive to the needs of pastoralists. One way of doing this is by facilitating the integration of emerging

technologies, distance education, and other alternative interventions in nomadic areas.

4. **Incorporate the nomadic pastoral production system into the national curriculum.** One of the objectives of education in Kenya is to foster nationalism and patriotism, and promote national unity. One way of doing this is by ensuring that the nomadic pastoral production system and lifestyle is incorporated/reflected in the approved national education curriculum.

5. **Strengthen and expand education institutions at all levels for increased access and transition to higher levels of learning.** The government can address this challenge by expanding the number of low-cost boarding schools in nomadic communities and increasing the number of feeder schools (ECDE and Standard I-III) to enhance proximity to school and also to serve as a catchment for boarding schools.

6. **Expand school feeding programs to all children in nomadic communities** to increase access and retention. Most of the homes in marginalized counties are food-insecure. Children are sometimes forced to participate in child labor in order to look for food.

7. **The government to sign the Refugee Bill, 2019.** The new Bill will revise the encampment policy to allow for a high level of freedom of movement. Refugees can then access education and economic opportunities beyond their camps.

8. **Review, adopt, and implement the curricula for Non-Formal Education (NFE) for increased access and completion.**

9. **Implement the Borderless Higher Education for Refugees (BHER) project** in Kakuma Refugee Camp and Kalobeyei Settlement to ensure equal access to tertiary education for all refugees living in Kenya.

References

Betts, A., Omata, N., & Sterck, O. (2018). *Refugee economies in Kenya*. Refugee Studies Centre, University of Oxford. https://www.refugee-economies.org/assets/downloads/refugee_Economies_in_Kenya_Report_for_website.pdf

Food Agricultural Organization (FAO). (2020). *Desert locust situation update 5 March 2020: New swarms forming in Somalia and starting in Kenya*. http://www.fao.org/ag/locusts/en/info/info/index.html

Kenya Ministry of Education (MoEST). (2014). *2014 Basic Education Statistics Booklet*. Nairobi: Government Printers.

Kenya Ministry of Education. (2016). *2016 Basic Education Statistics Booklet*. Nairobi: Government Printers.

Kenya Ministry of Health. (2016). *Kenya AIDs response progress report 2016*. https://nacc.or.ke/wp-content/uploads/2016/11/Kenya-AIDS-Progress-Report_web.pdf

Kenya Ministry of Health. (2017). *Kenya HIV county profiles*. https://nacc.or.ke/wp-content/uploads/2016/12/Kenya-HIV-County-Profiles-2016.pdf

Kenya National Bureau of Statistic (KNBS). (2015). *Kenya demographic and health survey, 2014*. https://dhsprogram.com/pubs/pdf/fr308/fr308.pdf

Kenya National Bureau of Statistics (KNBS). (2018). *Economic survey, 2017*. Nairobi: Government Printers.

Kenya National Bureau of Statistics (KNBS). (2019). *Economic survey, 2018*. Nairobi: Government Printers.

Mghenyi, C. (2018, August 14). *Over 850,000 children out of school in nine counties, Mandera leading*. The Star.

National Council for Population and Development (NCPD). (2020). *Teenage pregnancy in Kenya: Gloom and doom in education, health*. https://ncpd.go.ke/teenage-pregnancy-in-kenya/

Refugee Consortium of Kenya (2019). *Refugees and asylum seekers lament limited access to work permits in Kenya*. https://www.rckkenya.org/refugees-and-asylum-seekers-lament-limited-access-to-work-permits-in-kenya/

UNESCO. (2010). *UNESCO, Education for All: Global monitoring report 2010*. Paris: UNESCO.

UNESCO-UIS. (2015). *Fixing the broken promise of Education for All: Findings from the global initiative on out-of-school children*. Paris: UNESCO.

UNHCR Kenya. (2018). *Kalobeyei integrated socio-economic development programme*. https://www.unhcr.org/ke/wp-content/uploads/sites/2/2018/12/KISEDP_Kalobeyei-Integrated-Socio-Econ-Dev-Programme.pdf

UNHCR Kenya. (2020). *Figures at a glance.* https://www.unhcr.org/ke/figures-at-a-glance

UNICEF. (2019). *Rethinking education and training for youth in refugee hosting communities in Kenya.* UNICEF-Nairobi. Unpublished.

UNICEF. (2018). *Adolescent and youth employability in Kenya: Situational analysis report.* UNICEF. Unpublished.

Uwezo. (2020). *Are our children learning? The status of remote-learning among school-going children in Kenya during the Covid-19 crisis.* Nairobi: Usawa Agenda.

Save the Children. (2019). *Global childhood report, 2019.* https://resourcecentre.savethechildren.net/node/15264/pdf/global_childhood_report_2019_english.pdf

Afterword

The Challenge Ahead for Learning at the Bottom of the Pyramid

Rachel Hinton and Asyia Kazmi

The chapters within this book present a stark reality. Among other sobering statistics, in a high-income country, 9 out of 10 children will be able to read by age 10; in a low-income country, 9 out of 10 will not (UIS, 2019). And, in an indictment of the effectiveness of school systems, it is not just out-of-school children who are disadvantaged. The majority of those who aren't learning sufficiently are actually in school.

It's clearer now than ever before: In the push to achieve the United Nations SDG4—quality education for all—we must shift our focus from *access* to schools to the *quality* of learning therein, while paying particular attention to those who are typically under-served or left behind. This includes those who may be deprioritized due to income, locality, gender, disability, refugee status, or those not in school due to early marriage, homelessness, or other challenges. Those, in other words, at the "bottom of the pyramid".

The term "bottom of the pyramid" (BOP) acknowledges that there is a significant population of children with the least amount of power and resources. Naming this reality and making the scale of the challenge salient can play, as this book points out, a key part in catalyzing change. In every region, country, district, school, and class, there are those who fall behind or who are at risk of falling behind. It is how we identify, target, and support these children that marks a true commitment to equity, and a willingness to be held accountable.

As we examine how to reach children at the BOP, a critical issue to keep in mind is one raised by Beeharry (2021): namely, how can domestic spending of governments be most effectively deployed to address this worsening learning crisis? It is by supporting governments to implement policies informed by the evidence presented in this volume and elsewhere that policymakers can help ensure education systems reach, and effectively teach, the most marginalized.

This volume, in our view, supports the emergence of five key issues that are important for all educational systems in order to reach those at the BOP in a meaningful way. These include:

1. **Face the reality of the learning crisis:** Policymakers and funders need to appreciate the detrimental impact of poor literacy and numeracy skills on all other education and training priorities of their country. The global goal on learning is seriously off-track; and it is off-track for the large majority of children in the poorest countries. Systems must pivot so that policies address the needs of these children, and relentlessly and regularly ask, from the individual classroom to the national policy level, who is not learning and how to help them do so, aligning curriculum, assessment, and instruction in order to achieve this learning goal.

2. **Collect data to understand the problem:** These efforts require better quality and disaggregated data in order to see what is currently going wrong, where, and for whom. This needs to be accompanied by evidence that is produced locally by national researchers who understand the nuance of local issues, and are best placed to support uptake of findings. The gaps in funding and bias in the commissioning of research is a challenge that can and should be addressed.

3. **Act based on evidence of what is most likely to work:** We need to better incentivize the adoption of interventions that promote instructional coherence, namely, those that align curriculum, assessment, and teaching in order to rapidly improve learning outcomes. In this book there are many examples, such as utilizing assessment tools to continuously track students' learning and adapt instruction accordingly.

This should involve, for example, systemizing assessment-informed-instruction; providing ongoing support to teachers through coaching and ensuring that training provides teachers with practical experiences applicable in the classroom; supporting students with learning difficulties; providing mother-tongue instruction; and supplying trained teachers to rural areas.

4. **Support governments to implement effectively at scale:** Given the many urgent, competing priorities in the government's inbox, we need to be more effective and coordinated in communications to accelerate adoption of cost-effective policies and practices. There is increasing demand from policymakers (e.g., Building Evidence in Education group) for succinct and focused evidence synthesis, making better use of compelling data visualizations and smart technology to inform decision-making.

5. **Research the drivers of scale:** Finally, there is a need to understand how to scale up the many promising emerging innovations from civil society, the private sector, and government programs. We know a great deal about what works, but we need to learn from each other and advance the body of knowledge on how to improve learning outcomes at scale, for the most underserved. This will require support to implement science and replication studies in education, as is typically done in the health sector. We need to better understand not only which interventions work, but also the factors that create an enabling environment for successful scale-up and national adoption.

In sum, this volume in an important contribution to the global need for improved and time-sensitive information on key pedagogical issues, and better ways to understand how to improve outcomes for the underserved and the most marginalized in today's world. This process is complex, and involves many factors related to local historical, political, and economic contexts. As we move forward, collective efforts should focus on equipping all children with the learning of basic skills that are a gateway to much wider opportunities. This should be seen as a moral imperative for us all.

References

Beeharry, G. (2021). The pathway to progress on SDG 4 requires the global education architecture to focus on foundational learning and to hold ourselves accountable for achieving it. *International Journal of Educational Development, 82.* https://www.sciencedirect.com/science/article/pii/S0738059321000286

Building Evidence Funding Group. (n.d.). https://www.worldbank.org/en/topic/education/brief/building-evidence-in-education

UNESCO Institute for Statistics (UIS). (2019). *More than one-half of children and adolescents are not learning worldwide.* http://uis.unesco.org/sites/default/files/documents/fs46-more-than-half-children-not-learning-en-2017.pdf

List of Illustrations

Chapter 1

Fig. 1. Proportion of LMICs taking measures to include disadvantaged populations in distance learning during the COVID-19 pandemic in 2020. Source: UNESCO (2020).   14

Fig. 2. Access and learning by wealth over time in Ethiopia. Source: Created by authors with data from the World Inequality Database on Education.   18

Fig. 3. Budgetary interventions for primary and secondary school education for children with disabilities—selected states (millions of Rupees).   29

Chapter 3

Fig. 1. Ranking difficulty of teaching math topics.   82
Fig. 2. Ranking difficulty of teaching reading.   83

Chapter 4

Fig. 1. Differing levels of access to devices for low-, middle-, and high-income populations.   116

Fig. 2 Share of countries implementing remote learning policies at the pre-primary to upper-secondary levels of education, by technology and country income group, during COVID-19.   121

Fig. 3 Percent of countries reporting data for select education indicators at five-year increments, 1970–2013.   129

Chapter 5

Fig. 1. Comparison of Gini measures at t_0 and t_1 to chart improvement. 168
Fig. 2. Non-readers at t_0 and t_1. 170
Fig. 3. Mean reading fluency at t_0 and t_1. 170
Fig. 4. Changes in the mean and changes in inequality. 171
Fig. 5. Shifts in Lorenz curves in response to successful interventions. 173

Chapter 6

Fig. 1. Country mapping of learning exclusion relative to median score (PISA database). Note: Countries depicted are those that are present for all PISA cycles between 2009–2018. Median PISA scores are calculated by averaging the median score over all four cycles. Learning exclusion is operationalized as the percentage difference between the median score and 10th percentile for each country. 184

Fig. 2. Development of learning exclusion relative to median score between 2012 and 2018 – selected countries (PISA database). Note: For legibility, the only countries included were those above or below a specific threshold in terms of their development in relative median PISA scores or learning exclusion between the 2012 and 2018 PISA waves. The results for all other countries are available upon request. 185

Fig. 3 Development of the pyramid between 2000 and 2018— selected countries (PISA database). 187

Chapter 7

Fig. 1. Public education spending estimates, constant 2011 PPP dollars (billions), 1999–2017. Source: World Bank calculations based on World Development Indicators, UIS, and IMF online databases. Note: Total spending is estimated using income group averages of GDP and public education spending as a share of GDP. 195

Fig. 2.	Public education spending per child (constant 2015 PPP $), 1998–2001 to 2014–17. Real spending per child has generally risen in low-income and middle-income countries, but the gap between income groups has widened. Source: World Bank calculations using UIS and IMF online databases. Note: LIC = low-income country, LMIC = lower-middle-income country, and UMIC = upper-middle-income country.	196
Fig. 3.	Rapid population growth will put significant pressure on government education budgets. Source: United Nations Population Division (2019). Note: School-aged population includes children between 5 and 24 years of age. World Bank income group classifications are used to group countries and are as follows: LIC=low-income country, LMIC = lower-middle-income country, UMIC = upper-middle-income country. SSA = sub-Saharan Africa.	198
Fig. 4.	Education as a share of total government budget, and government spending as a share of GDP in low- and lower-middle-income countries (%), 2014–17. Fiscal space for mobilizing greater funding for education varies considerably. Source: World Bank calculations based on World Development Indicators, UIS, and IMF online databases.	200
Fig. 5.	Differences in education participation imply that public funding for education is distributed unequally. Source: Left-hand panel: UNICEF (2020). Right-hand panel: Burundi: Tsimpo & Wodon (2014). Pakistan: Asghar & Zahra (2012).	203
Fig. 6.	Education spending inequalities are large and can reinforce existing patterns of poverty and disadvantage. Source: Left-hand panel: Manuel et al. (2019) and various World Bank Public Expenditure Reviews. Right-hand panel: Manuel et al. (2019).	204
Fig. 7.	Association between spending per child and enrollment-adjusted learning. Source: World Bank calculations based on HCI, UIS, and IMF data. Note: The stochastic frontier is drawn from data and analytical work described in Al-Samarrai et al. (2019).	209
Fig. 8.	Elementary school per-student funding by source, 2013 and 2013/14 school year. MOOE refers to maintenance and other operating expenses. Funds that schools receive do not reduce inequalities in overall school funding in the Philippines. Source: World Bank (2016).	213

Fig. 9. Proportion of low- and middle-income countries by Public Expenditure and Financial Accountability (PEFA) rating, 2010–2015. Source: Public Expenditure and Financial Accountability database. Notes: A four-point ordinal scale based on specific criteria for each dimension is used to score country performance. 214

Chapter 8

Fig. 1. Percentage of general secondary school students at "good" and "excellent" levels in mathematics, by degree of involvement in the PMLE. Source: Data obtained from UPEPE (2012). 251
Fig. 2. Percentage of general secondary students at "good" and "excellent" levels in Spanish, by degree of involvement in the PMLE. Source: Data obtained from UPEPE (2012). 251
Fig. 3. Percentage of telesecondary students at "good" and "excellent" levels in mathematics, by degree of involvement in the PMLE. Source: Data obtained from UPEPE (2012). 252
Fig. 4. Percentage of telesecondary students at "good" and "excellent" levels in Spanish, by degree of involvement in the PMLE. Source: Data obtained from UPEPE (2012). 252
Fig. 5. Full-time schools, 2017–2019. Source: Prepared by the authors using varied sources. 255
Fig. 6. Puebla's ranking relative to both rich and poor states. Source: Data from SEP, ENLACE 2006 to 2013, and PLANEA 2015. 260

Chapter 10

Fig. 1. Linguistic diversity index of India. 297
Fig. 2. Distribution of languages in India—comparative strength. Source: the authors. 298
Fig. 3. A model of learning in diverse linguistic contexts of India. Source: based on the work of P. Banerjee (co-author). 303

Chapter 11

Fig. 1. Characteristics of indigenous knowledge. Source: the author. 313

Chapter 12

Fig. 1.   Net intake and enrollment rates in Ivory Coast from 2014/15 to 2019/20. Source: Ministry of National Education, Technical Education and Vocational Training (2014, 2015, 2016, 2017, 2018, 2019, 2020).   328

Fig. 2.   Repetition and dropout rates in Ivory Coast from 2016/17 to 2019/20. Source: Ministry of National Education, Technical Education and Vocational Training (2014; 2015; 2016; 2017; 2018; 2019; 2020).   329

Fig. 3.   Evolution of the number of Islamic schools integrated in Ivory Coast's public system from 2017 to 2020. Source: Ministry of National Education, Technical Education and Vocational Training (2018; 2019; 2020).   334

Fig. 4.   Evolution of the integration of children with disabilities in public schools from 2016 to 2020. Source: Ministry of National Education, Technical Education and Vocational Training (2016; 2017; 2018; 2019; 2020).   338

Fig. 5.   Number of children allowed to enroll without a birth certificate from 2015 to 2020. Source: Ministry of National Education, Technical Education and Vocational Training (2016; 2017; 2018; 2019; 2020).   339

Chapter 15

Fig. 1.   Distribution of study population by KCPE examination scores and type of primary school attended.   388

Fig. 2.   Distribution of school leavers by type of primary and category of secondary schools attended.   390

Chapter 16

Fig. 1.   Proportions of over-age, right-age, and under-age learners (KCPE 2016–2019).   408

Fig. 2.   Proportions of over-age, right-age, and under-age learners (KCSE 2016–2019).   408

Chapter 17

Fig. 1.	Primary Gross and Net Enrollment Rates for counties in Kenya (MoEST, 2014). Source: the author.	421
Fig. 2.	Secondary Gross and Net Enrollment Rates for marginalized counties (MoEST, 2014). Source: the author.	422
Fig. 3.	GER and poverty levels in education marginalized counties (KNBS, 2015; 2018).	425
Fig. 4.	Primary-level completion rate by gender.	427
Fig. 5.	Access to digital learning materials during the COVID-19 pandemic. Source: Uwezo (2020).	435

List of Tables

Chapter 2

Table 1. Mean scores for Lebanese students compared to OECD average (OECD, 2018a, p.1). — 58

Chapter 5

Table 1. Inequality measures. — 157
Table 2. Range of inequality measure results, PRIMR. — 164
Table 3. Range of inequality measure results, Tusome. — 166

Chapter 7

Box 1 Differences in district revenue result in large differences in education spending and quality in Indonesia. — 205
Box 2 The "pupil premium" in England. — 208

Chapter 8

Table 1. Percentage of children in poverty in Mexico (2018). — 227
Table 2. Students, teachers, and schools in preschool, primary, and secondary education (2018–2019). — 230
Table 3. Preschool, primary, and secondary education students and schools by type of service at national level and in rural localities (2018–2019). — 234
Table 4. Percentage of sixth-grade students by school type and level of educational attainment achieved in the domains evaluated in the PLANEA-SEN tests (2018). — 235

Table 5.	Percentage of third-grade secondary students by level of educational attainment attained in domains as assessed on Plan-ELSEN Tests by type of school (2017).	236
Table 6.	School attendance rate, percentage of population with complete education levels, and school attendance rate at educational level typically corresponding to age by selected subpopulation (2018).	239
Table 7.	Federal spending on basic education by budget program (millions of pesos) (spent in 2018; planned for 2019 and 2020).	245

Chapter 12

Table 1.	Girl's completion rates in primary and lower-secondary school in Ivory Coast from 2013 to 2019.	325
Table 2.	Overall birth registration rate.	326
Table 3.	Characteristics of COSS aged between 6 and 11 years old in 2012.	327
Table 4.	Children denied enrollment in CP1 in Ivory Coast from 2015–2019.	329
Table 5.	Levels of the compliance analysis for Islamic faith-based schools.	334
Table 6.	Number of school kits distributed to primary school students from 2016 to 2020.	336
Table 7.	Evolution of the number of open outreach schools from 2012 to 2019.	337

Chapter 15

Table 1.	Distribution of school leavers by type of primary school attended and KCSE examination year.	386
Table 2.	KCSE mean score distribution between top and bottom performance quarters by type of primary school attended.	386
Table 3.	Distribution of study population by KCPE examination marks and type of primary school attended.	387
Table 4.	KCSE mean grade distribution by marks scored in KCPE examinations.	388
Table 5.	Distribution of KCSE mean grade by category of secondary school attended.	389

Table 6.	Distribution of the study population by type of primary and category of secondary schools attended.	391
Table 7.	Regression model results based on Poisson Regression Model (probability of getting higher grade).	392

Chapter 16

Table 1.	Overall means for learners with and without disabilities for primary-school examinations (KCPE).	403
Table 2.	Overall means for learners with and without disabilities for secondary-school examinations (KCSE).	403
Table 3.	Examination means for the four disability categories at primary-school level (KCPE).	404
Table 4.	Examination means for the four disability categories at secondary-school level (KCSE).	404
Table 5.	Means for various categories of disability by gender for primary examinations (KCPE).	404
Table 6.	Means for various categories of disability by gender for secondary examinations.	406
Table 7.	Performance scores of right-age, over-age, and under-age candidates (2016–2019) at primary level (KCPE).	409
Table 8.	Performance scores of right-age and over-age candidates (2016–2019) at secondary level (KCSE).	409
Table 9.	Regression analysis of performance for learners with disabilities in primary (KCPE) examinations.	410
Table 10.	Regression analysis of performance for candidates with disabilities in secondary examinations (KCSE).	411

Chapter 17

Table 1.	Correlation between poverty and total fertility rate.	428

Index

6C model 304
21st-century skills 312
1951 Refugee Convention 49, 55, 62
1967 Refugee Protocol 62
1984 Cartagena Declaration on Refugees 62
2015 UN Millennium Development Goals 37
2017 Human Mobility Law (Ecuador) 62

accelerated education programs 94–95, 97, 103
access to quality teachers 77
Activity-Based Learning (ABL) program 283–284, 286–288
adaptive technology 353
Afghanistan 4, 22–24, 24
Africa 1–2, 18, 20, 31, 55, 57, 77–78, 81–83, 86–88, 90, 92–94, 119, 123–124, 127, 132, 139, 151, 165, 197, 201, 302, 314, 343, 349, 351–353, 363, 365–366, 372, 429
African Storybook Initiative 127
agile development 134–135
AIDs (acquired immune deficiency syndrome) 429–430
Albania 185–186
Allô Alphabet 350–351, 356
alternative education programs 20
analyses
 descriptive 400
 inferential 400
 regression 410–411
Andhra Pradesh 79, 279
Annual Status of Education Report (ASER) 79, 277, 282, 286, 289, 294, 306, 315, 363

Arid and Semi-Arid Lands (ASAL) 365, 367–369, 374, 430, 435
Armenia 55
Asia 57
assistive technologies 26
asylum seekers 47, 62–63, 431
Attendance, Permanence, and Learning (APA) model 258, 260–261
Australia 49

Bangladesh 212
Benito Juárez Basic Education Scholarship Program for Welfare 244
Bhojpur 295
Bihar 279, 295
Borderless Higher Education for Refugees (BHER) project 432, 436
Bottom of the Pyramid, Learning 1
Brazil 205–206, 352
Bridges to the Future Initiative 313
bridging program 346–347, 356
Bulgaria 184, 186
Burkina Faso 207
Burundi 87, 207

Carrera Magisterial teacher incentive program 90
cash transfer program 9, 244, 355
Chennai 283–284
children
 and attitudes to learning 29, 95
 asylum-seeking 53
 at risk 4
 laborers 57, 63, 229, 344, 354–355, 373, 426, 436
 migrants 4, 48, 53–54, 57, 63–64, 229, 231

monograde 84–85
out-of-school 13, 15–18, 20, 27, 35, 37, 63–64, 93–96, 113, 279, 324–325, 327–328, 331, 343, 346–347, 356, 397, 418, 420, 431–432, 439
China 91, 204
Citizen-Led Assessments (CLAs) 315
civil society organizations (CSOs) 8, 309–311
classroom interactions 33
class size 5, 21, 86, 124, 130, 205, 215, 349, 353, 432
Coahuila 234, 261
Code Club Pilot 318
cognitive development 17, 398
Colombia 61, 215
community-based schools 23–24
Complementary Basic Education (CBE) program 96–98
CONEVAL (National Council for the Evaluation of Social Development Policy) 226, 249, 270
COVID-19 pandemic 4–5, 10, 13–15, 17, 20, 22, 26, 34, 36, 61, 66–67, 113, 118, 121, 123, 131, 135–136, 138, 193, 196–197, 201–202, 216, 243, 247, 361, 374, 376–377, 430, 433–435
Critical Pedagogy approach 302
curricula
  competency-based 372, 376–377, 414
  differentiated 401
  national 84, 124, 232, 261, 330, 400, 436
  pace of 376
  reform 60, 362
cycles of deprivation 78

data challenges 52, 64, 68, 128–129, 393, 419, 440
data collection and analysis 138, 374, 377
data gaps 10, 16, 36, 45, 52, 58, 68, 81, 86, 129, 264, 399
data management systems 129
data processing and utilization 130–131, 137
Dausa 317
Delhi 286–287, 290, 295

de-schooling 302
Design Based Implementation Research (DBIR) 135
DIA human-chatbot hybrid 353–354
disability 8–10, 13, 15–16, 25–30, 36–37, 92, 225, 228, 262, 266, 295, 325–326, 337–339, 363–364, 370, 372, 374–375, 397–407, 409–410, 412–414, 417
  and rights 27
  investment in 29–30
  support 126
disadvantaged learners 4, 8–9, 13, 16, 24, 34–37, 59–60, 67, 77–80, 87–88, 91–93, 98–103, 203, 206–208, 242, 291, 325, 338, 343, 367, 370, 376, 394, 417, 419, 439
discrimination 54–55, 57, 62–63, 66, 137, 242, 278, 280–281, 290, 339, 373, 434
  and psychological wellbeing 66
disparities 22
District Primary Education Program (DPEP) 284, 310
diversity
  definition of 4
  of students 5, 91, 101, 294, 300, 376
  of teachers 4, 100
double shifting 56, 60

Early Childhood and Community Education Program 246
early childhood education
  and learning gaps 18–19
Early Grade Reading Assessment 6, 150, 160–161
East and Southern Africa 20
Ecuador 4, 46, 48–49, 54, 61–67, 69, 88, 90, 354
Ecuadorian Constitution of 2008 62
education
  access to 2, 4–5, 7–10, 14–20, 22–26, 28, 33, 36, 45–48, 50–51, 53, 56–57, 60–61, 63, 67–68, 78, 80, 92, 94, 97, 120, 137–138, 149, 182, 193, 197, 206, 211, 223–224, 229, 232, 237–238, 242, 261, 266, 269, 304, 318, 323–324, 339, 343–345, 349, 356, 362–366, 368–369,

371, 373–374, 381, 384, 393–394, 430–436, 439
and cultural norms 16, 23–24, 54, 351
and humanitarian contexts 37, 51
and identities 92, 95, 295, 301, 306
and income 24, 28
and local attitudes 30
and migration 46–48, 50, 68–69
and poverty 7, 25, 264
and refugees 45
and sanitation 22, 25, 370
as a right 16, 45–46, 49, 238, 267–269, 304, 311, 332–333, 337, 340, 372–373, 397
aspirations 263
completion 7, 19, 21–22, 26, 95, 149, 210, 224, 237–238, 246, 282, 324, 335, 370, 374, 401, 412, 426, 435–436
compulsory 7, 56, 223–224, 229, 237, 244, 258–261, 267–268, 311, 346, 372–373, 417
demand for 25, 35, 56, 90, 376
development goals for 1, 3–4, 6, 13, 77, 94, 104, 113, 117, 128, 138, 149, 182, 303, 305, 382, 394, 439
dropout rates 17, 22, 59, 77, 79–80, 93–94, 237–238, 242, 246, 254, 261, 325, 328, 336, 344, 367, 426–427
enrollment 6, 10, 16, 18, 21–23, 26, 28, 35, 45, 52–53, 56–58, 64, 67, 86, 136, 202, 206, 210, 215, 232, 260, 277, 282, 300, 324, 328, 330–332, 335, 337–338, 343, 345–346, 354–355, 370–371, 373, 381, 394, 398, 412–413, 418–420, 423–424, 427–428, 430–431
equitable 3, 6, 8, 15–18, 21, 86–87, 92, 138, 149, 182, 190, 205, 207, 210, 215–216, 243–244, 246–247, 258–260, 263–264, 268–269, 290, 304, 332–333, 362, 366, 368–369, 382, 390, 394, 439
exclusion from 26, 326
fees for 57, 60, 332, 350, 365–366, 370, 393–394, 424–425
goals for 6, 27, 80, 84, 114, 193, 197, 201–202, 214–215, 258, 317, 364, 369

government spending on 6–7, 14, 29, 34, 37, 60, 65, 193–199, 201–207, 209–210, 213, 215–216, 243–244, 247, 280, 335, 362, 367, 383, 395
grade repetition 237–238, 324, 328, 336, 346, 384, 391, 412
household spending on 195, 198, 201, 215
incentive schemes 248, 280, 349, 354–356, 370
inequality 15–16, 23–24, 118, 183, 189, 318, 323, 332, 361–362, 374, 383
integration 24, 333, 339
interventions 9, 24–25, 27–28, 30, 32–33, 36, 104, 114–115, 117–120, 122–126, 132–135, 155, 161–162, 168, 174–176, 186, 190, 208, 211, 232, 253, 279–280, 286, 313–314, 316–318, 335, 347, 349–350, 352–356, 369, 374, 394, 402, 413–414, 436, 440–441
late entry to 238, 412
public-private spending on 370–380
quality of 1, 4–5, 8–9, 13, 15–16, 21–22, 24–26, 37, 45–48, 56, 60, 68, 77–78, 94, 120, 136, 182, 197, 204–207, 210, 212, 215–216, 237, 277, 285–288, 290–291, 303, 305, 323, 330–331, 339–340, 343–345, 352–356, 362–363, 368, 376, 383–384, 430–432, 434–435, 439
standardization 288, 310
support measures 280
educational games 314
educational infrastructure 23, 54, 212, 237–238, 242, 247, 268–269, 277, 279–280, 328, 330–331, 373, 431
educational mainstream 304
educational policy xiii, 8–9, 15–16, 23, 27, 30, 68–69, 183, 215, 258, 261–262, 268, 295, 331, 365, 369, 372, 376, 393, 401, 441
Educational Technology (EdTech) 9, 114–115, 117–120, 122–123, 125–126, 131–132, 134, 137–138, 317–318, 345, 349–352, 354, 356
access to 122–123, 136, 318, 349–350
Education Commission 15, 25, 124, 197

Education for All 35, 103, 194, 261, 277–278, 282, 303, 305, 346, 365–366, 376, 381–382, 439
Education Management Information Systems (EMIS) 129–130
EduTrac program 131
effective questioning 80
ENLACE test 250, 254, 259, 267, 269
ethical AI use 137
Ethiopia 18–20, 79, 93–95, 97–98, 430
European Social Survey 53
examination accommodations 9, 398–400, 402, 412–414
EXCALE (Educational Quality and Achievement) test 267
existential inequality 119
exploitative working conditions 57
extreme poverty 201, 225–226, 228, 247–249, 424, 431–432

feedback loop 132, 253
female genital mutilation (FGM) 426, 429
financial crisis of 2008/09 201
foundational skills 15, 26, 79, 113, 126, 314–316
Full-Time Schools Program 244, 253–255, 264
Fund for the Development of Primary Education and Appreciation of Teachers (FUNDEB) 205–206
further/higher education
and examination score at school 394

Gaza 54
gender disparity 4, 13, 17, 21–22, 26, 37, 280, 282, 324, 330, 336, 339, 398, 406–407, 414, 426
gender parity 21, 337, 373, 426
geo-spatial data 21, 36
Ghana 35, 82, 84, 87, 91–94, 96–99
Gini coefficient 6, 151–153, 156–158, 163–169, 171–172, 174–175, 177, 183, 189, 344
Global 2030 Development Agenda 11, 394
global challenges 26

Global Compact for Migration 47
globalization 312
global learning crisis 13, 182, 382
Global Monitoring Report 85
Global North 48–51, 53, 127, 314
Global Partnership for Education (GPE) grants 214
Global South 46, 48, 50, 52–54, 69, 85, 137, 361
grade-based curriculum 83–84
Guinea 87
Gujarat 284
Gunotsav program 284–287, 289

Herfindahl-Hirschman Index 311
higher education
and examination score at school 388
and gender/socioeconomic status 15
and migrants 53, 431
higher-order skills 19, 33, 81, 85, 174
HIV (human immunodeficiency virus) 428–430
Homabay County 418
home-based ECE program 19
home-based training 19, 23
home/community-led education 376
home-school connection 35, 103, 211, 263, 301, 376
home support 32
human capital 248–249, 394
Human Development Index (HDI) 324

illiteracy/low literacy 32, 325, 343, 350, 363, 381–382
inclusion 1, 3, 26–27, 30, 48, 50, 56, 77–78, 96, 98–99, 101–104, 118, 137–138, 182–183, 237, 262, 264, 291, 300, 303–305, 332–333, 337–338, 362, 364, 366, 368, 372, 413, 432–433
India 4, 7–8, 26–30, 79, 84, 87–88, 90, 118, 210, 277–282, 287, 289–290, 293–303, 305–306, 309–311, 313–316, 319, 347, 352
indigenous children 7, 225, 227–228, 230–232, 238, 263
indigenous or traditional knowledge 309, 312

indigenous populations
  and learning achievement 7, 227, 232, 246, 261
  and poverty 228, 246
indigenous technologies 314
Indonesia 204–205, 207, 210–211
information and communication technologies (ICTs)
  and innovations 8
  and personalised/adaptive learning 11
  and quality education 9
  data collecting and monitoring 5
  mobile phones 2, 5, 132, 349–351
Instituto Nacional para la Evaluación de la Educación (INEE) 227–233, 258, 265–269
instructional coaching 33, 122, 176, 178
Integrated Child Development Services (ICDS) 27, 30, 281
Interactive Radio Instruction 120, 122
internally displaced people (IDPs) 45, 47, 50, 55–56
International Common Assessment of Numeracy (ICAN) 315–316
International Development and Early Learning Assessment (IDELA) 17
International Monetary Fund (IMF) 34, 197, 201
investments 22
Iraq 55
Item Response Theory (IRT) 154
Ivory Coast 1, 8–9, 207, 323–326, 328, 330–333, 335, 337, 339, 343–356

Jordan 50, 54, 186

Karnataka 284, 287–288
Kenya 1, 4, 6, 9–10, 26, 31–34, 50–51, 81–82, 84–85, 98, 151, 161, 177, 211, 361–365, 367–377, 381–384, 386, 393–394, 397–402, 412–414, 417–418, 420, 424–425, 427–436
Kenya Education-Sector Support Program (KESSP) 368
Kenyan Sign Language 402, 413
Kerala 278

Kiambu 161
Korea 186, 189

Laboratorio Latinoamericano de Evaluación de la Calidad de la Educación (LLECE) 261, 267
Lamu 418, 427
language deprivation 398, 413
language diversity 8, 295
language of instruction 4, 7, 15, 30–33, 36, 50, 54, 57, 80, 83, 85–86, 93, 95, 117, 126, 238, 263, 301, 347, 364, 373
language policy 31, 33–34, 372, 376
  implementation of 33, 295, 303, 306
language-rich home environments 413
languages
  foreign 30–31
  home 3, 93, 117, 123, 126
  indigenous 227–228, 263, 266–268
  local 2, 31, 33, 92, 95, 120, 296, 311, 319, 347
  of instruction 2, 30, 97, 127, 133
  standard 294
Lao 199
last mile problem 132–133
Latin America 54–55, 65, 153
learning
  analytics 131–132
  and attendance 104, 131, 238, 258, 345–346, 352, 354–355, 370–371
  and diversity 4–5, 7, 15, 35, 103, 119, 126, 227, 242, 293, 295, 297, 299–300, 306, 372
  and information and communication technology (ICT) 8, 11, 61, 114–115, 117, 126
  and technology 2
  barriers to 8, 10, 16, 25–26, 28, 33, 50, 53–54, 57, 59, 63, 67, 93, 113–115, 120–121, 128, 195, 229, 237, 242, 281, 295, 306, 323–324, 336, 349–351, 354–355, 364, 400–401, 412, 432–433, 439
  by doing 312
  collaborative 97–98
  context of 1

continuity 20
crisis 13, 78–79, 85, 354, 361, 382, 398, 440
deficit 277, 289
delays 27–28, 36, 301, 412
disparities 3–4, 9, 14, 22, 47, 49–50, 60–61, 64, 66, 68–69, 88, 117, 194, 202, 204, 206, 208, 212, 302, 339, 344, 363
effective 13, 80–81, 95, 98
engagement in 8, 19, 25, 28–29, 35, 93, 96, 98–99, 132, 316, 318, 347, 351–352, 356, 372, 376
environments for 2, 69, 96, 115, 120, 434
equity 1, 3–4, 9–11, 13, 15, 21, 37, 87, 90, 119, 135, 138, 182, 210, 264, 277, 361–362, 364–365, 368, 373, 375, 382, 394, 433
experiences 16, 68, 95, 317
gains 19, 21, 65, 84–85, 91, 93, 95, 120, 154–155, 169, 206, 255, 277, 313–314
gaps 3, 6–7, 9–10, 15, 18–19, 26, 36, 52, 54, 66–67, 78–79, 83, 87, 94, 103, 136, 172–174, 182–183, 189, 194, 197, 202, 206, 208, 267–269, 280, 289, 311, 346, 382, 390, 392, 398, 409–410, 431
inequality 150, 156, 183, 323, 375, 395
intercultural 264
investment in 4, 25, 27, 37, 195, 375
(lack of) opportunities for 9, 14, 91–92, 99, 138, 181–183, 194, 247, 253, 261, 363, 368, 375–376, 382, 390, 394, 412–413, 432, 436
ladder 283
loss 14
metrics 5–7, 154, 160, 189
peer 283, 286
potential 84, 91, 343–344, 354, 413
synchronous 128
through play 312
worlds 3
learning achievement 4–5, 78, 80, 223, 266, 407

and aboriginal ethnic groups/ scheduled tribes 37, 278–280, 293, 363
and age of learner 392, 398–399, 407, 409–412, 414
and castes 92, 278–280, 293
and disability 402–403
and disability type 398, 404
and discrimination 66
and EdTech 122, 318
and educational funding 65, 211
and gender 22, 155, 280–282, 392, 399, 405–406, 411
and grade repetition 391
and lack of attendance 97, 346
and life satisfaction 53, 432
and malnutrition 248, 262, 281, 371
and migration 4, 46, 48, 51, 53–54, 60–61, 64–65, 67–68, 242, 262
and parental educational level 66, 262, 375, 383
and parental engagement 351
and poverty 15–18, 79, 206, 262, 324, 326, 335, 346, 355–356
and quality of education 355, 384
and religious minorities 278–279
and resilience 53
and sense of belonging 4, 53
and societal norms 22
and socioeconomic status 17, 19, 59, 66–67, 79, 87, 155, 175, 259, 290, 374, 384, 399
and teacher support 351
and type or location of school 15, 79, 392–393, 399, 420
and wellbeing 4, 36, 54
learning assessments 21, 65, 152–153, 382
and tracking progress 84, 181, 237, 287, 374, 440–441
citizen-led 315
competency-based 414
cross-national 315
diagnostic 289

end-of-cycle 10, 362, 398
external 289
formative 5, 95, 127, 138, 176, 399
high-stakes 399
large-scale 21, 68, 288–289
national 294
periodic 376
smaller, quicker, cheaper (SQC) 5, 149–150, 152, 177
standardized achievement tests 46, 58, 69, 232, 247, 249, 255, 260–264
summative 127, 130, 176, 375, 399–400
learning exclusion 6, 182–186, 189–190
learning levels 29, 80, 83–84, 238, 332, 432
learning needs 9, 36, 47, 49, 69, 77–78, 80, 84, 91–92, 97–104, 137–138, 207, 280, 332, 344–346, 354, 356, 363, 365–366, 375, 397–398, 402, 414
learning outcomes 1, 3–4, 6–7, 9, 13–23, 25–26, 36–37, 46–48, 50–51, 54, 58–60, 64–68, 77–79, 81–82, 84, 88, 90–91, 95, 97, 100, 104, 114–117, 122–123, 125, 130, 132, 151, 153, 155, 157, 182–183, 189, 197, 209–211, 230, 265, 268, 282–287, 289–290, 301, 309, 311, 313–316, 345, 347–349, 352, 354–356, 363, 367, 375, 377, 382, 398–399, 413, 434, 440–441
learning poor 153, 181
Lebanese Labor Law 57
Lebanon 4, 46, 48–50, 52, 55–61, 69
lifelong learning
  of children 8, 306, 364, 368
Linguistic Diversity Index (LDI) 297
literacy development
  and language 31–32
  community reading activities 19
locust invasion 430
Lorenz curve 157, 167, 172, 174
lower scores 242
low-income countries
  and access to remote learning 17
  and children at risk of exclusion 14, 17, 22

and learning gap 7, 13, 17, 20
and migration 48
and out-of-school rates 16
low-income parents
  and access to resources 27, 330
low-literacy population 32

Macao 186
Madagascar 91, 198
Madhya Pradesh 28–29, 279
Maharashtra 317–318
mainstream schooling 26
Malawi 21, 36, 198
Mali 30, 82, 91
marginalization 3, 8, 10–11, 30, 34–35, 37, 69, 77–81, 85–86, 89–92, 101, 113–114, 117, 119, 125, 133, 181, 216, 225, 246–247, 255, 257, 260, 262, 264, 277, 279–281, 289–290, 296, 301–302, 304–306, 310, 323, 362, 376, 381–382, 398, 423–427, 429–436, 441–442
materials
  culturally relevant 31
Mauritius 86
measurement
  of learning 2, 5–6, 10–11, 34–36, 123, 153, 285
Mentor Teacher program 286–287, 290
Mexico 1, 7, 87, 90, 206, 223–228, 230, 232–233, 253, 256, 260–267
micro data 150–151, 155–156
Mid-Day Meal (MDM) program 281–282
Middle East 51, 55
migrants
  economic 47, 49–50, 63
  South-South 46
migration
  and legal protection 56
  and sustainable development 47
  internal 61, 426
  internal displacement 49, 55
  irregular 53
  mixed 45
  outward 49, 55, 61

perception of 69
return 61, 266
rural-rural 229
rural-urban 300
seasonal 229
Millennium Development Goals 21, 149, 381
minimum education level 332
Moldova 199
mother-tongue education 8, 31–34, 92–93, 96, 103, 293, 295, 441
Mozambique 81, 89
multigrade teaching 231, 242, 246, 254, 262–263
multilingual classroom 33, 96
multilingualism 33, 93, 126, 294, 301
multilingual learning environments 93, 294
Murang'a 161

Nairobi 161, 431–432
Nakuru 161
nali kali project 284, 287–288
National Achievement Survey (NAS) 286, 289, 294, 306
National School Effectiveness Study (NSES) 78
natural resource wealth 200
New York Declaration for Refugees and Migrants 47
Niger 206
Nigeria 81–82, 201
non-government organizations (NGOs) 1, 23, 27, 63, 119, 309–315, 333, 346–347, 355
Northern Kenya 417

One Laptop Per Child Initiative 122
Open Educational Resources (OER) 125, 127
OER4Schools 125
open learning 316–317
Organic Law on Intercultural Education (LOEI) 63
Organization for Economic Cooperation and Development (OECD) 17,
45–46, 48, 52–53, 58–59, 65, 79, 181, 183, 207, 261

Pakistan 84, 90
Palestine 49, 52, 54–56, 58–59
parents
  attitudes to disability 28
  attitudes to learning 26, 28, 32, 35
  attitudes to disability 28
  literacy skills 32
pastoralism 418, 426, 430, 435
patriarchal societies 24
pedagogy 9, 27–28, 35, 64, 78, 81, 83–84, 90, 94–99, 101, 103, 113–114, 116, 125–126, 130, 136, 138, 155, 175, 231, 242, 256, 262–263, 268, 283–284, 286–288, 312, 330–331, 333, 344, 346–347, 351–353, 441
People's Action for Learning (PAL) Network 315–316, 375
percent below a learning floor 150–152, 154–156, 165, 171–172, 174, 177
Peru 122, 131, 186
Philippines 88, 181, 210, 212–213
PLANEA tests 232–233, 247, 260, 267, 269
pluriculturalism 294, 296
Poisson regression model 384–385
polarization of society 382
policy continuum 49
policy-practice connection 30
poverty
  and access to electronic devices 115
  index 2
  intergenerational 94, 381–382, 428
  multidimensional 226, 324
poverty of learning 152, 159, 180–182, 189, 383, 394–395
PraDigi Open Learning program 8, 316–318
Pratham 8, 84, 310, 313, 315–318, 347–348, 352
pregnant students 22, 246, 248, 324–325, 336, 339, 425–427
pre-primary education
  and disabilities 25, 27

and future outcomes 9, 311, 393
and language of instruction 31
and learning gaps 78
indigenous 232, 254, 266
Primary Math and Reading Initiative (PRIMR) 33, 160–162, 166–167, 172, 174–176
primary school
  and disabilities 25
  and language of instruction 31–32, 93, 103
  and migrants 53
  and teacher quality 80, 82
  indigenous 231–232, 254, 266
Principles for Digital Development 123
Problem Driven Iterative Adaptation (PDIA) method 134
Program for International Student Assessment (PISA) 6, 17, 51, 53–54, 58–59, 65, 79, 152, 181, 183–186, 189, 261, 267, 287
Program for the Development of Meaningful Learning in Basic Education 247
Program for the Improvement of Educational Achievement 249–250, 252–253, 256
programs
  enforcement of 26
  for literacy development 32
  implementation of 26–27
Progresa-Oportunidades-Prospera 248–249, 264
Public Expenditure and Financial Accountability (PEFA) assessments 213
public financial management systems 194, 213
public policy 3, 368
Puebla 258–261
Pupil Completion Rate (PCR) 419
pupil premium 208
Pyramid, Bottom of the 1

Qatar 186

Rainbow Spectrum initiative 88
raising the floor 3–4, 10
Rajasthan 279, 317
Ranga Reddy 313
Reaching All Children with Education (RACE) I and II 60
read to learn 80, 94
Refugee Bill 436
refugee children 45, 53
  and social stigma 66
remedial action 100, 289, 311, 314, 347
remote learning 5, 10, 14, 17, 36, 61, 67, 115, 118, 121–123, 128, 136, 349, 361, 434, 436
Research on Improving Systems of Education (RISE) 153
residential family training 28
responsibility sharing 48
Rift Valley 418
right to equality 278, 332
right to work 49, 54, 434
rigid curriculum 85
rote teaching 120, 242, 262

Samarpan Early Intervention Center model of Madhya Pradesh 28
Sarva Shiksha Abhiyan (SSA) program 26–27, 29–30, 82, 94, 279–280, 310–311
Saudi Arabia 200
Save the Children 14, 17, 19, 21, 37, 61, 347, 427
scheduled castes 298
scheduled tribes 299
school funding formulas 206–207
schools
  free 9, 13, 32, 56, 223, 268, 311, 330, 332, 346, 362–363, 366, 368, 371–373, 381–384, 393–394, 417, 419
  non-formal 175
  outreach 336–337
  private 56–57, 59, 61, 67, 161, 294, 310, 330, 362, 371, 382–387, 390–393
  public 6, 14, 52, 54, 56–61, 63–64, 67, 93, 95, 97, 103, 161–162, 197, 202, 208–209, 215–216, 232, 254, 301,

310–311, 331–332, 338, 346, 362, 370, 374–375, 383–387, 390–394
rural 1–2, 9–10, 15, 19, 23, 25, 27, 33, 79, 84, 86–91, 96, 101, 133, 212, 225–232, 235, 242, 248–249, 254, 261–262, 280, 282, 314–316, 324, 327, 330–331, 336–339, 343–344, 349–350, 352–353, 355, 362, 366, 385–387, 390–392, 394, 431, 441
rural vs. urban 2, 227
and teacher quality 81
urban 2–3, 19–20, 27, 33, 79, 81, 87, 132, 226–228, 231–232, 235, 242, 248–249, 254, 261, 294, 327, 337, 339, 347, 355, 385–386, 391–392, 431
secondary school
and disabilities 25, 29
and migrants 53
and teacher quality 82
Senegal 81–82, 197, 199
Service Delivery Indicators (SDI) survey 90
Sierra Leone 130–131, 212
Sierra Leone Education Attendance Monitoring System (SLEAMS) 130
silently excluded 78, 97–98, 100, 102, 104
Singapore 186, 189
Slovak Republic 186
Slovenia 186
social debt 7, 224
socializing processes 426
social mobility 394
social vulnerability 7, 224–225, 229, 235, 237
sociocultural development 302
Somalia 430, 432
Sonora 261
South Africa 1–2, 78, 94, 119, 132, 165, 314
South Africa Annual National Assessment (ANA) 2
South Asia 79, 201, 302, 309
special schools 27, 413
Speed School program 95, 97–98
spending equity 6, 215

State Report on the National Education System (RESEN) 324, 327
Statistical Analysis Report 2018-2019 328, 333
stigmatization 30
student retention 206, 258, 339, 423, 435–436
student-teacher ratios 86, 90, 205, 210
studies
analytical 290
evaluation 95–96
longitudinal 79, 95
qualitative 98
RCT 23, 32, 35, 84, 90, 133–134, 211, 351–352
subject matter experts 8, 102, 310
sub-Saharan Africa 77, 81–83, 86–88, 92–93, 124, 151, 197, 201, 302, 343, 349, 352–353
Sudan 55, 203, 430, 432
Support for Diversity in Indigenous Education Program 247
Sustainable Development Goals (SDGs) and resources 6
Sweden 186
Switzerland 186, 189
Syria 46, 49–52, 55–60

tailored learning opportunities 92, 318
Tamil Nadu 4, 29, 284, 287–288
Tanzania 15, 81–82, 87, 215
targeted help 85, 91, 155, 176, 208, 279, 398, 414
teacher community assistants (TCAs) 85
Teacher Development Programme (TDP) 82
teachers
absenteeism 88–89, 101, 124, 242
access to 81
accountability of 290
allocation of 21, 33, 85–90, 135, 211, 266, 431
and subject content knowledge 81–83
and support given 36, 54, 69, 352–353

attendance of 88, 114, 130
attitudes/beliefs of 26–28, 91–92, 125
competency of 85, 285
contract teachers 60, 90–91
expectations of 88
experience 26
housing and transportation 88
incentives for 211
motivation of 86, 90, 253, 288
number of 77–78, 86, 88, 90, 124, 281, 295, 331, 374, 376, 393–394, 431
pay 88–89, 124, 195, 265, 330–331, 353
quality of 5, 54, 65, 77, 80–82, 85–87, 89–91, 101, 120, 124, 223, 376, 441
recruitment of 86, 100, 102, 124, 300, 374, 431
retention of 85–86, 423, 430–431
working conditions of 90
teachers' attitudes 26–27
teacher-student language matches 33
teacher training
  and absenteeism 88
  and attitudes 91
  and EdTech 122
  and literacy skill development 19
  and parental awareness meetings 35
  continuous professional development 34, 87, 91, 100–102, 115–116, 122, 125–126, 176, 287, 290, 344, 352–353
  formal training 80–82, 91–92, 100
  in foreign languages 31
  in languages 8, 31, 33, 93, 103, 231, 294
  lack of 77–78, 81, 124, 130, 242, 262, 265, 330–331, 345, 352
  needs 285
  on basic school subjects 82
  on disabilities 26–28, 30
  on migrants 50
  teacher education programs 28, 33, 78, 80, 83, 85, 87, 92, 99–101, 104, 125, 238, 262, 286, 306, 333, 348, 352–353
Teaching at the Right Level (TARL) 83–85, 102, 346–350, 352–354, 356

telesecondary schools 230–232, 235–236, 246, 252, 254
Third Regional Comparative and Explanatory Study (TERCE) examination 65
This School Is Our School 246
Togo 81, 207
transition
  complex 117, 242, 336
  smooth 93, 95, 97
  uninterrupted 238
transition effects 67
transition rates 29, 336, 367, 371, 374, 381, 419
transition support 32
Trends in International Mathematics and Science Study (TIMSS) 54, 152, 154
Turkey 50
Tusome 160–162, 166–167, 175–176
Tutoring Networks (TN) 256–257

Uganda 50–51, 81–82, 89, 199, 203, 206, 430
United Nations 1, 45, 47, 113, 124, 381, 439
  United Nations Children's Fund (UNICEF) 14, 16–18, 21, 37, 52, 63, 121, 123, 136–137, 203, 227–228, 230, 258, 282–284, 328, 333, 335, 432–433, 445
  United Nations Convention on the Rights of Persons with Disabilities (UNCRPD) 25, 397
  United Nations Educational, Scientific and Cultural Organization (UNESCO) 1, 4, 13–14, 21–22, 26–29, 45, 47, 52–54, 65–66, 77, 79, 81, 85–87, 89–90, 94, 113, 117–118, 121, 123–124, 126, 129, 147, 197, 202, 216, 261, 297, 300, 343, 346, 361–364, 374, 417–418, 420
    UNESCO Institute of Statistics (UIS) 77, 80–81, 86, 94, 113, 195–196, 200, 209, 439, 444
  United Nations High Commissioner for Refugees (UNHCR) 45–46,

48–49, 51–54, 56–58, 60, 62, 76, 431, 433
United Nations Office for the Coordination of Humanitarian Affairs (OCHA) 61
United Nations Relief and Works Agency (UNRWA) 52, 54, 56, 58
United Nations Sustainable Development Goals (SDGs) 1, 6–7, 13, 47, 113, 136, 149, 193, 197, 202, 302, 362, 368–369, 382
United States (US) 49, 60, 64, 67, 163, 186, 189, 227, 230, 267, 412
universal education 7–8, 13, 15–16, 22, 63, 207, 224, 238, 278, 300, 367–368
Uruguay 122, 186
Uttar Pradesh 29, 279, 317–318

Venezuela 46, 49, 62, 64
Vision 2030 368–369, 371, 394, 434–435
vulnerable learners 1, 9, 14, 49, 60, 69, 104, 225, 237–238, 264, 280–281, 332, 335, 355–356, 362, 366–367, 369–370, 374, 377

West Africa 349
West Bank 54
West Bengal 279
West Godavari 313
World Bank 4–5, 13, 16–17, 21, 26–27, 51–52, 54, 80, 82, 90, 94, 114, 120, 129, 150–151, 153, 155, 165, 181, 189, 193, 201, 204, 207, 210–212, 214, 300, 343, 355, 361, 366, 398
World Development Report 77, 151
World Economic Forum 22, 318
World Food Program (WFP) 335
World Health Organization (WHO) 397

xenophobia 62

Youth-in-Action program 20

Zambia 84, 89, 125, 200, 215
Zimbabwe 2, 86, 125

About the OBP Team

Alessandra Tosi was the managing editor for this book.

Rosalyn Sword and Melissa Purkiss proof-read and indexed the manuscript.

Anna Gatti designed the cover and created the visuals. The cover was produced in InDesign using the Fontin font.

Luca Baffa and Melissa Purkiss typeset the book in InDesign and produced the paperback and hardback editions. The text font is Tex Gyre Pagella; the heading font is Californian FB. Luca produced the EPUB, AZW3, PDF, HTML, and XML editions—the conversion is performed with open source software freely available on our GitHub page (https://github.com/OpenBookPublishers).

CPSIA information can be obtained
at www.ICGtesting.com
Printed in the USA
LVHW071204290822
727087LV00004B/18